ORE *and* EMPIRE

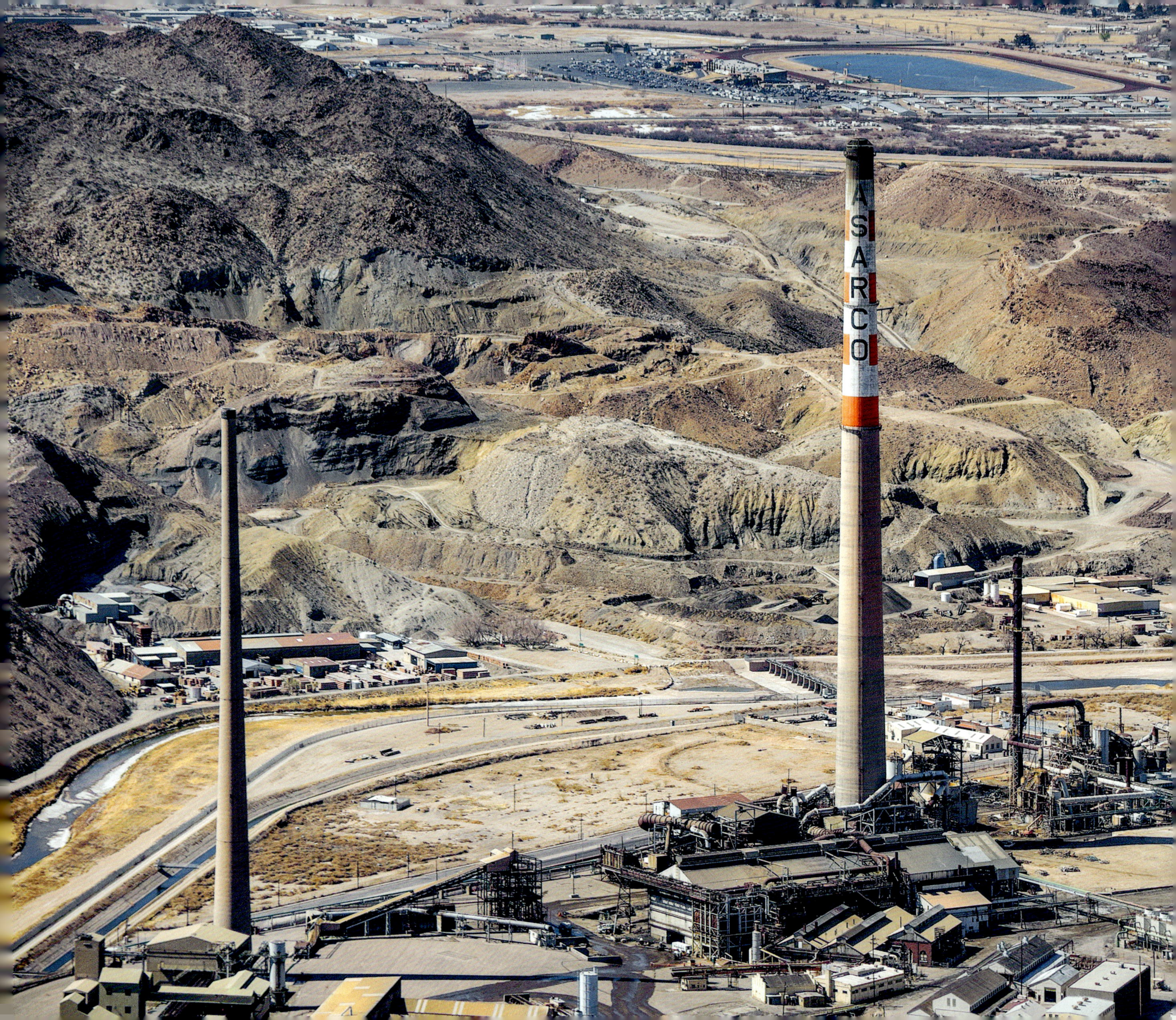
ASARCO

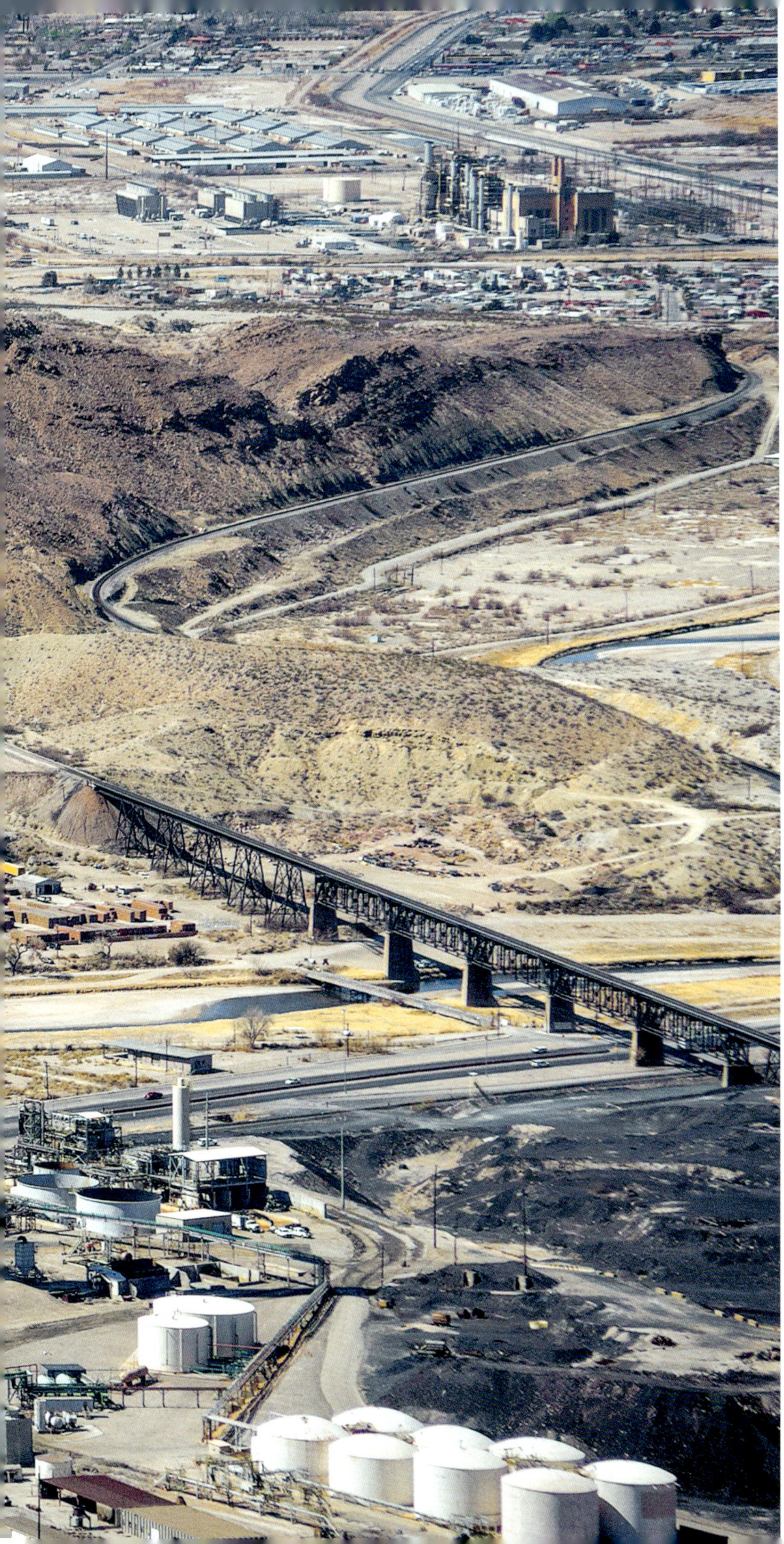

ORE *and* EMPIRE

Conquistadors to Guggenheims on the Camino Real

MARTIN STUPICH

FOREWORD BY DAGOBERTO GILB

University of New Mexico Press | Albuquerque

For David Wright Vaughan

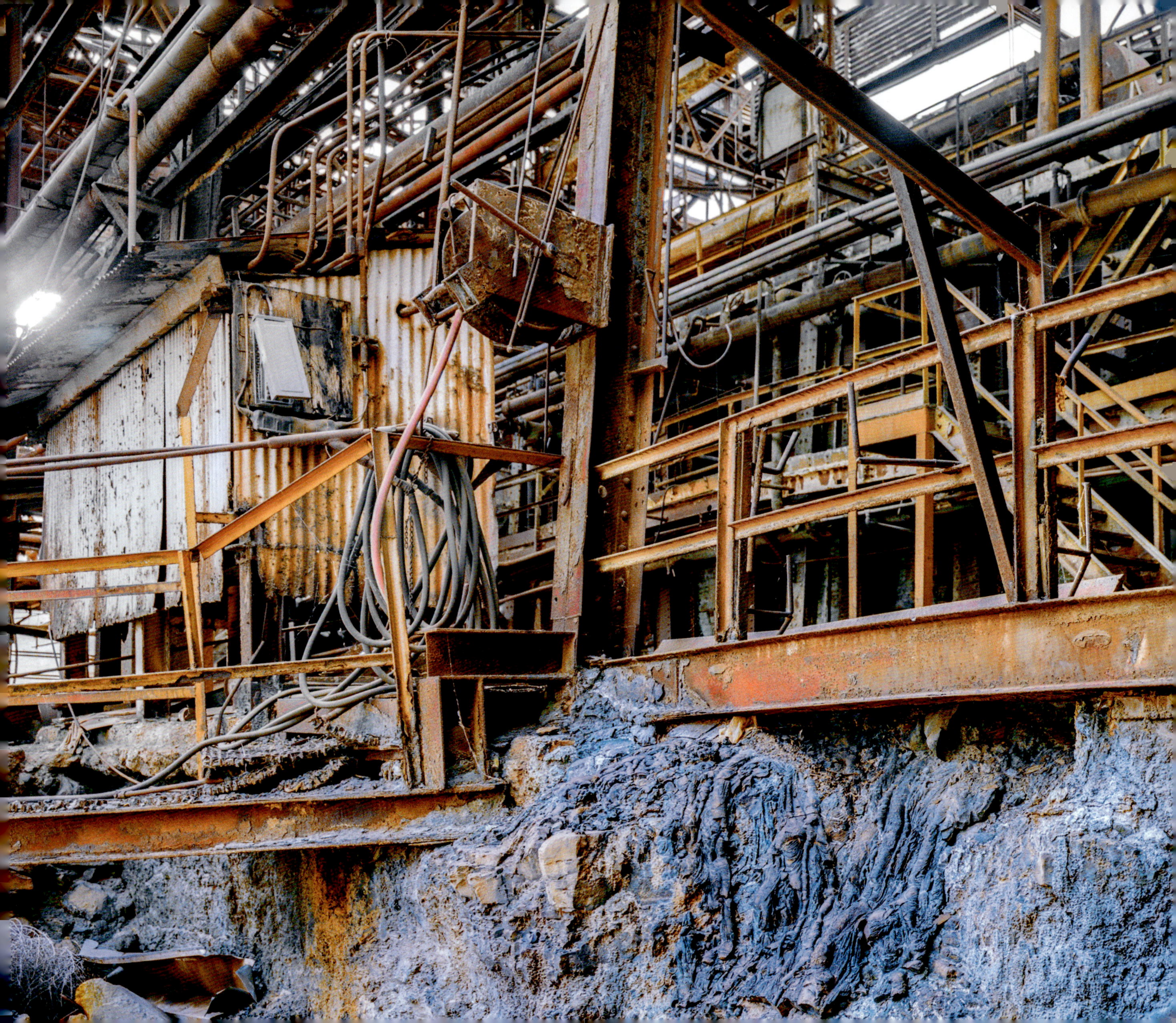

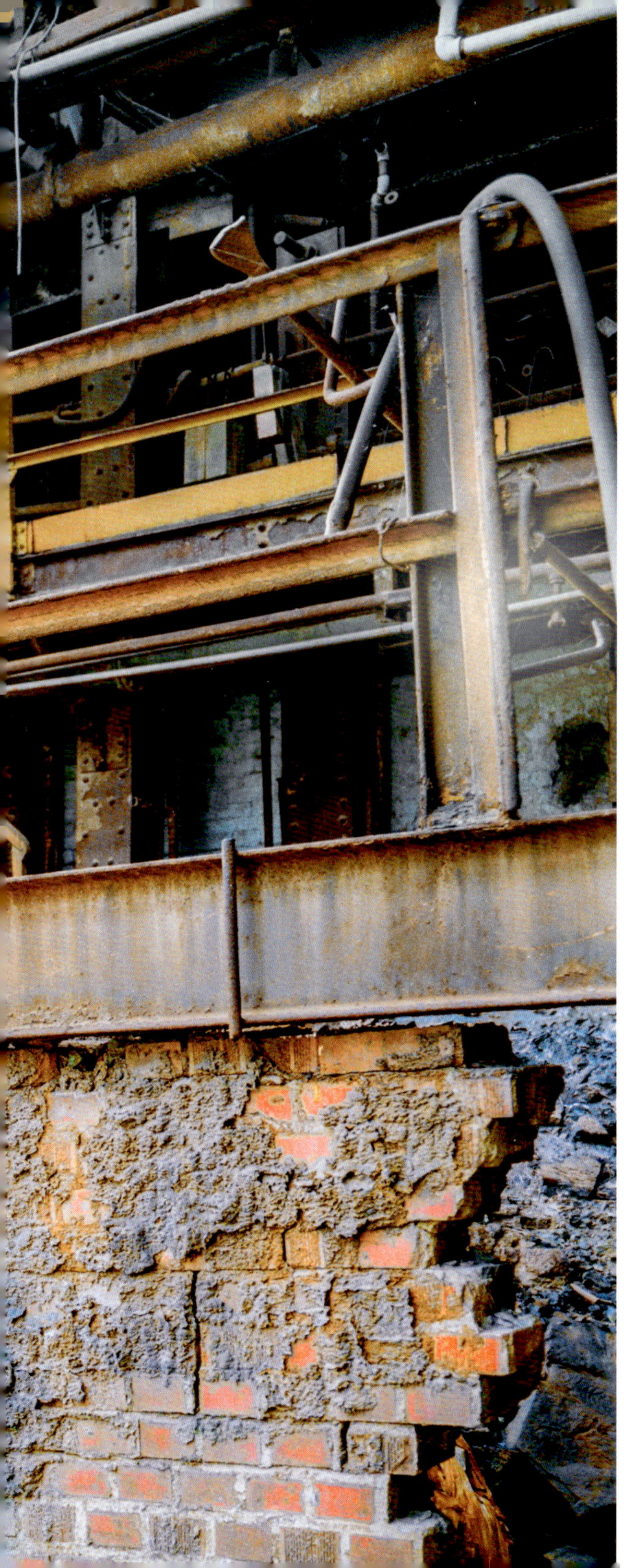

Contents

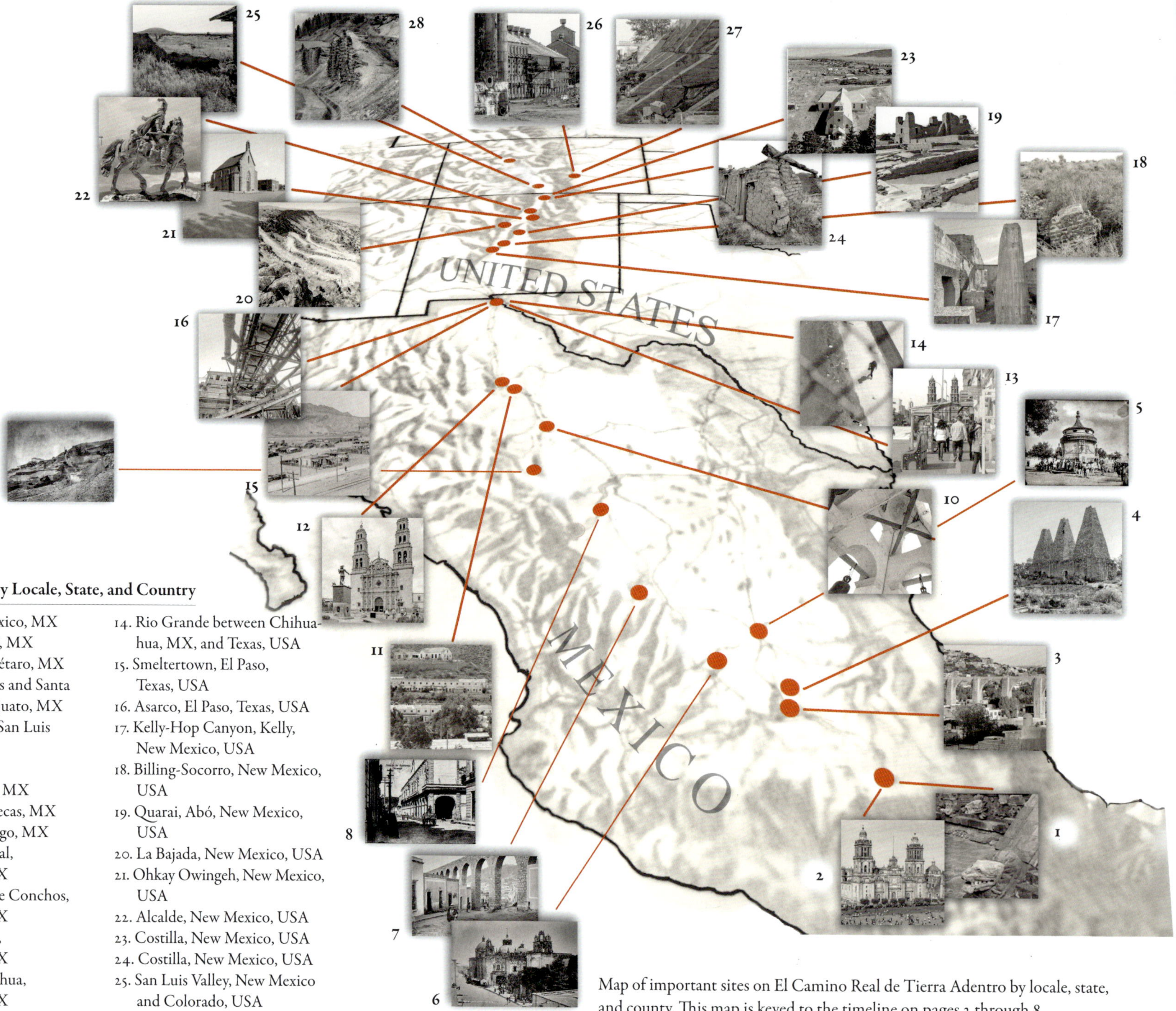

Important Sites by Locale, State, and Country

1. Teotihuacán, Mexico, MX
2. Mexico City, DF, MX
3. Querétaro, Querétaro, MX
4. Mineral de Pozos and Santa Brígida, Guanajuato, MX
5. San Luis Potosí, San Luis Potosí, MX
6. Aguascalientes, Aguascalientes, MX
7. Zacatecas, Zacatecas, MX
8. Durango, Durango, MX
9. Hidalgo del Parral, Chihuahua, MX
10. San Francisco de Conchos, Chihuahua, MX
11. Santa Domingo, Chihuahua, MX
12. Ciudad Chihuahua, Chihuahua, MX
13. Ciudad Juárez, Chihuahua, MX
14. Rio Grande between Chihuahua, MX, and Texas, USA
15. Smeltertown, El Paso, Texas, USA
16. Asarco, El Paso, Texas, USA
17. Kelly-Hop Canyon, Kelly, New Mexico, USA
18. Billing-Socorro, New Mexico, USA
19. Quarai, Abó, New Mexico, USA
20. La Bajada, New Mexico, USA
21. Ohkay Owingeh, New Mexico, USA
22. Alcalde, New Mexico, USA
23. Costilla, New Mexico, USA
24. Costilla, New Mexico, USA
25. San Luis Valley, New Mexico and Colorado, USA
26. Pueblo, Colorado, USA
27. Pueblo, Colorado, USA
28. Leadville, Colorado, USA

Map of important sites on El Camino Real de Tierra Adentro by locale, state, and county. This map is keyed to the timeline on pages 2 through 8.
Map by Martin Stupich.

Foreword

DAGOBERTO GILB

For almost two decades I worked construction, most of those jobs at high-rise sites. Dirty, sweaty, muscle work. Hard hat and boots required. Hours as early and long as ants, duration on feast or famine terms. Fences surrounded the area to warn innocent, curious pedestrians to not stroll into the work-zone dangers. Besides the splintered, chapped, calloused hands, a dozen tie-wire cuts and scabby wounds on arms, and animal-scented men (in my time, only a rare woman), there were many other gigantic mechanical beasts that tore open the earth, pounded and scooped and discarded it. It was another vision being created, a land and time that we who worked there came to know well, way past the onset, the first close encounter. Look down, look up. Big holes and long, tall ladders. Torches sparking, discs grinding, machines torquing. Stacks of scaffolds here, what will become floors there; manlifts attached, steel beams weighing hundreds of pounds swinging high and wide sky bound. At floor 15, stand at the edge and feel the vertigo shift in dimension like new age artwork. At 23, more at 32, stars light up below.

For me, with union gigs in the capital city of the Southwest, Los Angeles, it was giving in to the call of the wild. It was volunteering to board a ship to cross the barely known seas to find the unknown. It was working in icy Alaska on a desolate pipeline, riding a horse on a few-months-long cattle drive. It was heading to the mountains of Mexico to search for gold. A construction gig was dropping into in the Wild West—semicivilized, raw as just-cut meat. Beyond the jobsite cage—usually like two football fields square—a modern, opulent civilization thrived for miles in all cardinal directions, and its comfortable citizens could watch us, like prehistoric birds of prey through peepholes and photo-friendly landings.

One day, close to quitting time, it'd be way up high, a wind blowing through, swaying the skeleton building, the sun hitting and coloring the horizon, the sky closer than the ground, and a dude from another crew would walk over: "Hey, didn't we both work that pyramid job together too?" We laughed in the air as fresh as it is at this height—maybe as clean as it was in those ancient workdays. My Wild West job, years into it by then, became a window to view our almost-hidden-away human activity—to rip open the skin and gut the living earth in order to celebrate, adorn, worship, make our world outside luxuriant. We want shiny awe, need magnificent awe. We want silver, gold, copper. From domestic towers to temples and pyramids and domes, amulets and pendants, monuments of and for gods and lovers and rulers, this commerce of luxury comes from the depths of the treasure-chest earth.

As most who will have the enormous pleasure of encountering this book, I strain to find a description for the abandoned remains of an industrial slaughter ground for minerals. Not a geologist or scientist, I see myself still and only as one of those workers connecting to those of past and long past. Now, as wordless with wonder as I'd get up high in the steel bones of a high-rise—stopped, not using my body—it's almost as one being chosen to be allowed to view and learn the insights inside this book. An El Pasoan for so many years, I'd been an average pedestrian, too simple to realize what the ASARCO smokestack was beyond its ugly spew, doing what it did to those who lived nearby. Never occurred to me what it was in the large, in the human history. It had only been the giant marker that told me I was a few more curves of the Rio Grande and highway from home to my family.

Look through these photographs, be struck by what is shockingly beautiful to the mind. It's as if we are seeing through a deep space and time microscope. We aren't only the time we experience at that moment, but far more ancient. Yes, in the graveyard of ASARCO, this hidden life of our human species is glimpsed. Almost a man-made geologic form itself. But no, it's more: the startling talent of Martin Stupich's art, of course. With it, he shows us the whole of this human effort of want and need, across time and cultures, that leaves this detritus as something that bears a unique human marking, often in sight. Always a mysterious world, fenced off, but a world of creation, of high risk and cost—for beauty, luxury, betterment for all, and only dangerous work for the unseen poor.

Preface

MARTIN STUPICH

If joined together, History and Geography crown our reading with delight and profit; if parted, they threaten both with a certain shipwreck.

—Dr. Peter Heylyn, *Cosmographia* (1649)

A good book, to engage me fully, has within its first five pages a map showing the geography described between the covers, or a graphical timeline dissecting the sweep of the story that I am about to enter. Often the best of these illustrations is as compelling as the author's narrative or the pictures filling the book I'm holding. It is a simple preference, like my favoring aerial photographs over portraits or historical biographies over memoirs.

"The long view," whether through the Hubble telescope or a rearview mirror, is a useful voice for storytelling. *Ore and Empire* is an example of this artist learning on the fly a swath of the world by trusting that it offers more than what's scattered about in plain view. The El Paso American Smelting and Refining Company (ASARCO) smelter, in all its visual cacophony, would alone have been an engaging photographic subject. But from its place on the Rio Grande, in the thin, brilliant Chihuahuan desert air, ASARCO feels not just like a "place" but like a small piece of a vast whole—one part of ten million acres of raw geography delineated by the continent's mountain spine and the green ribbon of one of its great rivers, El Rio Bravo (the Rio Grande).

When it was completed in 1966, the world's tallest industrial smokestack punctuated the skyline of El Paso–Ciudad Juárez from ASARCO's smelter site on the Rio Grande. Though the eighty-three-story-tall double-shelled concrete chimney held that world record for less than two

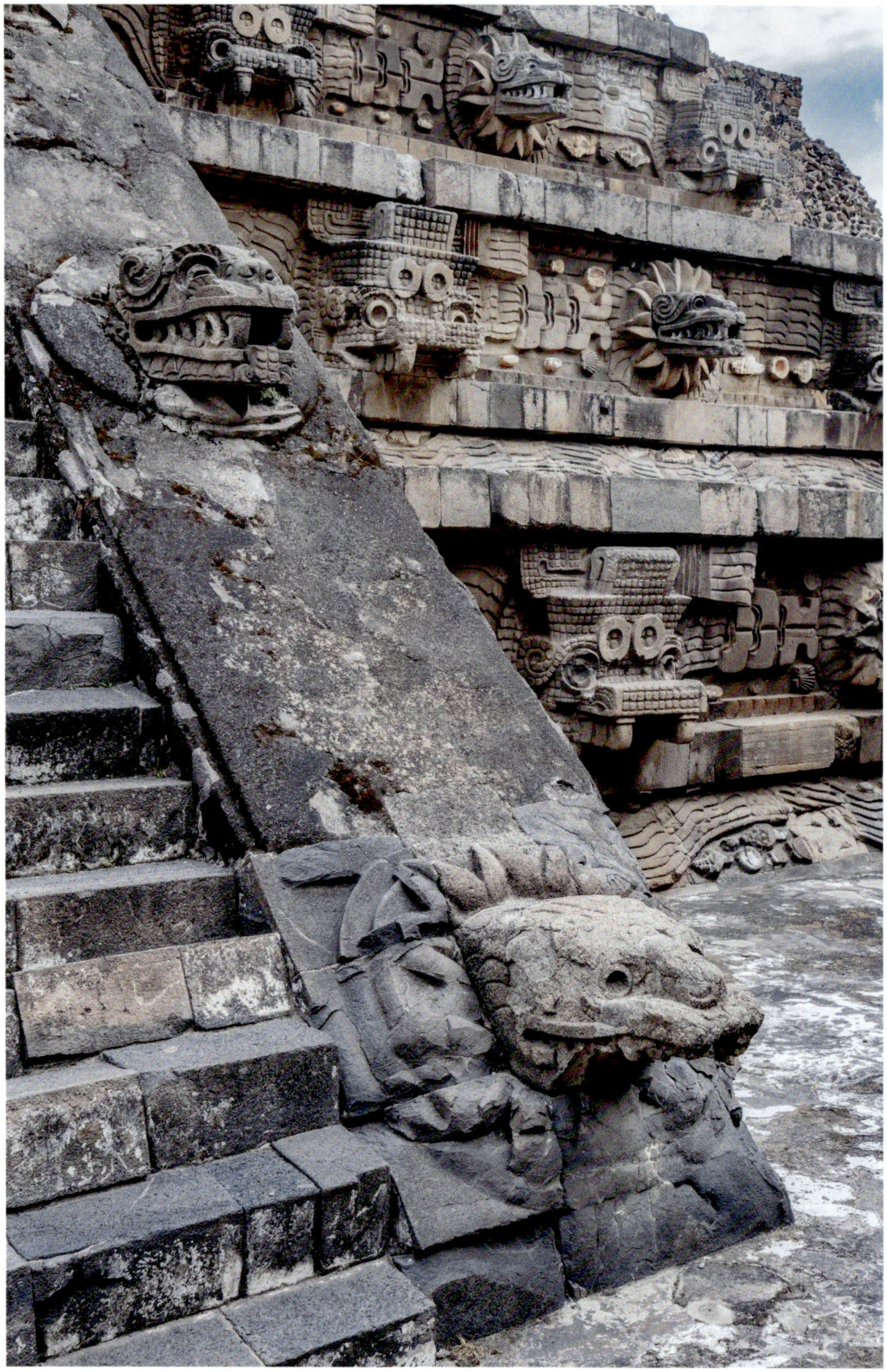

Aztec Temple of Quetzalcoatl (Temple of the Feathered Serpent) near Mexico City, Mexico, 2020. Partly intact and partly restored, this temple stands in a complex of several Teotihuacán pyramids in the Valley of Mexico. It predates by centuries the temples and pyramids thirty miles to the southwest that were demolished by the conquistadors in the sixteenth century in order to obliterate, with mixed success, native religion. The Spaniards replaced human sacrifice with genocide and pyramids with cathedrals.

years, it remained a regional icon for forty-seven. In 2013 it fell in a seventy-second burst of timed detonations, ending decades of local pride as well as derision. Environmentalists cheered as they watched the tower crash to the ground, while in the same breath warning of its poison ash and the dust cloud now slowly drifting east toward downtown El Paso. Others alerted citizens to the hazards lurking in the pulverized concrete and twisted rebar jumble of the two fallen stacks—whose mangled shells now lay precisely as planned in their nine-hundred-foot-long graves, awaiting burial. Also watching the stack-drop were some whose families had for generations depended on smelter wages. A few shared their thoughts (I was there with them). Some spoke in nostalgic, whispered fragments, almost inaudible through tears. "Finally," one said to me, "it's over."

By then I had been photographing on the ASARCO demolition site for more than three years, a process I naïvely thought would end when the infamous stacks fell. But life doesn't unfold neatly in chapters. As I closed in on making my last pictures in El Paso, my research led me to a time before ASARCO's beginning, back a century and a half to Meyer Guggenheim's early years as a genius entrepreneur patriarch; to his sons building a worldwide conglomerate, starting with the incidental investment in 1880 in two small Leadville, Colorado, mines.

From there the story leapfrogs southeast to Pueblo and south across the Rio Grande to central Mexico, where in 1902 M. Guggenheim Sons bought the flourishing lead and silver mine at Santa Eulalia in southern Chihuahua State. Here they tapped the same lodes that, in 1652, had been worked by the Spanish crown's army of proxies and local Indians. Santa Eulalia's mountain of silver had funded construction of the magnificent regional capital of Ciudad Chihuahua, whose grand cathedral dates from 1725. In the twentieth century the same mine fed Guggenheim coffers, helping to underwrite a century of brash exuberance.

Artifacts, and the departed, don't easily give up their stories. As an artist, the best I can do is to photograph remnants of their ephemeral landscape: El Paso's smelter (and next door its workers' cemetery), California Gulch in the Colorado Rockies, Santo Domingo in the desert canyon above Ciudad Chihuahua. This history reaches across 1,600 miles. But nowhere to be seen, not even as mirages over the horizon, are Peggy Guggenheim's Venetian palace, or El Museo Guggenheim Bilbao, or Frank Lloyd Wright's Solomon R. Guggenheim Museum in Manhattan. Almost involuntarily, I see myself magically lifting and transporting it, Frank Lloyd Wright's 5th Avenue spiral gem,

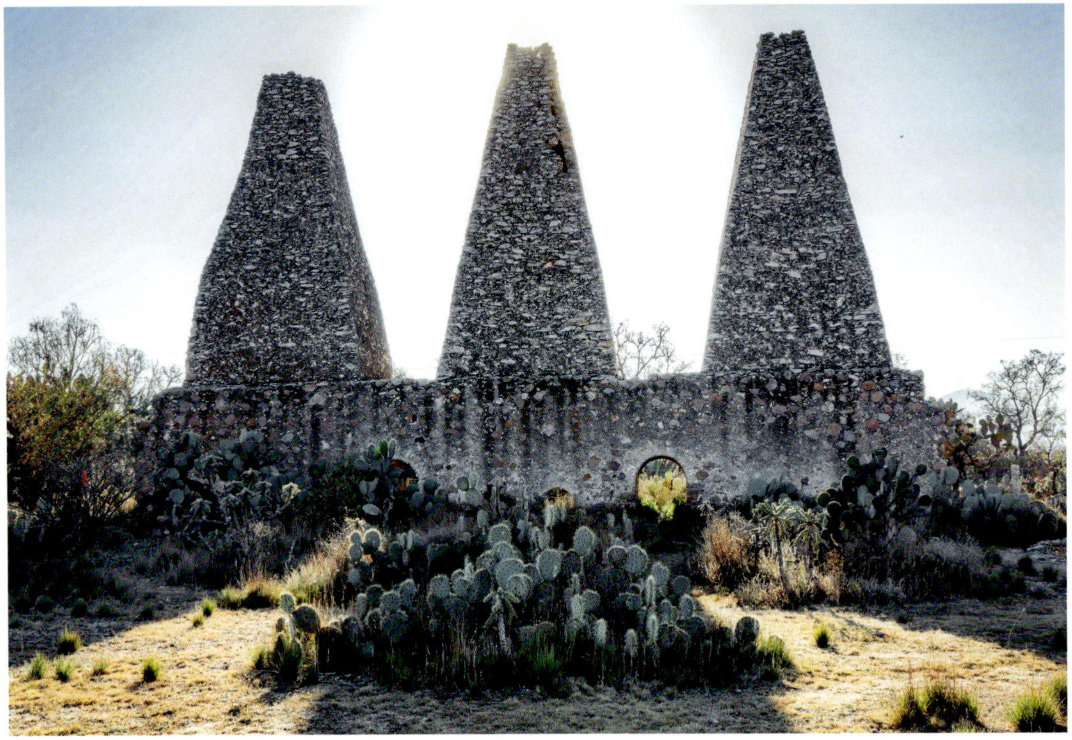

Silver Smelter at Santa Brígida, Guanajuato State, Mexico, 2018. The story of smelting begins more than 3,500 years ago almost simultaneously in Sumer (modern southern Iraq), in China, in Egypt, and in Mesoamerica. The fundamental elements of smelting remain unchanged, evolving only in sophistication and in scale. Simply stated, crushed metal-bearing rock (ore), heated sufficiently, will give up its treasure—copper, iron, silver, or gold. The earliest smelters were mere fire pits, which eventually included crude bellows. Their modern descendants might be massive oxygen-charged gas-fired rolling cylinders, or rows of towering coke-fueled blast furnaces. From any epoch and at any scale, they command attention on the landscape. This photograph from Santa Brígida makes that point, the smelter's three spires dominating an isolated desert valley straddling El Camino Real de Tierra Adentro in central Mexico. In 1595 Indians, working for Jesuits licensed under Spanish King Felipe II, built this elegant silver smelter. Its hornos (ovens) and stacks are made of native stone and mud, their interiors are finished with plaster stucco. The handiwork is so splendid that this three-story marvel seems mere decades old, not four centuries.

two thousand miles southwest, to carefully perch it on a tailings dump in Santo Domingo. Then I invite the town's mineros in to wander—to marvel at what they and their ancestors have built.

The twentieth-century Guggenheim trail doesn't go cold in Chihuahua. Farther south in Mexico, ASARCO miners and smelter crews working the Conquistadors' historic claims ceaselessly transformed hard rock into treasure. I finally saw it: a modern map of Guggenheim's industrial empire, its imprint on the world, fits perfectly atop the seventeenth-century map of Spanish conquest. In places, conquistadors and Guggenheims had mined the same lodes (exactly!), traveled the same roads (exactly!), and depended for labor on families whose ancestors worked these same veins centuries earlier. Today, abandoned pits and shafts, Baroque cathedrals, hacienda ruins, and anonymous graves mark the way across mountains and deserts

Oñate Monument near Alcalde, Rio Ariba County, New Mexico, 2019. This bronze equestrian monument on the historic pueblo of Ohkay Owingeh commemorated "the last conquistador," don Juan de Oñate, and his 1598 founding of the first capital of Nuevo México—which he named San Juan (for himself and his patron saint). After a long career of conquest, murder, and lesser cruelties, he was prosecuted by Spain for atrocities—most famously for those against the Acoma. Banished from Nuevo México and exiled from Mexico City to Spain, he died there in 1626. Installed in 1994, this statue stood at the Northern Rio Grande National Heritage Center on the Camino Real 1,200 miles north of Mexico City. Three weeks after George Floyd's death in 2020, amid national demands for racial justice, the sculpture was forklifted off its pedestal by county commissioners and removed "temporarily."

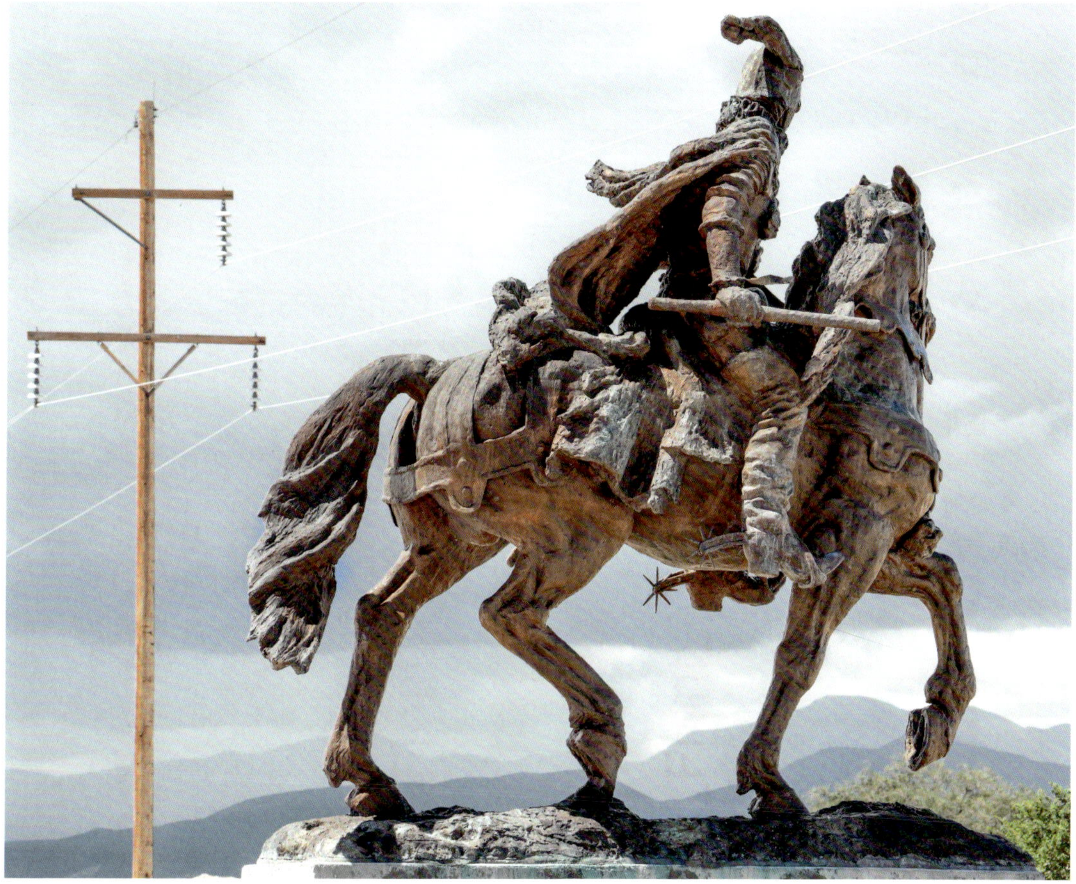

between Leadville, Colorado, and central Mexico. Each of these thousand remnants holds a story we will never hear. I meet that silence by making this collection of photographs. As such, my work is a sort of forensic poetry. Pure curiosity sparked this project years ago. Now my regard for simple beauty sustains it—and me—in this exhausted yet inexhaustible sublime landscape.

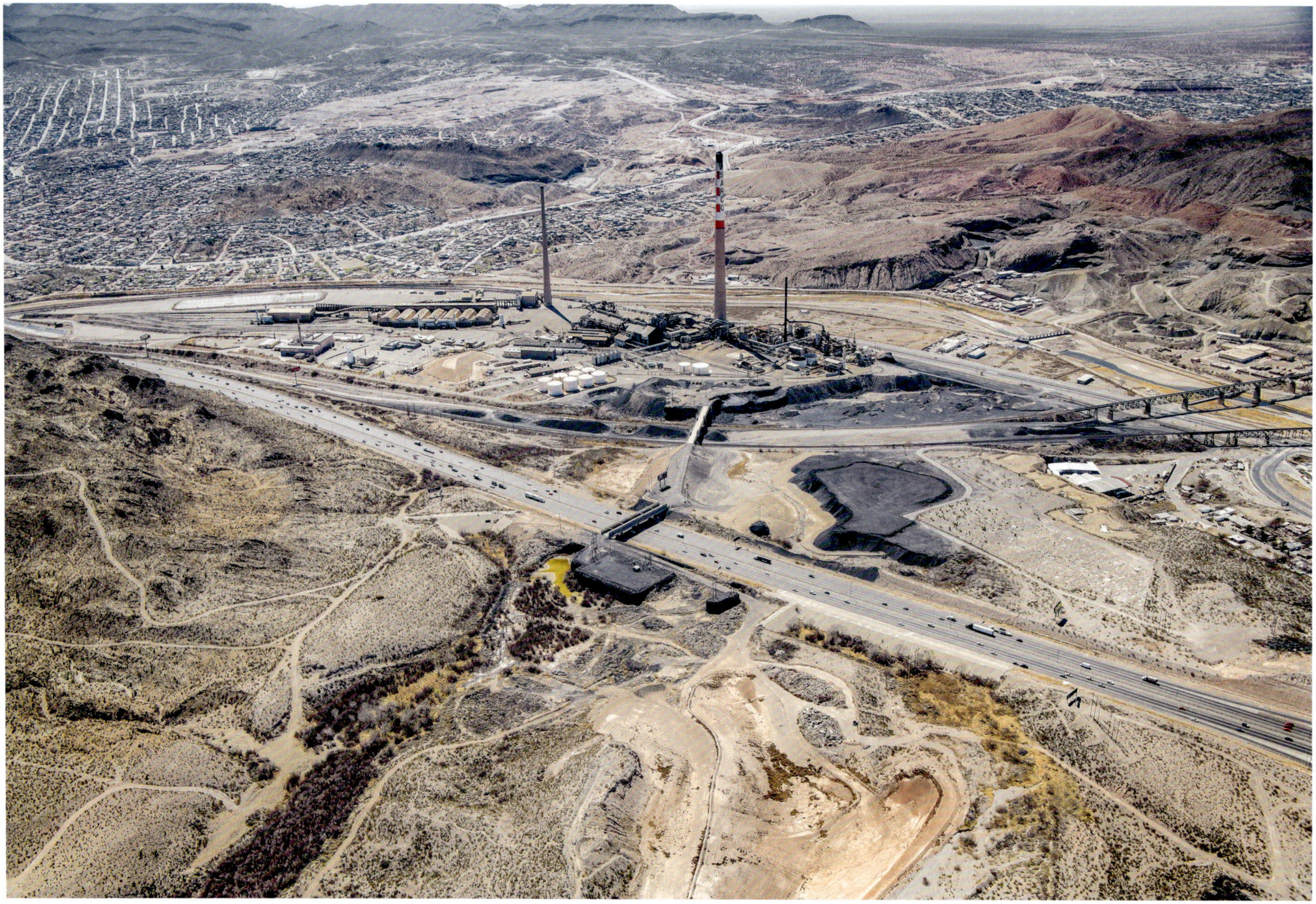

Ciudad Juárez is the backdrop in this view of the entire ASARCO site.

Introduction

MARTIN STUPICH

The Principals

This story hangs on the framework of centuries of history; but its robust twin arms are the nineteenth-century reach of the Guggenheim mining and smelting empire and, before that, the sixteenth- and seventeenth-century exploits of Spanish and Mexican conquistadors.

Conquistadors (1519–1600)

In the Americas, Spain's conquistadors were at first explorers—among them Francisco Pizarro, Hernán Cortéz, Francisco Vásquez de Coronado, and Mexico-born don Juan de Oñate. Their disciplined, well-armed legions thrust forth from Cuba to Peru and as far north as present-day Colorado, propelled by rumors that in América, untapped lodes of silver and gold and ancient royal treasure troves were theirs for the taking. From 1519 forward, greed and entitlement turned these fortune hunters inevitably into predatory warrior-conquerors, licensed by Spain's crown to pillage, exploit, baptize, and govern the civilizations whose land they occupied. Conquest was swift; it took Cortéz less than two years to subdue Montezuma II and conquer the Aztec capital, now the site of Mexico City.

By 1600 conquistadors had overpowered centuries-old cultures, from the Taíno in the Caribbean to the Inca in Peru's Andes (where in the 1500s, at Potosí, most of the world's silver was mined). Farther north, in modern New Mexico, mythical cities of gold and heathen souls needing salvation bedazzled Spain's royal and papal armies, drawing the conquerors deep into the

American interior. Five centuries on, the imprint of the armies and the caravans of emigrants who often accompanied them—from the southwestern United States to the far tip of Chile—endures in their language and religion.

Guggenheims (1880–Mid-Twentieth Century)

During the Gilded Age, though most of the era's robber barons traded in railroads, oil, steel, and coal, the family name dominating the copper mining and smelting narrative is Guggenheim—not a single entrepreneur, but a dynasty spanning five generations, a century, and two continents.

In his seventy-seven years, Meyer Guggenheim transformed himself from young Swiss immigrant lace wholesaler in Philadelphia into modern international mining mogul. By the time he was fifty, Guggenheim had fathered ten children, built and grew fortunes, and forged a family-run empire, and he ensured its stamina by training five of his seven sons in finance and in the business of running a modern consortium—one of the world's first multinational corporate success stories.

The Guggenheims built their fortune on risk and skill. With no mining background, in 1880 Meyer Guggenheim paid five thousand dollars for a minority interest—sight unseen—in two

This timeline is keyed to the map on page viii.

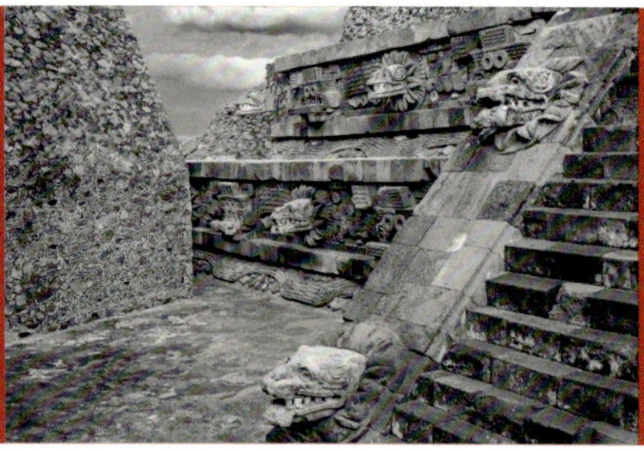

1. **Teotihuacán, Mexico, MX.** Until the sixteenth-century Spanish genocide and its imposition of Christianity on the survivors, great pyramids dominated the spiritual and civic landscape—both here and thirty miles southwest at the site of modern Mexico City.

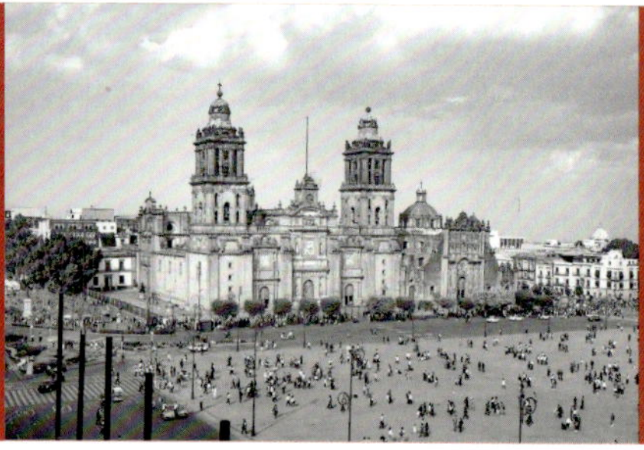

2. **Mexico City, DF, MX.** Mexico City's massive Metropolitan Cathedral is built atop the rubble of Aztec sacred sites. It is still the largest Catholic cathedral in the Americas.

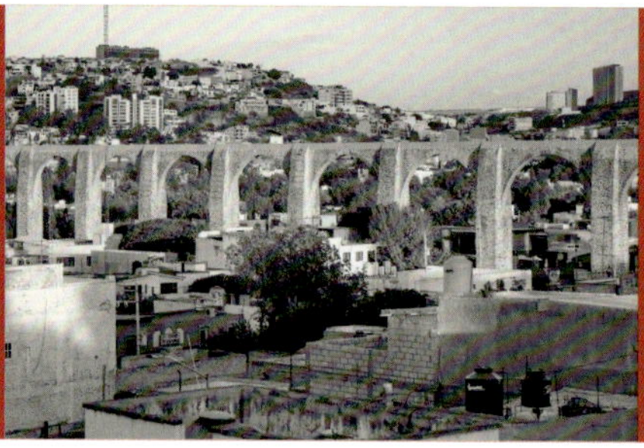

3. **Querétaro, Querétaro, MX.** In the seventeenth century, when north-bound travelers set out from Mexico City into the great interior desert of northern Mexico, Querétaro was their last taste of civilization until Ciudad Chihuahua—about midway to Santa Fe.

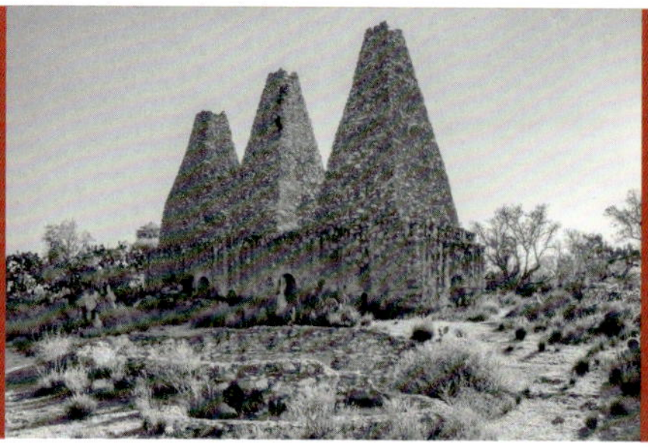

4. **Mineral de Pozos and Santa Brígida, Guanajuato, MX.** Mineral de Pozos comprises a virtual museum of mining history on the Camino. Sixteenth-century smelter ruins and excavations share the landscape with remnants dating from the 1920s.

small, underperforming mines in Leadville, Colorado. Within a year, based on prospects for success, the family formed M. Guggenheim Sons.

The Colorado works prospered; soon the company was acquiring more mines and building smelters—and railroads to connect them—from Mexico to Alaska. In 1899 ten US mining and smelting interests combined to form the American Smelting and Refining Company (ASARCO). Within two years and in fiscal disarray, ASARCO was purchased by the Guggenheims, who went on to develop mineral claims in Latin America—in Peru, Chile, and Bolivia, with some of their most active investments in central and northern Mexico, closer to US markets. Mexico's mines, their proximity to El Paso, Texas, and the Guggenheims' mastery of Mexico's Revolutionary Period politics ultimately ensured the success of the El Paso ASARCO plant—the centerpiece of this photographic project.

The Setting

This visual chronicle reaches from 1595 to 2022. The story of ASARCO, copper, and industrial-scale mining and smelting starts not at its beginning but near the story's middle—in the

On this timeline, sites 5 through 9 have not yet been visited by the photographer.

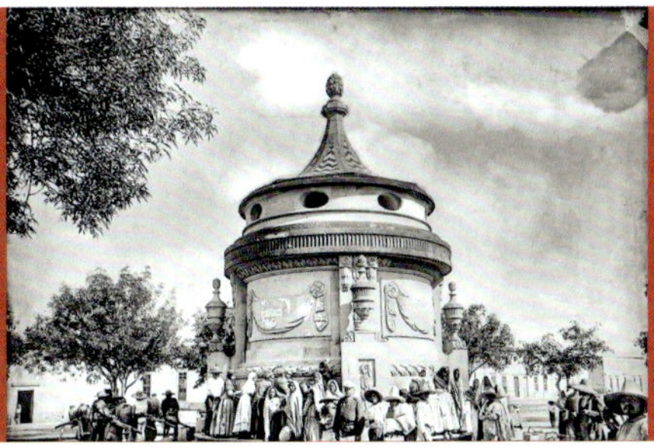

5. **San Luis Potosí, San Luis Potosí, MX.** In 1592 gold and silver drew Spaniards to Potosí, named for the conquistadors' fabled Bolivian silver mine. By 1890 San Luis Potosí was the perfect place for Americans to build crusher mills and smelters. Courtesy of the Library of Congress.

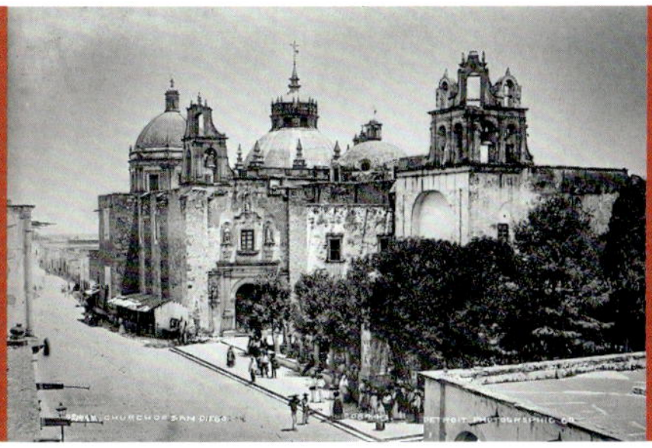

6. **Aguascalientes, Aguascalientes, MX.** By 1575 Spaniards had established a presidio on the site. In 1893 Guggenheim built a smelter here to process orders from Tepezela and Asientos mining districts. Courtesy of the Library of Congress.

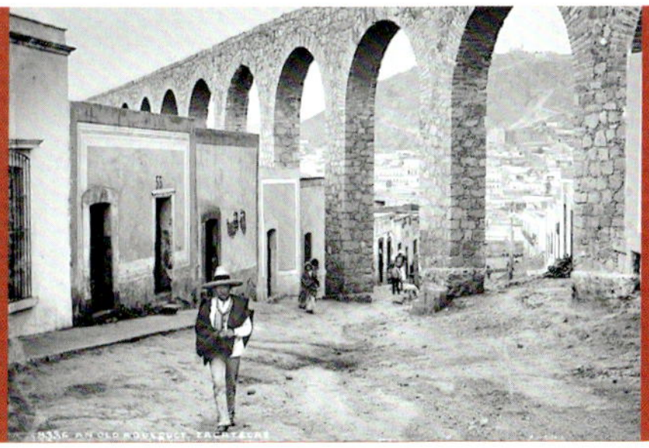

7. **Zacatecas, Zacatecas, MX.** Don Juan de Oñate was born here in 1550. By 1605 Zacatecas mines were the source of 20 percent of the world's silver. Courtesy of the Library of Congress.

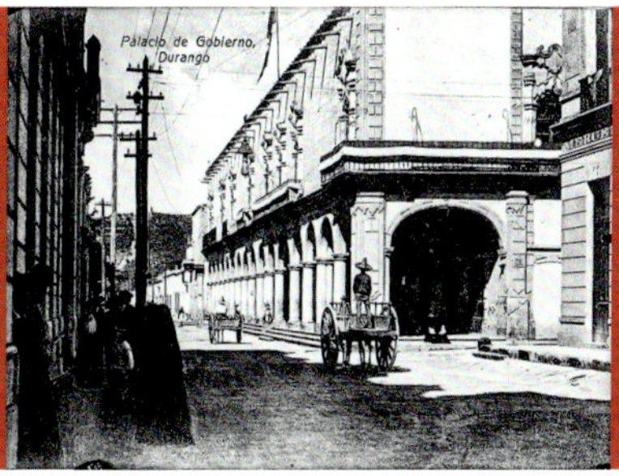

8. **Durango, Durango, MX.** In 1564 Spain built a regional capital here, on the Silver Road—the Camino de la Plata—linking Mexico City to northern mining districts. Courtesy of the Library of Congress.

nineteenth century. Its epicenter straddles the Mexico-Texas line where the Rio Grande and El Camino Real de Tierra Adentro intersect, then merge. The saga unfolds on a multilayered map and over a tangle of timelines spanning half a millennium and embracing a mosaic of nations, native and ancient and recently drawn. It reaches from El Paso south to Mexico City and north to Colorado. Parts of the story overlap and mingle like a watercolor's transparent washes, populating one expansive diorama.

The earliest layer, the first landscape, is of sixteenth-century Spanish North America, where European "contact" with Indigenous peoples and treasure led to conquest (exploitation, assimilation, religious conversion, or extermination). During this long moment—the Age of Discovery—treasure extracted from central Mexico's (and Peru's) fabled silver lodes sailed off to Spain, funding history's first truly global empire. In North America, El Camino Real defines this vestigial sweep of historic land, from Mexico to beyond Santa Fe, its hard-trod earth the stage for this centuries-long narrative. Few physical traces of the Spanish onslaught remain. Crude surface excavations and hand-dug silver and copper mines have long since eroded, collapsed, or been subsumed ages ago by larger digs. Among the few early mining artifacts still standing, the most splendid is the thirty-five-foot-tall stone and stucco smelter oven and its three pyramidal-peaked

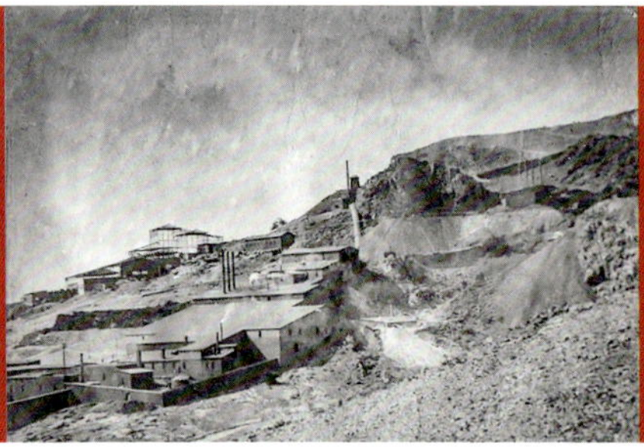

9. **Hidalgo del Parral, Chihuahua, MX.** A once-prosperous mining district, in 1640 Spain's King Felipe IV berated Parral's declining fortunes by proclaiming neighboring Santa Barbara the "capital of the world of silver." Courtesy of the University of California San Diego.

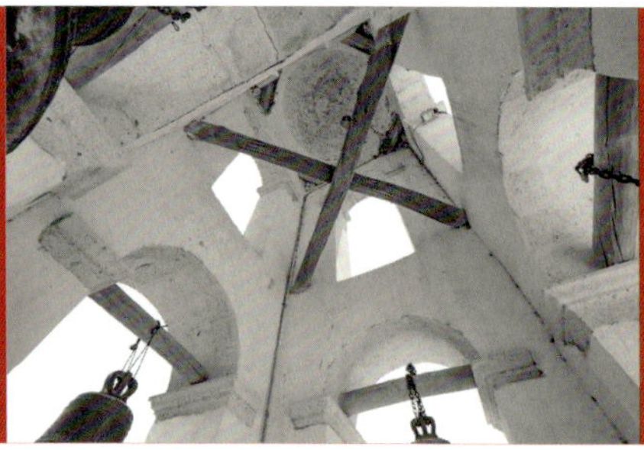

10. **San Francisco de Conchos, Chihuahua, MX.** In 1604 Spanish missionaries settled here. As a security measure along the Camino, in 1685 a presidio was built near the mission church to protect commerce along the route—especially its ore-laden wagons, headed to northern smelters and the treasury in Mexico City.

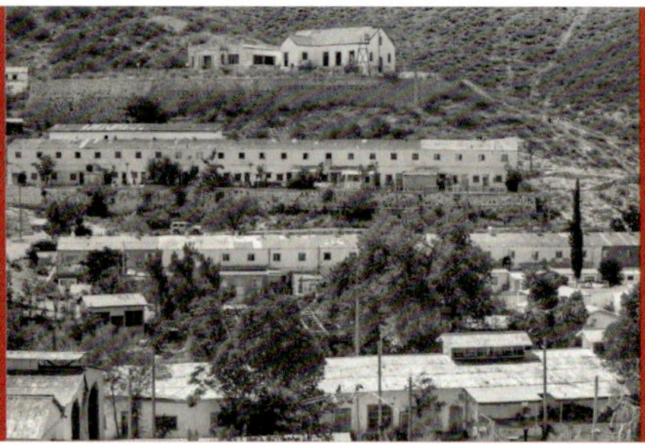

11. **Santa Domingo, Chihuahua, MX.** Worker housing hugs terraces cut into the steep slopes. As with company towns everywhere, housing in Santa Domingo was uniform, cramped, and a short walk from work. These rows of adobe buildings, conforming to the canyon's contour, consist of dozens of connected one- and two-room units.

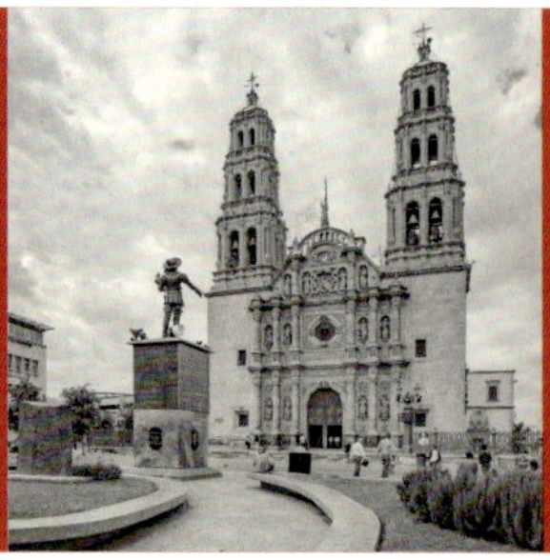

12. **Ciudad Chihuahua, Chihuahua, MX.** The treasure extracted from the region called for a cathedral commensurate with the conquistadors' newfound wealth. Two centuries later this place was the backdrop for "cooperation" agreements between Pancho Villa's armies and Guggenheim mining interests.

chimneys at Santa Brígida near Mineral de Pozos in Guanajuato State, Mexico (see pp. xiv and 149–50). Built in 1595 by Indians for Jesuits licensed by the Spanish crown, the Santa Brígida smelter was more than four centuries old in 2013 when ASARCO's 828-foot El Paso smelter stack, a modern marvel, was toppled after standing for less than five decades.

Four hundred years before I began photographing Paso del Norte's smelting landscape, conquistadors traversing it on horseback waded north across the wide, silty Rio Bravo (the Rio Grande in the United States) where it cuts a gash through the Franklin Mountains. The lure was silver, gold, and pagan souls—all promising generous returns for the trouble. By the mid-nineteenth century, El Camino Real, joining Mexico City to Santa Fe through today's El Paso, was well-worn. Stretches of its rutted, parched landscape were infamous, first blazed by Indigenous hunters and traders, then by Spanish soldiers, Catholic missionaries, and migrants, and after them, mining engineers, railroad surveyors, and captains of industry hoping to claim the treasure the conquistadors had missed.

Two centuries into the Conquest, by 1750, a continuous flotilla joined Veracruz on Mexico's eastern Gulf Coast with Spain's port at Sevilla, its galleons groaning with bullion smelted from Mexican ores. But not all the freshly forged treasure left New Spain. Conquistadors retained enough to fund grand royal and papal ambitions in América. Political and church clout clustered

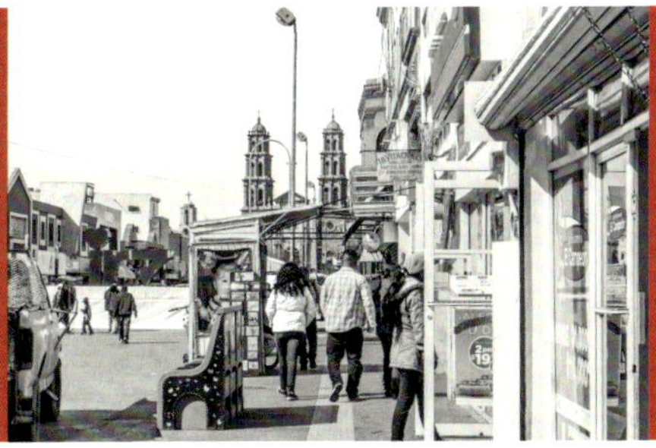

13. **Ciudad Juárez, Chihuahua, MX.** A decade before Oñate waded on horseback north across the Rio Bravo, Spanish fortune hunter Castaño de Sosa was probably the first European to see this place. This paso through the mountains was the gateway to the fabled treasures of northern New Spain. Franciscans established a settlement here, and by 1659 a mission church was rising in the heart of the new colony.

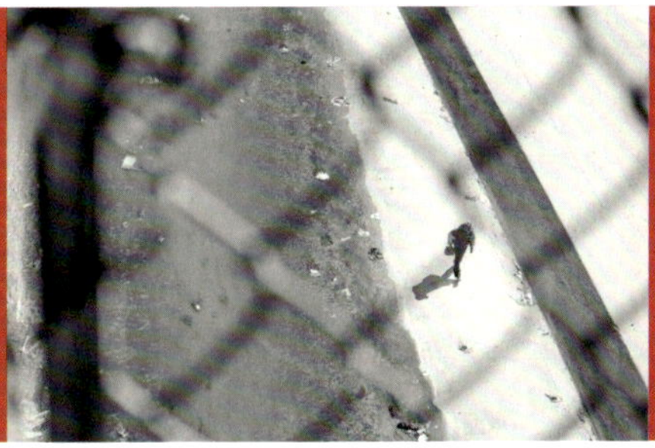

14. **Rio Grande between Chihuahua, MX, and Texas, USA.** In the mid-nineteenth century the river became the border between Mexico and the United States. By the 1980s this section of the international boundary was a fortified barrier, and the once-unruly river had become a fetid debris-strewn trickle confined to a concrete-lined gutter.

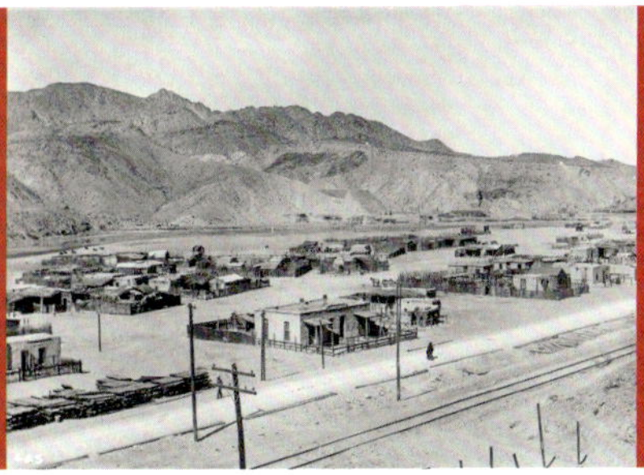

15. **Smeltertown, El Paso, Texas, USA.** It was common for laborers in late nineteenth-century industrial landscapes to live in dense "company towns" sometimes mere steps from where they worked brutal twelve-hour days. Smeltertown was such a place. The Rio Grande separated the adobe neighborhood on the floodplain from the slopes of Cerro de Cristo Rey. Photograph by O. A. Aultman, ca. 1910. Courtesy of the Otis A. Aultman Collection, El Paso Public Library.

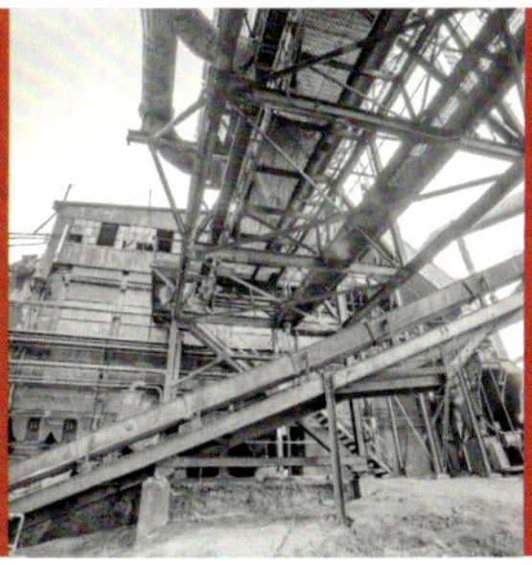

16. **ASARCO, El Paso, Texas, USA.** Built, rebuilt, expanded, and reconfigured to meet the demands of the market, ASARCO's efforts at environmental stewardship were insufficient to elude its eventual closure and bankruptcy.

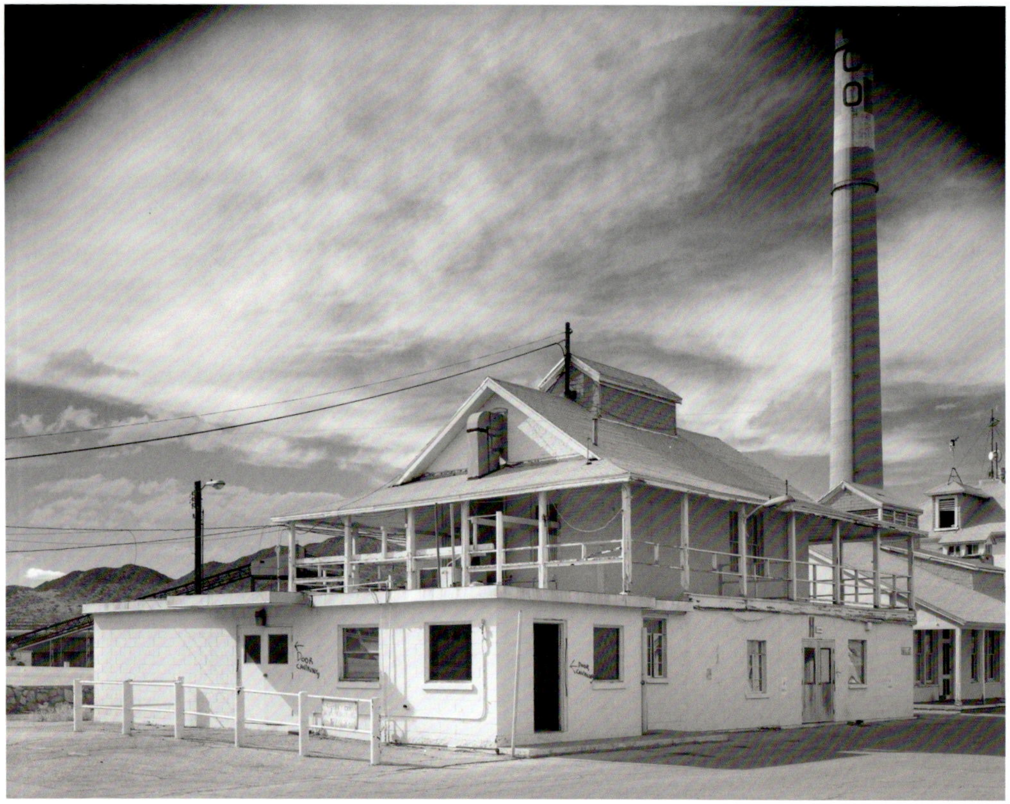

El Paso ASARCO site, 2010. In the 1880s, the first smelting to occur on this site was done in a small mud-brick building whose tiny scale soon made it obsolete. Larger facilities were built, but the original adobe structure survived (with modifications shown here), serving first as the on-site ASARCO office and later as the field headquarters during ASARCO's multi-year demolition and environmental remediation.

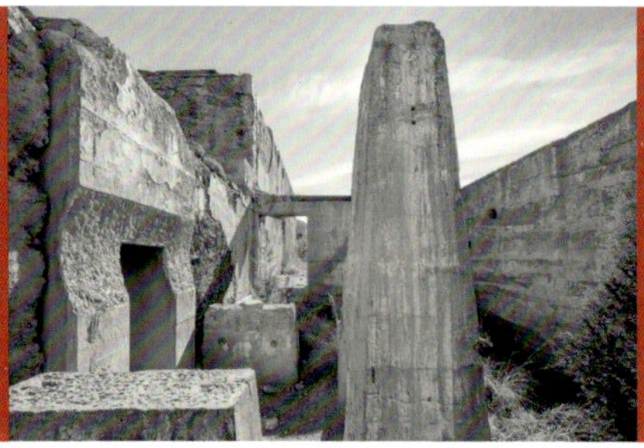

17. **Kelly-Hop Canyon, Kelly, New Mexico, USA.** In New Mexico, above the town of Magdalena, mining flourished starting in the 1880s. Wealth from lodes of zinc, lead, and silver supported a population of two thousand, a bank, schools, churches, saloons, and a clinic. The ruins pictured here are from 1913. ASARCO owned this property from 1943 until 1950. By then, nearby Kelly was a ghost town.

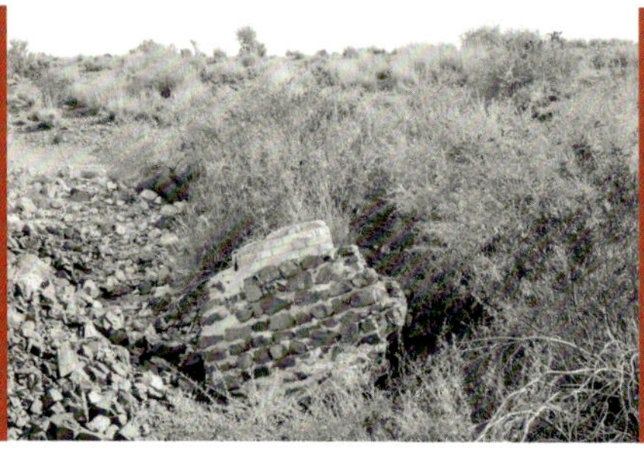

18. **Billing-Socorro, New Mexico, USA.** Crushed ores from the Hop Canyon Mill were hauled (first by cart, later by rail) twenty-five miles downhill to the Billing Smelter, a mile west of Socorro in the Rio Grande valley. This brick chunk of building fragment is one of few architectural remnants to be found in a twenty-acre Superfund landscape characterized by smelter slag.

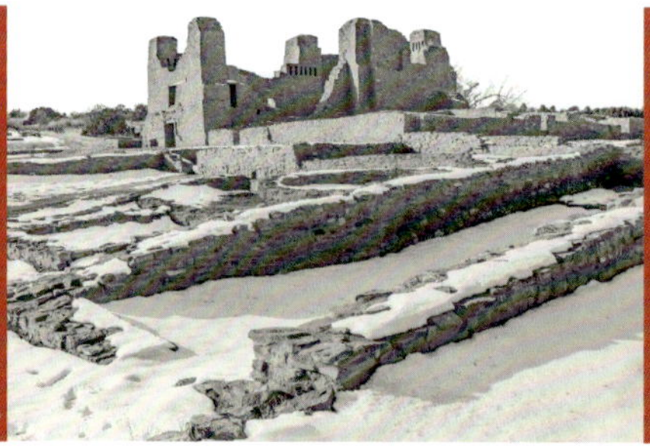

19. **Quarai, Abó, New Mexico, USA.** One of three Salinas Pueblo missions built in the 1620s by Spain's army of conquistadors and native Tompiro and Tanoan, Quarai served as the ecclesiastical headquarters for the Catholic pope's Inquisition in Nuevo Mexico. Abandonment and ruin followed the Pueblo Revolt of 1680.

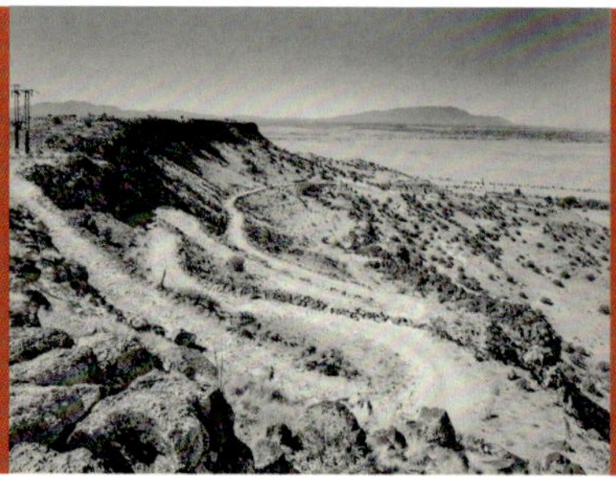

20. **La Bajada, New Mexico, USA.** On the journey from Mexico City, a basalt escarpment southwest of Santa Fe was for centuries a traveler's most daunting obstacle—a great rampart jutting six hundred vertical feet from the valley floor. In 1598 Oñate's convoy climbed this steep trail, which by the 1920s was known as Route 66.

where mines flourished along the southern Camino Real on a section known as Camino de la Plata. This Silver Road linked the country's rich mining and smelting districts to its power center at Mexico City. Along the entire route the church (and Spanish royals) staked claim to their conquered provinces, branding them with flamboyant civic and liturgical architecture—the stamp of Empire—thereby bolstering their dominion over peoples and lands. Today those colossal European-influenced Baroque "silver cathedrals" and sprawling public plazas remain the Crown's and the Vatican's unambiguous mark on the cultural topography of the New World. Mexico City, Puebla, Querétaro, Zacatecas, San Luis Potosí, Aguascalientes, Parral, Chihuahua, and Ciudad Juárez each has at its center a version of this bold exclamation point—distinguished by soaring bell towers and a prominent dome festooned inside with gold- and silver-gilt saints and martyrs and topped outside with a crucified Christ. A map of this corridor through modern Mexico is a concise geographic guide tracing the course of riches flowing through, and pouring out of, the New World.

Spain's influence in the Americas diminished greatly through the nineteenth century under pressure from both sides of the Atlantic. By the late 1800s American east-coast speculators had reshaped the continent's mountain spine from Montana to southern Mexico, much of it along

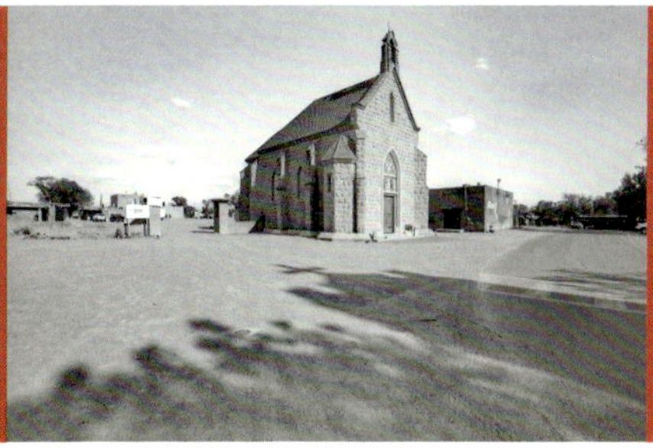

21. **Ohkay Owingeh, New Mexico, USA.** This French chapel occupies a spot at the center of an ancient Indian pueblo claimed by a Mexican general working for a Hapsburg king enthroned in the Spanish capital. Don Juan de Oñate christened it the Seat of Government of New Spain. Within two years Oñate, guilty of atrocities against his Indigenous "subjects," was banished, exiled to Mexico. The capital was moved to the site of today's Santa Fe.

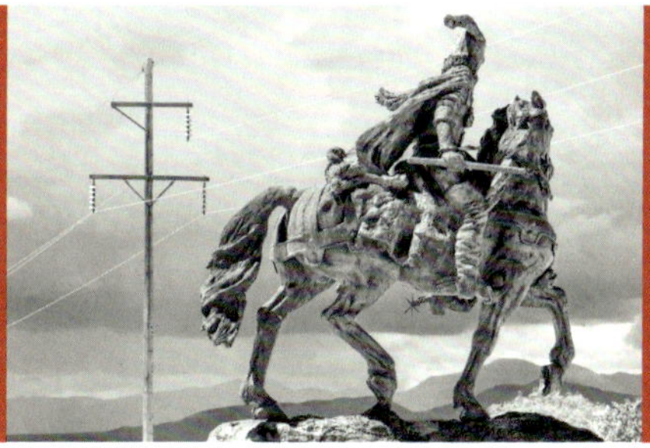

22. **Alcalde, New Mexico, USA.** Don Juan de Oñate y Salazar crossed into Nuevo Mexico in 1598. Within months his marauders had enslaved and murdered scores of Natives along the way, mostly in present-day northern New Mexico, between Acoma and Ohkay Owingeh. This monument was unceremoniously removed in 2020.

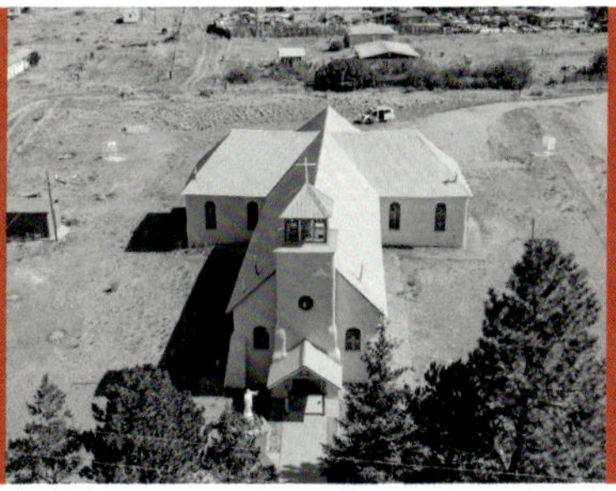

23. **Costilla, New Mexico, USA.** Along the Camino from Mexico City to Costilla, almost every settlement has a church. Some are grand basilicas, but most are humble chapels. This Mission Church of the Sacred Heart is New Mexico's northernmost, sited just a few hundred yards south of the Colorado line.

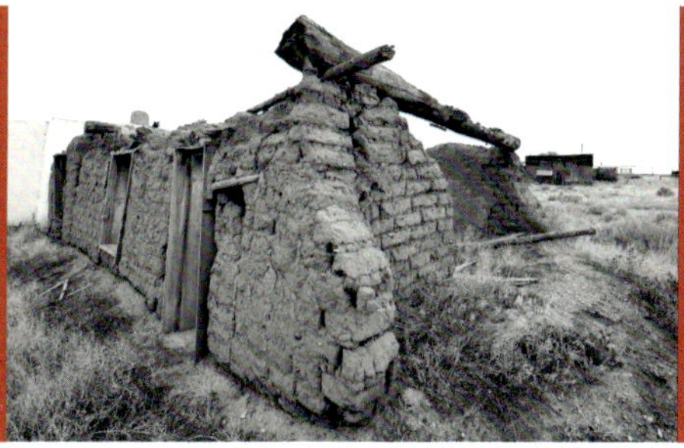

24. **Costilla, New Mexico, USA.** In the 1840s families from old Mexico, bound for the far-northern vestigial end of the Camino, emigrated north to Santa Fe and Taos. Their abandoned traditional adobe homes continue to gradually vanish, taken down by the elements or by demolition.

the historic Camino route (its north half no longer a part of Mexico). Wilderness morphed into industrial landscape, linking scores of mines and smelters by a network of new railroads to deep water ports and world markets.[1] Controlling most of it, either by influence or outright ownership, were a half dozen Gilded Age icons: Clark, Hearst, Heinze, Huntington, Rockefeller,[2] and Meyer Guggenheim, founder of M. Guggenheim Sons and eventually owners of American Smelting and Refining Company. That rowdy era was as much clad in copper as gilt in gold. Copper—its mining, smelting, and refining—was at the heart of enormous new fortunes, Guggenheim's primary among them. The family name, after more than a century, remains a synonym for high drama, philanthropy, arts patronage, and implausible wealth.

From south to north on the Royal Road, fewer than two lifetimes stand between us and those who survived (or did not) service to the princes of industry, church, or crown. Along the way, the most poignant ruins are still-legible artifacts. For the length of El Camino in Mexico, the ordered civility of grand haciendas (actually planned company towns) anchored crowded one-story adobe or wood shanty workers' ghettos. Thousands of feet beneath them were shafts and timber-braced tunnels, and within a short haul was the din of ore crushers and smelters. Farther north the settlements of Kelly in New Mexico and Leadville in Colorado played similar roles. Today their crumbling remains

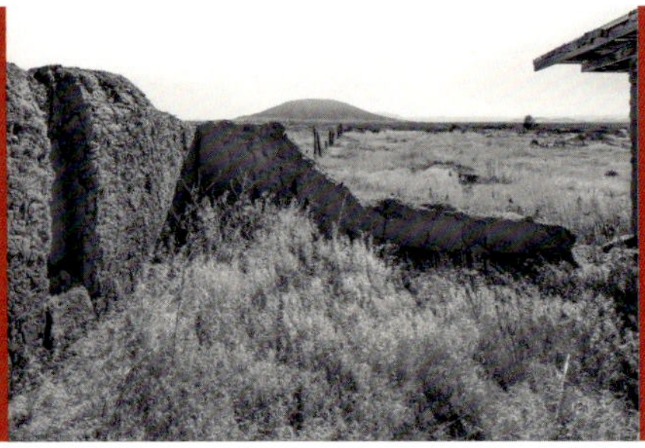

25. **San Luis Valley, New Mexico and Colorado, USA.** Spanning the present-day New Mexico–Colorado line, this was the de facto northern limit of Hispano settlement along the 1,600-mile historic trade route between Mexico's capital and northern New Mexico. This view looks across the southern part of the valley—one of the most expansive in the American west—from Garcia, Colorado, southwest to Ute Mountain in New Mexico.

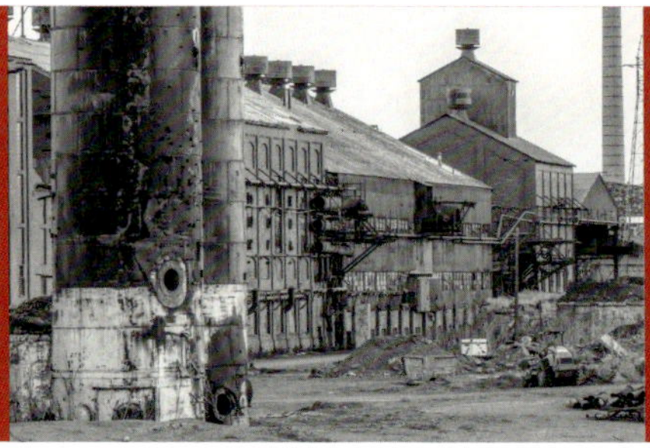

26. **Pueblo, Colorado, USA.** In the 1880s the Guggenheim-ASARCO smelter was Pueblo's largest. But it was obsolete by 1909 and was subsequently demolished. A contemporaneous industrial icon, the Colorado Fuel and Iron Company, still stands a century later, hinting at the nature of Pueblo's late nineteenth-century Arkansas Valley smelter landscape.

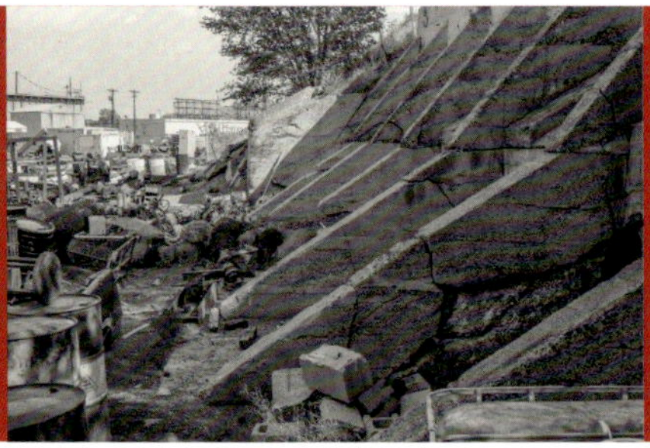

27. **Pueblo, Colorado, USA.** The Guggenheim-ASARCO smelter, its buildings leveled more than a century ago, has for decades been an active Superfund environmental remediation site. Other than a prominent slag mesa, this concrete remnant, on the north side of the ASARCO tract, is one of the last visible artifacts from Pueblo's Guggenheim-ASARCO period.

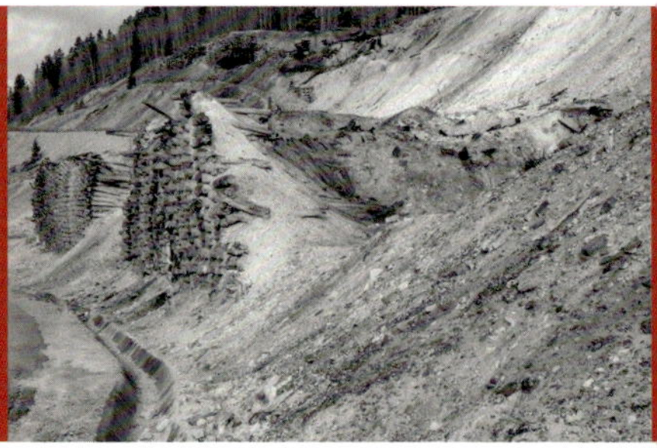

28. **Leadville, Colorado, USA.** In 1880 M. Guggenheim Sons bought an underperforming lead and silver mine. Within a few years its great success encouraged the company, new to the minerals business, to invest in more mines and in state-of-the-art smelters in Leadville, Pueblo, El Paso, and central Mexico. In 2025 Leadville and the upper Arkansas River watershed are a half century into an environmental restoration effort.

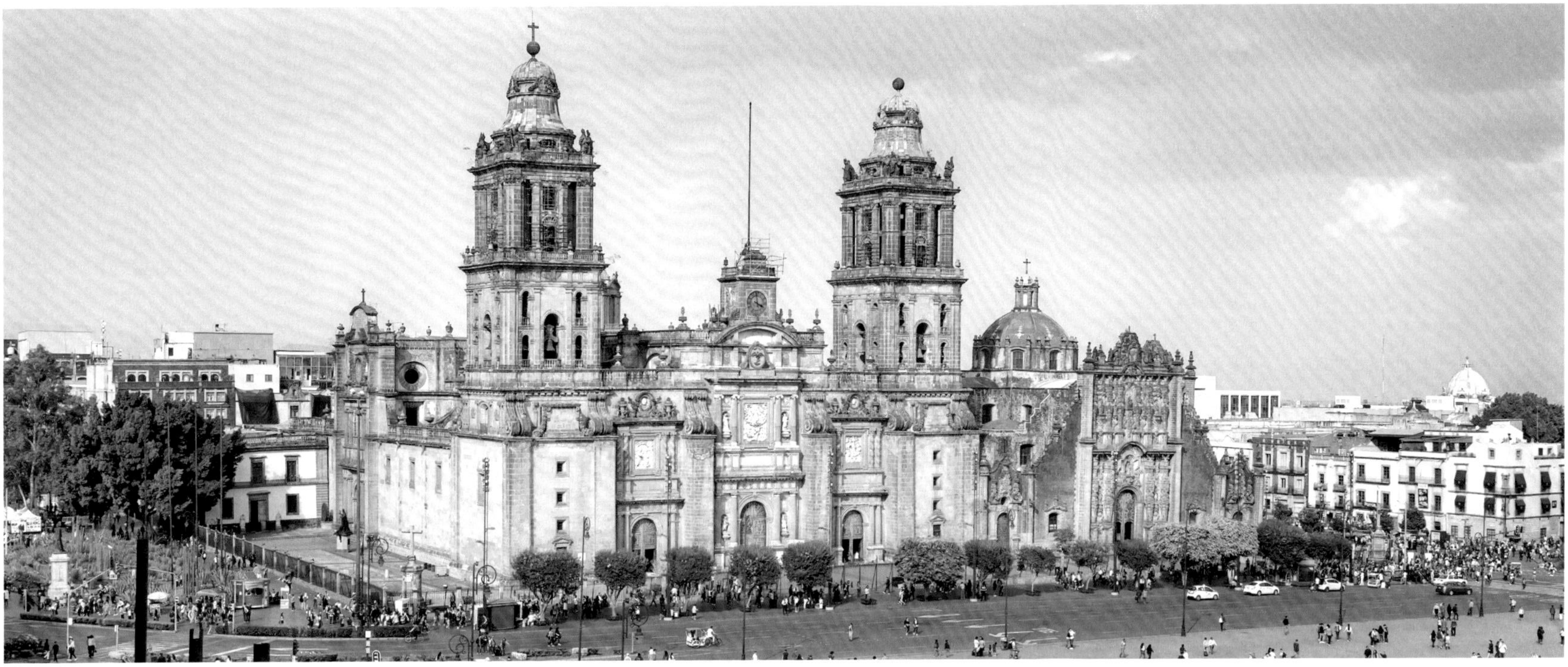

Metropolitan Cathedral, Mexico City, Mexico, 2020. Under construction for two and a half centuries starting in 1573, Mexico City's Metropolitan Cathedral is built atop the rubble of Aztec sacred sites. To obliterate pagan influence, conquering Spaniards demolished massive pyramids and temples dating from centuries earlier. Conveniently, the recycled stone, already quarried and dressed, was ready for reuse in building what is still the largest Catholic cathedral in the Americas.

speak, though faintly, with an eloquence unique to archeological ruins. Scattered from Pozos to El Paso, from Magdalena to Pueblo, their rusting hulks, melting stone foundations, and toxic-slag mountains are the headstones honoring generations of *trabajadores* and their families.

The Land atop a Treasure Vein

Environment is another way of saying context. The El Paso ASARCO smelter, America's largest, rose where it did and succeeded so completely for so long because the natural setting and political landscape favored it and because ASARCO took prudent advantage of both.[3] To put it simply (and Michael Romero Taylor's essay elaborates on this idea), the Rio Grande cutting through a mountain range to form El Paso del Norte was for three centuries crucial in steering North America's destiny.[4]

Every cultural artifact on any landscape owes a debt to nature. And every natural element in that same landscape bears culture's heavy imprint. Other authors, artists, and activists articulate that topic more fully than I.[5] My goal in this photographic project is to understand the big complex picture by responding to beauty in its many facets wherever I encounter it.

Within three miles of the El Paso smelter site, the stunning range of topographic variety is incomparable, though subtle. A binational urban grid, with its population of three and a half million, fans out from a point where in 1598 don Juan de Oñate crossed Rio Grande del Norte into Nuevo México. Half a millennium later the perimeter of this sun-bleached metropolis abruptly halts, the frayed edges of Juárez–El Paso opening onto searing desert for hundreds of miles in all directions. And like islands rising from a sea of gypsum, mesquite, and chamisa, mountains beyond number punctuate the glare to the horizon. This is the landscape at the crossroads of the continent where, after campaigns of conquest, exploitation, and salvation, cultures converge and now thrive. El Paso del Norte, a narrow slit cut by a shallow silty stream through an isolated desert mountain range, is also the pivot point for one of North America's historic chapters—a complex, ongoing narrative centuries in the making.

Industrial landscape is ephemeral. At least that is nature's perspective—one that, at a leisurely pace, sees tectonic plates collide and black holes gobble up galaxies. But our timetable is different, and our priorities more urgent. We live, build, learn, explore, populate, and cultivate, measuring our progress by tracking how much or how fast or how big or how many. Industry is a noun conjuring loud, gritty machines in hulking buildings blighting vile neighborhoods in polluted cities. But industry, as an attribute, connotes an exemplary human trait. To be industrious, to practice industry, is to be unlazy, hardworking, and resourceful. In our time, a culture's success is measured in industrial output. Applying our personal industriousness to industry is the same as good citizenship.

As an artist (and a former farmhand and steelworker) I not only understand labor, I honor it. The work we do shapes our autobiographies. It helps to define our lives. This is true of individuals and of peoples.

I use the common term *cultural landscape* to understand the physical world outside my window, stretching as far as I can see. Making these pictures conjures for me a sprawling map with El Paso at its center, a map reaching deep into Mexico and extending north to embrace much of what we know today as the American West. It is a topography strewn with clues to the story—the history—of the lives of heroic but often unnamed souls.

Sometimes the most complex subjects are the most subtle, like the debris field of artifacts scattered in history's wake: adobe villages melting into hillsides, smelter foundations and aqueducts, and cemeteries, cathedrals, and railroads. Their place-names are descriptive (Smeltertown; Leadville) and honorific (Santa Eulalia; El Camino Real). They have this in common: everything I see was built by someone, by some community, by some person multiplied by the thousands over the centuries—persons whose names are lost. The names we do remember are of people who paid or owned or commanded the laborers and the miners. Oñate, Juárez, Villa, Guggenheim. But the unnamed legions of workers binding a dozen generations are invisible to us.

My task here is to look for, then to make tangible, the remnants left by these anonymous thousands over half a millennium. It is to their industry that I feel most indebted.

Artifacts vanish, turned to powder due to either to time or to human mischief. These photographs, made in this most remarkable landscape, are my stab at learning the stories they might reveal—learning the stories and then passing them on.

Notes

1. Monica Perales, *Smeltertown: Making and Remembering a Southwest Border Community* (University of North Carolina Press, 2010), 5, 32, 36 (map).

2. Michael P. Malone, *The Battle for Butte: Mining and Politics on the Northern Frontier, 1864–1906* (University of Washington Press, 1981), 133–38.

3. C. L. Sonnichsen, *The Pass of the North: Four Centuries on the Rio Grande*, vol. 2 (Texas Western Press, 1980), 72.

4. The name "El Paso del Norte" is cited by various scholars as a reference to the most convenient river crossing (of El Camino Real de Tierra Adentro) in the north of Mexico; it is also a reference to the canyon cut by the river, forming an east-west passage through the region's north-south mountain chain.

5. Betsy Fahlman, "The Muse of Enterprise: The Industrial Landscapes of El Paso" (this volume) and Toby Jurovics, "The Old Topographics" (this volume).

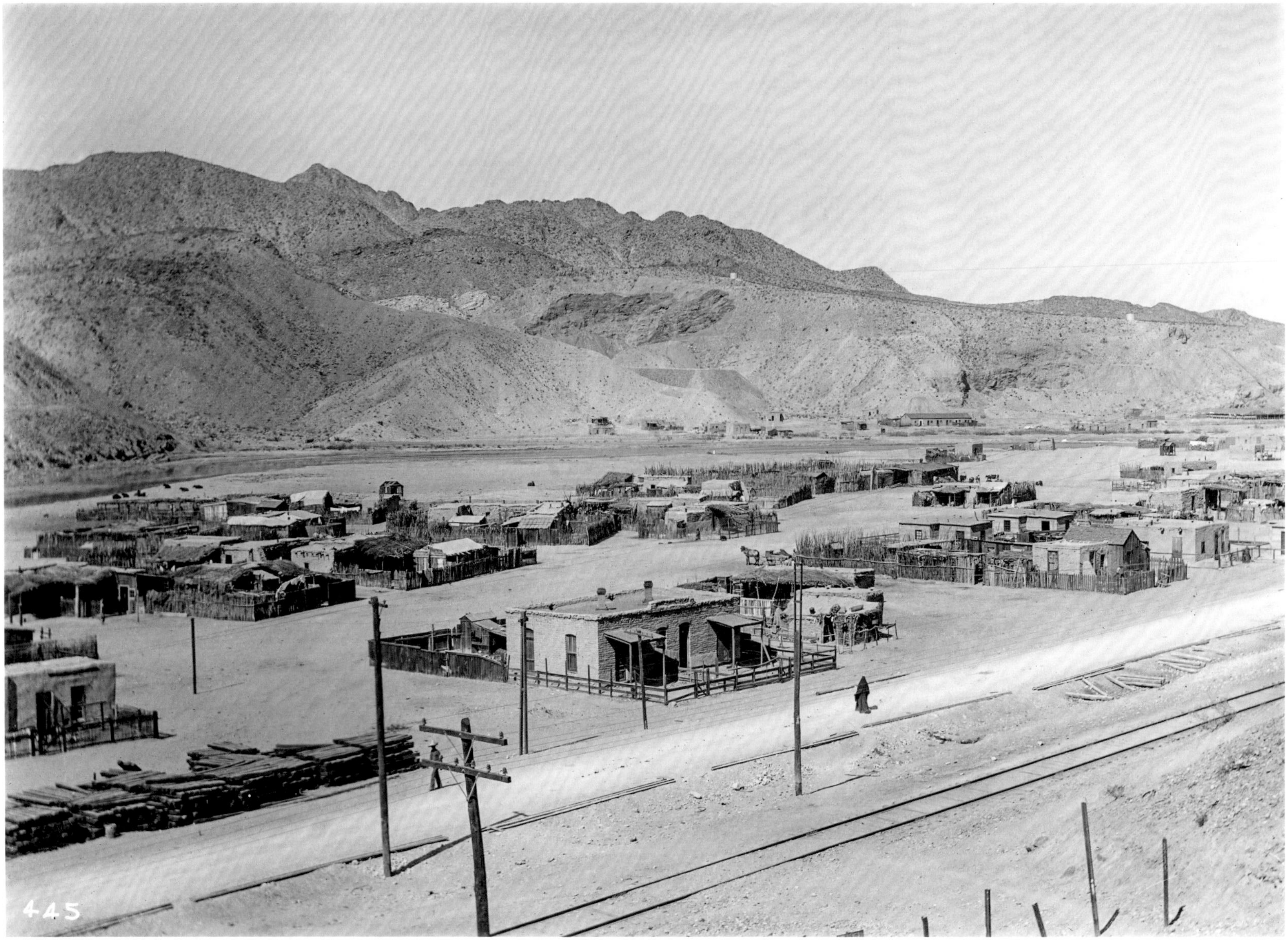

Smeltertown, early twentieth century. This photograph was made from the ASARCO slag mesa east of the county road (now Paisano Drive). The view looks west toward the Rio Grande and Mount Cristo Rey. Smeltertown was demolished in the 1970s, its community scattering to resettle elsewhere in El Paso neighborhoods and beyond. Photograph ca. 1910. Courtesy of the Otis A. Aultman Collection, El Paso Public Library.

A Brief History of El Paso del Norte

MICHAEL ROMERO TAYLOR

EVERY TIME I DRIVE BY the site of the old American Smelting and Refining Company (ASARCO) plant, I am reminded of the special place that it is. The now-leveled landscape has been broken, but if you use your imagination and strip away the asphalt, concrete, and razor-wire border fences near the site, you can read the layers of history that blanket the area where ASARCO once stood proud at El Paso del Norte, the Pass of the North, the location of alternating intrigue, turmoil and tranquility for thousands of years. A pass where the movement of man and nature has always taken place—a kinetic landscape, a crossroads. A place where one had to have patience, since the temperament of the river could paralyze families, and entire armies waiting to cross, until the floods subsided, especially in the spring months when the mountains far to the north would release their snow melt.

The Pass of the North is part of who I am. When we were children, our family would travel south to El Paso down the Mesilla Valley to visit relatives; my parents would point to the largest ASARCO stack and remark, "That's the tallest smokestack in the world." We seven kids in the back of the Volkswagen bus were always soundly impressed by this pronouncement. Whether or not it was really the tallest is irrelevant. And at the time, so was the pollution it spewed. For young boys like me, ASARCO was the epitome of the erector-set industrialized world. The smokestacks were our datum point for approaching El Paso from the Mesilla Valley, thirty-five miles upriver where we were raised; and at night, hundreds of feet high, their blinking red lights served as our beacon heading back north. I have experienced moving through this pass for the past sixty-eight years, lingering enough to try to comprehend its significance.

Our mother, Mary Daniels Taylor, spent her childhood in the 1920s and early 1930s in company housing right next to ASARCO where her father, Albert Milton Daniels, was foreman at the Southwestern Portland Cement Plant. It defined the edge of Smeltertown, on the east bank of the Rio Grande, just to the north of the iconic 1917 train trestles. My mother's daily life on this part of the border, the scene of much drama then and in prior centuries, had a profound influence on her later work as a respected scholar of border studies. Besides being mother to seven children, she was an avid historian, getting up at four in the morning before the house awoke to research the history of the Mesilla Valley and El Paso. She taught us from a young age the respect that she had for the Pass of the North, the place where people for millennia had been crossing El Rio Grande del Norte (the Great River of the North). Occasionally she would take us to the Pass near ASARCO, the place where she spent part of her childhood looking for ruins and landmarks like the historic river ford now marked by an abandoned park, its granite slabs inscribed with snapshot histories of the Pass; or the site of the old Custom House at Frontera across the river in Juárez, or the Zach White School where she attended elementary classes and later taught.

El Paso–Juárez is home to one of the largest border populations in the world, now approaching three million. What made it this way? The Pass of the North is a tale of two inseparable cities in two countries, a demographic that embraces a unique borderlands passion, and experience expressed (in part) through an amalgam of Spanish and English language, smoothly woven together during everyday conversations into the "Spanglish" that many of us speak. The entangled place-names at the Pass exemplify its complexity: the original seventeenth-century settlement of El Paso del Norte was in Ciudad Juárez's historic plaza center, about three miles across the Rio Grande and to the south of the ASARCO site. A nineteenth-century Anglo American settlement of Franklin sprang up from the 1823 Juan María Ponce de León ranch on the north side of the river. El Paso del Norte, Mexico, changed its name in 1888 to Ciudad Juárez to honor the charismatic president Benito Juárez who led the Mexican Republic from there in the 1860s. In 1873 Franklin changed its name to El Paso to acknowledge its location at the Pass of the North.

What was this landscape like before the Industrial Age, before the building of the railroad and the ASARCO smelter? It was indeed a pass—six miles long, shouldered by mountains and hills on both sides of the river. In the past century it has been chewed up by mining and by cement and brick plants and the massive smelting operations of ASARCO, and it has been paved over by shopping centers, urban sprawl, and interstate highways. The river is now in a straightjacket of dams and levees and border fences. At night the river frontier is illuminated by glaring security lights as bright as day, monitored 24-7 from land and air by border patrol in SUVs and helicopters. Compared to the unbridled terrain that existed before the arrival of Euro-Americans, it is a jarring scene.

This Pass has long been part of a very significant cultural route. Even the name connotes movement—the Pass of the North, the gateway upriver to what is now northern New Mexico. The Rio Grande that cuts through the Pass was a riparian lifeline along which people and wildlife had traveled for millennia prior to the arrival of the Spanish. The river was vital for sustaining life in natural cycles that alternately brought drought and floods. Its rich soils nurtured a green ribbon teeming with life, incising the otherwise parched landscape. Archaeologists believe that people were hunting large mammals such as bison and gathering plants here as far back as ten thousand years ago. The river terraces in the area were being used by seasonal hunters and gatherers of plants and were dotted with habitations dating to 4,500 years ago.[1] In my early years as an archaeologist, I conducted a survey on the west mesa overlooking the Pass, and I recorded incredible Archaic period campsites and a multiroom earthen pueblo site dating to AD 900–1400. Occasionally I would take time to pause and gaze over the river to imagine the caravans, armies, trading expeditions, shamans, and priests that had maneuvered the Pass.

When Juan de Oñate's colonizing expedition from deep in Mexico crossed the river through the Pass in 1598 bound for northern New Mexico, the route became part of the Camino Real de Tierra Adentro, the "Royal Road to the Interior Lands," the earliest Euro-American trade route in what is now the United States. Directly tying Spain's colonial capital at Mexico City to its northern frontier in distant New Mexico, the Camino Real spanned three centuries, two countries, and 1,600 miles. It not only connected the Pass to Mexico City; through its maritime routes it connected to Spain and the rest of Europe as well as to the Philippines and the Far East, making Spain, through its complex network of roads and shipping routes, one of history's earliest global economies. In the shadow of what would later become the ASARCO plant, countless travelers moved along this global cultural route.

Oñate and his colonizing expedition were in search of a new home far to the north. They hoped to better their lives, maybe even to find hints of the type of wealth found at Tenochitlán, the site of today's Mexico City, 1,200 miles to the south, the beginning of the Royal Road. What a scene, and what a cacophony Oñate's expedition must have been to the local Manso Indians at the Pass four centuries ago: 400 men, 130 of whom brought their families, traveling in 83 creaking wagons and carts laden with an incredible variety of provisions, much of which had never been seen before in these far reaches of New Spain, and accompanied by 7,000 over-excited animals thirsty for water.[2] It is said that the caravan went as fast as a pig could trot. When Oñate's mobile city reached the Rio Grande in the vicinity of today's San Elizario, Texas, twenty-four miles downriver from the ASARCO site, it stopped to take possession of the lands in the watershed of the Rio Grande for King Philip II in faraway Spain, adding what is now much of the southwestern United States to the Spanish Kingdom. The river, with its game and fish, was a welcome respite for the exhausted expedition after crossing the Chihuahua desert from the south. From San Elizario, Oñate sent scouts upriver to find a suitable crossing. The Mansos led them to a time-worn, rocky ford at the narrows of the Rio Grande where the present-day Franklin Mountains yielded to the river, forming the cut, and joined the riverbed, near the site of where ASARCO would later be located. It took days for the entire caravan to cross the river, which it did with assistance from the Mansos, who helped ferry the laden wagons through the swift current.[3] Members of the Oñate expedition, and subsequent colonizers who used this Pass heading north, are the ancestors of many present-day Hispanic residents in New Mexico and the El Paso area. I am one of those descendants on my father's side. But the Pass did not see only Spaniards during the colonial period. Enslaved Indians who were forced to work in the silver mines of Zacatecas, seven hundred miles south on the camino, also came through the Pass, as did thousands of mestizos (Spanish for "persons of mixed race," in this case Spaniards and Indians).

Thus began the documented historic use of the Pass, starting with 223 years of dominance over the region by the Spanish empire initiated by Oñate's entrada. We know through various journals, ledgers, and other documents that for more than four hundred years the Pass has been witness to many events that tell stories of struggle, joy, heartbreak, fortune, and poverty, the most recent being the incredible story of ASARCO and Smeltertown.

The gorge at the pass did not offer an easy route for much of the seventeenth and eighteenth centuries. Seasonal flooding often made the ford impassable. The foothills northeast of the river were difficult to traverse by wagon since the adjacent Franklin Mountains precipitously dropped to the river's edge. Travelers crossed at Oñate's southern rocky ford and continued along the very rough eastern bank of the river up through the Pass. The Camino Real continued north hugging the river, generally along the same route as today's Paisano Drive.

This stretch of the camino was one of the more difficult ones, until road improvements and railroad construction made the route more passable thanks to modern machinery that could blast, haul, and grade the rocky terrain. Some travelers detoured around the rugged mountains by way of Camino de los Muleros (Road of the Muleteers) to the west along the base of Cerro Cristo Rey, then joined the river and the main camino again near today's Sunland Park at a ford about six miles north.[4]

By the early 1600s Franciscan missionaries were working with Indigenous people at settlements near the center of today's Ciudad Juárez. In 1659, with the establishment of Nuestra Señora de Guadalupe de los Mansos (Our Lady of Guadalupe of the Mansos Mission) at the Pass, the area became an important stop on El Camino Real de Tierra Adentro.[5]

About this same time, Spaniards built a dam on the river below today's ASARCO site that diverted water through an acequia (ditch) to El Paso del Norte. In addition to localized traffic, the Pass witnessed caravans coming from far south in Mexico every three years on the way north to supply the missions in faraway New Mexico. These were major events that brought not only much-needed supplies but also news and correspondence from within and beyond the Americas.

Among seminal events that the Pass experienced was the mass exodus of Spaniards who survived the Pueblo Revolt of 1680 in northern New Mexico. After eight decades of Spanish mistreatment and exploitation in scattered settlements and missions, the Pueblo Indians revolted and killed several hundred settlers. This drove almost two thousand remaining Spaniards and Indian captives and allies out of the region along the camino three hundred miles to the south, eventually reaching the Guadalupe Mission at El Paso del Norte. The population pressure, created by this sudden influx of refugees, forced the Spanish officials to establish new settlements downriver from the mission on more irrigable lands and provide room to minimize social strife. Today, the settlements of Ysleta del Sur, Socorro del Sur, Senecú, and San Elizario are surrounded by the greater metropolitan area of El Paso and Ciudad Juárez, but they still retain their identities with their founding three centuries ago.

By the middle of the eighteenth century, the valley at the Pass of the North was an incredibly busy trading center, sustained by rich farmlands watered by miles of acequias irrigating extensive gardens, fruit orchards, fields of corn and wheat, and vineyards that produced good wines and brandies, both sacramental and secular. Trading caravans traversing the Pass created a constant stream of interaction, communication, and exchange of news, traditions, and lifestyles.[6] The sights, sounds, and smells of agriculture, ranching, commerce, and transportation created a lasting impression on travelers passing through the area. In the 1760s, it was estimated that five thousand people lived in the villages, ranches, and farms scattered below El Paso del Norte for about twenty miles. The settlement and surrounding farms and hamlets offered some protection and safety in numbers, but it was by no means a peaceful, bucolic environment during the Spanish Colonial period, which witnessed much conflict with the surrounding nomadic Indians and with in-fighting among the Spaniards, Pueblo Indians, and mestizos. The settlements at the Pass were located far from the centers of power in larger cities to the south, such as Zacatecas and Mexico City, and as a result El Paso del Norte did not receive the attention it needed to maintain enough Spanish soldiers and sufficient funding.

Until the early nineteenth century, there were no Euro-American settlements on the north side of the river, but in 1823 Juan Ponce de León established a farm in what would later become downtown El Paso. The settlement reportedly included a flour mill at the falls where the Rio Grande emerged from the Pass, very close to the ASARCO site.

Another seminal event at the Pass was the Mexican American War, a historic pivot point that changed the region forever. In December 1846, 1,200 Mexican soldiers and peasants camped near the ASARCO site in anticipation of marching north to meet the American army head-on.[7] A few days later at Bracito, about thirty miles upriver from the Pass, the Mexican Army was defeated, and after subsequent battles in Chihuahua and Mexico City, the Mexican government conceded.

The result was a new boundary between the two nations, one that transferred almost half of Mexico's territory to the United States, through the 1848 Treaty of Guadalupe Hidalgo. The Rio Grande, at a point opposite the ASARCO site, became the new natural international border, from the Gulf of Mexico to the Pass. Today, on the west side of the river, a large limestone obelisk marks the first boundary monument set in place in 1856 after binational negotiations determined the latitude where the boundary leaves the Rio Grande and heads west to the Pacific.[8] The Pass quickly became an important crossing on the new international border.

After the new boundary was determined, the Pass saw a torrent of Anglo travelers heading west on the heels of the discovery of gold in California in 1849. Thousands of these gold seekers camped near La Frontera, on the north side of the Pass, on their way to the gold fields. Stage lines and mail service from the east, many of which had major stops and offices in El Paso, followed this stream of adventurers heading west.[9] The El Paso area was one of the few relatively safe and well-watered stops for travelers, where they could rest after traversing hundreds of miles of west Texas desert to resupply provisions before continuing. Several of the main streets in El Paso today retain the nineteenth-century names that reflect these destinations and westward migration: San Antonio, Santa Fe, San Francisco, Overland, and El Paso (the road to Ciudad Juárez, old El Paso del Norte).

The historic river ford at the south end of the Pass, where Oñate's 1598 expedition had crossed, became the location of Hart's Mill, where Juan Ponce de León had his original mill a few years earlier. Originally from Kentucky, Simeon Hart married a Hispanic woman from the area and became a very successful merchant, trader, and social figure in El Paso. By 1850 his property was comprised of his expansive residence, the mill, a stage stop, and a restaurant, and it was one of the first permanent compounds in American El Paso.[10] Part of Simeon Hart's complex, from 1881 to 1883, was the fifth site of Fort Bliss. The sixth and current Fort Bliss is located northeast of the city, and today is a major economic anchor in the region.[11] Part of the old Hart residence still exists and served as a restaurant called La Hacienda up until the early part of this century. It was one of those wonderful Mexican restaurants where ice-cold beer, *bolillos*, and delicious bargain lunches were enjoyed by thousands over the years.

The railroad arrived in 1881 and changed everything at the Pass. The population exploded from a small ranching town to a city. With the railroads came smelting and mining—now the powerhouse of El Paso's economy for over a century. The rails passed directly through old Fort Bliss and what would later become Smeltertown, where generations of ASARCO's workers' families would live. The railroad shifted the major transportation routes from the footpaths and wagon roads of the ancient Pass to new bridges that crossed the river and linked with Mexican railways to the interior. For El Paso, the arrival of the railroad meant a new global linkage; it became a hub of transportation and trade that was key in connecting North America north to south and east to west, adding a new dimension to the already diversified border. With the building of the International Brick Company across the river from ASARCO in New Mexico in 1897 and the Southwestern Portland Cement Company adjacent to ASARCO in 1907, concrete and brick building materials changed the skyline of El Paso, which by then offered most of the amenities of other large cities in the United States.[12] In 1916 cement from the Southwestern Portland Cement Company was shipped north by rail to build Elephant Butte Dam, one hundred miles above the Pass. The dam enabled unprecedented irrigation and the expanded cultivation of crops in the Mesilla and El Paso valleys, and it provided a more reliable water source for the ever-increasing Rio Grande valley population.

Important sieges and battles of the Mexican Revolution also played out at the Pass of the North.[13] Across the river from ASARCO in 1911, Mexican revolutionaries under Pascual Orozco's command camped and eventually entered the historic core of Ciudad Juárez under cover of the acequia that tiered off from the river opposite Hart's Mill. Thousands of curiosity seekers on the US side watched pitched battles take place in Ciudad Juárez from rooftops and railroad cars in the vicinity of Smeltertown.

Through the symbiotic relationship between autos and highways, new transportation routes were built on top of or adjacent to the ancient camino that had brought travelers through the Pass for centuries. Paisano Drive (Highway 85) and the Pan American Highway pass right by the front door of Smeltertown, and the 1970s Interstate passes adjacent to and to the eastern border of the site. Every day, thousands of people from diverse backgrounds share this narrow corridor through the Pass of the North with the river, freight and passenger trains, and highways. Speeding along the interstate through the gauntlet of overpasses, train trestles, and interchanges, it is hard for one to imagine the stories concealed by this scoured landscape at the Pass.

The area is much transformed since the early nineteenth century. Layers of history have been stripped from the surface by the raging river and by intense mining over the past 150 years, leaving us with a confusing vista that is hard to decipher. But the fact is that the Pass of the North is pivotal to the narrative of the United States and Mexico. This place, as jumbled as it seems today, is one of the most historically rich sites in the United States. It has been a crossroads of ideas and customs for centuries, a place that has witnessed countless stories of daily life. Even though most of the physical remains of Smeltertown have been scraped from the landscape, telling vestiges still serve as touchstones for the people who once lived in the shadows of its smokestacks: the forty-three-foot limestone statue of Cristo Rey overlooking the valley, the river, the train trestles and tracks, the cemetery, Paisano Drive, and remnants of the surrounding Pass. The Camino Real de Tierra Adentro, the long-distance route that for centuries carried so many travelers through the Pass, is the same route used by generations of workers who sought employment at ASARCO, and it is the same route used today by thousands of people heading north and south through El Paso and across the international border. How many millions of people have passed through here? Where were they going? Where were they coming from? How many individual orbits have coincided, collided, intersected, exploded, and shared life and emotions? Imagine the stories they could tell! The Camino Real de Tierra Adentro is still alive and well through the Pass of the North. This place represents a true crossroads for the continent, a place where energies and forces have converged. My family history is tied up like a ball of string around this nexus.

As I am funneled into this narrow corridor when I travel to El Paso, I always glance toward the river where my mother spent her childhood. Feelings are good here in this zone, at this special crossroads that physically and figuratively has been, and remains, so much a part of me. I relish its rush, its power, its significance, its cleansing, its swath of history, of things that transpired here that are part of its mystery. It is a strong, spiritual, and always humbling place. I often try and decipher its secrets. Sometimes I think too hard about it, try to analyze what I am feeling. But most of the time I catch myself, and gratefully I just experience it, basking in the enigma of the place.

Notes

1. Thomas C. O'Laughlin, "The Keystone Dam Site and Other Archaic and Formative Sites in Northwest El Paso, Texas," *Publications in Anthropology* no. 8, El Paso Centennial Museum, the University of Texas at El Paso, 1980.

2. "Oñate Expedition," Texas State Historical Association, accessed December 20, 2016. https://tshaonline.org/handbook/online/articles/up002.

3. Sonnichsen, *Pass of the North*, 17

4. Sonnichsen, *Pass of the North*, 32.

5. George D. Torok, *From the Pass to the Pueblos: El Camino Real de Tierra Adentro National Historic Trail* (Sunstone Press, 2012), 71.

6. Torok, *From the Pass to the Pueblos*, 72.

7. Sonnichsen, *Pass of the North*, 112.

8. Torok, *From the Pass to the Pueblos*, 113.

9. Torok, *From the Pass to the Pueblos*, 98.

10. Torok, *From the Pass to the Pueblos*, 111.

11. Perales, *Smeltertown*, 22, 31.

12. Perales, *Smeltertown*, 229.

13. Sonnichsen, *Pass of the North*, 397.

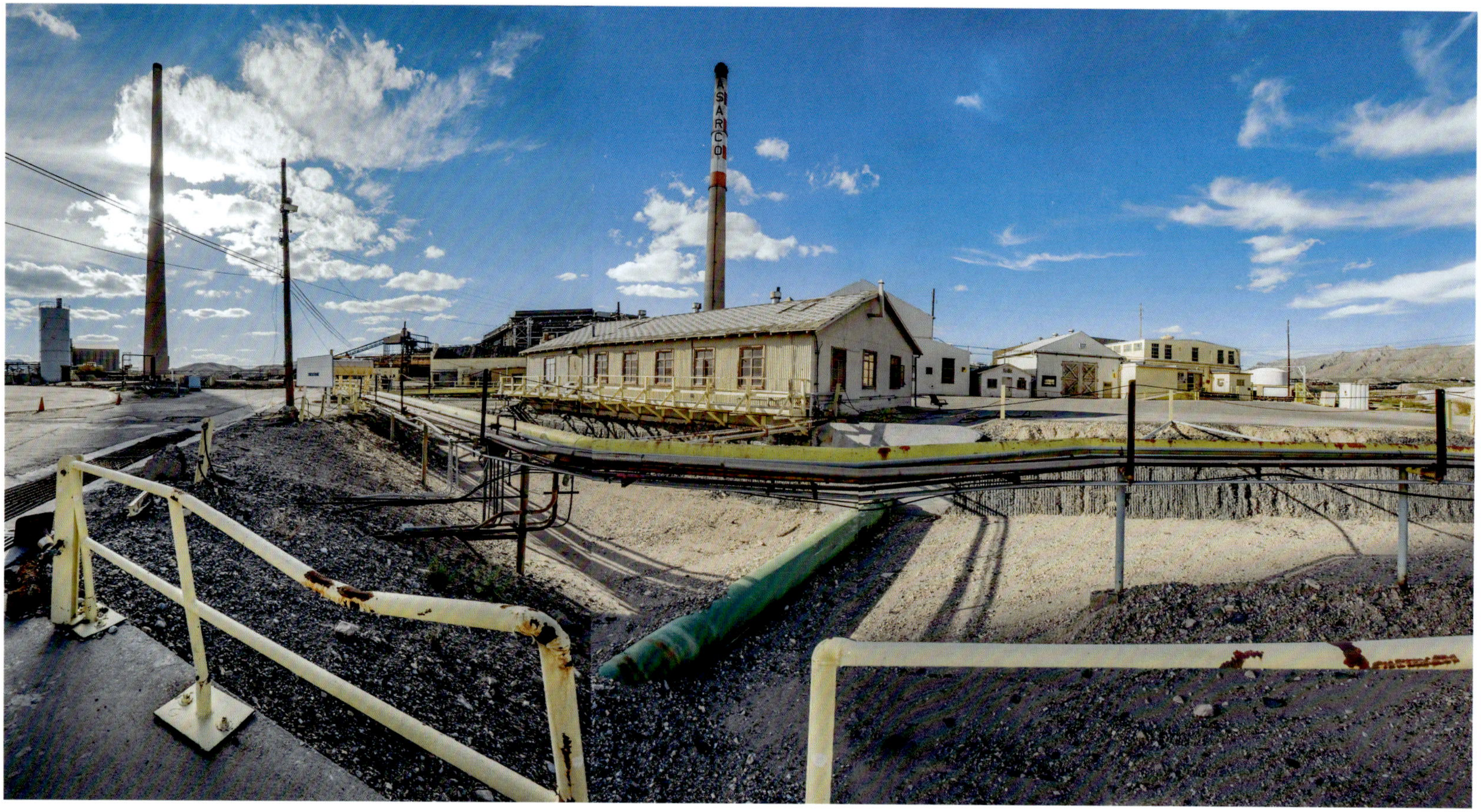

A pre-demolition view of the El Paso ASARCO site. This composite panorama was made at the geographic center of the smelter property. In the foreground is a once-natural stream bed that drains into the Rio Grande channel. The camera is shielded from the sun's glare by the shadow of the sixty-story lead stack seen on the left, three-hundred yards away.

The Muse of Enterprise

The Industrial Landscapes of El Paso

BETSY FAHLMAN

ONE WRITER POETICALLY DESCRIBED THE American Smelting and Refining Company's one-hundred-foot-tall sheet-iron smokestack "built in a wooden frame supported by a cross-work of timbers" as providing visitors with "an Eiffel Tower effect."[1] El Paso, situated at the border of Mexico, does not immediately conjure art, but rather a gritty border city whose most significant industry was once the American Smelting and Refining Company (ASARCO). The city lacked the deep historical resonances found in the landscape and Native peoples that attracted artists to the art colonies of Santa Fe and Taos. Nor did it possess the seaside charms of the many picturesque coastal towns in California overlooking the Pacific Ocean, which attracted many artists to settle there, either seasonally or permanently, offering popular art classes during the summer months. Many remember El Paso for its environmental pollution, where the tallest stack in America spewed toxic yellow smoke filled with sulfur dioxide and heavy metals into the air when the smelter was in full production.[2]

Nevertheless, beginning in the late nineteenth century, a small group of artists were inspired by the unusual beauties of El Paso's Industrial landscape.[3] Not surprisingly, these artists received no commissions from ASARCO. Industrialists who became patrons of art generally did not want to see canvases celebrating the source of their wealth and its environmental depredations (though smoky skies denoted jobs and prosperity), preferring conservatively safe aesthetic choices such as comfortingly placid French Barbizon landscapes and peasant views, or academic figure paintings of mythological and historical subjects. El Paso was not a place known for wealthy collectors, and the city's art museum was not established until 1959. Nevertheless, the artists who ventured to El Paso found both pleasant and dramatic scenes to capture their interest.

In 1885 French artist Léon Trousset (1838–1917) painted a handsome panoramic view of El Paso as seen from the Mexican border.[4] The artist employed common landscape conventions typical of the European art historical canon, which American artists translated into the conventions of the Hudson River School in the nineteenth century, by framing the scene with trees and placing figures in the foreground to establish scale. This practice also included a single man cutting down a tree, a common trope of the ever-westward advancement of civilization impelled by Manifest Destiny. In the far background, the prosperous and expanding city of El Paso is visible at the base of the Franklin Mountains; between 1880 and 1890, the city's population increased thirteen-fold. Above the mountains are dramatic clouds that convey the energy of the enterprise unfolding below (which would later include the smoke of pollution), and the artist includes several standard signifiers referencing the progress of a civilization whose industry could thrive in a pastoral context. On the right side a train steams across a wooden bridge over the Rio Grande, a common reference to the "machine in the garden" of the fruitful harmony of industry within the context of landscape.[5] On the left we see in the far distance the stacks of a smelter ejecting a plume of white smoke. The ASARCO facility dates from 1887, but smelting on that site dates back even earlier. By the time Trousset had completed his large canvas, El Paso had become a busy commercial and railroad hub, and trains passed through from all directions: the Southern Pacific to the west, the Santa Fe to the north, and the Texas Pacific and the Galveston-Harrisburg-San Antonio to the east, and the Mexican Central Railroad headed into Ciudad Juárez across the border.

The landscape conventions employed by Trousset continued into the first quarter of the twentieth century and may be seen in *View of El Paso at Sunset* by Audley Dean Nicols (1875–1941), which dates from about 1922. The artist, who was born in Pittsburgh, moved to El Paso in 1919 for health reasons, and he remained in the city until his death in 1941. Once settled in the Southwest, he made numerous views of his favorite subjects—desert scenes in Texas, New Mexico, and Arizona. For him, these sere regions were full of color, as Nicols observed of the typical landscapes he painted:

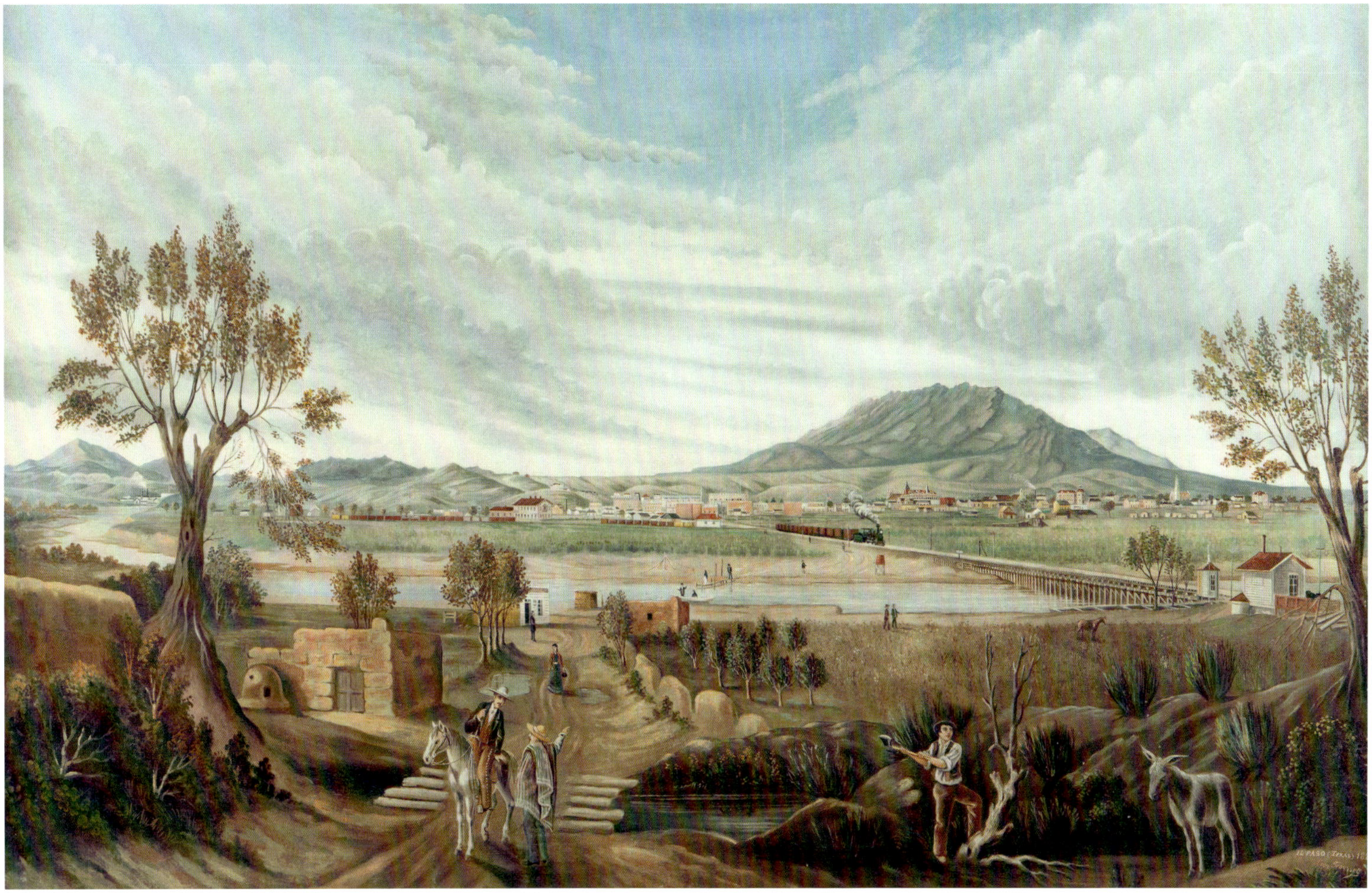

Léon Trousset (1838–1917), *View of El Paso*, 1885, oil on canvas, 39 × 60 in. Courtesy of the El Paso Museum of Art, gift of Mr. and Mrs. J. Sam Moore Jr. and family.

> The so-called gray of the desert is a mistake. The desert is everything but gray. There are fresh blues in the skies, pinks and yellows in the sunset, opalescent purple, rose, and lavender in the distant mountains, dull greens of every shade in the vegetation, and reds and yellows in the rocks and earth—but never gray.[6]

His atmospheric panoramic landscape is lyrical in color, and it represents an optimistic view of the region at a time of great prosperity. The attractive hazy lavender tones that infuse the painting led to him becoming the center of a group that by the 1940s had become known as the "Purple Mountain Painters."[7]

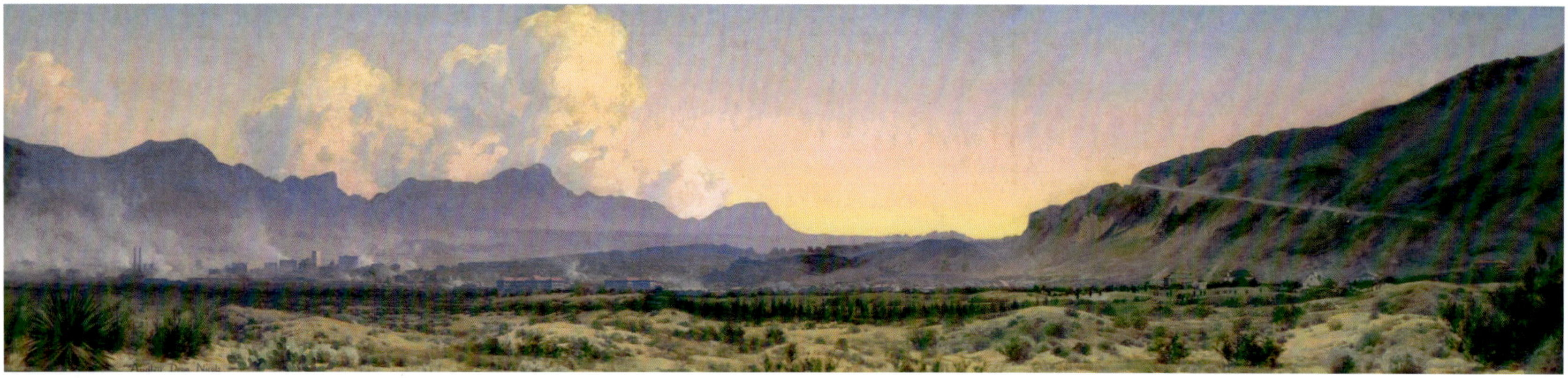

Audley Dean Nicols (1875–1941), *View of El Paso at Sunset*, 1925, Oil on canvas on panel, 45 × 193 in. Courtesy of the El Paso Independent School District, on long-term loan to the El Paso Museum of Art.

Nicols's large canvas presents the modern landscape of El Paso during a period of economic growth and population expansion. The stacks of ASARCO are emphatically present at the left. In the middle of the composition is the city of El Paso itself, whose skyline is punctuated by some of the many handsome commercial buildings that the architectural firm of Trost and Trost designed in the city between 1903 and 1933.[8] At the right are several of the early buildings of the College of Mines and Metallurgy of the University of Texas, founded in 1914.[9] That school offered its students a highly practical education, in contrast with the training of teachers at normal schools or the broad liberal-arts curriculum found at other colleges and universities. El Paso's institution of higher education was grounded in the industrial source of the prosperity of the city and was focused on training the next generation to work for the city's major employer.[10]

Several notable New Mexico–based artists ventured across the Texas border and found inspiration in the city's typical features. Born in the remote mining town of Virginia City, Montana, Fremont Ellis (1897–1985) had an unsettled childhood. His father was an itinerant dentist who eventually saw some success in mining. He later pursued a career in vaudeville and the management of motion-picture theatres before settling in El Paso, where his son Fremont briefly pursued an unsuccessful career as an optometrist. He had more success as an artist, and in January 1919 thirty of his paintings were exhibited at the University Club in El Paso. It was his first one-man show, and his work sold so well that he decided to become a full-time artist.

Ellis painted *El Paso Smelter at Night* in 1919. His canvas represents a very different sort of view of the ASARCO site than the more traditional images portrayed by either Trousset or Nicols.

It certainly does not capture "the very spirit, soul, and poetry of the desert" that one critic had admired in the work Ellis had shown at the University Club.[11] Instead of a distant, pastoral view, he has taken a vantage close to the smelter. Apocalyptic in mood and dramatically lit, it captures the spectacular night sky illuminated as it was when the facility was in full production. Smoke pours out from the three stacks, and the scene is ablaze with fiery colors, the sky full of smoldering grey, purple, red, and orange clouds from the smelter. The thick application of paint conveys a powerful texture suggesting the emotional charge of the scene. The buildings appear as heated to near molten, and the foreground landscape crackles with volcanic eruption. A critic writing in the *El Paso Morning News* observed in 1919: "He delights in indulging in a riot of melting colors, all blending in exquisite harmony and glowing in subtle lights and shade so characteristic of the far reaches of the arid plain."[12] This description parallels that which appeared in the 1940 WPA guide to Texas, whose writer was decidedly painterly in characterizing the changeable colors of the ASARCO plant: "A tawny cloud of smoke and jets of snow-white steam hover about the brick and sheet metal buildings by day, while at night the regular dumping of white-hot slag weirdly illumines the scene."[13] The same year Ellis painted *El Paso Smelter at Night*, he moved to Santa Fe where he would remain for the rest of his career. In 1921, with four other painters, he founded Los Cinco Pintores, a school whose members worked in modernist styles grounded in representational modes.

One of the founding members of the Taos Society of Artists in 1915, Ernest Blumenschein (1874–1960) remains best known as a painter of northern New Mexico scenes. With the exception of a series of railroad paintings he made during the 1950s, late in his career, he rarely produced scenes that could be thought of as industrial. His small 1935 painting, *El Paso Industry*, presents a painterly and highly expressive view. In his several canvases of the freight yards in Albuquerque, he was struck by the scenes, characterizing them as "a dramatic movement of the masses and lines with certain qualities of light and color" that captured its "character, strength, and virility."[14] These are elements also evident in *El Paso Industry*. Despite the small scale of his canvas, Blumenschein effectively conveyed the raw power of the smelter during the daytime. With expressive energetic brushstrokes, he moves the viewer through the scene from the train tracks in the foreground highlighted with an electric light blue, to the orange-brown rusty

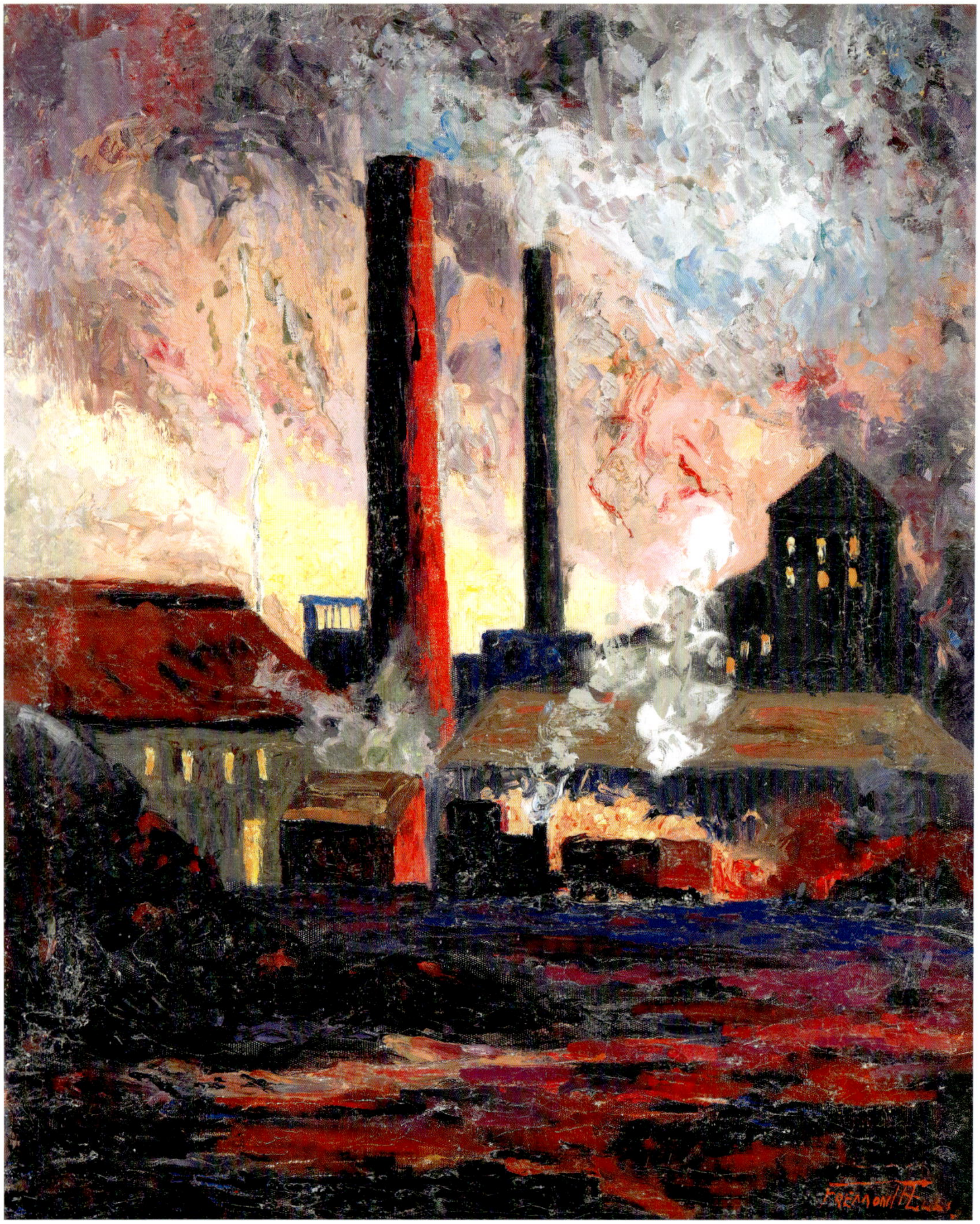

Fremont Ellis (1897–1985), *El Paso Smelter at Night*, 1919, oil on canvas, 36 × 30 ⅛ in. Courtesy of the El Paso Museum of Art, gift of the Artist (1971.5.1).

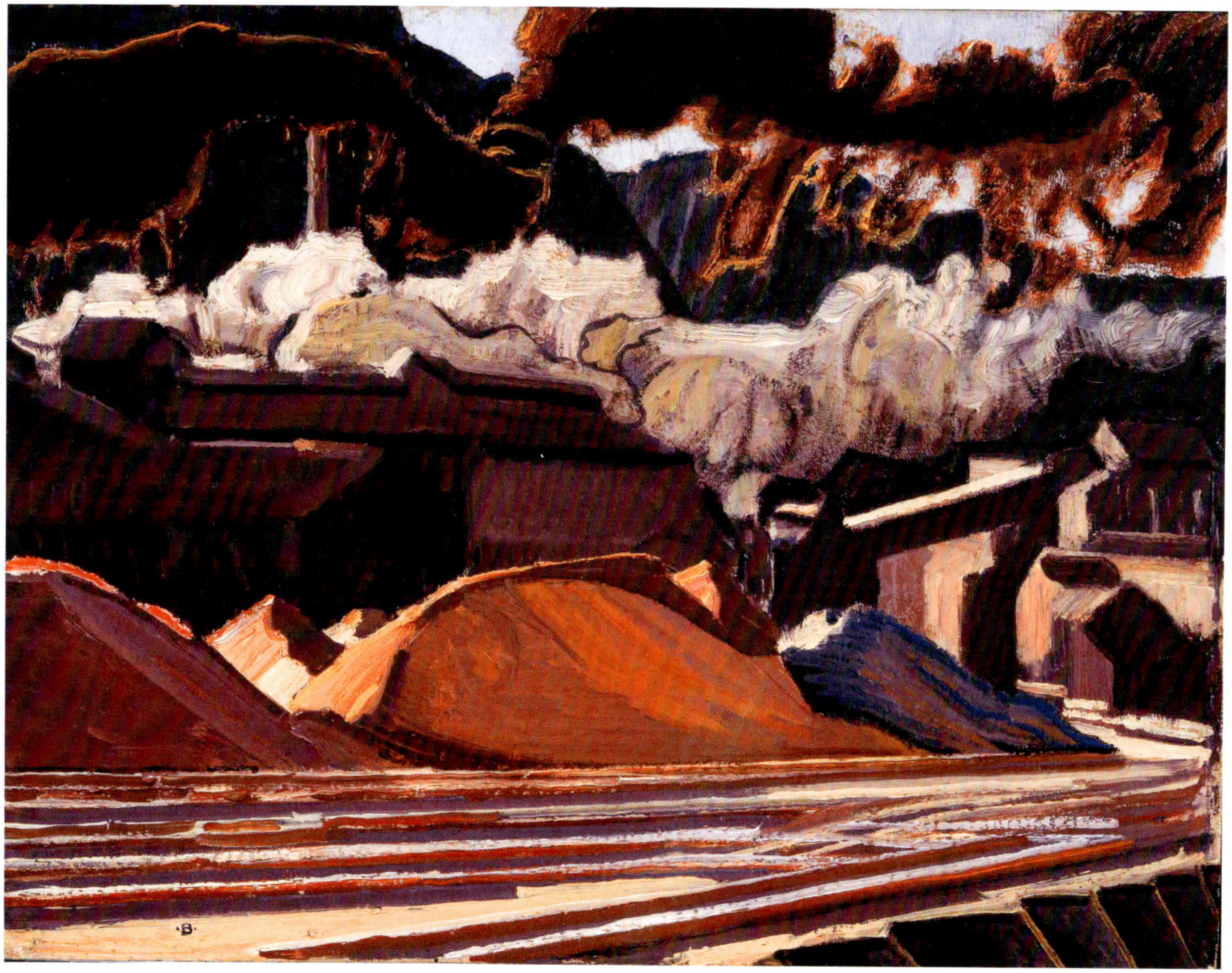

Earnest Blumenschein, (1874–1960), *El Paso Industry*, 1935, 11 ⅞ × 13 ⅞ in. Courtesy of the El Paso Museum of Art, gift of Dr. Reginald Fisher (1960.2.1).

looking slag heaps, to the smelter itself with billowing white and brown smoke, its stack in the background nearly obscured. The dark colors of his palette convey the rough beauty of the scene.

During the thirties, New Deal art programs with their emphasis on representational styles and regional themes encouraged several El Paso artists to portray local industrial subject matter, including the smelter. Some did this through government-sponsored art projects under federal cultural initiatives aimed at providing relief for artists during the Great Depression, including the Public Works of Art Project (PWAP), the short-lived predecessor to the more famous WPA.[15] The PWAP, which only lasted six months, was locally administered, and as a result the works were often exhibited in or installed in unsecured venues such as public schools (highly visible post-office murals were major federal commissions and generally remained in situ). Unframed works on paper, particularly highly portable prints and watercolors, were also more likely to disappear once the government programs ended in 1943. In 1934, supported by the PWAP, Beth MacLafferty Blake (1901–1993) produced watercolors and lithographs of industrial scenes. Her works (now lost) *Smelter from Scenic Drive* and *Globe Mills* were placed on exhibition in El Paso public schools. When she toured the smelter, she complained that she "was constantly choked with fumes and peppered with grit."[16]

Also supported by the PWAP were the two murals painted by Emilio García Cahero (1897–1939)—*Mining* and *Metallurgy*—for Holliday Hall at what was then the College of Mines and Metallurgy. Each was 14 feet by 120 feet and covered 3,360 square feet of wall space.[17] Born in Veracruz, Cahero taught art for many years at the Academia de San Carlos in Mexico City before establishing his studio in El Paso in the 1930s. The artist was part of the Mexican muralist movement, and during the twenties he was one of a group of artists who painted murals in the Colegio de San Ildefonso in Mexico City. Diego Rivera, David Alfaro Siqueiros, and José Clemente Orozco were among those who contributed to this project, which numbered forty-one murals.

Despite the prominence of the ASARCO complex within the local landscape, El Paso's most notable artist (and a native of the city), Tom Lea (1907–2001), only painted a single work of the site: his 1936 *The Smelter, From Mesa Road*. Described as "a desert Southwesterner to the bone,"[18] Lea was a significant regionalist artist, but his heart was not with the new West of commerce and vigorous industrial production but rather with its rich historical narrative and the sunbaked landscapes of west Texas. His mural in the United States Courthouse in El Paso is comprised of two panels picturing the theme of the city's history and development. His goal was to portray "the giants who came trying to tame the desert mountain country" of West Texas, and his grand narrative features the region's early explorers and settlers set against Coronado and his conquistadors, a Franciscan monk, a vaquero, Apache scouts, a frontier couple, a cowboy, a prospector, and

Tom Lea, (1907–2001), *The Smelter from Mesa Road,* 1936, oil on prepared heavy paper, 9 × 13 in. Courtesy of the Collection of Adair and Dee Margo, El Paso, copyright James D. Lea.

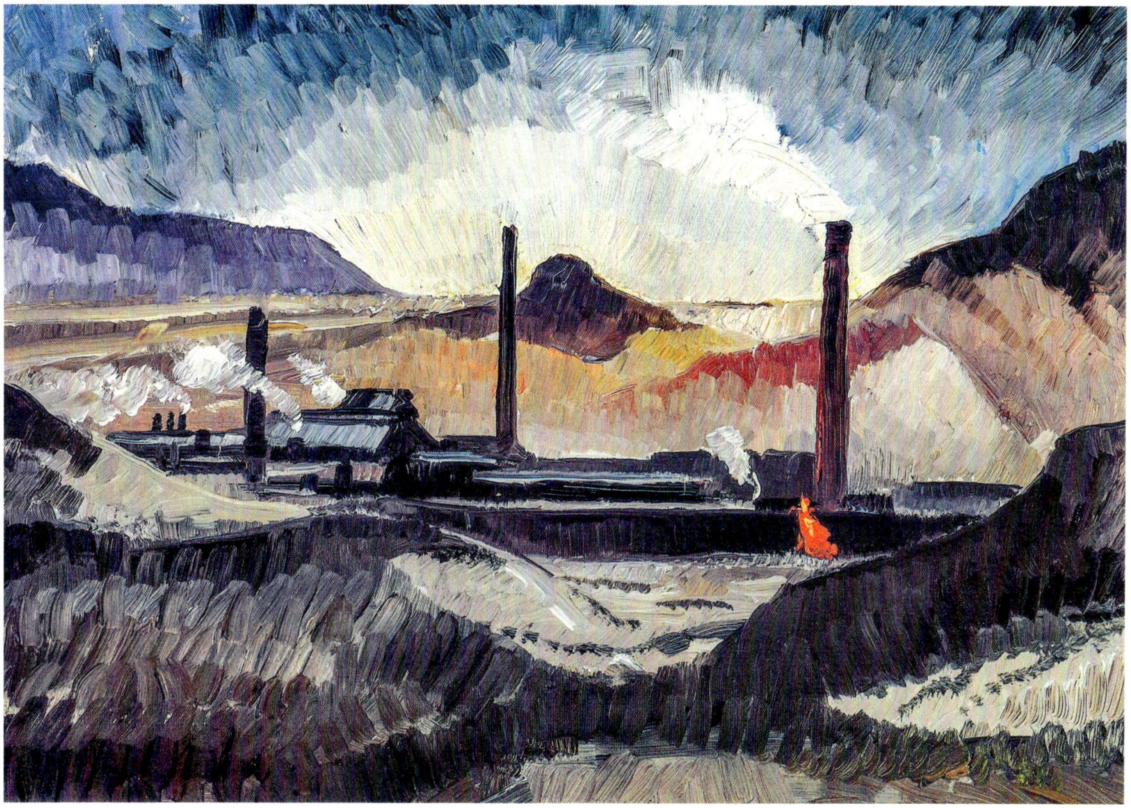

a lawman.[19] Lea spent considerable time away from El Paso during the twenties and early thirties, including moving to Santa Fe in 1933 (he had become friends with Fremont Ellis), but he returned to El Paso for good in 1936, the same year as his painting of the smelter. Lea was an active muralist under the New Deal, but only in the mural he executed for the El Paso Federal Court House in 1938 does he make a reference to the local industry: he included an old miner with his pickax and mule as one of several stock characters in his mural.[20] He noted that "these old desert rats with their burros" could "live on coffee, cornmeal and Jackrabbits."[21]

One of three high schools in the city, El Paso High School was constructed in 1914, and by 1930 it had 1,500 students. In 1930 the students of Eula Harlacker's 2B art class put together a booklet titled "El Paso in Block Print," which featured images of notable local structures and some typical residents, including the Austin and El Paso high schools, the Cortez Hotel, a Native American from one of the three regional tribes in a feathered headdress, the Juárez Mission just across the

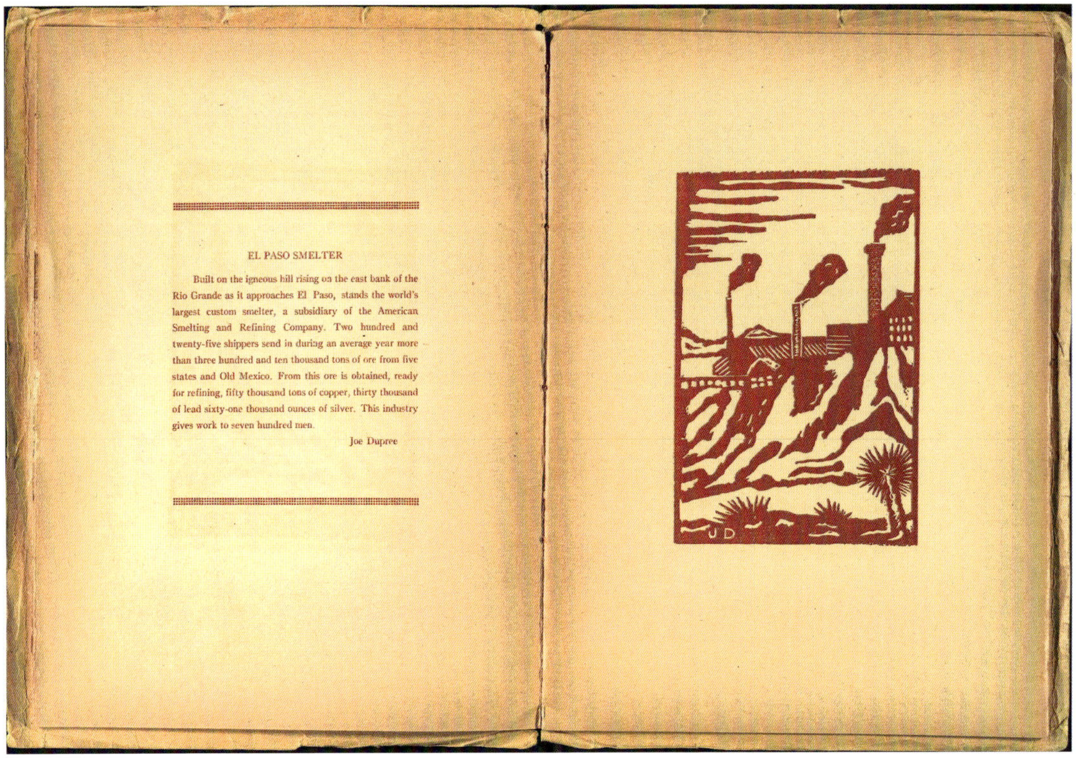

EL PASO SMELTER

Built on the igneous hill rising on the east bank of the Rio Grande as it approaches El Paso, stands the world's largest custom smelter, a subsidiary of the American Smelting and Refining Company. Two hundred and twenty-five shippers send in during an average year more than three hundred and ten thousand tons of ore from five states and Old Mexico. From this ore is obtained, ready for refining, fifty thousand tons of copper, thirty thousand of lead sixty-one thousand ounces of silver. This industry gives work to seven hundred men.

Joe Dupree

El Paso in Block Print, 1930, created by the 2B Art Class, El Paso High School, under the direction of Mrs. Eula Harlacker. Printed by the Vocational Print Shop, El Paso, Texas. Courtesy of the University of Texas at El Paso Special Collections.

border, Mexican dancers doing the Fandango, a Mexican woman food vender, Mount Franklin, a Fort Bliss polo player, and the Isleta Mission. A cowboy was characterized as one of the "Riders of the Range": "The cowboy is not just a colorful figure of the West, but a necessity of the cattle industry." Produced by the vocational Print Shop, the publication contains a surprisingly diverse group of images with thoughtful captions written by the students. For his caption for the El Paso Smelter, Joe Dupree wrote,

> Built on the igneous hill rising on the east bank of the Rio Grande as it approaches El Paso, stands the world's largest custom smelter, a subsidiary of the American Smelting and Refining Company. Two hundred and twenty-five shippers send in during an average year more than three hundred and ten thousand

> tons of ore from five states and Old Mexico. From this ore is obtained, ready for refining, fifty thousand tons of copper, thirty thousand of lead, sixty-one thousand ounces of silver. This industry gives work to seven hundred men.

Not all of the artists who visited El Paso and portrayed industrial themes focused on ASARCO. In December 1942 Fritz Henle (1909–1993), employed by the Office of War Information, the agency that succeeded the Farm Security Administration, came to El Paso on assignment and made eighty-two photographs of the Phelps Dodge Refining complex.[22] Born in Germany, a commission from Time-Life led to the publication of some of his photographs in *Fortune*, and he moved to the United States in 1936, where he became an early contributor to *Life* magazine, publishing more than fifty picture essays. He became a United States citizen in 1942, the same year he came to El Paso.

Located east across town from ASARCO, construction of the Phelps Dodge refinery began in February 1929, and the first refined casts of copper were made in March 1930. The complex "was once one of the largest refiners of electrolytic copper in the U.S.," and it was a major local employer.[23] There, "copper was refined and formed into a continuous-cast rod, which would then be turned into electric wire and cable."[24] Henle's extensive series documenting this facility reinforces how important producing large amounts of copper was for the war effort. In one photograph, three workers are posed with balletic precision standing above the huge electrolytic tanks "in which sheets of pure copper are formed." These were later melted and cast into ingots. The furnaces in the casting house were hot, and the space was filled with smoke that poured into huge pipes in order to recover any remaining copper. Conveyors transferred the ingots to the loading yard.

This essay gives historical context to Martin Stupich's decade-long photographic documentation of the ASARCO complex in El Paso, which began in 2010 and extended past the day the big stacks—one 828 feet tall and the other 612—were taken down with three hundred pounds of explosives on April 13, 2013.[25] Stupich continued his site work while expanding his project to include the mining and smelting landscape stretching from the central Rocky Mountains south to Mexico City. At once both factual and artful, he captures the deep historical and contemporary

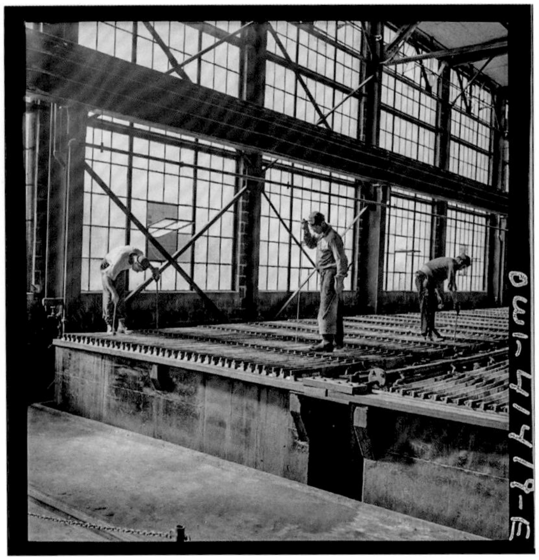

Fritz Henle, (1909–1993), *Phelps Dodge Refining Company, El Paso, TX*, 1942. Courtesy of the Office of War Information Photograph, Prints and Photographs Collection, Library of Congress (LC-DIG-fsa-8d34657; digital file from original negative).

resonances of a powerful industrial landscape. His photographs present not only what the site and its many highly practical structures looked like, but also what it felt like to be there, confronted by a colossal and implausible artifact that would soon disappear after more than one hundred years of operation.

Stupich's images go beyond mere documentation to a deeper understanding of a complex that was once an immense site of industrial production before it transitioned to what is termed "Dead Tech."[26] These are structures that cannot be readily reclaimed: they do not lend themselves to adaptive reuse (and not just because of toxic industrial waste). Permitting them to crumble into colossal ruins of the post-machine age was not a risk-management option. Yet it is important not to let these industrial colossi disappear from memory, for when they are lost a vital part of American history vanishes. Representing both a Progressive Era confidence in the benefits of modern industry (without questioning their environmental and human costs) and arrant capitalism, they are examples of the industrial sublime, true "wonders of work" in the words of printmaker Joseph Pennell, who was inspired by similar scenes during the first two decades of the twentieth century. Stupich's photographs guarantee that the visual character and meaning of the site will endure. As a new landscape replaces it, the old one is preserved in his images.

The narrative of ASARCO is a complicated—and often vexed—chronicle in which the company's mining and smelting operations, within a broad geography, become a more epic tale than the mere documentation of the industrial archaeology that generated an immense fortune. Stupich's handsome color photographs may be read as modern history paintings, honoring the labor that built the complex structures that once housed ASARCO's smelting operations and the Gordian knot of its historical legacy. His work emphatically pictures the New West. It derives not from the hallowed tropes of Manifest Destiny grounded in the classic beauties of the first discovery by artists commissioned by the great government and railroad surveys, but rather from a New Industrial "New Topographics" that portrays the human-altered landscape of the contemporary west.[27]

Acknowledgments

I am deeply grateful to Martin Stupich, a fellow traveler in industrial archaeology, for giving me the opportunity to pursue my quirky interests in the relationship between American art and industry by introducing me to El Paso. I would like to acknowledge the invaluable assistance in my research of the following individuals and institutions: Special Collections, University of Texas at El Paso (Claudia Rivers and Abbie Weiser); El Paso Museum of Art (Patrick Shaw Cable, Christian J. Gerstheimer, and Michelle Villa); and the El Paso Public Library.

Notes

1. Isaac F. Marcosson, *Metal Magic: The Story of the American Smelting and Refining Company* (Farrar, Straus and Company, 1949), 150.
2. See John Burnett, "A Toxic Century: Mining Giant Must Clean up Mess," NPR, February 4, 2010. https://www.npr.org/templates/story/story.php?storyId=122779177. Phelps Dodge and ASARCO produced 29 percent of America's refined copper. See W. H. Timmons, *El Paso: A Borderlands History* (University of Texas at El Paso, 1990).
3. For more on the art history of El Paso, see Carol Ann Price, *Early El Paso Artists* (Texas Western Press, the University of El Paso, 1983); Carol Price Miller and Holly Thurston Cox, *Guide to Early El Paso Artists: With Biographical Sketches and Early Art Exhibits and Galleries* (Early El Paso Art Project, 1999); and Carol Price Miller et al., *Into the Desert Light: Early El Paso Art 1850–1960* (El Paso Museum of Art, 2010). See also Mary A. Sarber, *Photographs From the Border: The Otis A. Aultman Collection* (El Paso Public Library Association, 1977).
4. Trousset painted scenes of other towns in New Mexico, California, Texas, and northern Mexico. One other industrial scene has been located: a view of the Park City and Billings Smelter (Socorro Public Library, 1886). The smelter was located near Socorro, New Mexico.
5. See Leo Marx, *The Machine in the Garden: Technology and the Pastoral Ideal in America* (Oxford University Press, 1964).

6. Audley Dean Nicols, quoted from a 1972 *El Paso Times* article in Sara Sanchez, "An El Paso Treasure That Spent Time in a Janitor's Closet Now Hangs in Art Museums," *El Paso Times*, February 5, 2019.
https://www.elpasotimes.com/story/news/education/episd/2019/02/05/el-paso-painting-audley-dean-nicols-goes-from-janitors-closet-to-museums/2678044002/.

7. See Miller et al., *Into the Desert Light*, 16.

8. The firm was one of the most notable in the Southwest. Henry Charles Trost (1860–1933) was the firm's chief designer. Between 1899 and 1903 he established a successful architectural firm in Tucson. In 1903 he moved to El Paso, which he had first visited in 1901, joining his brother Gustavus Adolphus Trost (1876–1950), and together they established the architectural firm that bore their names. In 1908 Gustavus's twin brother, Adolphus Gustavus Trost (1876–1957), joined the firm as the chief engineer. For more on the firm, see Lloyd C. Engelbrecht and June-Marie F. Engelbrecht, *Henry C. Trost: Architect of the Southwest* (El Paso Public Library Association, 1981).

9. In 1967 it became the University of Texas at El Paso.

10. One other artist is known to have painted the smelter in the twenties. New England painter Aldro T. Hibbard (1886–1972) met Winifred Jackman (1898–1986) in 1923 when she was a student in his summer school in Rockport, Massachusetts. She was from El Paso, and in 1924 he visited her family there (they married in 1925). It is likely on this trip that he painted the AS&R Smelter (later ASARCO). The work has not been located.

11. Barbara Spencer Foster, with Bambi Elizabeth Ellis, *Fremont F. Ellis: Last of Los Cinco Pintores of Santa Fe* (Sunstone Press, 2010), 38–39.

12. Patrick Shaw Cable, ed., *Renoir to Remington: Impressionism to the American West* (El Paso Museum of Art, 2014), 21.

13. *A Guide to the Lone Star State*, comp. by Workers of the Writers' Program of the Works Projects Administration in the State of Texas, American Guide Series, Sponsored by the Texas State Highway Commission (Hastings House, 1940), 565.

14. "Blumenschein Explains What Makes a Painting New," *Santa Fe New Mexican*, September 13, 1953, quoted in Elizabeth J. Cunningham, "In Contemporary Rhythm: The Search for Final Perfection," in *In Contemporary Rhythm: The Art of Ernest L. Blumenschein*, by Peter H. Hassrick

and Elizabeth J. Cunningham (University of Oklahoma Press, in Cooperation with the Albuquerque Museum of Art and History, Denver Art Museum, and Phoenix Art Museum, 2008), 275.

15. Established by Franklin Delano Roosevelt in 1935, the Works Progress Administration was renamed the Work Projects Administration in 1939. The WPA was ended in 1943.

16. Price Miller and Thurston Cox, *Guide to Early El Paso Artists*.

17. The frescoes were unfortunately destroyed in the early 1960s. See Fernando Leal, "Los frescoes de Garcia Cahero en el Paso E.U.," *El Nacional: Diario Popular* (Mexico City), January 20, 1935. Also in the thirties he completed two murals at the School of Construction Engineers in San Antonio. Returning to Mexico, he died in Mexico City in 1939.

18. John O. West, "Tom Lea: Artist in Two Mediums," *Southwest Writers Series*, no. 5 (Steck-Vaughn Company, Publishers, 1967), 1.

19. West, "Tom Lea," 2. The only other industrial theme he pursued was for a 1946 commission from *Life* magazine to do a series of paintings on the cattle industry. For this assignment, his travels ranged from the Chicago stockyards to ranches in Mexico. The series was never published, and the eleven paintings he produced were given by the magazine to the Dallas Museum of Art in 1950. See *Western Beef Cattle: A Series of Paintings by Tom Lea* (Dallas Museum of Fine Arts, 1950).

20. For more on thirties era work in Texas, see Patrick Stewart, *Lone Star Regionalism: The Dallas Nine and Their Circle, 1928–1925* (Texas Monthly Press, 1985); Robert L. Reid, *Picturing Texas: The FSA-OWI Photographers in the Lone Star State, 1936–1943* (Texas State Historical Association, 1994); and Philip Parisi, *The Texas Post Office Murals: Art for the People* (Texas A&M University Press, 2004). Portrayals of heavy industry in the murals in Texas post offices and courthouses relate mostly to oil (these are located in Amarillo, Electra, Graham, Houston, and Kilgore).

21. Tom Lea to Edward Rowan, October 9, 1937, quoted in Parisi, *The Texas Post Office Murals*, 56.

22. On this same trip he traveled to Morenci, Arizona, to photograph the mining and processing operations at the Phelps Dodge facilities there.

23. El Paso Copper Refinery, Texas, Center for Land Use Interpretation. http://clui.org/ludb/site/el-paso-copper-refinery. The complex is now owned by Freeport-McMoRan, which acquired Phelps-Dodge in 2007. In September 1942, Russell Lee visited the Anaconda Copper Mining Company's electrolytic copper refinery in Great Falls, Montana, and described the process in his caption: "Refining tanks in which the anodes of impure copper are refined by electrolytic means to the pure cathode copper. The anodes are placed in the tank as they are received from the Anaconda smelters; between these anodes are suspended starting sheets which are thin sheets of electrolytic copper; the cathode sheets remain in the tank until sufficient copper from the anode has been deposited on the cathode to give it a weight of approximately 170 pounds."

24. El Paso Copper Refinery, Texas, Center for Land Use Interpretation. http://clui.org/ludb/site/el-paso-copper-refinery.

25. See Erica Orden, "El Paso Says Goodbye to Landmark: Asarco Smokestacks Are Demolished as Part of Effort to Clean Up and Redevelop Industrial Site," *Wall Street Journal*, April 14, 2013.

26. See Manfred Hamm et al., *Dead Tech: A Guide to the Archeology of Tomorrow* (Sierra Club Books, 1983).

27. "New Topographics: Photographs of a Man-Altered Landscape" was the title of an exhibition organized by the George Eastman House in Rochester, New York, in 1975.

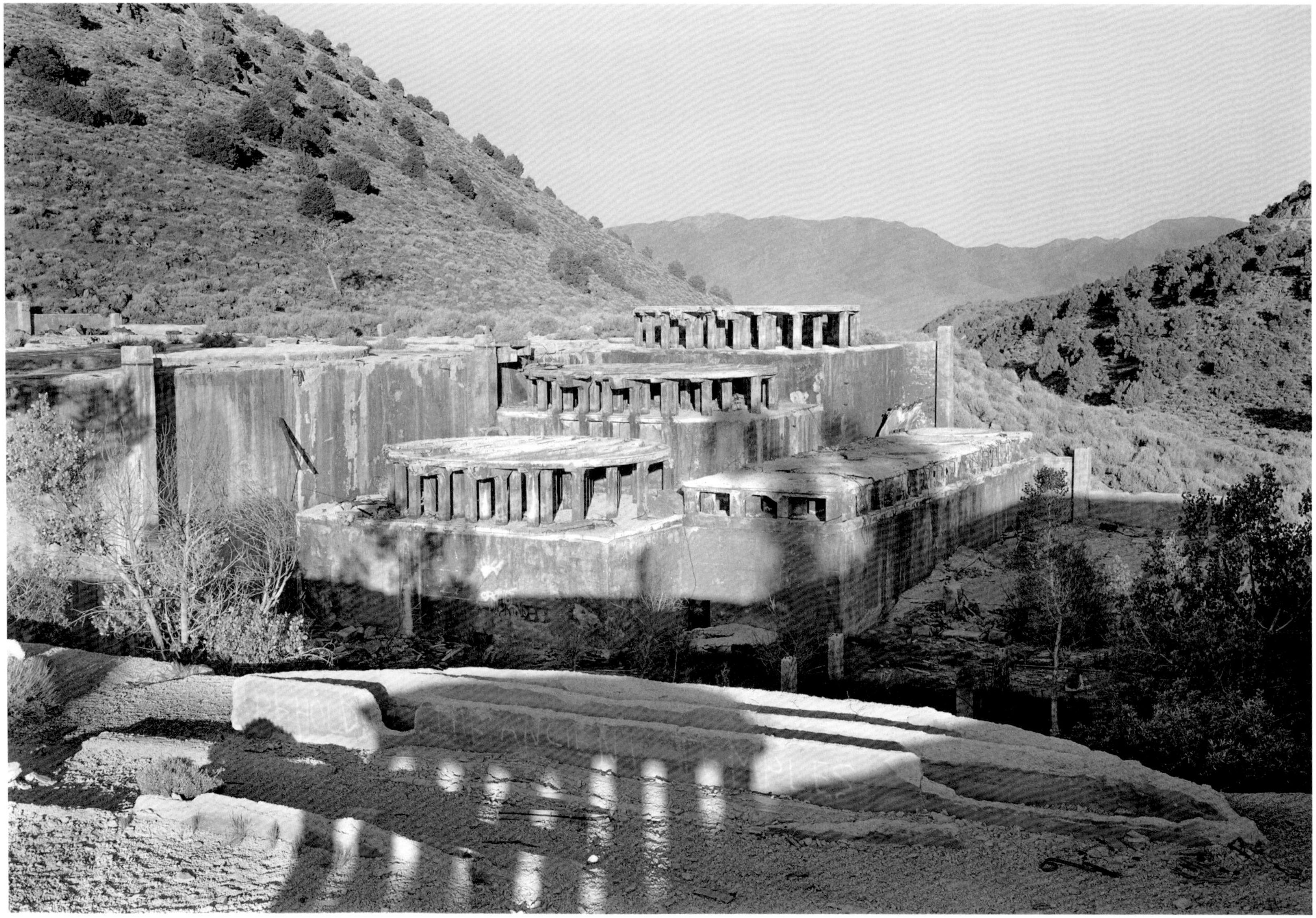

Martin Stupich, *Mill Ruins with Shadow at American Flat, Nevada, 1980*, medium-format negative.

The Old Topographics

TOBY JUROVICS

IN A MESSY WORLD, WE gravitate toward neatly defined, linear packages, ordering our existence in centuries and decades, wanting events to fit like wooden pegs neatly aligned in a row of square holes. Conveniently, by that measure, 2020 marked Martin Stupich's fortieth year making photographs in the American West. I noted this fact while counting another interval backward, one that doesn't fit quite as evenly but that vibrates in my imagination like a telegraph line stretched tight between two moments in time—1867 and 1980—yet somehow also affixed to the same geographic point: the Comstock Lode in Virginia City, Nevada. At each end stands a view camera on a tripod, Timothy H. O'Sullivan behind one and Stupich the other. Or perhaps one might imagine two tin cans and a century plus of string, Stupich's ear pressed tightly at one end as he awaits a faint message from his forerunner. But Mr. O'Sullivan did not seem the type to have spoken at a whisper—rather, I suspect he bellowed. And I imagine that other young photographer, the Nevada landscape upside down and backward on his ground glass, pulling his head out from under his dark cloth and hollering back.

It is remarkable to imagine that the medium of photography can be contained within the lifespan of three or four not particularly old people. It has been a brief yet potent inflection in how we describe and comprehend the world around us. In the late nineteenth century, when photographers supplanted painters and draftsmen on the geographic and geologic surveys of the American West, it had the virtue of being relatively fast, efficient, and easily reproducible. O'Sullivan also understood that a camera, in the right hands, could capture narrative, metaphor, and geologic time. A lot could be packed into that frame, and there are times looking at his photographs that it seems a miracle his ground glass didn't shatter. Three words come to mind: tension, structure, and rigor. A century later, they are the same words I would use to describe Stupich's photographs. To cinch the load down a little more tightly, I'll borrow a phrase from his own assessment of the cultural landscape of nineteenth-century Nevada: "pragmatism ruled."[1] I cannot offer a more knowing or succinct summary of Stupich's career than the one he has already written, and I encourage readers to find his essay, "The Historic American Engineering Record and Me: 1980 until Now."[2] In it, he describes a career defined by the pragmatic, governed by a string of federal acronyms: HABS (Historic American Buildings Survey), HAER (Historic American Engineering Record), and HALS (Historic American Landscapes Survey) as well as the more familiar NPS and DoD. These were assignments that came with rules and expectations—to create visual documents that fit within fixed parameters and clearly render the required information. One might assume that this would lead to dozens of photographers making thousands of indistinguishable images, but reading the directions again carefully, one finds no prohibition against working thoughtfully, methodically, or gracefully. Just as it has been wrongly suggested that O'Sullivan's government commissions were a hobble rather than an opportunity, it is often misunderstood that one must create a document stoically, without care or inflection. To paraphrase the photographer Frederick Sommer, when doing a job, one should do it no less well than they possibly can.

Landscape photography has been similarly misunderstood, the prevailing impression being that it is easily done, the horizon placed neatly in the middle of the frame and the shutter released. In its simplest sense, landscape is an art of topography, the literal description of a recognizable place notable for both its dramatic scenery and its absence of people, intended to evoke a reaction of awe or wonder and perhaps a little ire that more hasn't being done to protect or conserve its presumed "wilderness-ness." In other words, landscape photography was believed to be a style without a great deal of inherent conflict. The questions it asked were pro forma, answered with a simple pronouncement of "beauty." This all changed in the 1970s, when photographers were no longer willing to suffer this particular fiction, to endorse the equation "landscape = wilderness." Much has been written on this moment, as if photographers everywhere suddenly realized that the compass had been set for magnetic rather than true north and simultaneously adjusted the declination. The exact spot where photography pulled over to check the map has been clearly circled—George Eastman House, Rochester, New York, 1975, the exhibition, "The New Topographics: Photographs of a Man-altered Landscape." The break, however, was not complete, and photographers continued to find beauty in the quotidian, in subtle rather than heroic horizons, in places that had been damaged or abused but still carried with them the possibility of hope or redemption. But as hope becomes less and less a part of our dialogue, glancing back at that map on the seat beside us we might notice a narrow road, just past the Sinclair station, veering off in another direction.[3]

As an undergraduate and graduate student in the 1970s, Stupich was taught by lyrical, poetic artists who used the camera in deeply personal ways: Emmet Gowin, John McWilliams, and Elaine O'Neal. This was one of photography's richest moments, a time of serious picture making, high expectations, and earnestness as well as burgeoning attention from museums and universities. It was also a time of fairly set expectations, and after completion of an MFA, it was assumed that one would embark on a teaching career, passing along the same care and attention that one had been given by their mentors. But this is where Stupich left the highway, and instead he spent three years working on a National Endowment for the Arts commission to photograph Atlanta's MARTA subway system under construction, which he described as "a dynamic engineered landscape"—a subway has never sounded more interesting.[4] From there, a friend suggested he apply for a job "out west" with the Historic American Buildings Survey / Historic American Engineering Record: "I was first put to work for HAER in 1980, collaborating with National Park Service historians and a group of young hires like myself. Our summer working in Nevada's Comstock historic mining landscape immersed me for the first time in the world of projects with real performance expectations, guidelines, and—most importantly—unambiguous transmittal criteria."[5] This was not the language of "fine-art photography," but those first months set his compass for the next forty years: "That summer job in Virginia City, Nevada, was a baptism by fire. My role was to document 260 sites with a medium-format view camera: commercial buildings, a town's main street, an opera house, residential structures, locomotive and freight sheds, head frames, open pit mines, mine adits, shafts, tailings piles, and a stamp mill."[6] This list could as easily substitute for the table of contents for the volume now in your hands. *Mill Ruins with Shadow at American Flat, Nevada, 1980* feels like an anchor being set for everything that would follow. Nestled into a shallow valley, Stupich photographed the supports for long-gone cedar tanks that had held cyanide solution for leaching gold and silver from the ore with the same respect and admiration as if its columns were from Sardis or Palmyra. Awash in warm afternoon light, a literal shadow of the past slips into the foreground, echoing the silhouettes of an ancient forum. The site feels not like an imposition on the landscape but rather as if it had always been there, its presence the cause of neither surprise nor alarm.

Stupich developed a practice almost unique among his peers—he worked without antipathy toward the built environment. More importantly, he drew no distinction between what some considered intrusions or affronts into the landscape and the landscape itself. There was no purity test, nor did he judge the landscape based on notions of its grandeur or hospitality. His catalogue reads as a history of the modern American endeavor, from rails to the space age, in no particular order: steel mills, bridges, played-out mines and open pits, ICBM silos, the Panama Canal, Cape Canaveral, and western dams. *Roosevelt Dam, Before Entombment in Concrete Monolith, Arizona, 1988* sits in perfect balance, no element carrying either favor or bias. Much like O'Sullivan's photographs of Nevada and Utah, Stupich arrests geology, freezing the angled thrust of the canyon wall, tense with latent energy. The uplift's strata are mimicked by the terraced face of the dam, gracefully arcing in the opposing direction. The weight of the Salt River can be felt against the dam's upstream face, and, within the realm of "transmittal criteria," we are given a sense not just of the dam's appearance but of how it functions. His photographs of the Roosevelt, Parker, Hoover, Glen Canyon, and Bonneville Dams capture not just their physical form but why they were constructed as they were, their place within the immediate landscape, and their role as part of a larger system. Seen together, they become a rubric of the hydrology of the West, the ambitions and hubris of the Bureau of Reclamation, our successes and failures, and our inability to recognize the inevitable.

If that first summer in Nevada fixed his course, revealing the possibility of a particular kind of life in photography, more time in the field led to a more expansive and holistic understanding of these systems and their intricacies. Between 2003 and 2006, Stupich documented "the transformation of Wyoming's Red Desert from the largest roadless area in the contiguous United States into a natural gas field." This comment might be regarded as flippant, but it is simply a statement a fact. Within its 2.5 million acres, the Red Desert Basin encompasses a geologic, natural, and

Martin Stupich, *Roosevelt Dam Before Entombment in Concrete Monolith, 1988*, large-format negative.

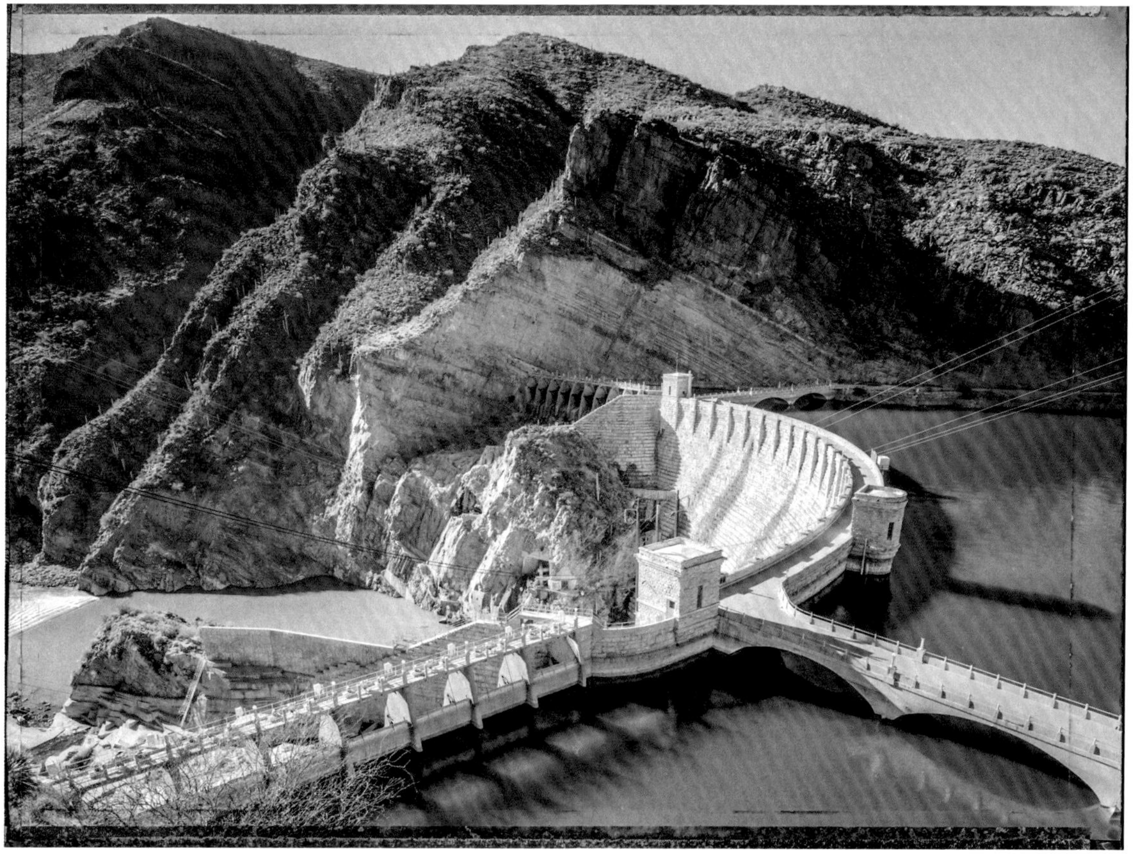

human history that came to a very particular late twentieth-century point: that the value of any place is ultimately measured by how easily one can access its fossil-fuel reserves. Of course, this is most easily accomplished when out of sight. Unless you happened to be driving through Wyoming in the summer of 2001 and noticed all the Halliburton equipment staged along the highway, you might not have had any sense of what was coming. Stupich's photographs of the Red Desert document what happens when a landscape collides with twentieth-century enterprise, the shadows of emigrant trails crisscrossed by freshly laid gas pipelines. A photograph of rocks migrating down a wash, moved by wind, water, and gravity, is captured with the same equanimity as the open-pit coal mine feeding the Jim Bridger power plant—arguably, the only difference is one of speed and scale. Writing of a photograph he made of the Phelps Dodge Pit No. 4 in Morenci, Arizona, a site that he has returned to on numerous occasions, Stupich wrote, "The Morenci copper pit is a spectacle, visible from the moon (I am told), and is part of your autobiography and mine. We drive cars, use electricity, have plumbing, collect pennies. We all use copper, silver, gold. So we all helped dig that hole, and all the others like it from Peru to Mexico to Zambia. In that respect, my 'message' is 'look at what we had someone do for us.' It is partly about acknowledging that each of us helps create the world we live in, whether you choose to call our deeds abominable scars or engineering marvels."[7] What happened in the Red Desert, in a few short years, cannot be "undone"—it wasn't only allowed to happen, but, for better or worse, we gave our consent.

The ASARCO Smelter makes one fact emphatically clear: geology is destiny. Looking at a map, the two-hundred-acre site is a pushpin on the Rio Grande as it cuts through a low gap, a placemark along an international border marking El Paso–Ciudad Juárez, Fort Bliss, transcontinental rail lines, and the rough midpoint of El Camino Real's 1,600-mile-long route traveled by Spanish conquistadors and Guggenheims alike. The surrounding desert appears barren and inhospitable, especially when seen through the windshield of a car traveling eighty miles an hour along I-10 in one-hundred-degree heat. It is a landscape that encourages little empathy, the terraced hillsides and manmade river channel obscuring its profile. But Stupich uses his camera like the blade of a pocket knife, leveraging something shiny out of the dried mud of a riverbed. To be fair, it didn't take much effort to figure out where to start photographing—the pushpin of the smelter towers was impossible to miss and made explicitly clear why the smelter site was here and what its purpose was. We have become accustomed to industrial scale, from warehouses and overpasses to skyscrapers and factories, but the immensity of the ASARCO facility was physically intimidating—its towers were landmarks for dozens of miles in all directions. And as Stupich approached the site with his camera, his careful documentation unfolded the superhuman scale of the ASARCO works. Even akimbo and off their mounts, the flywheels and buckets and turbines and furnaces suggest a place that must have been terrifying for the people that worked there. It isn't easy to imagine the clamor, the heat, and the constant threat of physical harm, because most of us have never been in such an environment. The photographs convey a place indifferent to human scale, one that appears even less hospitable than the desert landscape beyond its gates, every shift an ongoing assault.

Images like the south end of the No. 1 furnace (p. 104) emerge as a postmortem to the photographs made almost a century earlier by Charles Sheeler at the Ford Motor Company's River Rouge Plant. In 1927 Sheeler received a commission from Ford to document what was at the time the largest integrated automobile factory in the world. His photographs capture the sheen of a monumental new industrial era, an aesthetic he continued to celebrate in his subsequent paintings *American Landscape* (1930) and *Classic Landscape* (1931). His faith in Ford's colossal edifice could not have been more conspicuous. The seventy-five thousand workers who ran the plant almost entirely absent, his images rise with a heroic grandeur that celebrates the triumph of American industry, innocent or ignorant of its cost. We recognize the same forms at ASARCO, equally void of its human presence but now encrusted with soot and slag and rust—the archaeological ruin of this earlier promise and progress.

Writing this essay during the first months of 2021, it is clear that many of our expectations and understandings about the world are no longer relevant as we enter fully into the twenty-first century. Indeed, the presumptions from which Stupich worked throughout his career have been slowly chipped away and shattered. When he first planted his tripod in the Nevada dust, he was chronicling sites and artifacts from a past that, although in ruins, had laid the foundation of our present. Nineteenth-century forays into the silver veins of the Comstock Lode, dug by hand and hammer, became the open pit mines that provided the raw materials Apple used to make my iPhone—they are both recognizable parts of the same system, we just became more adept at scale. Whether leaching invisible traces of gold from ore in cyanide vats or excavating with earth movers rolling on thirteen-foot-high tires, the photographs in *Ore and Empire* have simply stretched Stupich's vision to a continental scale. The collapse of the ASARCO smelter tower, with its sonic concussion and rising clouds of dust, was a closing parentheses on a short chapter in our history. Learning his craft on what was essentially a nineteenth-century work of technology—a 4 × 5-inch view camera, one that with an hour or so of practice Timothy H. O'Sullivan would have been able to familiarize himself with—Stupich has captured the rise and fall of an industrial culture so vast and pervasive it has laid the groundwork for our undoing—one that is everywhere, and inescapable.

My career as a photography curator was set on its course in the windowless basement of the Solomon R. Guggenheim Museum on New York City's Upper East Side, and my office for the

2010s was a short walk from the site of a former ASARCO lead refinery that operated for a century on the banks of the Missouri River. I welcome Betsy Fahlman's clever adjustment—the "New *Industrial* Topographics"—as it fits Stupich's photographs precisely. Almost twenty years ago, he wrote the following, and it has remained constant: "A subtext that runs through these decades of work is my uneroded belief that the cultural landscape, and all that occupies it (these *elements of geography*), render a true likeness, our best chance at a faithful collective self-portrait."[8] Stupich was once called out by a colleague for making images that were too beautiful, that seemed to suggest he *liked* these places. He does. The Hoover Dam *is* beautiful, a graceful concrete parabola just downstream of Black Canyon, flooding the site of some of the most elegant photographs made in the nineteenth-century West and holding back a century of folly and greed and willful ignorance of hard Western fact. All of this doesn't mean you make an indifferent photograph, nor is recognizing its beauty an acquittal. Rather, it is an act of acknowledging what is before your lens by making the best photograph one possibly can, and thereby honoring the landscape, its history, and our place within it.

Notes

1. Martin Stupich, "The Historic American Engineering Record and Me: 1980 until Now," *The Journal of the Society for Industrial Archaeology*, 44, nos. 1 and 2 (2018): 180.
2. Stupich, "Historic American Engineering Record," 179–93.
3. See Toby Jurovics, "Same as it Ever Was: Rereading the New Topographics," in *Reframing the New Topographics*, edited by Gregory Foster-Rice and John Rohrbach (Center for American Places, 2010).
4. Stupich, "Historic American Engineering Record," 179.
5. Stupich, "Historic American Engineering Record," 179.
6. Stupich, "Historic American Engineering Record," 179.
7. Email to the author, 2011.
8. Martin Stupich, "Introduction," in *Cameraman Obscura: Thirty Years Sneaking Around in Broad Daylight* (PGI Photo Gallery exhibition catalogue, 2000).

Photographs

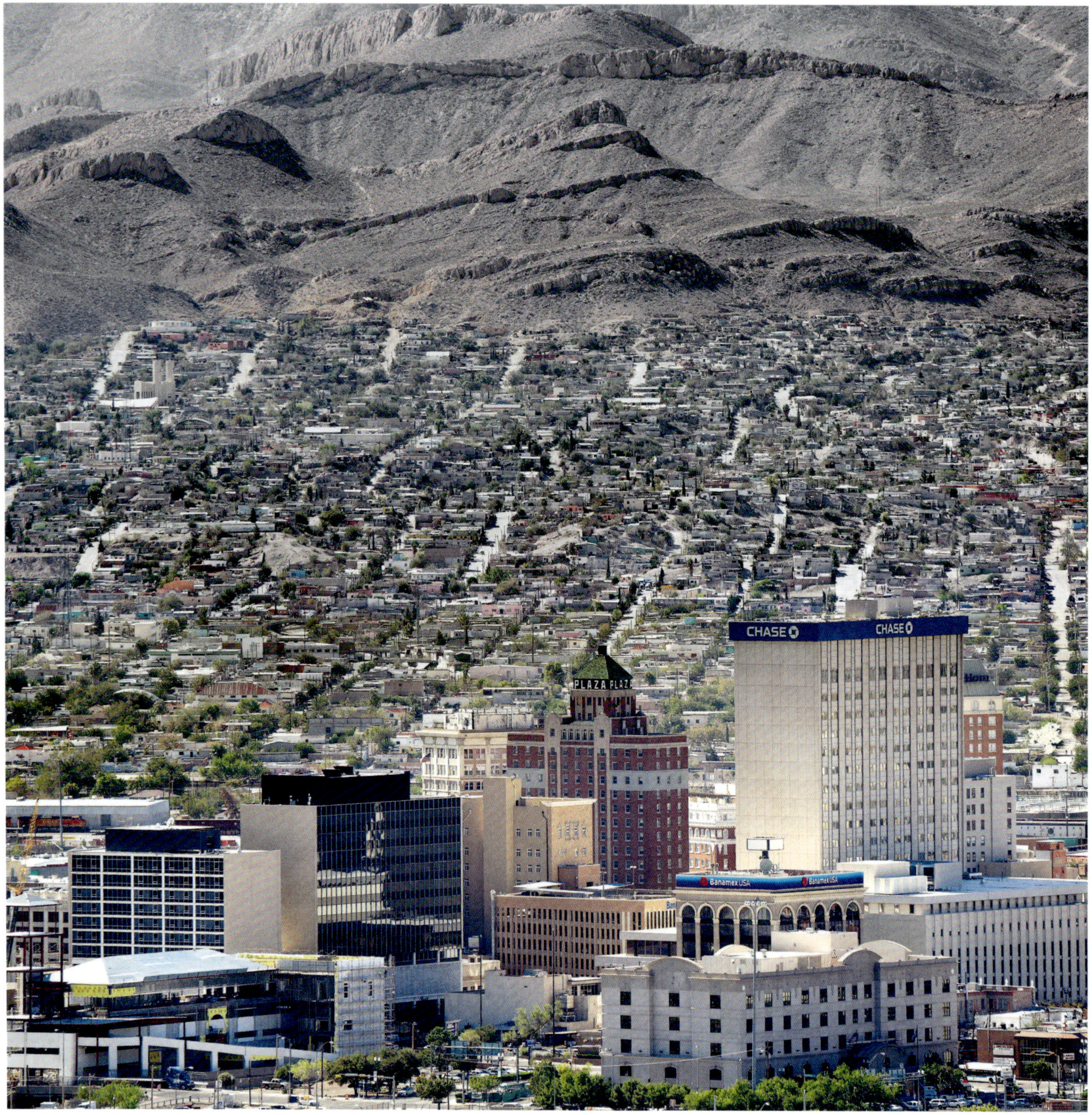

El Paso, Texas, with Ciudad Juárez, Mexico, as a backdrop. Until 1848 Juárez and El Paso were one big city with a wide shallow river running through it. Now, a concrete-lined drainage ditch against a looming steel wall, dreamed up by civil and social engineers, cuts the metropolis in half. These crude public gestures fail to dilute the vitality of this binational community. Juárez and El Paso defy outsiders' expectations by thriving on the synergy of a population of three million unused to incivility.

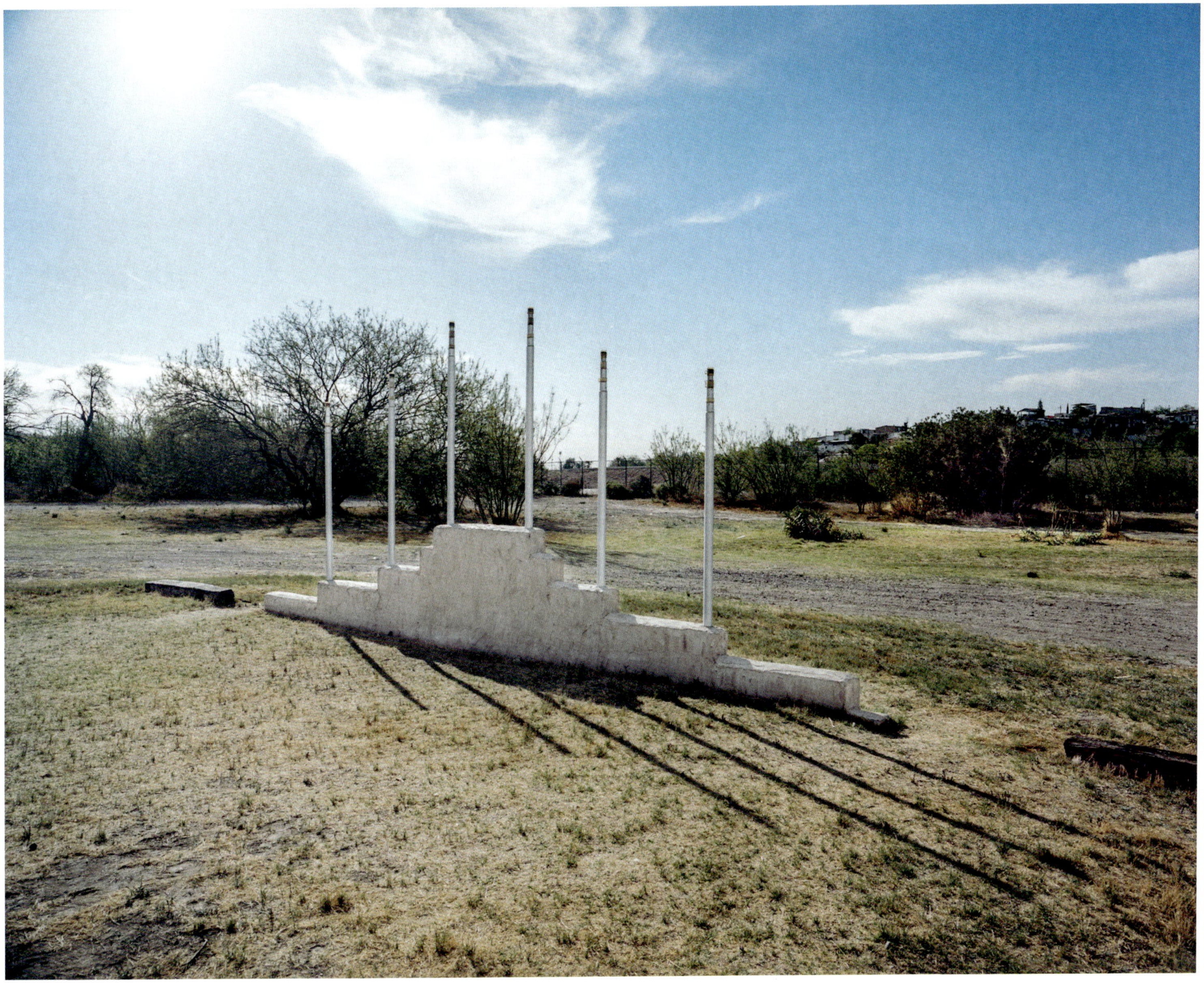

Oñate Crossing, El Paso, Texas. This derelict, little-used public park near downtown El Paso is where, in 1598, don Juan de Oñate crossed the Rio Bravo from Old Mexico to execute his colonization of Nuevo Mexico. The history of the subsequent five centuries of commerce, race politics, immigration, land ownership, religion, and civil discourse in the western United States pivots on that moment. A visit to the site does little to underscore its importance or its legacy.

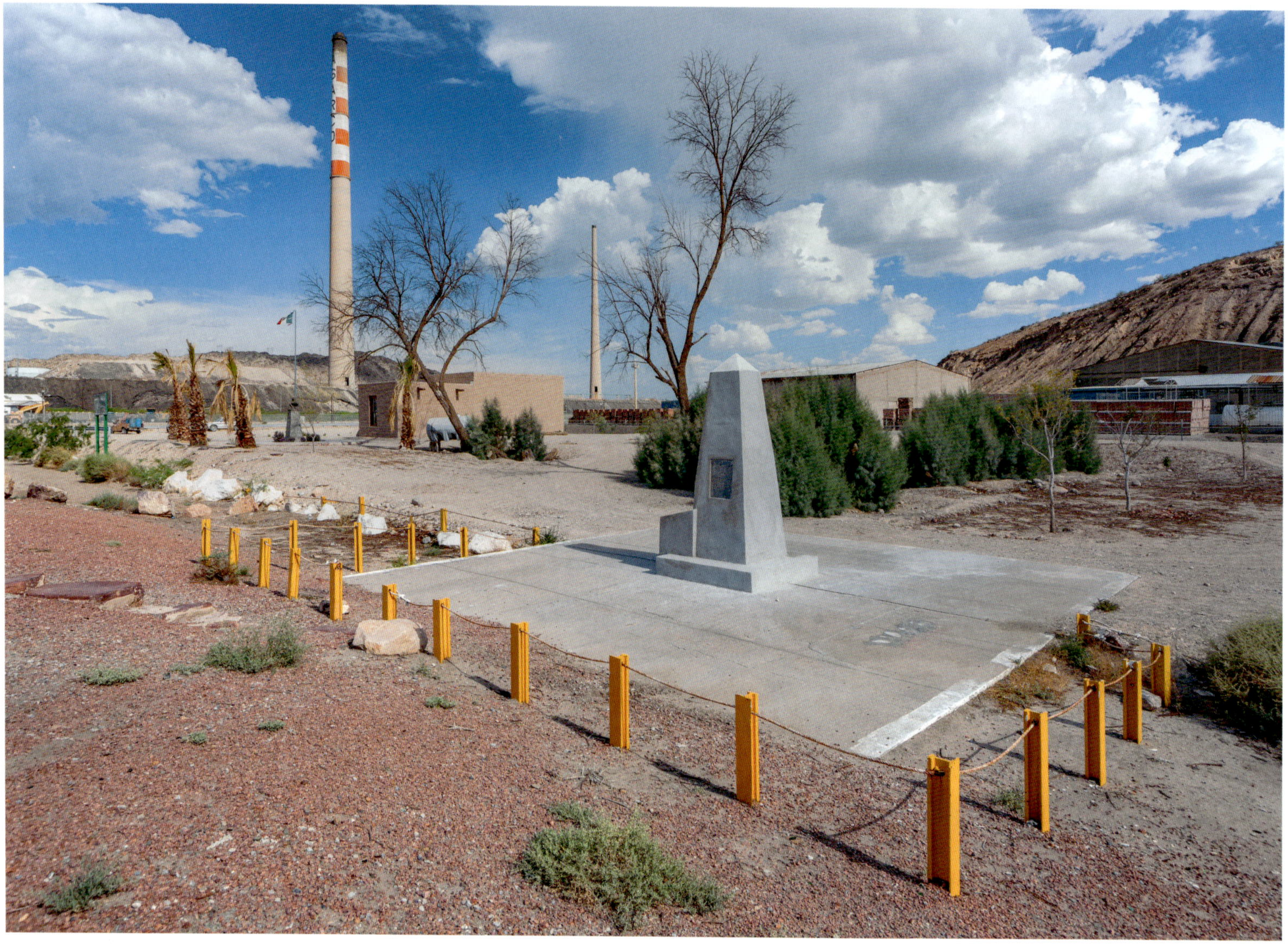

International Boundary Monument No. 1. This is one of 276 obelisks marking the Mexico–United States border reaching from the Rio Grande at El Paso to the Pacific surf at Tijuana–Imperial Beach. This view illustrates the simple complexity of the El Paso–Juárez border region: the camera is in New Mexico pointing southeast toward the boundary monument on the international border, across a sliver of Mexico, aiming at the ASARCO stacks in Texas.

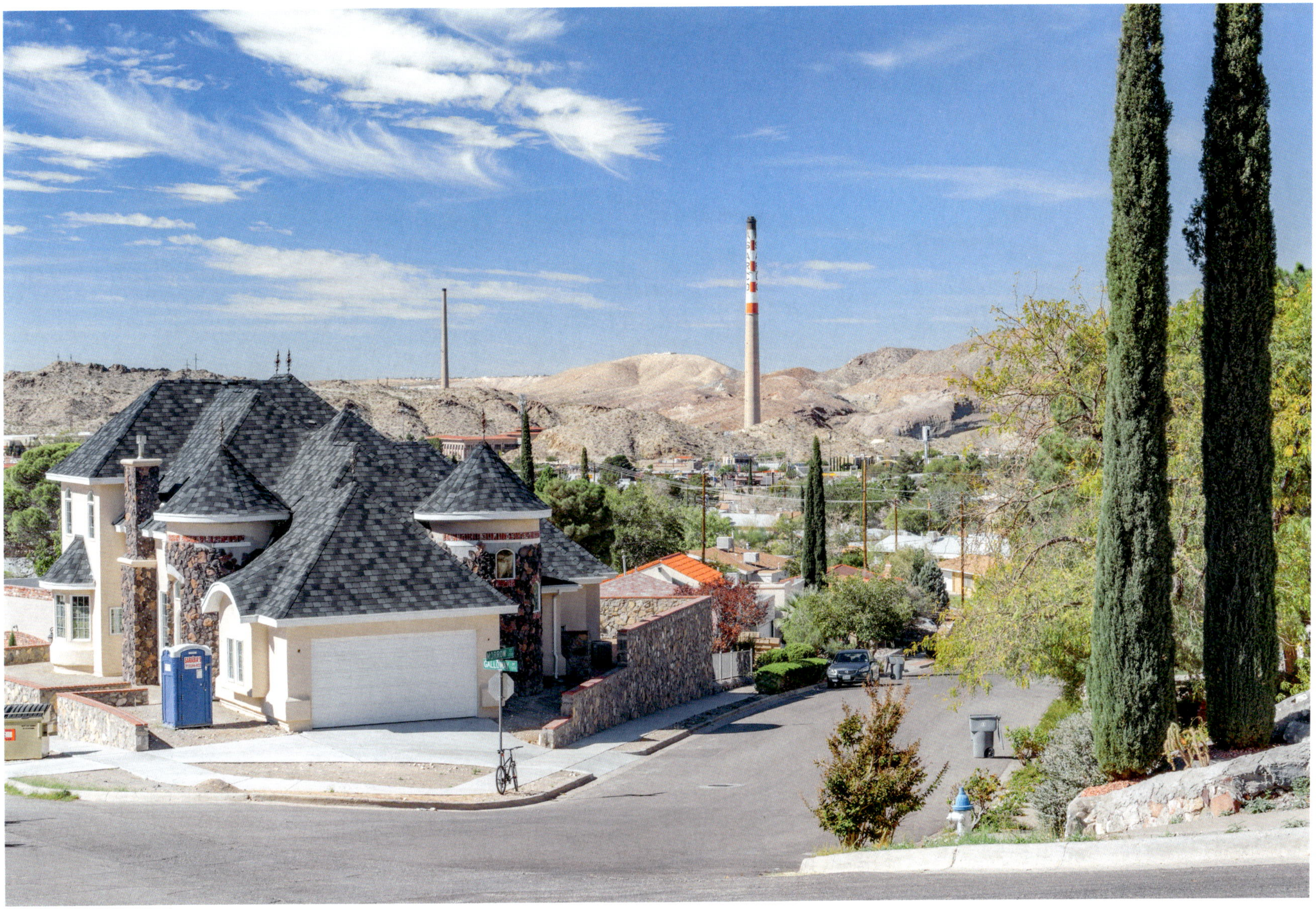

The El Paso ASARCO site viewed from a residential neighborhood. For more than a century ASARCO smokestacks, in their many sizes and iterations, dominated the west horizon of El Paso. This picture was made six months before the "stack drop" that took place on April 13, 2013.

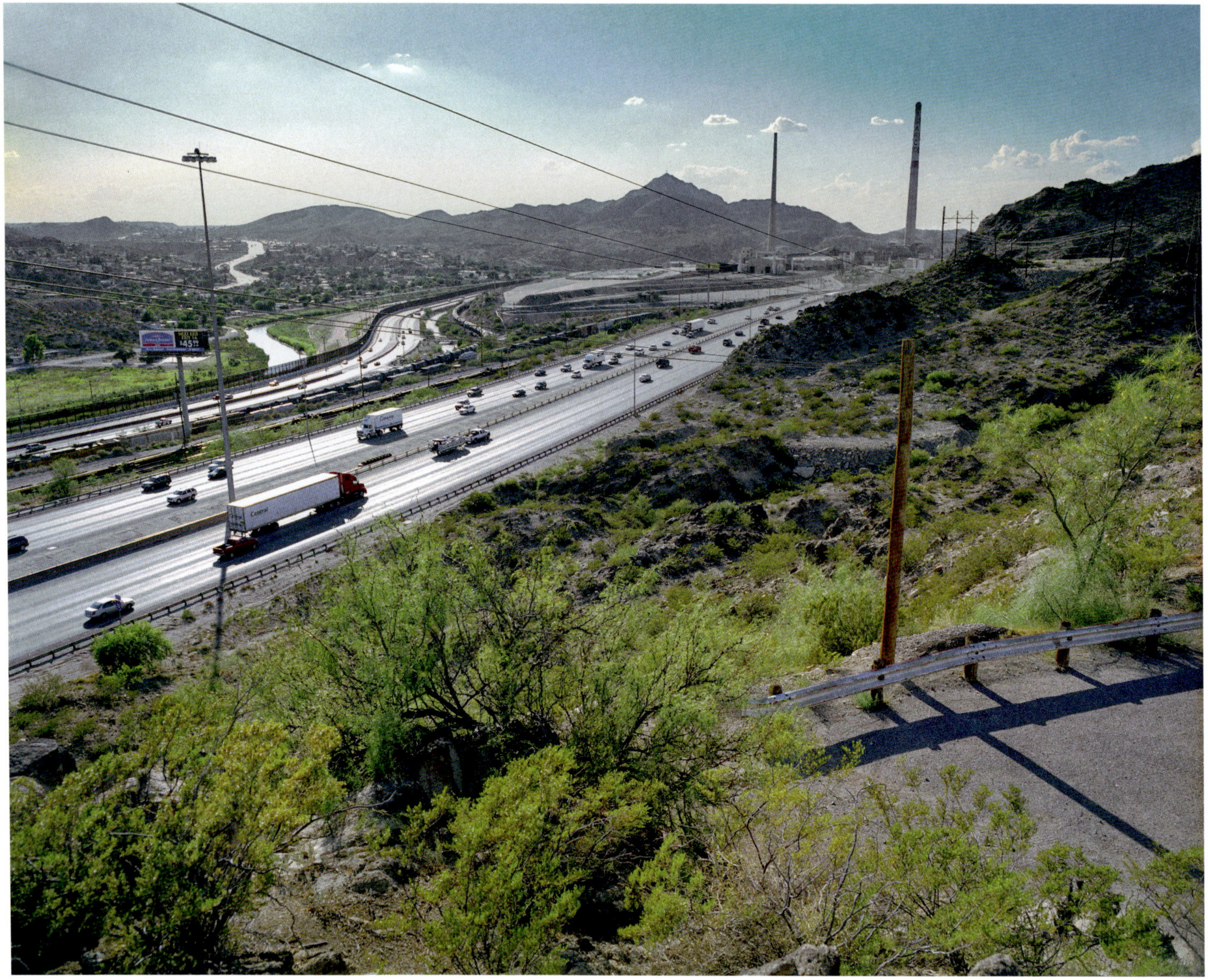

The El Paso ASARCO site in context, from the University of Texas El Paso Sun Bowl. This late-afternoon view illustrates the tight squeeze required at Paso del Norte. The natural geologic cut (with man-made alterations) accommodates the Rio Grande, three active railroad rights-of-way, US Highway 85, Interstate Highway 10, several brick and cement plants, a sprawling smelter operation (before its demolition), and the sites of a (now leveled) company town, and its cemetery.

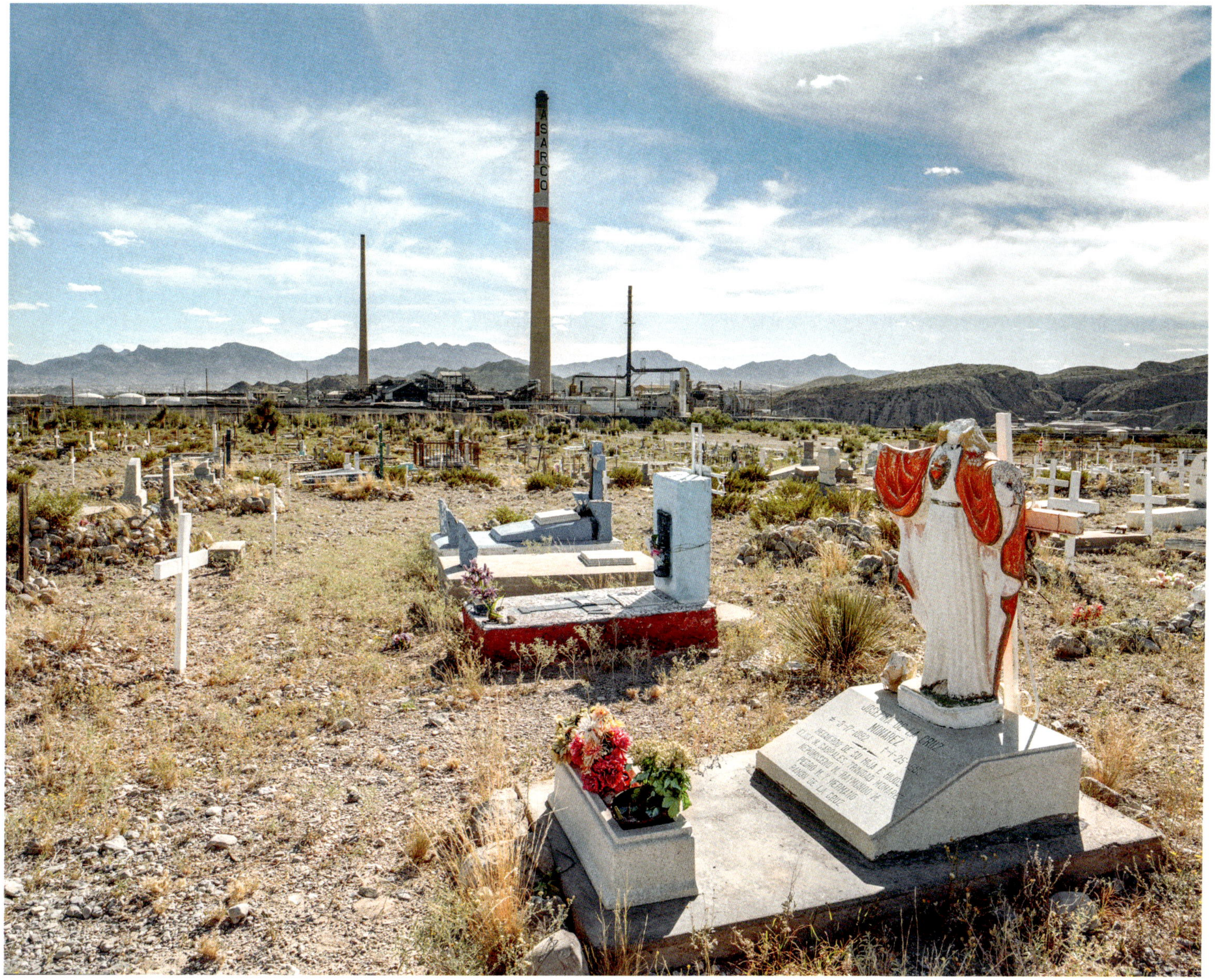

Smeltertown Cemetery, prior to the El Paso ASARCO demolition. Smeltertown Cemetery occupies land adjacent to the ASARCO slag dumps at the north end of the smelter site. The first smelter workers' graves here date from the 1880s, and the cemetery remains a social center for their families, the now long-dispersed ASARCO Smeltertown community.

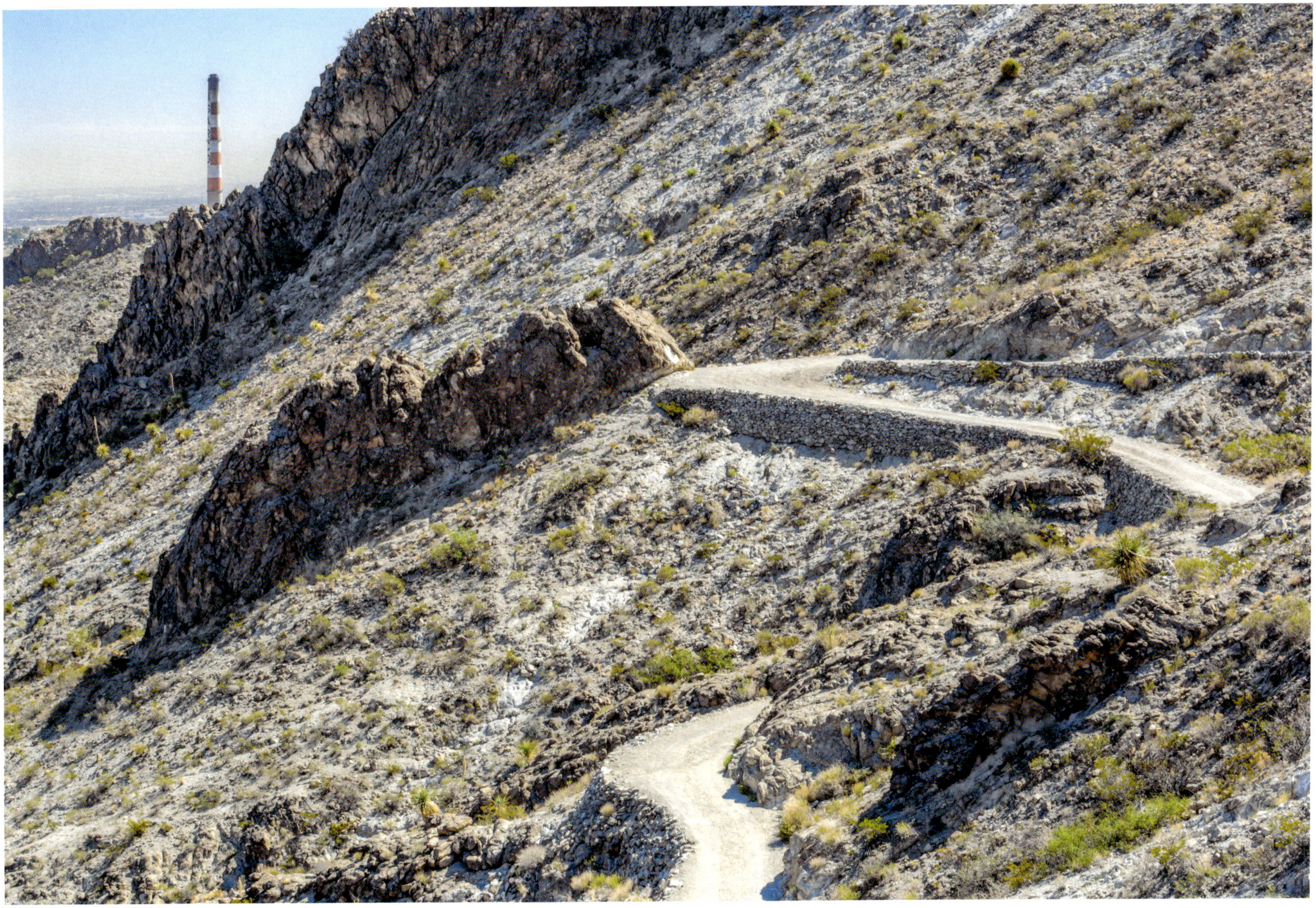

Mount Cristo Rey (Cerro de Cristo Rey), Sunland Park, New Mexico. This 4.5 mile pilgrims' footpath climbs the 650 feet from near river level to a 3-story-tall limestone statue of Christ, completed in 1940. For decades the towering statue shared the horizon with ASARCO's monumental eighty-three-story stack, which then rose nearly two-hundred feet higher than the mountaintop shrine.

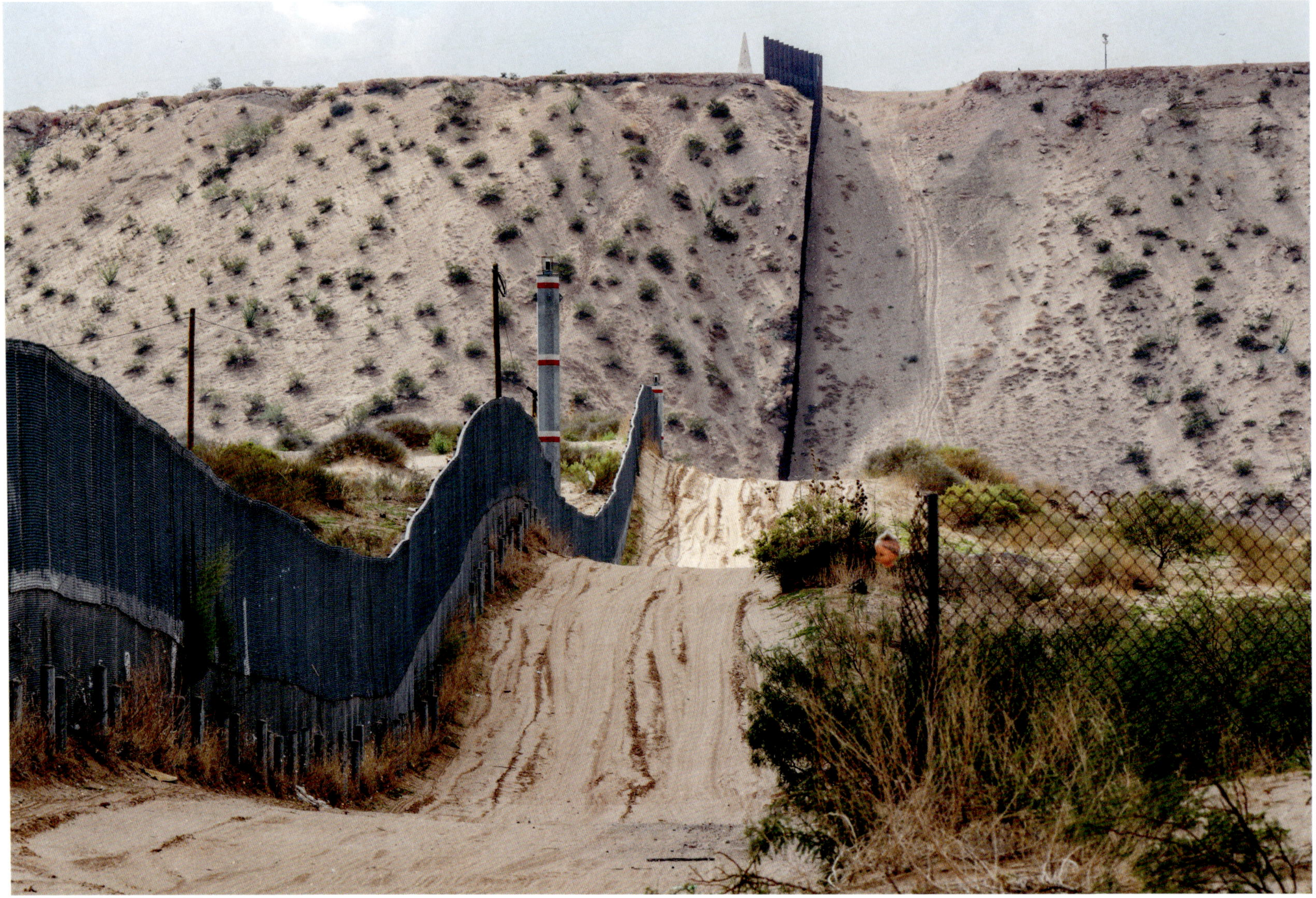

Border fence separating Chihuahua, Mexico and New Mexico, United States. In the southwest, El Paso is synonymous with "the border." About two miles west of ASARCO, on the northwest outskirts of Ciudad Juárez, a thick-link chain-mail fence separates the barrio of Anapra in Chihuahua (on the left) from Sunland Park in New Mexico. At the horizon's center is International Boundary Monument No. 3, three miles from where, on the Rio Grande, the states of Chihuahua, Texas, and New Mexico meet.

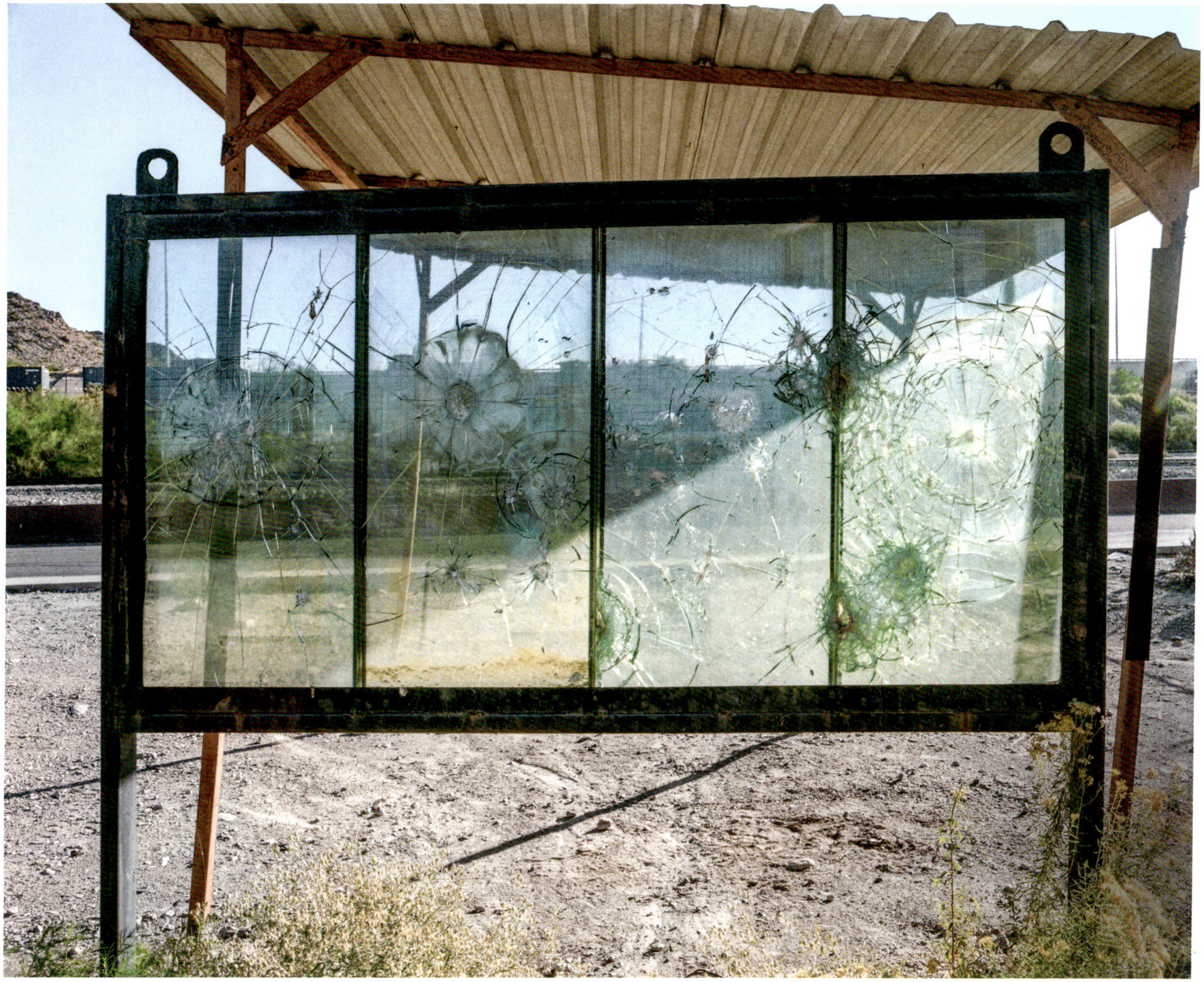

Paisano Drive, El Paso, adjacent to ASARCO. This roadside sun shelter backs up against the border with Mexico, five feet behind the camera. The view is to the southeast, facing ASARCO and the University of Texas–El Paso campus.

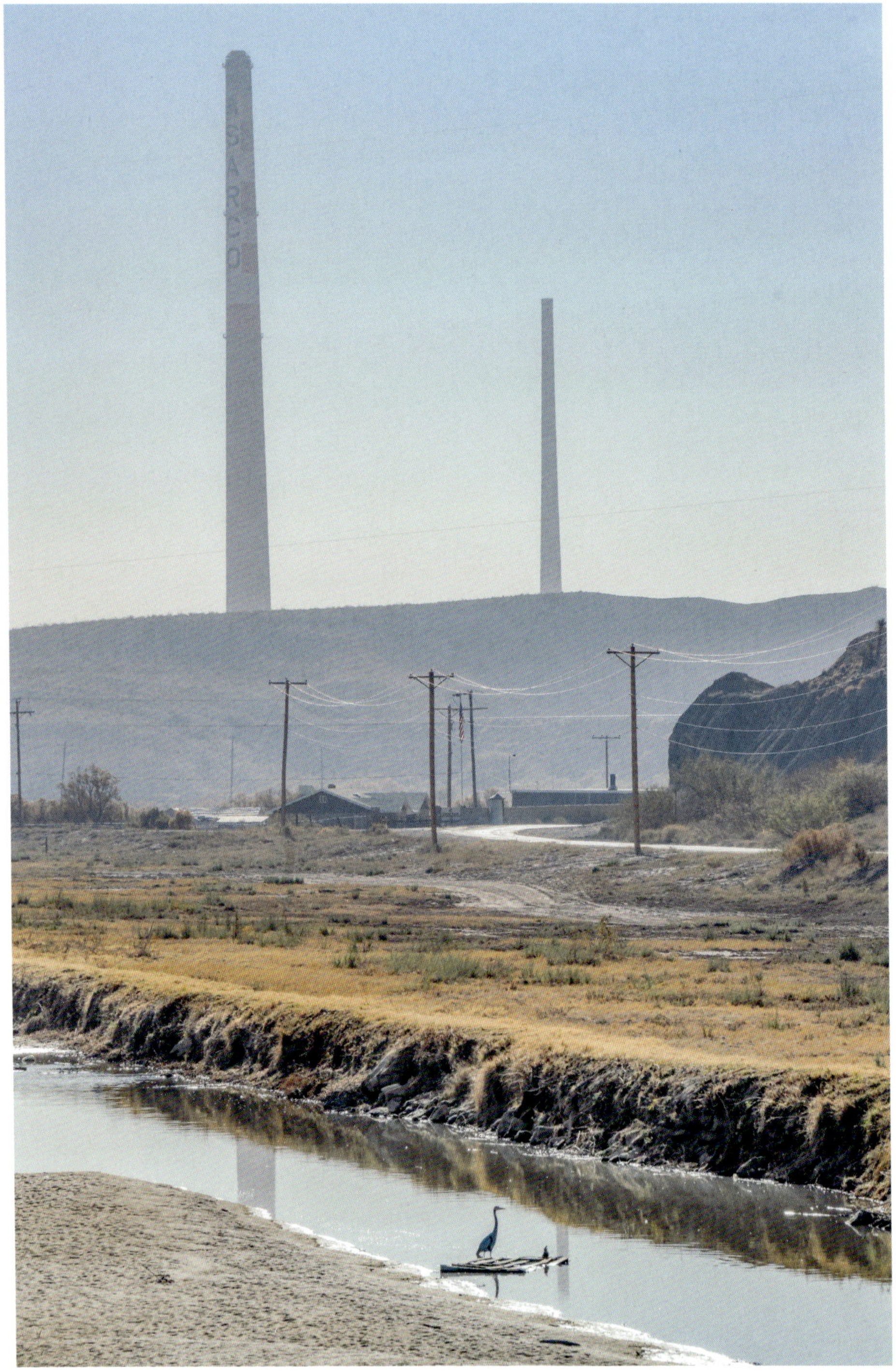

The Rio Grande, El Paso, Texas, and Sunland Park, New Mexico. Periodically, depending upon rainfall and agricultural demand upstream, the Rio Grande can change within hours from a chain of stagnant pools to a swift bank-to-bank torrent. This picture was made at the end of a season of peak demand, so water is being held back upstream at Elephant Butte Dam in anticipation of next season's irrigation draw.

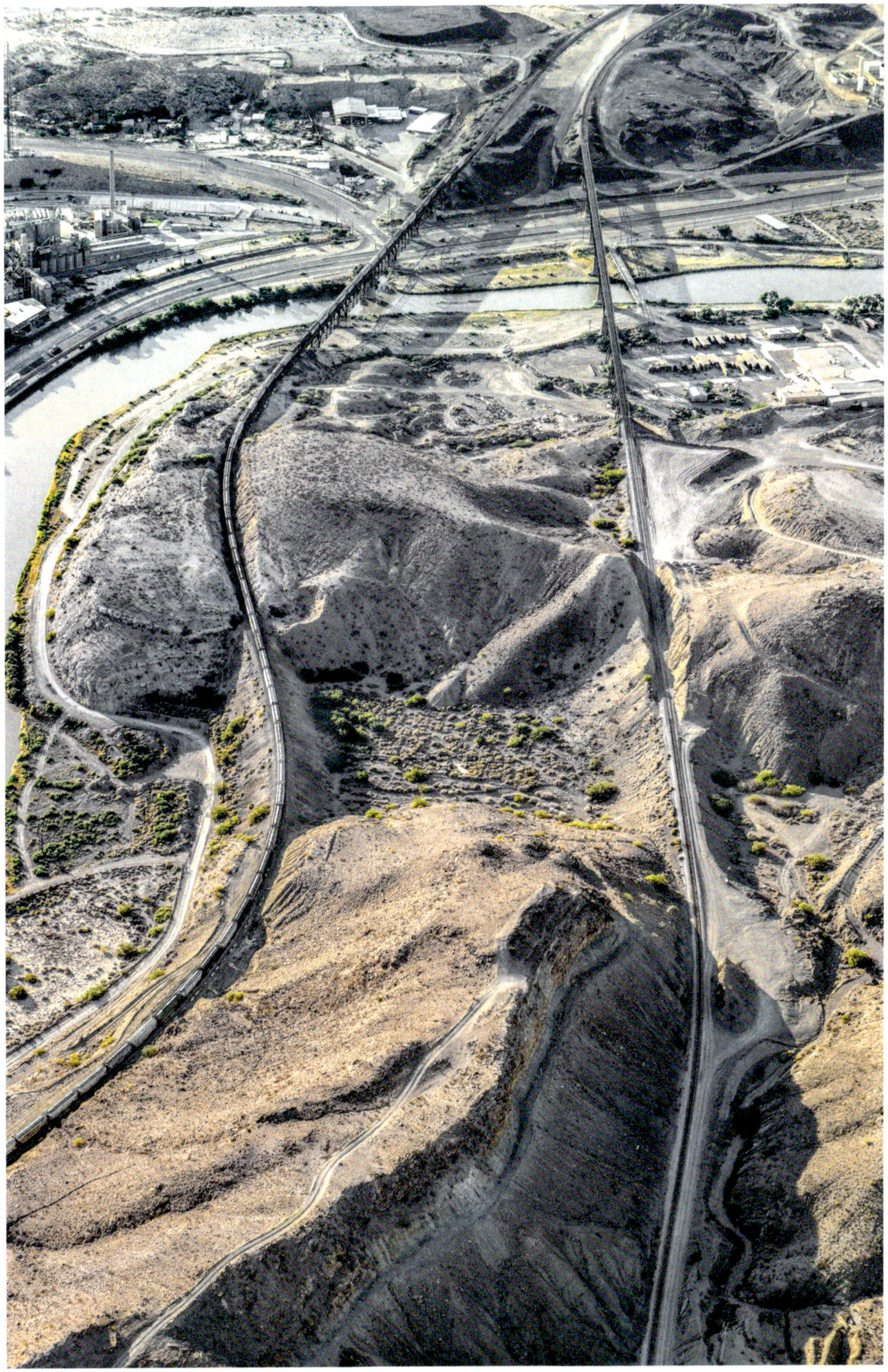

An aerial view north of the El Paso ASARCO site. Visible here are the transcontinental railroads at Paso del Norte. From left to right: the BNSF (the historic El Paso and Southern) and the UP (the historic Southern Pacific) run parallel to each other, wedged close to share the narrow canyon carved by the Rio Grande. In places the two railbeds come within a few feet of touching, to squeeze through the natural pass cut by the river. In the foreground the undulating hills at the base of Cerro de Cristo Rey (in New Mexico) are separated from Texas by the Rio Grande, at the top of the image.

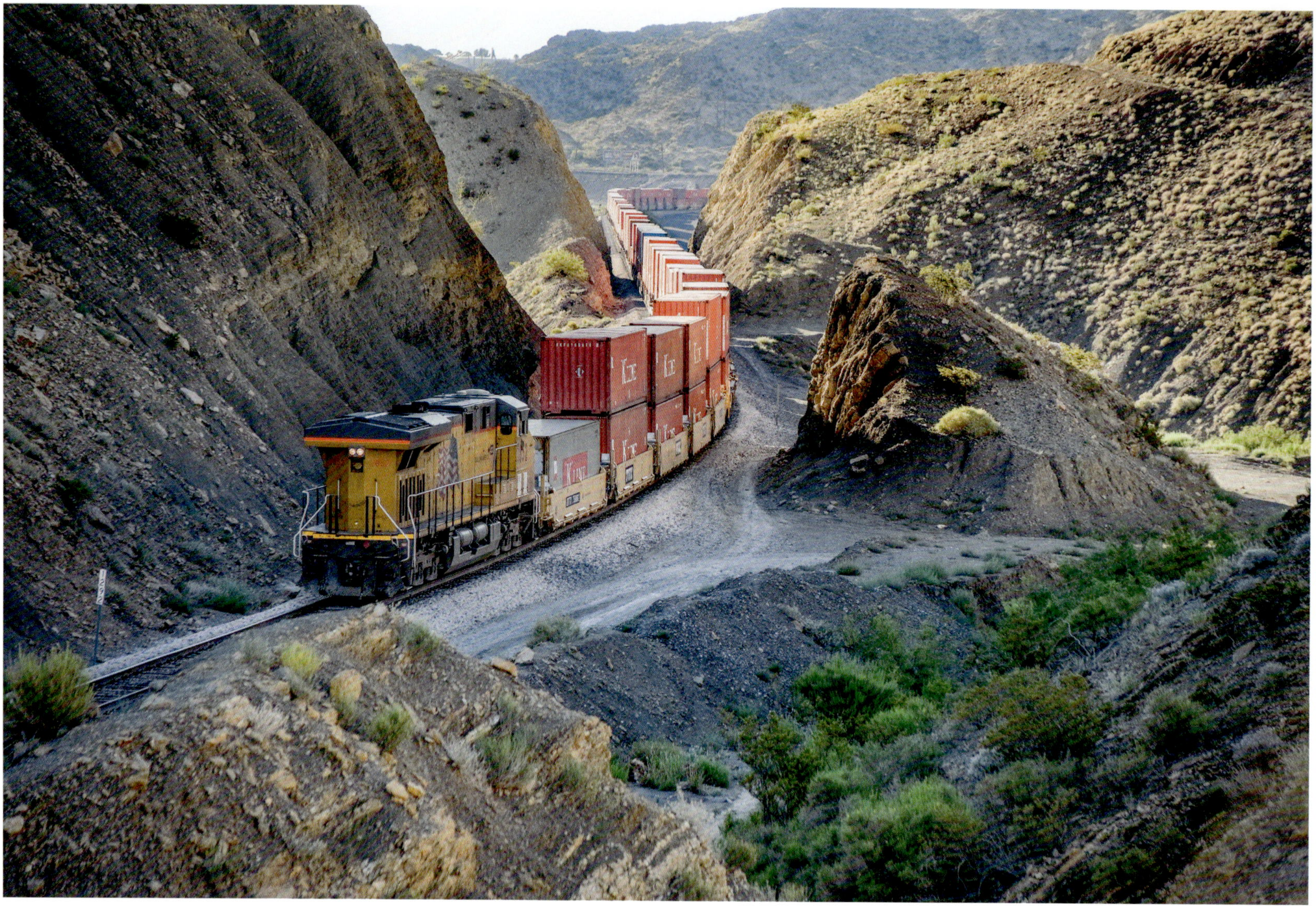

Railroad cut, Sunland Park, New Mexico. The Southern Pacific (historically the Union Pacific) right-of-way stretches cross-country east-to-west, bordering the El Paso ASARCO site. Here a freight train passes west through a cut at the base of Mount Cristo Rey after skirting ASARCO then crossing the Rio Grande (out of view in the distance).

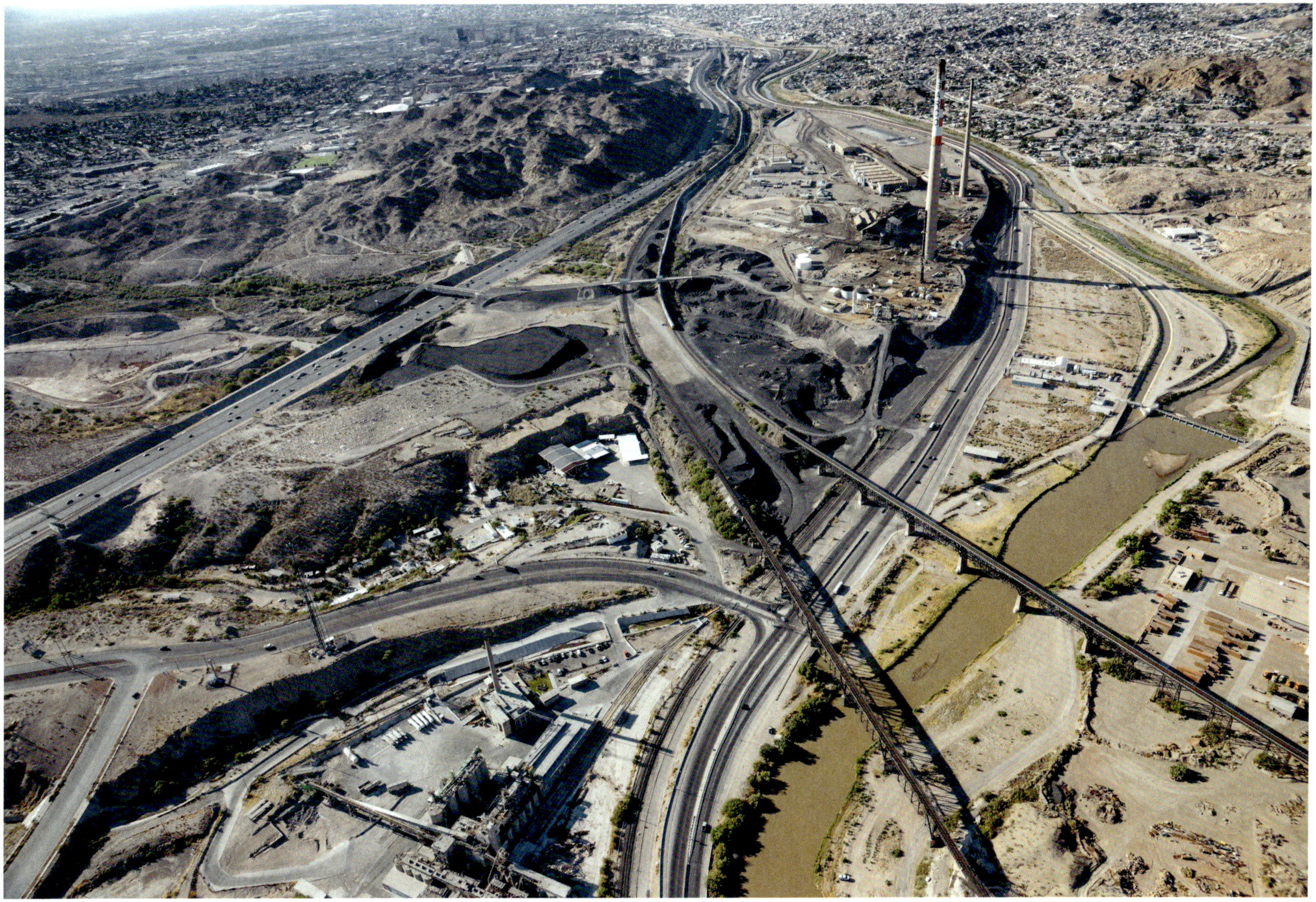

An aerial view of the El Paso ASARCO site. Virtually the entire property appears here in context. From the upper left: the city of El Paso and the University of Texas–El Paso campus east of the low hills skirted by Interstate 10. Parker Brothers' Arroyo is at the center left; west of Interstate 10 is Smeltertown Cemetery and the sprawling ASARCO site, bounded by Interstate 10 and railroads on the left and Paisano Drive on the right. Until the 1970s Smeltertown occupied the bare crescent bound by Paisano Drive and the Rio Grande channel. Ciudad Juárez is in the upper right immediately west of the river. The Grupo Cementos de Chihuahua cement plant is at the picture's bottom center.

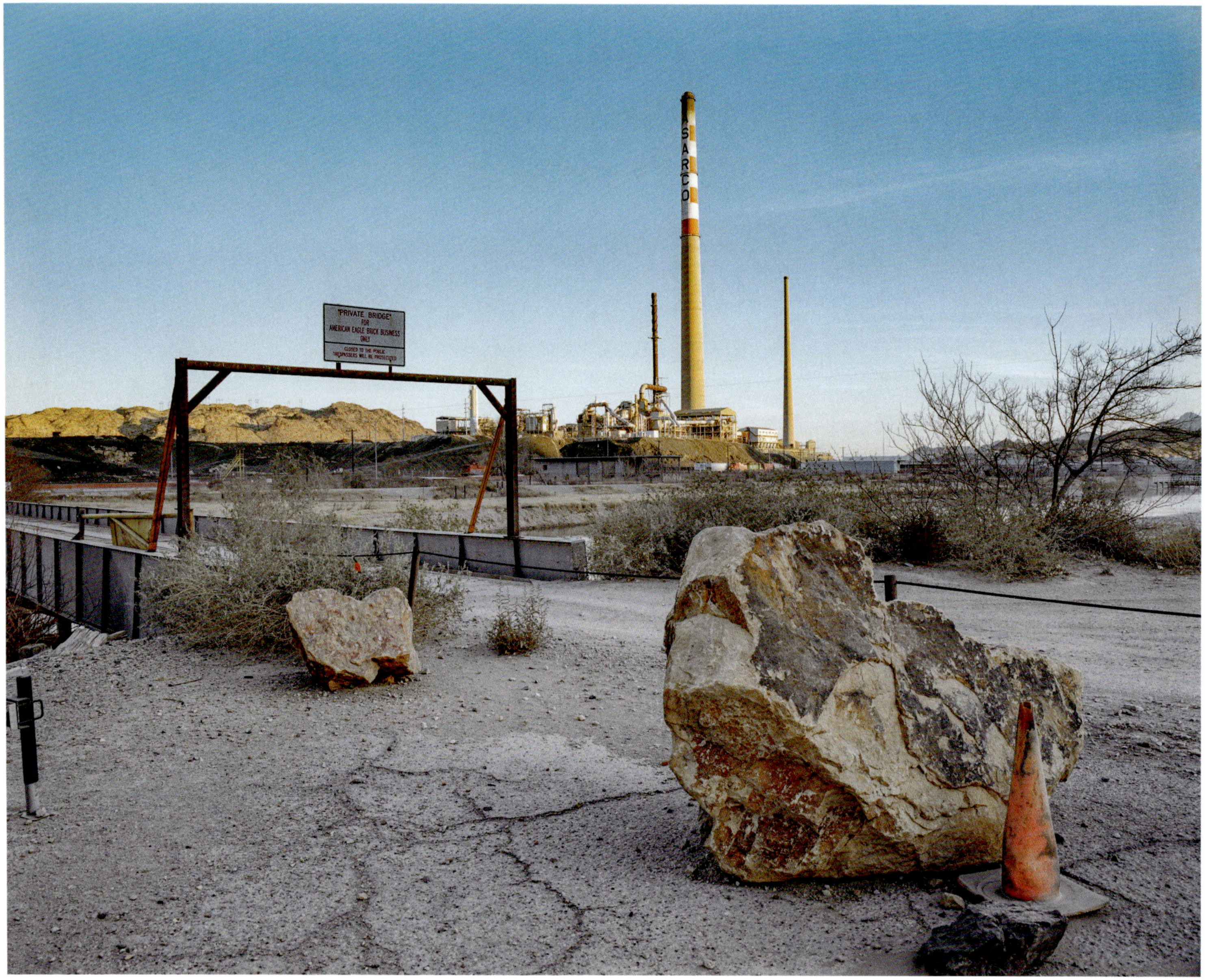

Sunland Park, New Mexico, toward the El Paso ASARCO plant. A small, private one-lane bridge spans the Rio Grande, linking the El Paso Brick Company in New Mexico to markets in Texas. A few hundred yards to the right is the border between New Mexico and Chihuahua.

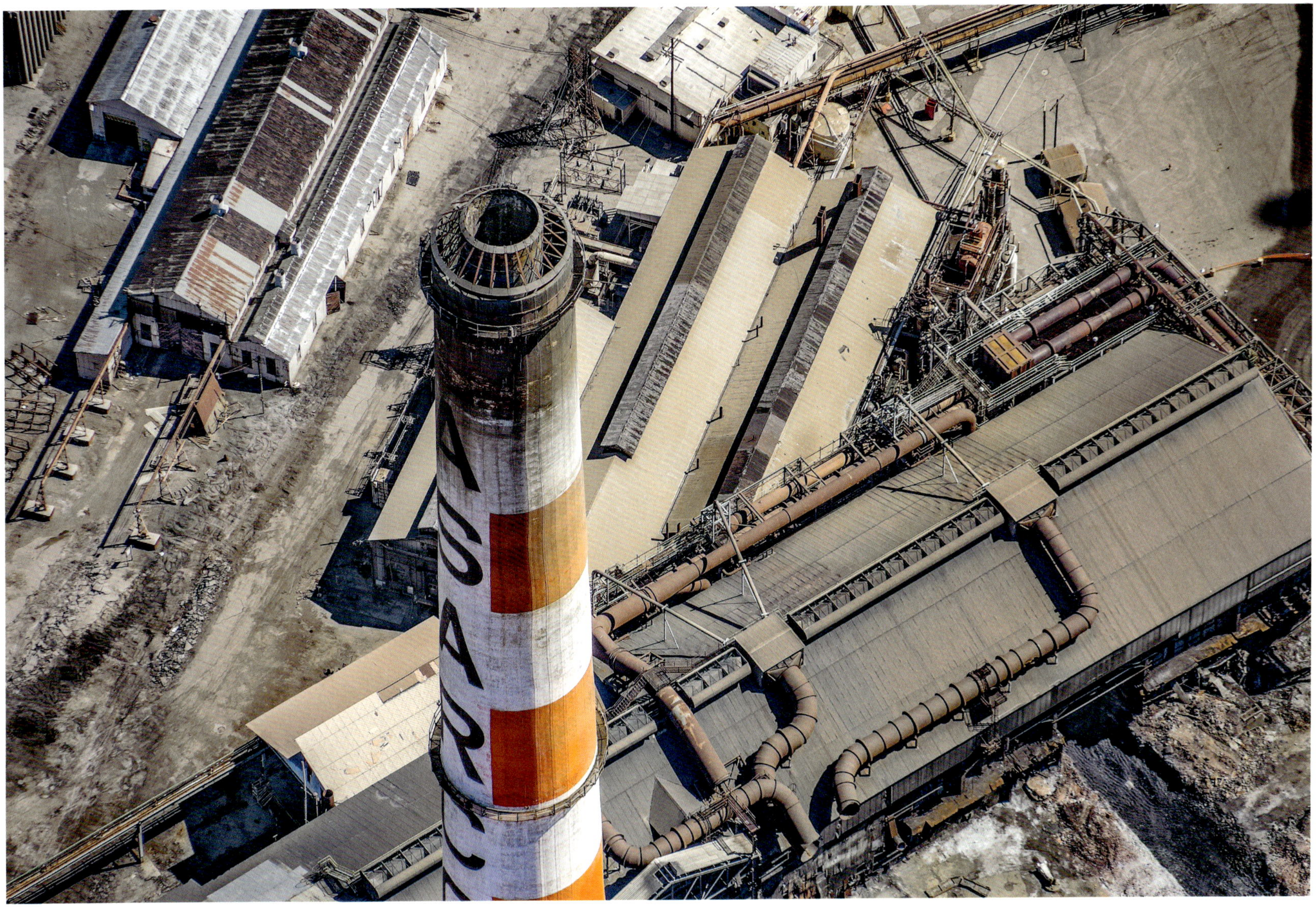

The copper stack at the El Paso ASARCO plant. This aerial view looks down onto the main 828-foot-tall double-walled concrete stack, showing the inner and outer concrete tube structures. The inner concrete stack projects slightly above the outer shell. On the ground, the boiler shop is left of the "R" in ASARCO, the powerplant is at the center right, and the main copper converter building (housing the copper smelting furnace) is in the lower right.

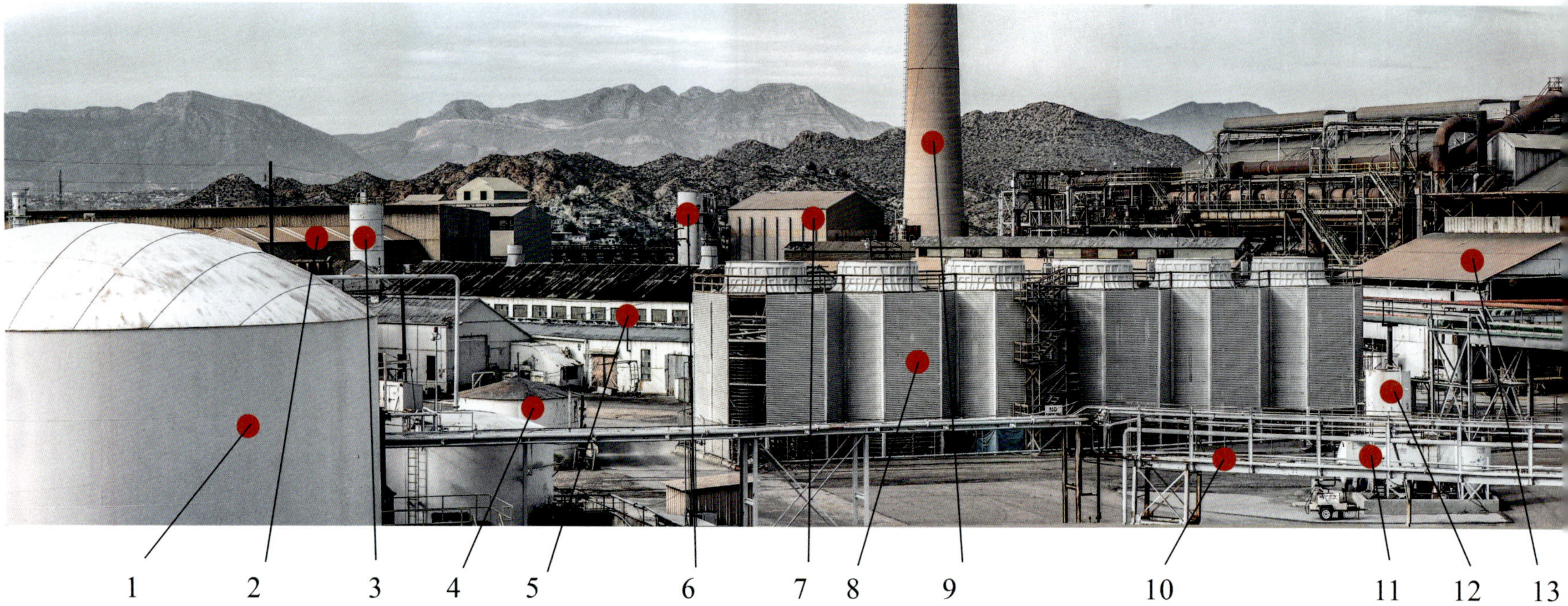

1. The SO_2 storage tanks.
2. The ore bedding building.
3. The unloading silica tanks.
4. The oleum tank.
5. The long white building with the row of windows is the boiler shop.
6. The vertical structure near the back is the sinter plant ventilation plenum silo.
7. The blocky pitched-roof building right of the silo is the sinter machine hot Cottrell.
8. The bank of vertical panels shields the six-cell array of the powerhouse cooling towers.
9. The 610-foot stack dating from 1950.
10. The H_2O and SO_2 pipe rack.

11 and 12. The vertical tank is the fuel station; the horizontal tank is for diesel storage.

13. The pink shed roof covers the anode casting area.

This panorama is stitched together from ten separate medium-format negatives. The view is from the north end of the site toward the southwest. Ciudad Chihuahua, Mexico, is the hilly backdrop.

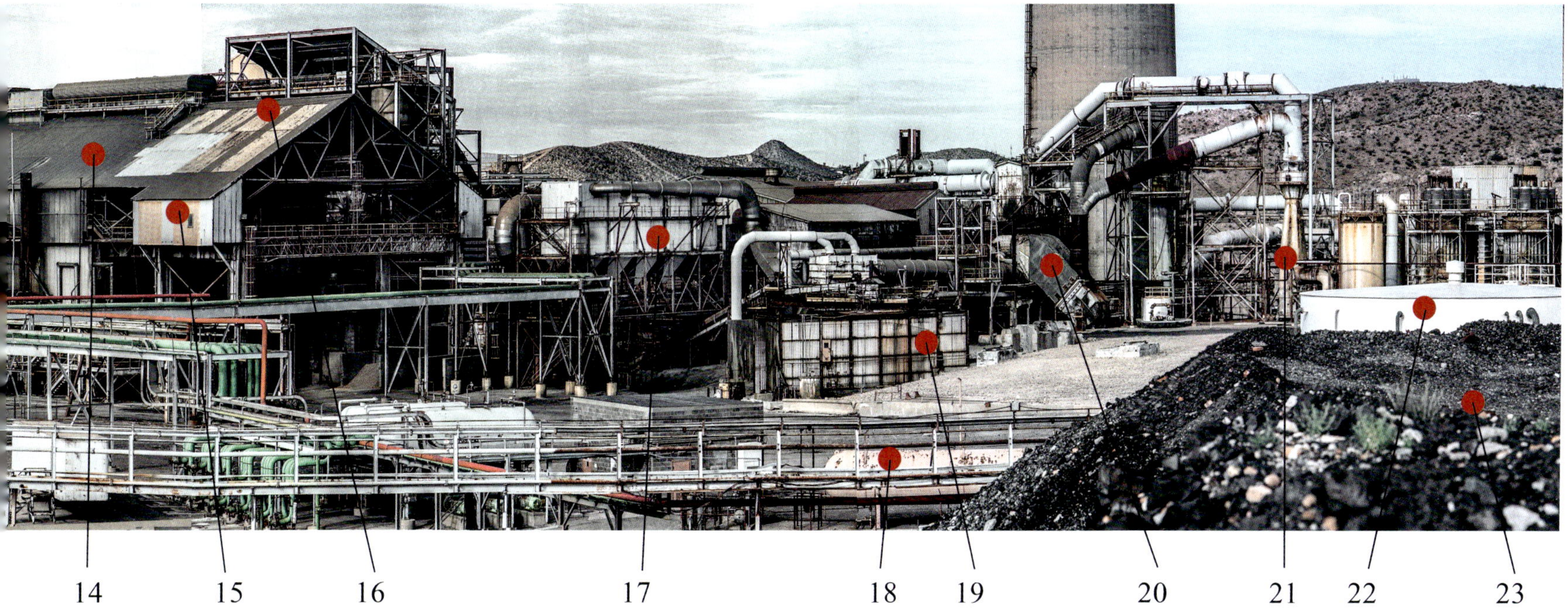

14. The main building mass is the converter building.
15. The shed projecting from its roof is the converter crane service bay.
16. The highest roof slope covers the contop.
17. The contop five-cell bag house.
18. The horizontal tank in the foreground behind the pipe rack is the compressed air receiver thank.
19. The cube above the compressed air tank is the Cottrell ventilation-dust collection and loading area.
20. Ducts from the No. 1 and No. 2 acid plants obscure the base of the 828-foot copper stack in the background.
21. The No. 1 acid plant.
22. One of a pair of stormwater storage tanks.
23. Slag.

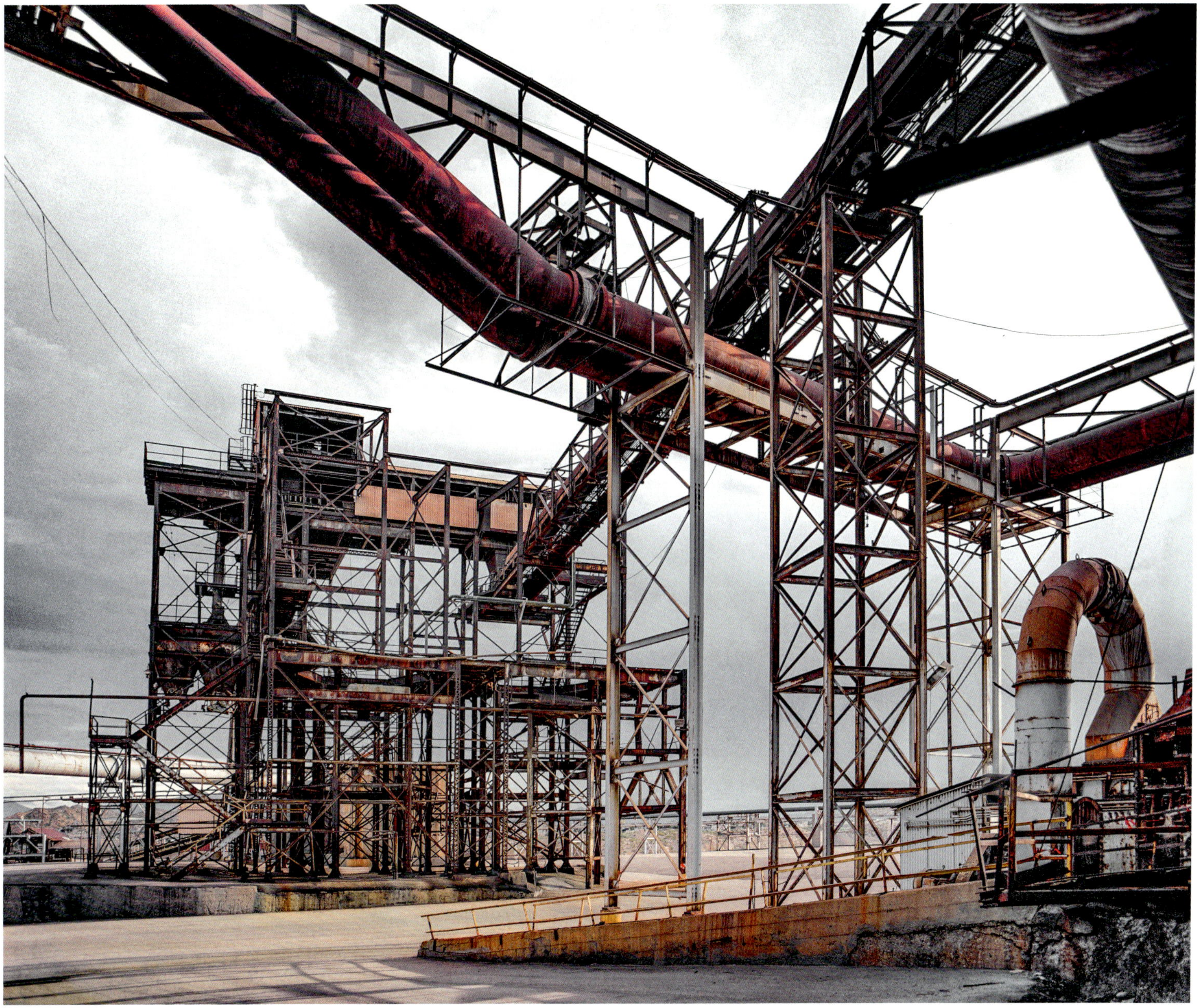

A pre-demolition view of the El Paso ASARCO plant. The image shows the No. 25 conveyor and high velocity flue.

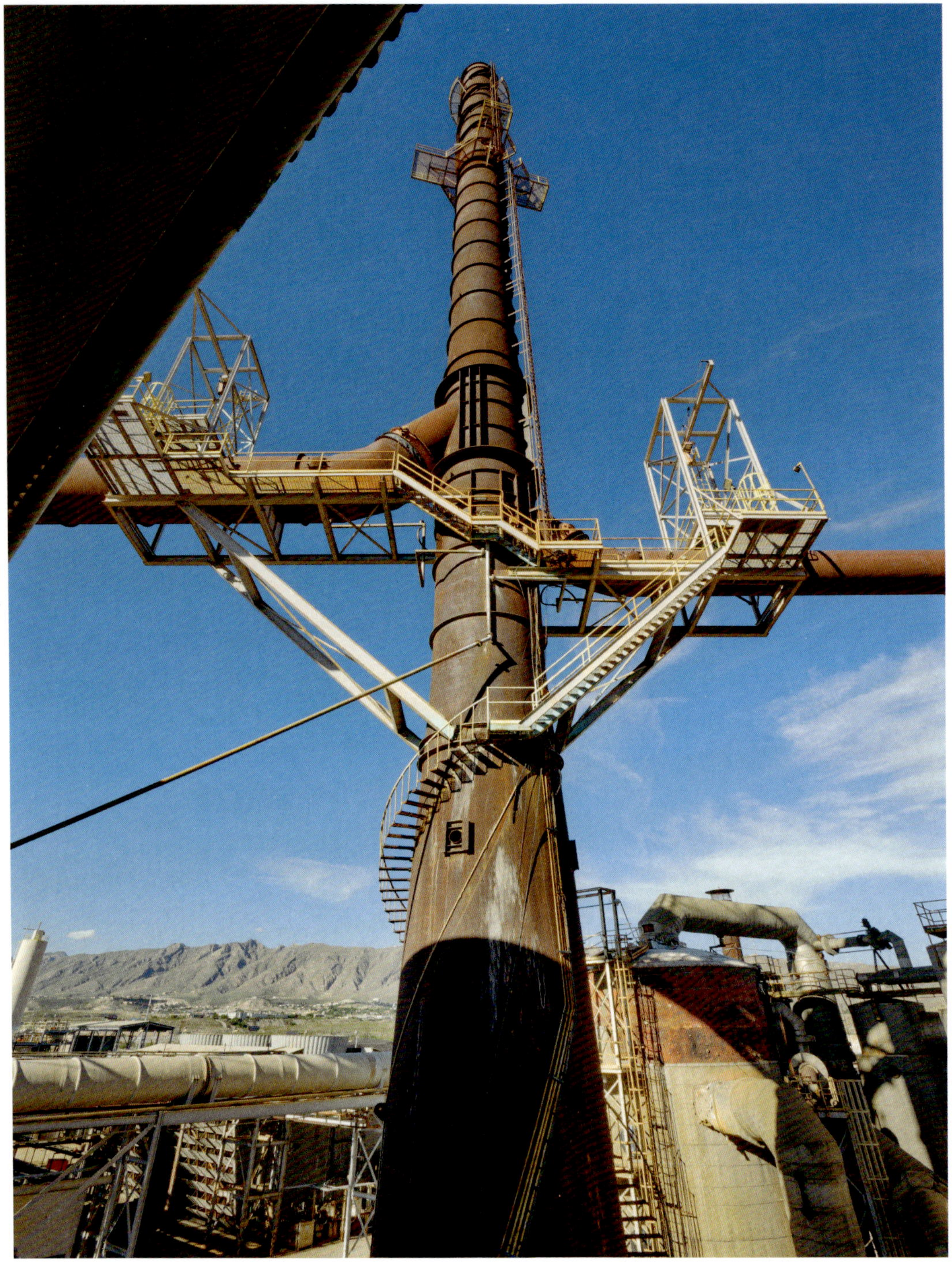

A pre-demolition view of the El Paso ASARCO plant. This is the flue, or tail gas stack, serving the No. 1 and No. 2 acid plants. One of the site's most unusual elements was the innovative design of this stack: its upper third was wrapped by a spiral steel flange that, in high winds, stabilized the relatively thin steel tube, preventing the formation of invisible "Kármán vortex sheets," whose oscillation could cause the structure to vibrate, sway, and fall.

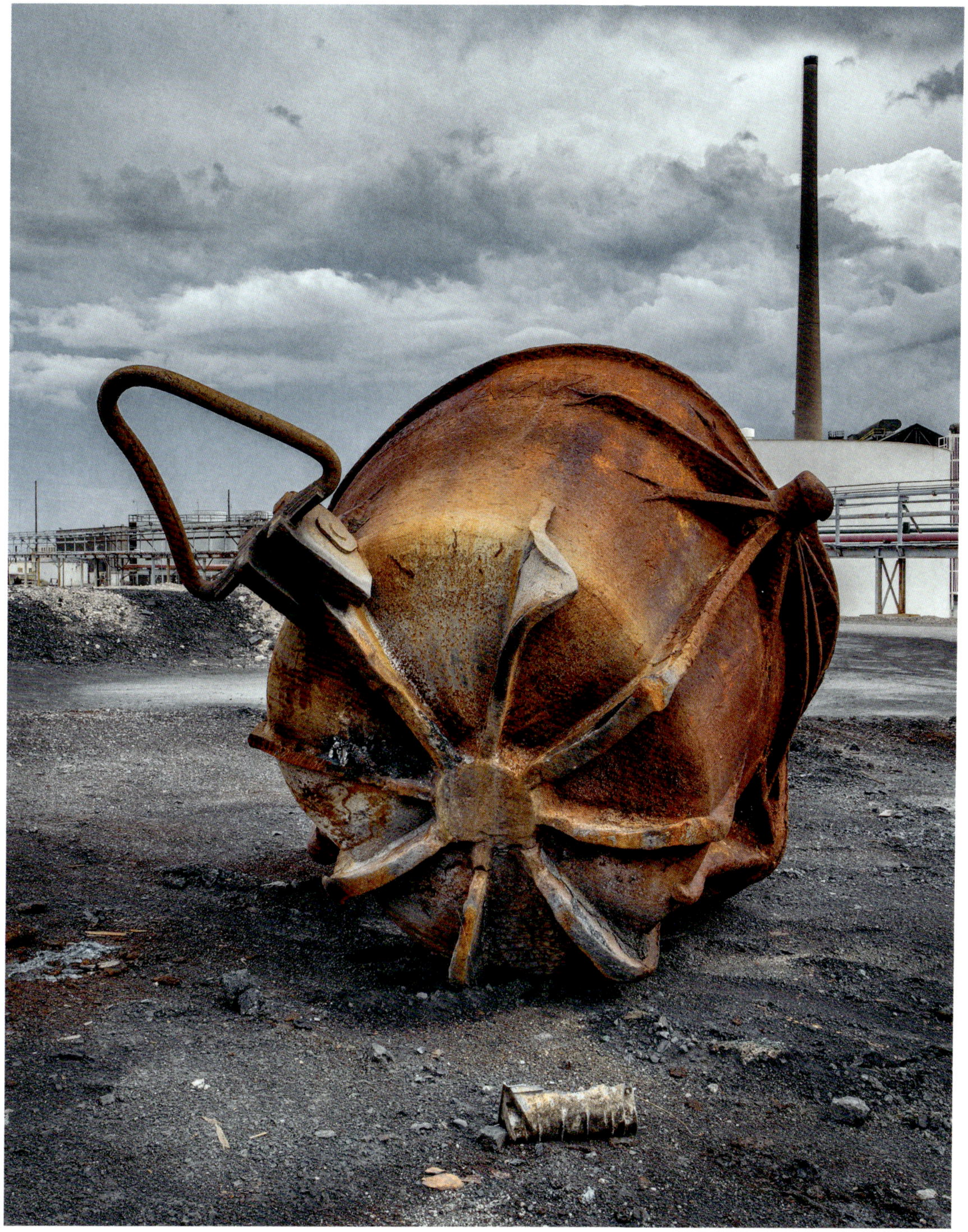

A pre-demolition view of the El Paso ASARCO site. The image shows one of the last two matte ladles on the site, awaiting salvage.

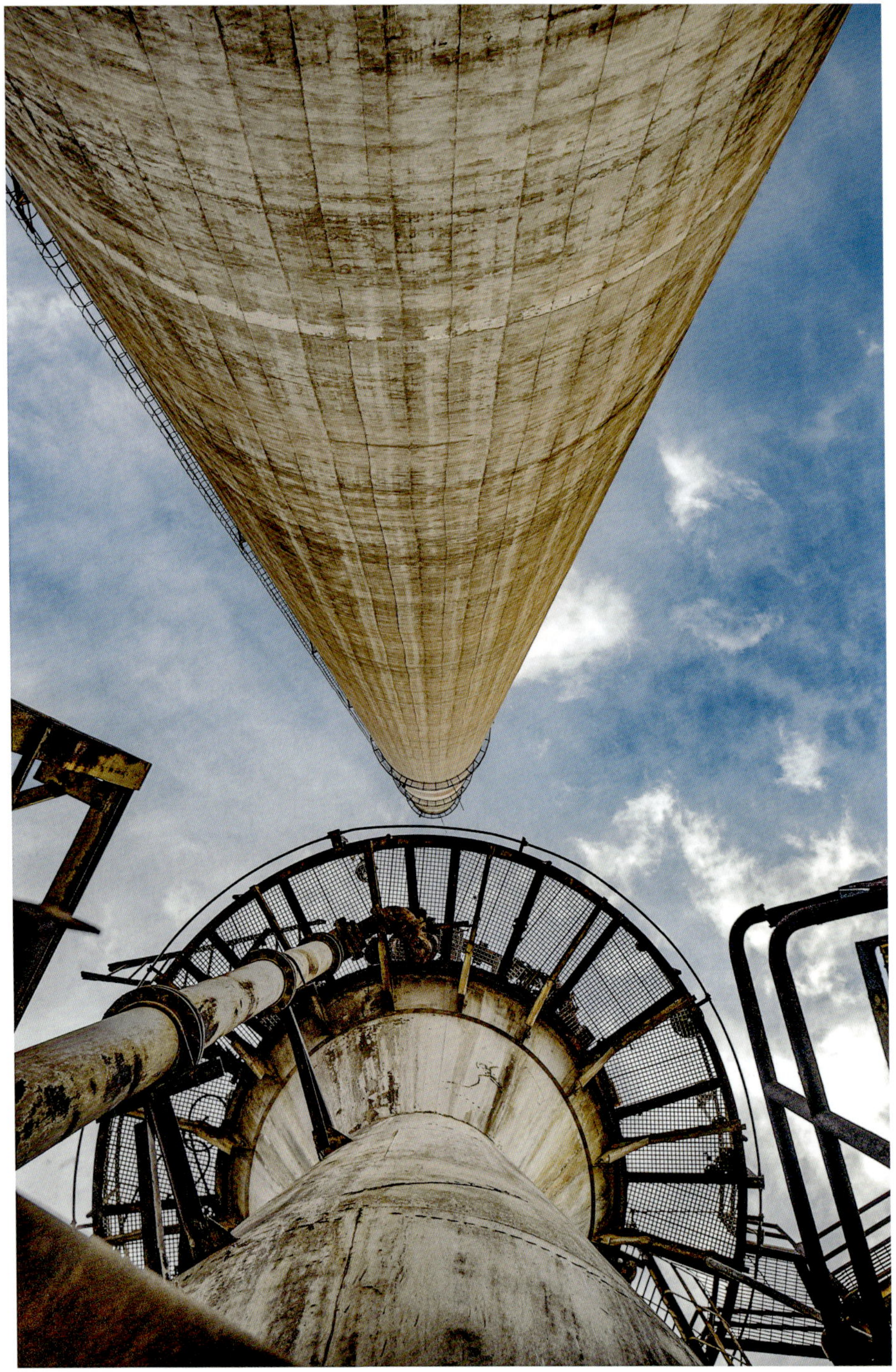

A pre-demolition view of the El Paso ASARCO plant. This is a skyward view from between the main copper stack and one of the two Venturi scrubbers.

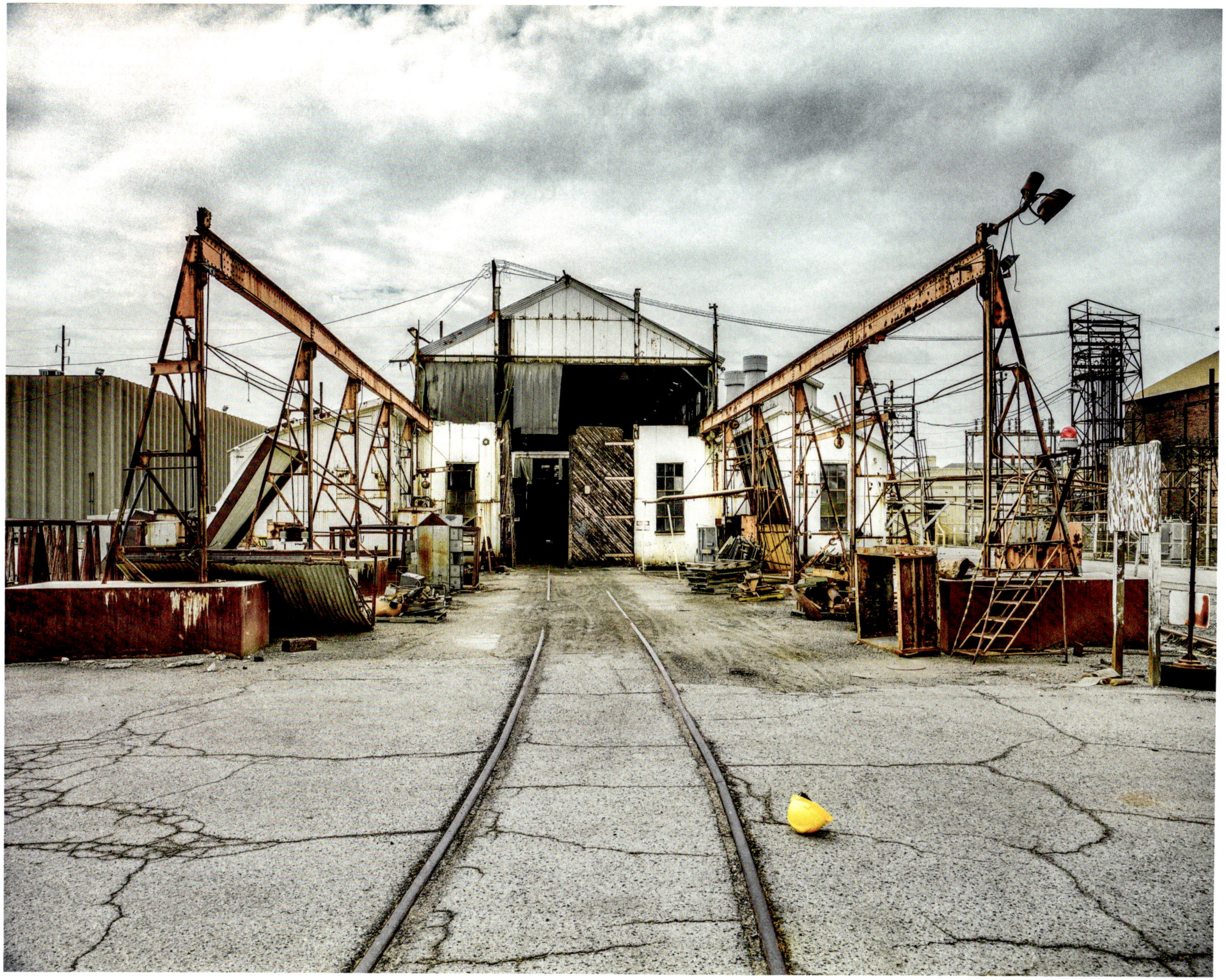

A pre-demolition view of the El Paso ASARCO plant. The image shows the welding shop building with its overhead crane rails, north of the power plant in the far right center.

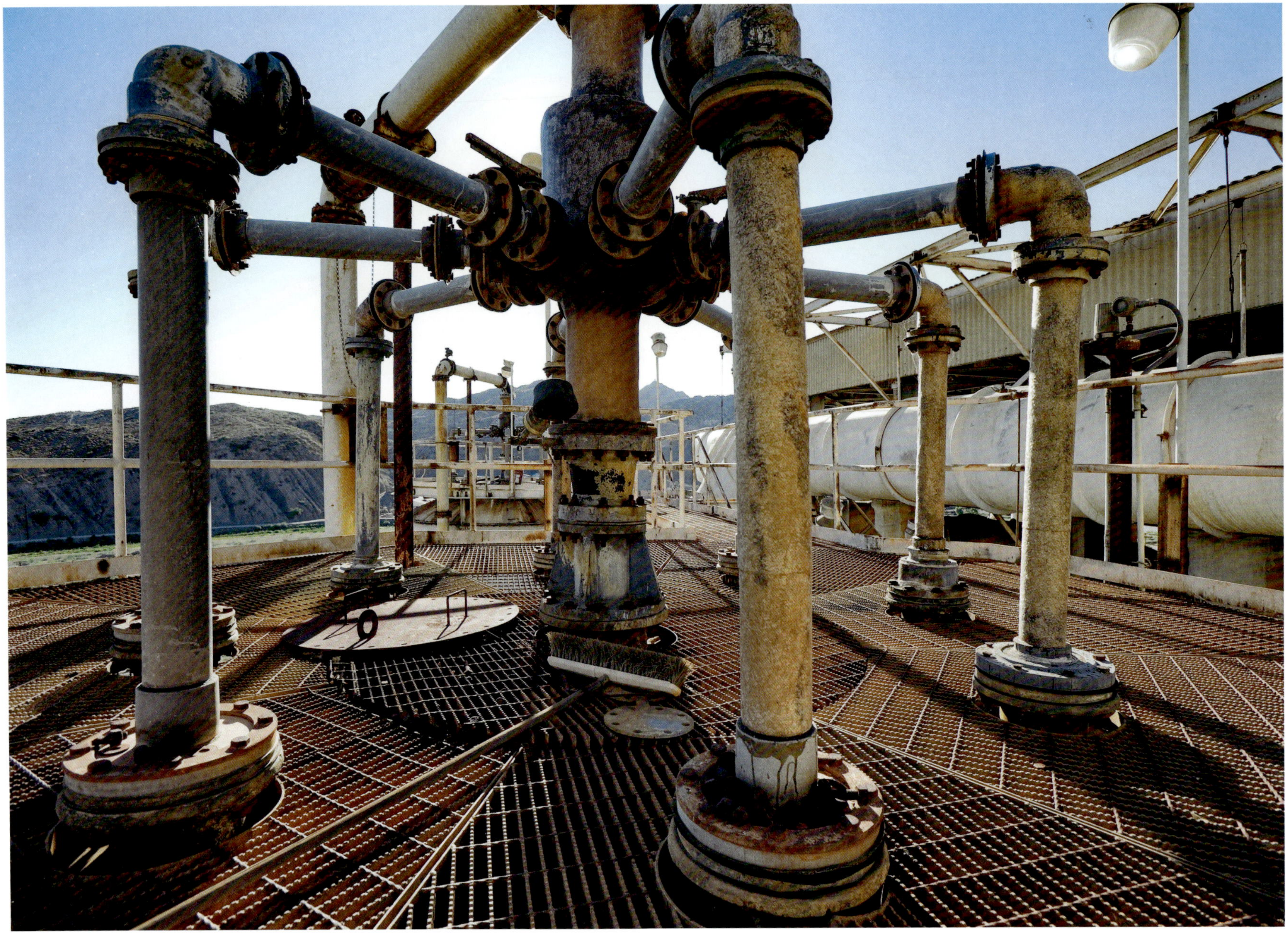

A pre-demolition view of the El Paso ASARCO plant. On the catwalk above the No. 2 acid plant, this view shows the pack scrubber distribution manifolds. The view is west toward Cerro de Cristo Rey.

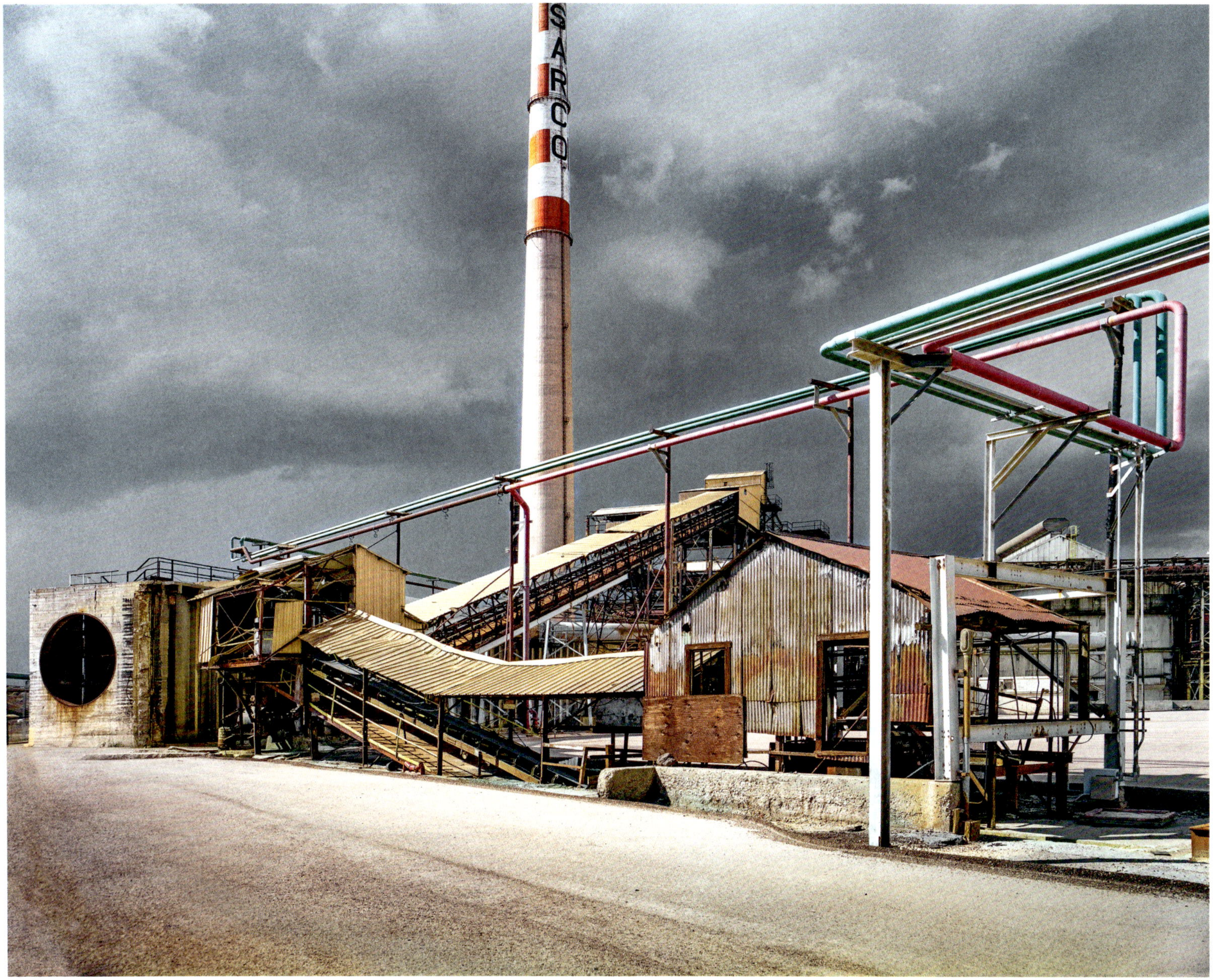

A pre-demolition view of the El Paso ASARCO plant. This image shows the No. 13 incline belt conveyor, with its overhead color-coded gas delivery bus. This photograph was made in August 2010, during the photographer's first week of working on the property. In hundreds of hours of fieldwork over the following decade, this was the only time lightning and monsoon deluge threatened to cut the day short.

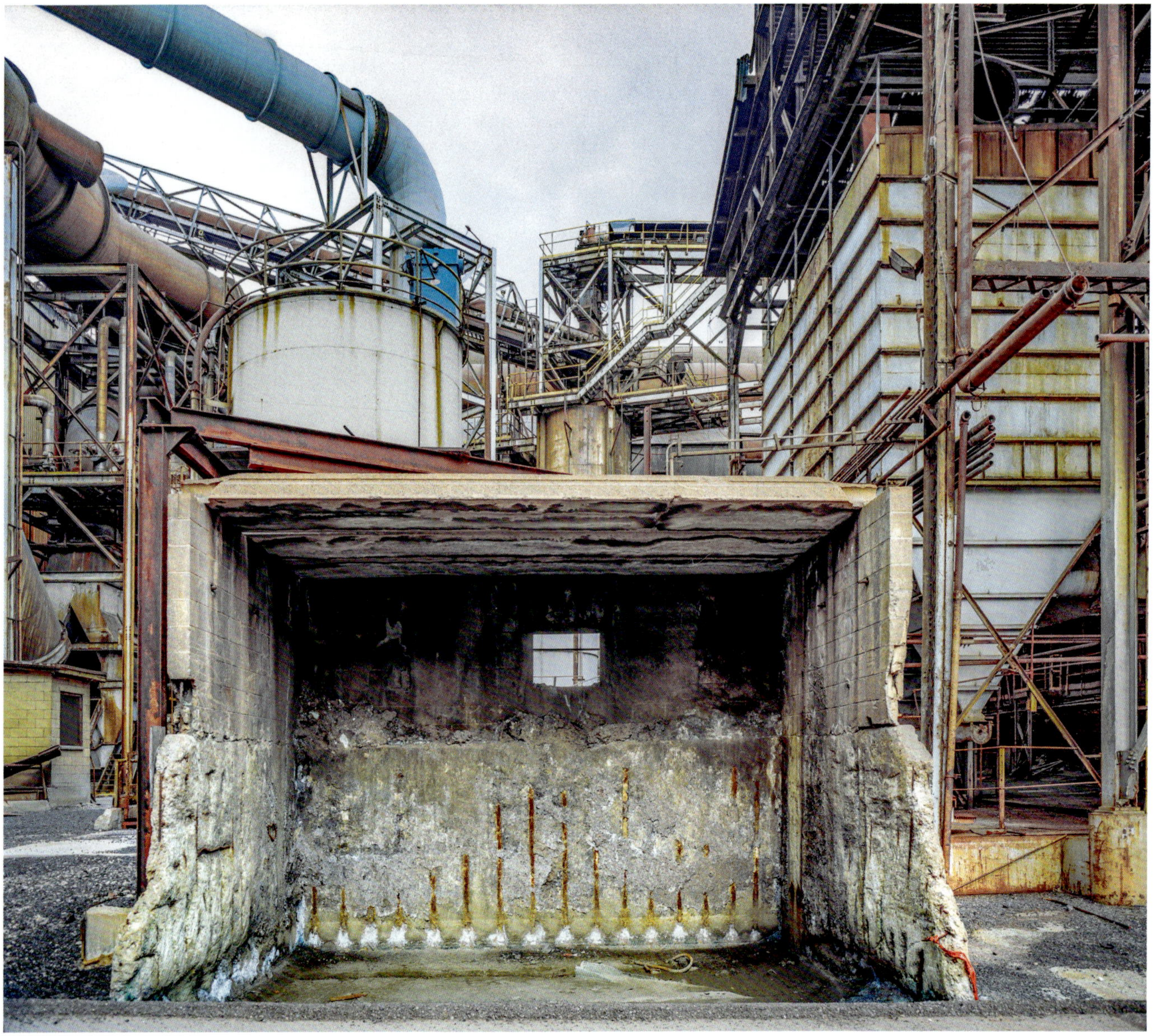

A pre-demolition view of the El Paso ASARCO plant. The image shows an open concrete bin west of the main copper converter building.

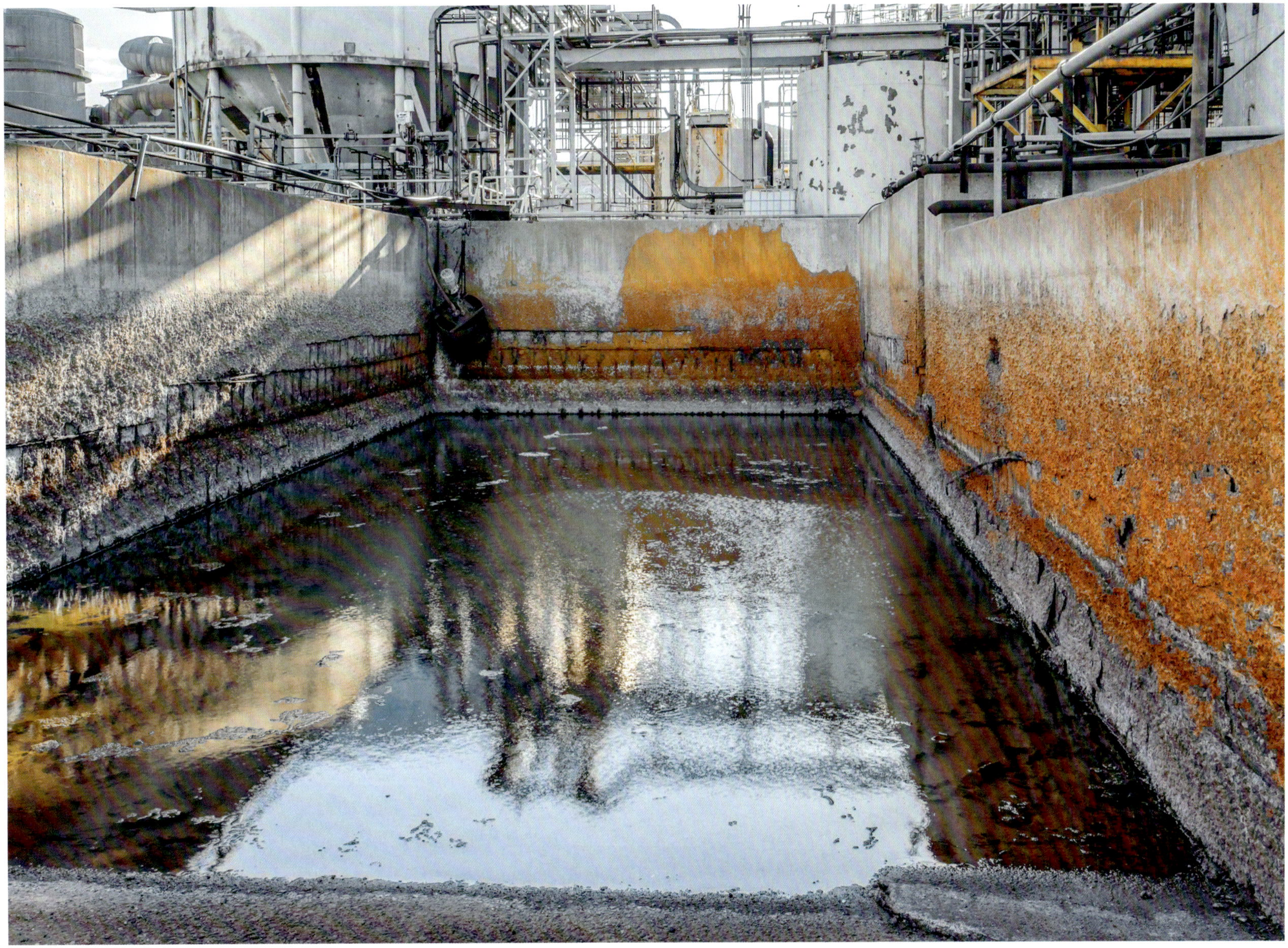

A pre-demolition view of the El Paso ASARCO plant. The image shows standing water in the subgrade pit at the cadmium plant.

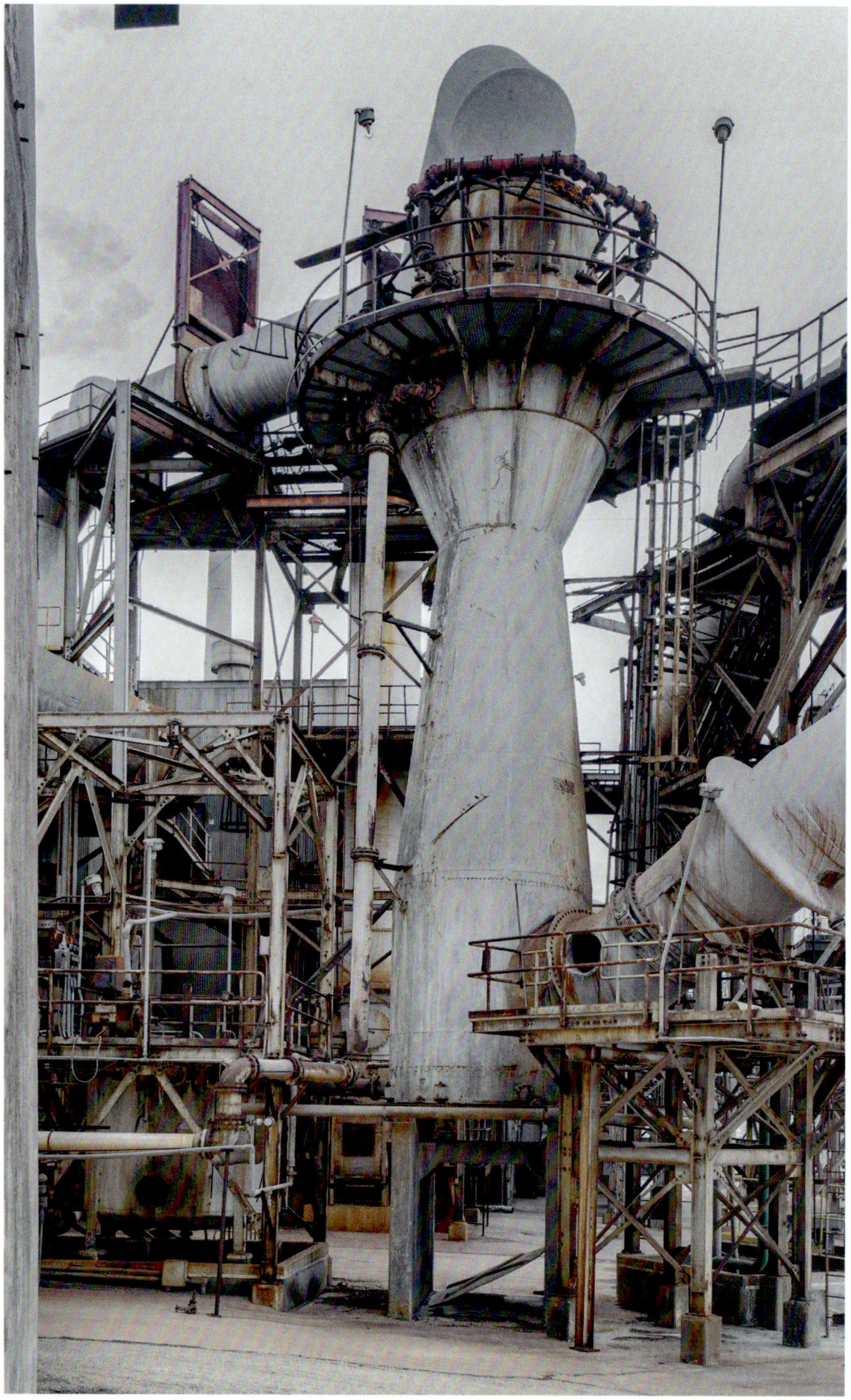

A pre-demolition view of the El Paso ASARCO plant. The image shows one of two Venturi scrubbers associated with acid plant No. 1. Venturi scrubbers capture raw smelter gasses, then tap the energy from the resulting newly introduced high-velocity gas stream to "scrub" the incoming gas of most pollutants, before ejecting the unburdened gasses into the atmosphere via the much taller main stack.

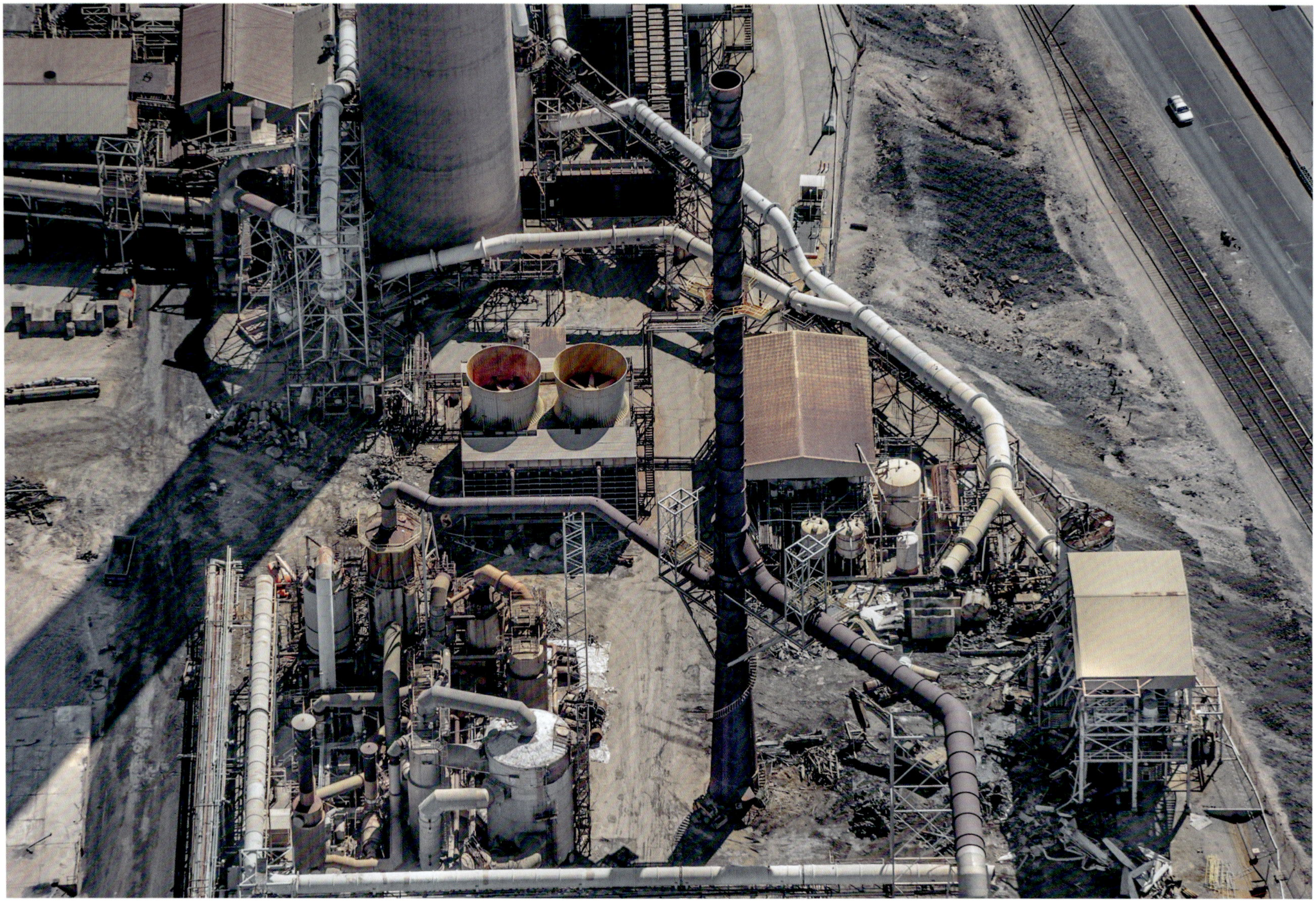

An aerial view of a section of the El Paso ASARCO plant. This view shows the acid plant prior to its demolition, featuring the complex system of "scrubbing" equipment at the base of the main copper stack in the upper left.

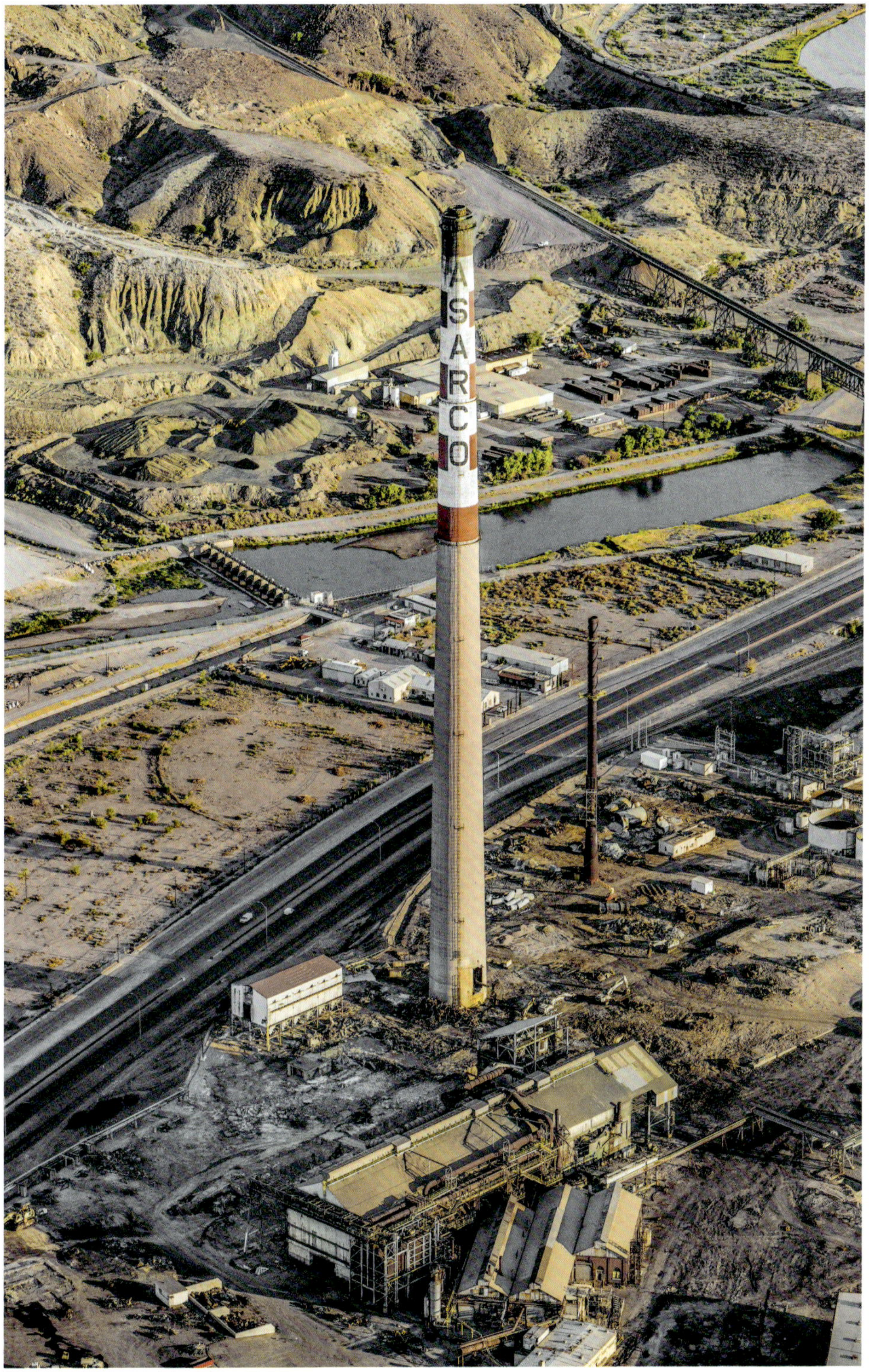

An aerial view of the El Paso ASARCO plant. The main copper stack stands surrounded by the rubble of the acid plant, whose distinctive steel stack will soon fall.

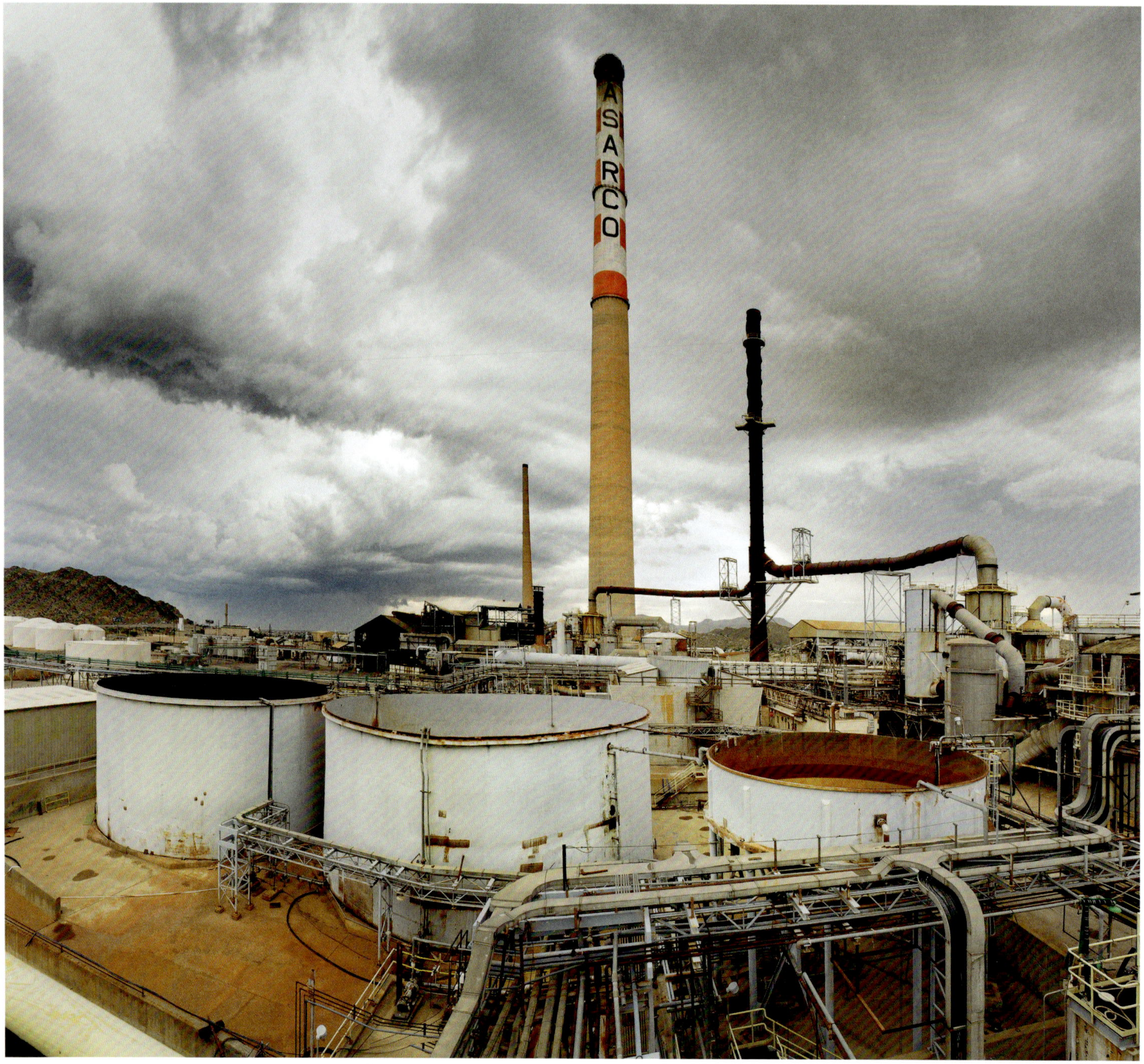

A pre-demolition view of the El Paso ASARCO plant. The view is east from the acid plant, before large-scale demolition was evident. From this vantage point at the site's north end, the complexity and density of the smelter infrastructure suggested that its demolition and removal would be impossible. But in less than twenty-four months, everything in this photograph except the stacks had been pulled down, cut up, and sold for scrap.

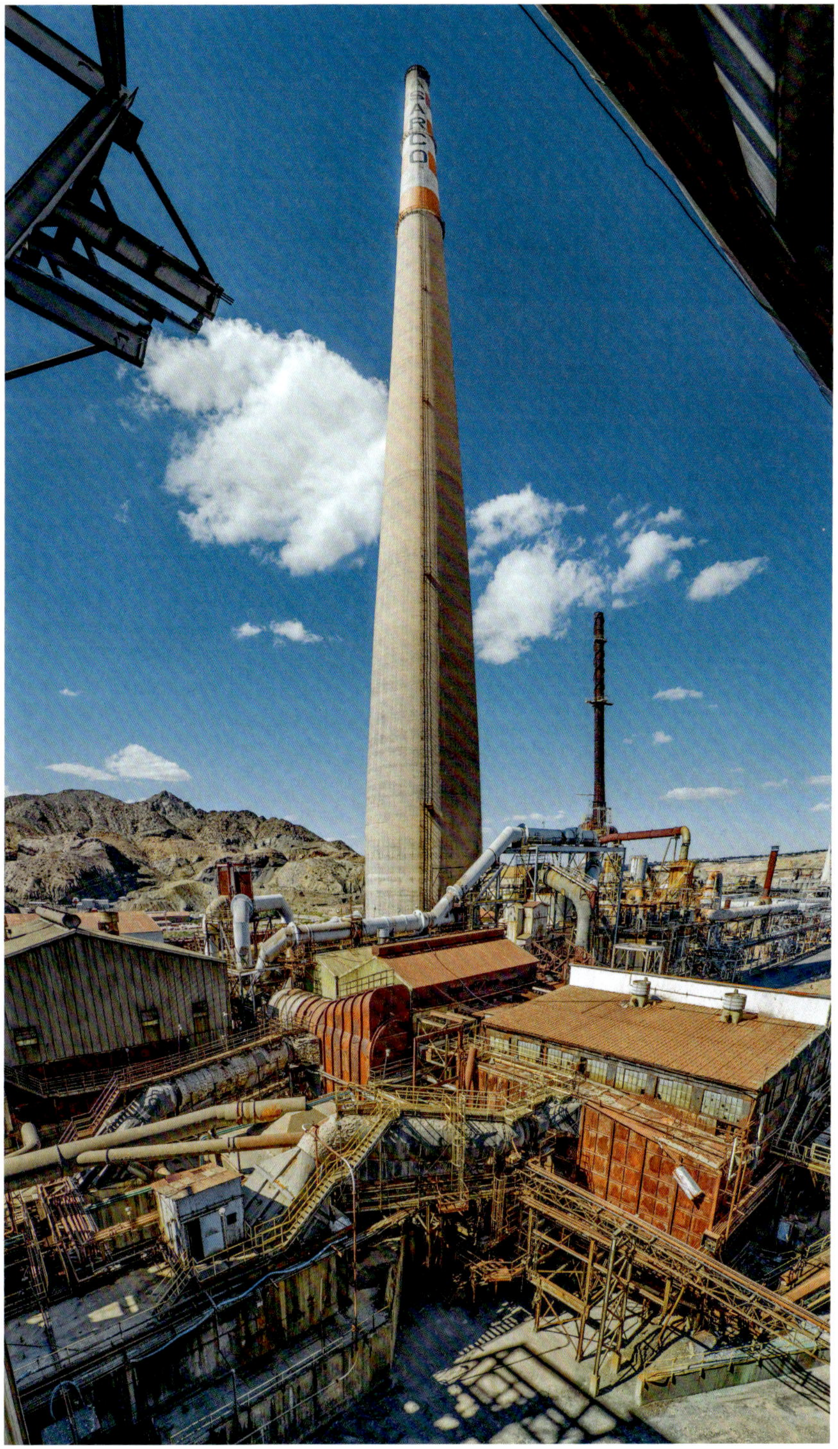

A pre-demolition view of the main "copper" stack at the El Paso ASARCO plant. The view looks west from the main converter contop (continuous smelting and top ventilating) building. The spray chamber is in the lower left, in the upper left is the 1970 Cottrell, and in the lower right is the 1929 Cottrell. Cerro de Cristo Rey is at the horizon at the center left.

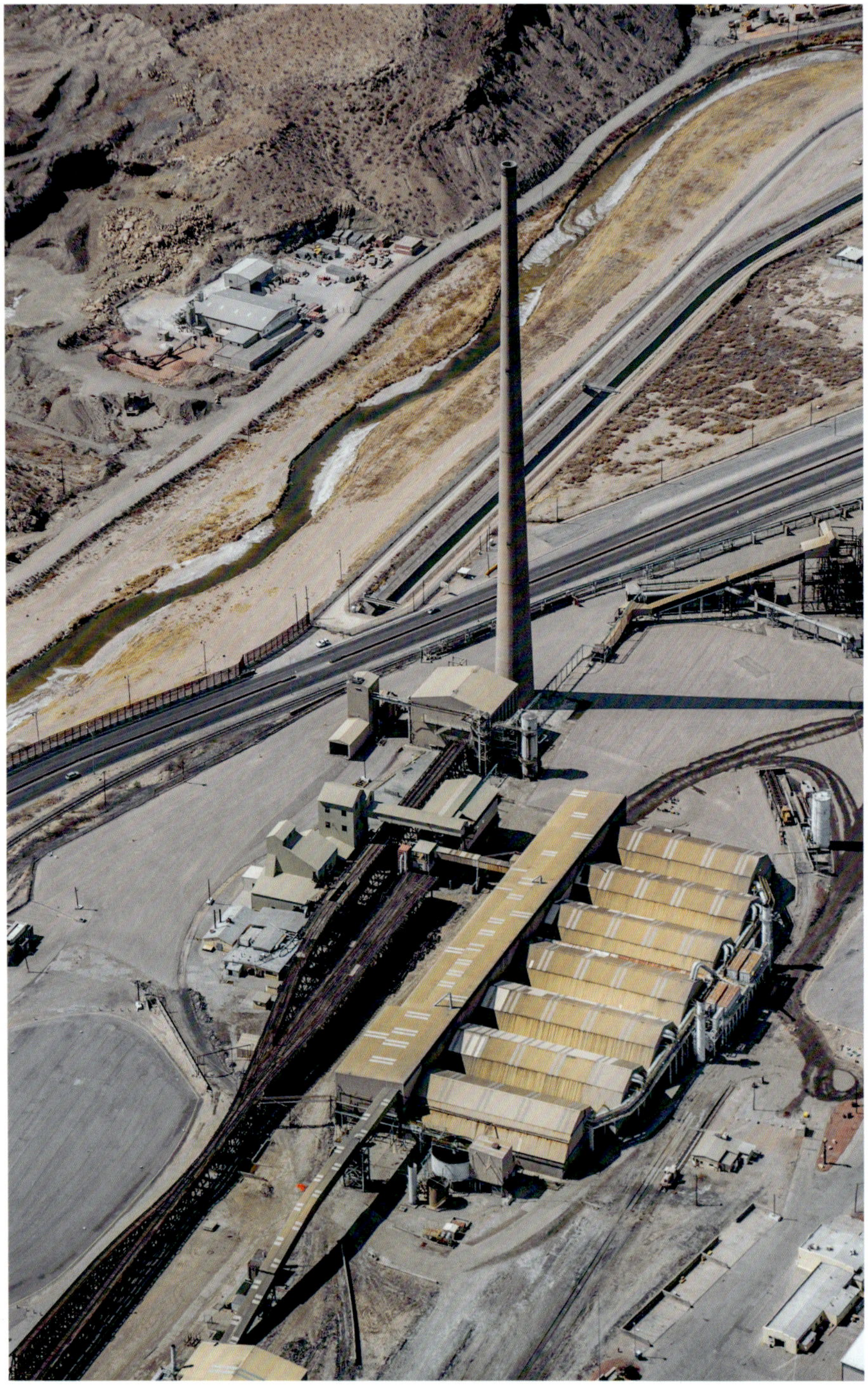

An aerial view of the El Paso ASARCO plant. The photograph features the "lead stack" at the center, the seven-bay ore bedding building in the lower right, the rail trestle in the lower left, and the mill building at the base of the concrete stack. The Rio Grande and a brick plant in Mexico are in the upper left.

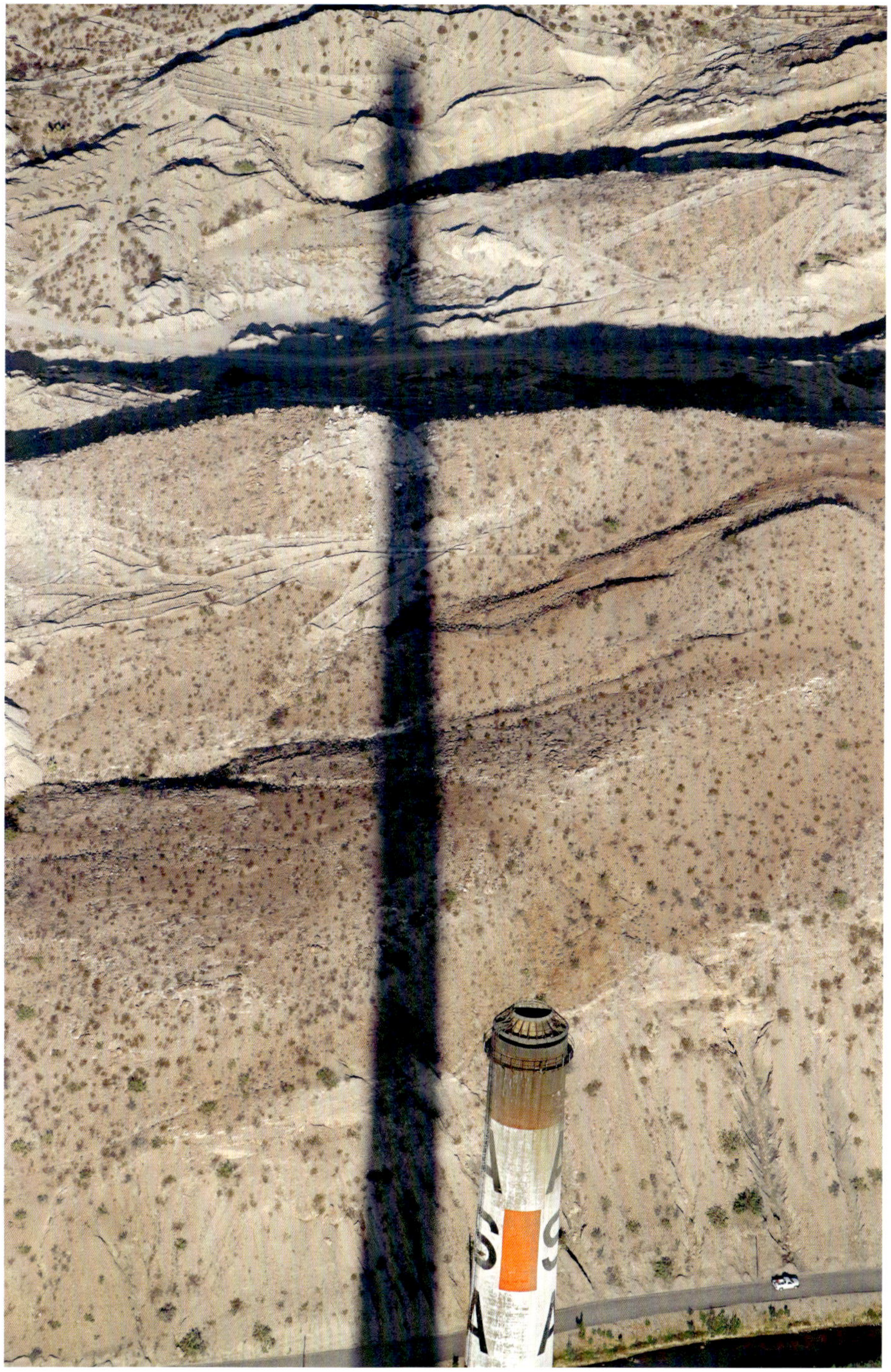

An aerial view of ASARCO's copper stack with its shadow. In this morning view, the shadow of the 828-foot towering stack spills across the Rio Grande and the base of Cerro de Cristo Rey into Ciudad Juárez.

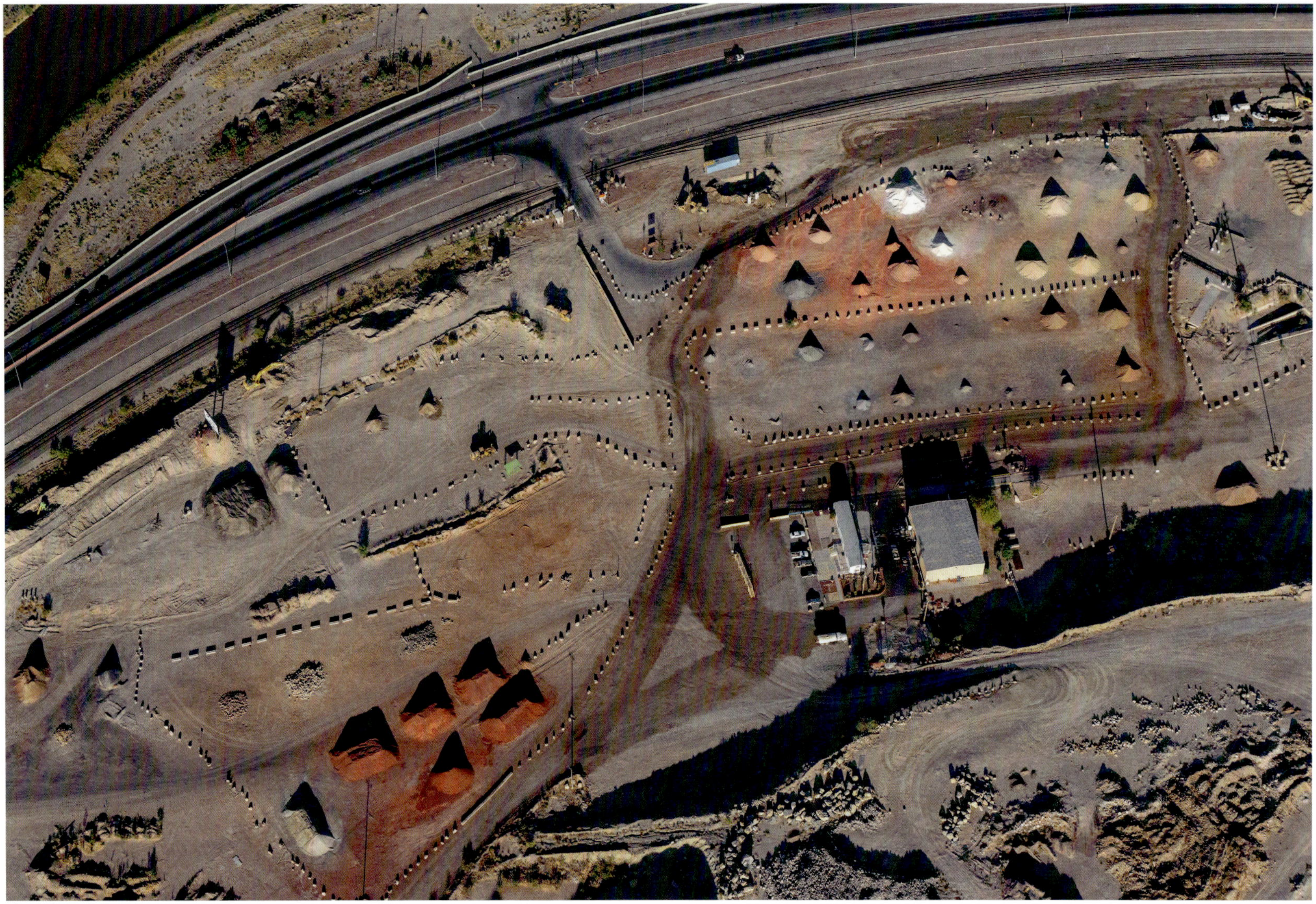

An aerial view near the El Paso ASARCO site. This active gravel yard is just northwest of the ASARCO smelter tract. A cement plant has operated here since the 1880s. The historic pass, after more than a century, still supplies limestone, gravel, and brick to the region's construction trades. Elephant Butte Dam, completed in 1915 and located one hundred miles upstream in New Mexico, is made of material quarried from Paso del Norte. Grupo Cementos de Chihuahua currently owns this operation.

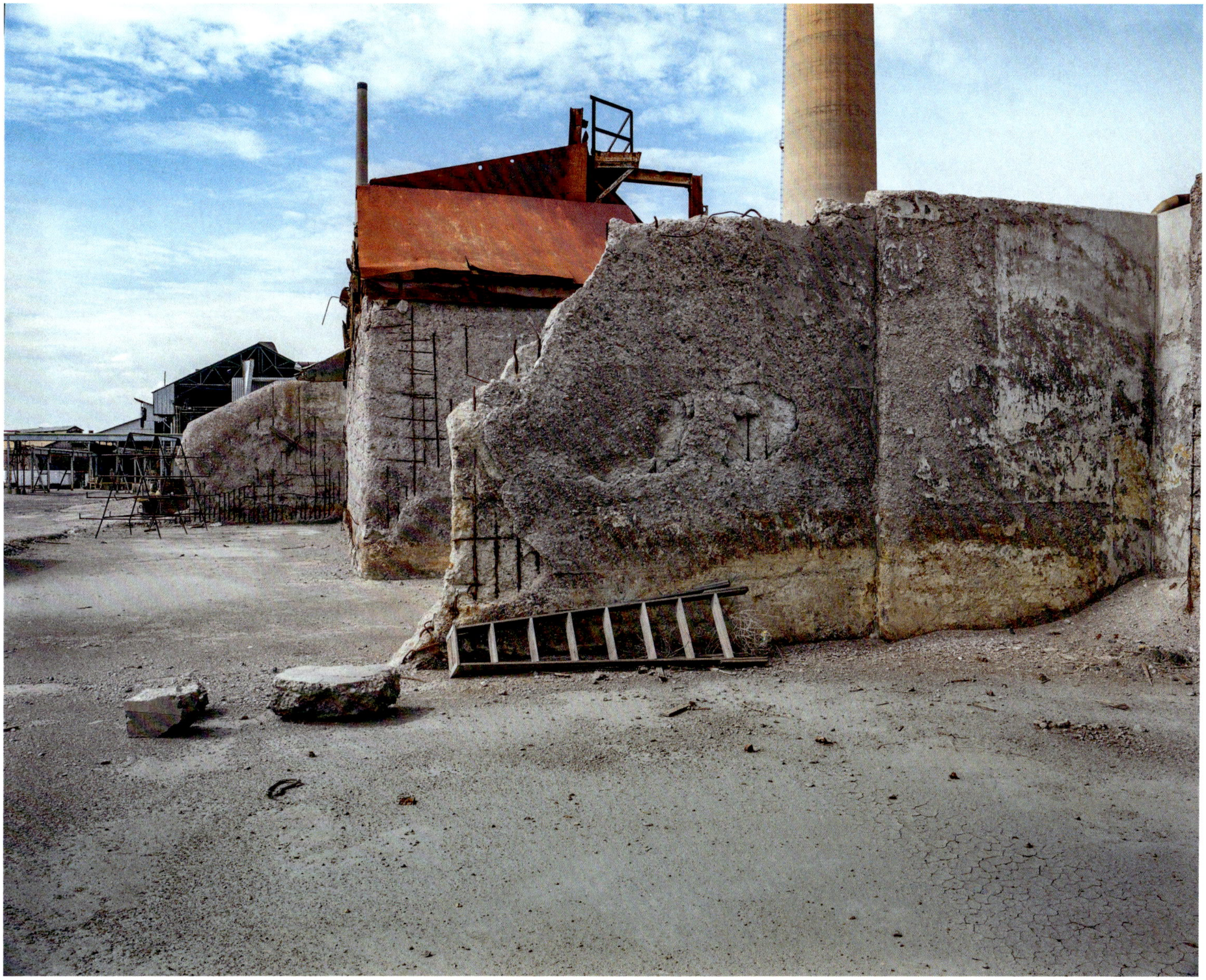

A pre-demolition view of the El Paso ASARCO plant. The image shows the concrete remains of a scrap bunker, north of the main converter building.

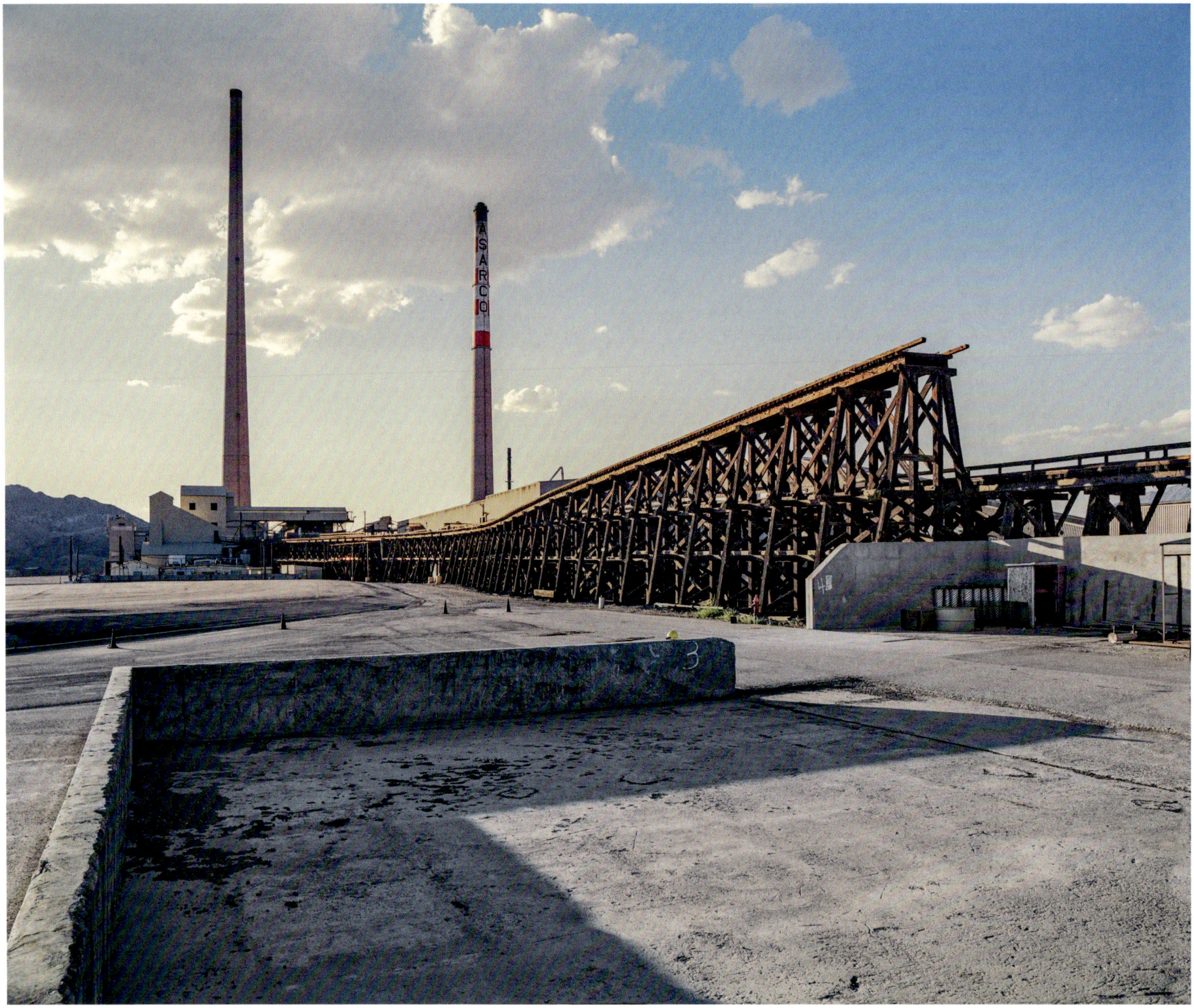

A pre-demolition view of the El Paso ASARCO site. The image shows a timber rail trestle and ramp. More than eighty years after its construction, much of the trestle—its wood having never been treated with creosote—was in such fine condition that after its disassembly and removal from the site, could be re-milled and sold as "architectural" or "restoration grade" lumber.

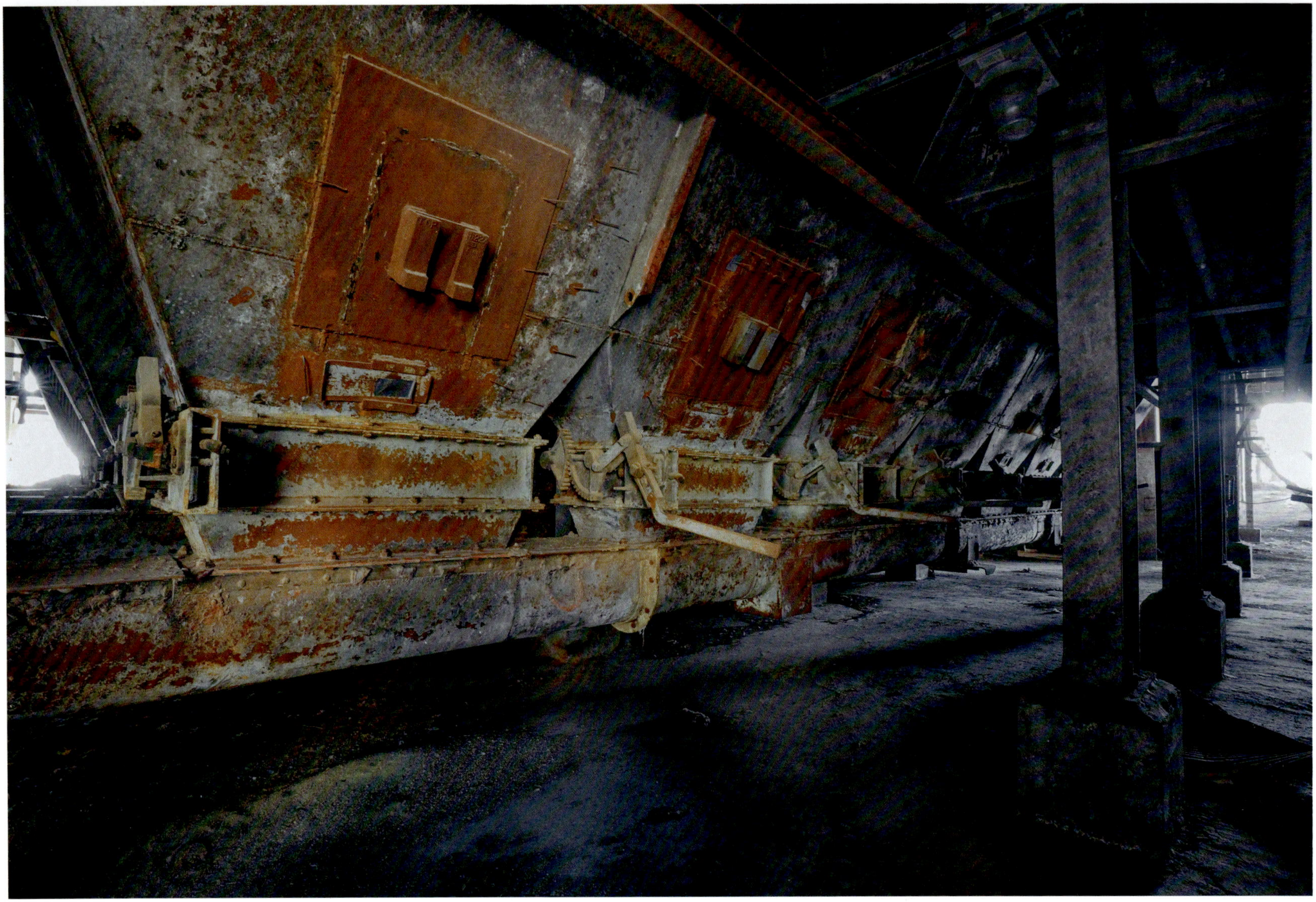

A pre-demolition view of the El Paso ASARCO plant. This image shows one of several rows of Cottrell hoppers with screw conveyors dating from 1929.

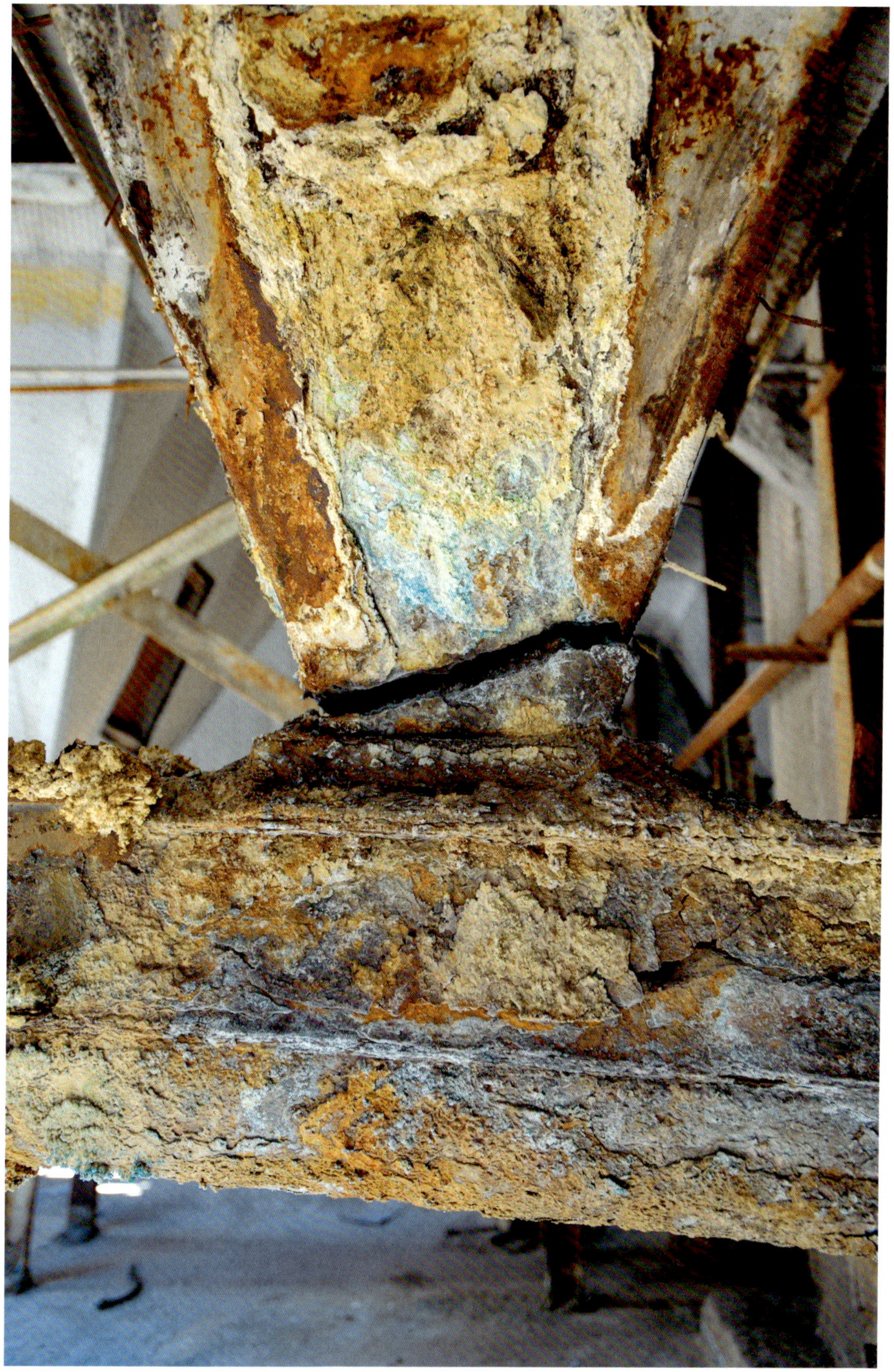

A pre-demolition view of the El Paso ASARCO plant. This image shows a detail of the corroded ore hopper.

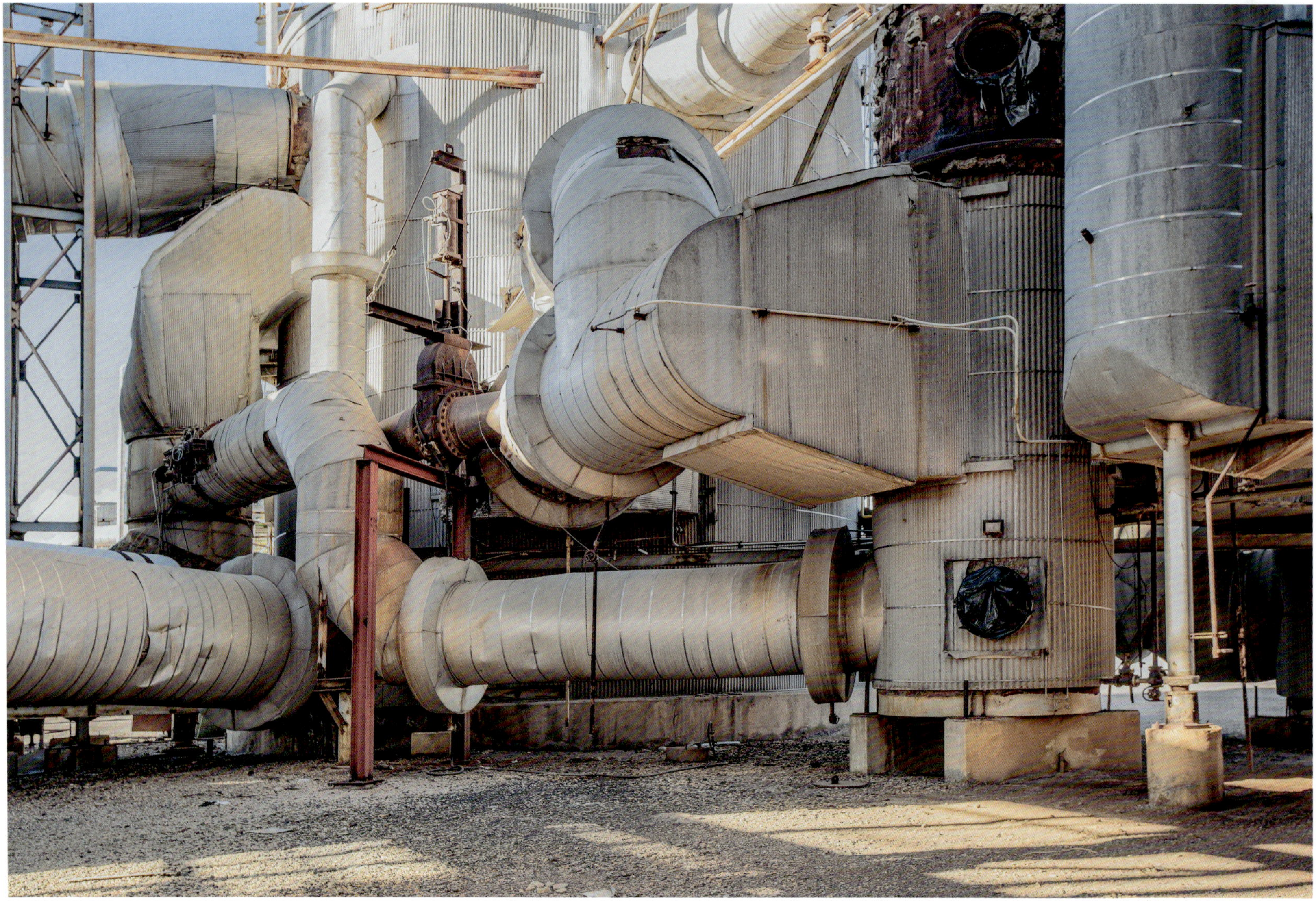

A pre-demolition view of the El Paso ASARCO plant. The image shows the acid plant's high-velocity blower ductwork.

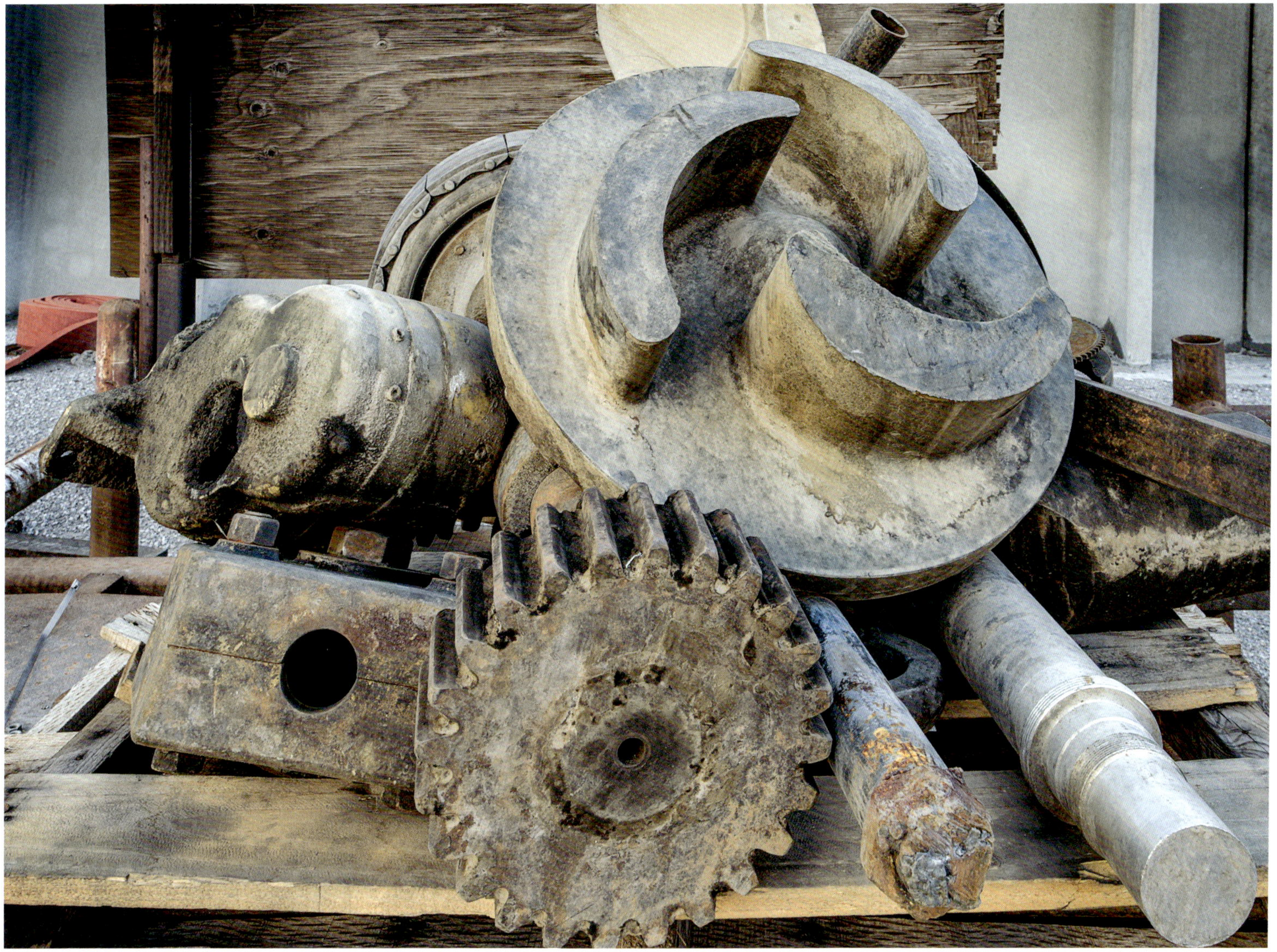

A pre-demolition view of the El Paso ASARCO plant. In this image, scrap recovered from machinery awaits recycling. Prior to demolition, machine parts, plumbing, matte ladles, and anything else of value for reuse or recycling was sold and removed from the site.

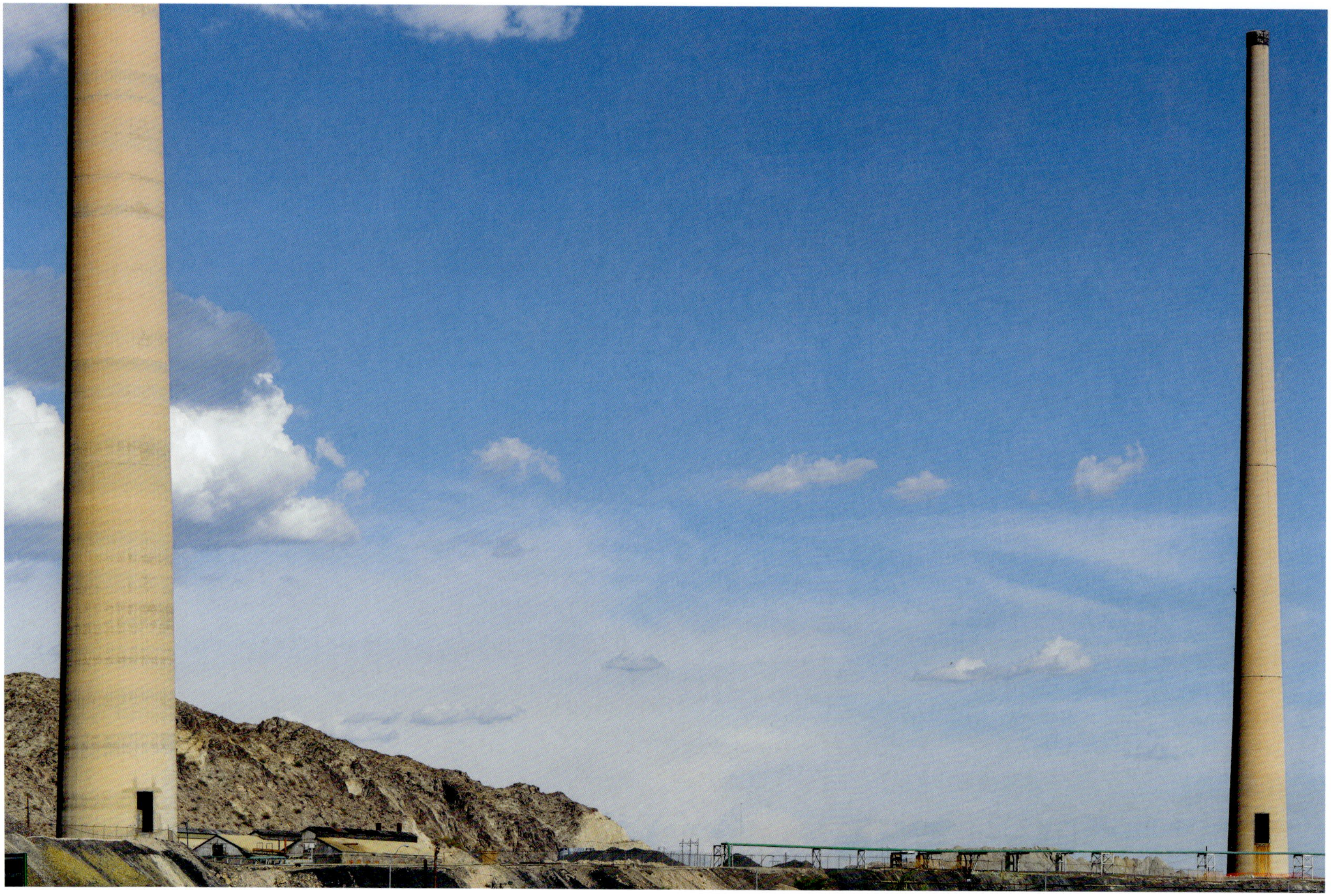

The El Paso ASARCO plant. This image shows the copper and lead stacks. Because it was thinner by comparison, from some vantage points the single-walled "lead" stack in the far right gave the impression of being taller than the bulkier 200-foot taller "copper" stack, which dominated the site and the skyline for miles around.

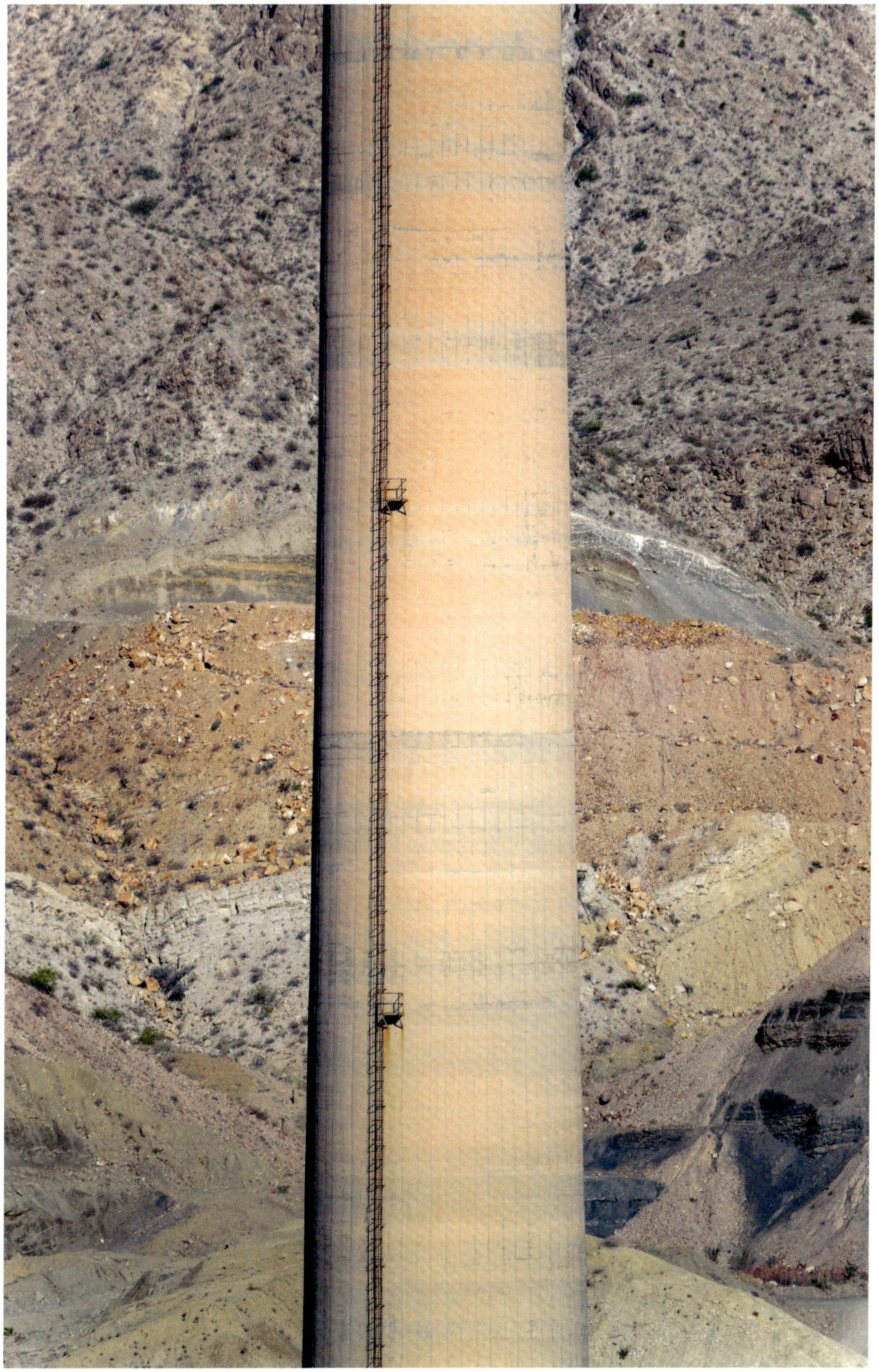

A pre-demolition view of the El Paso ASARCO plant. Here the main stack was photographed from a half mile away on a University of Texas–El Paso mountain. Suggesting the geologic timeline of the pass, the cast-in-place concrete structure is made of limestone quarried from the same landscape on which it stands.

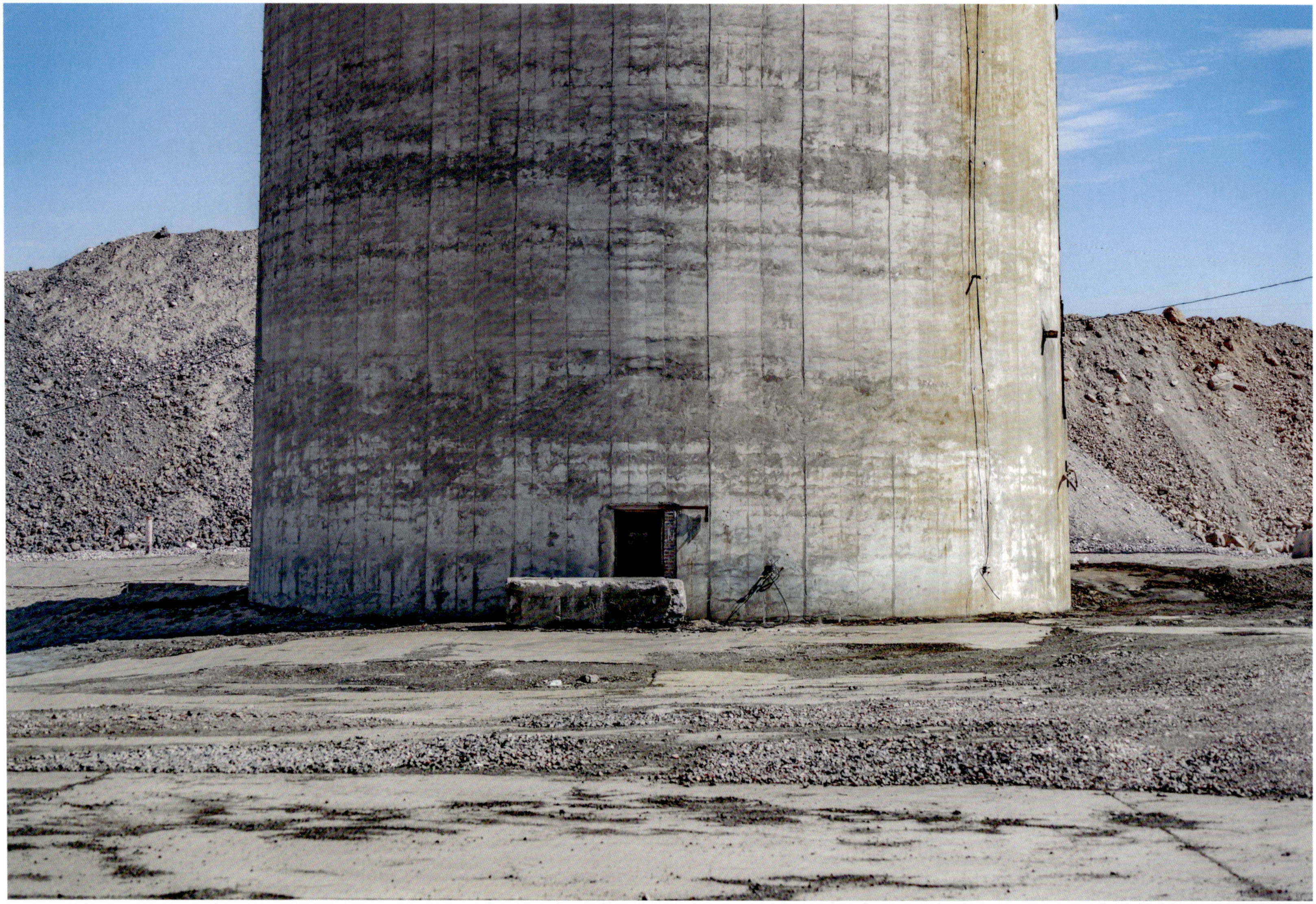

A view of the El Paso ASARCO plant. In this view of the base of the main stack, its scale can be extrapolated by comparing its mass to the seven-foot-high "person-scale" doorway opening.

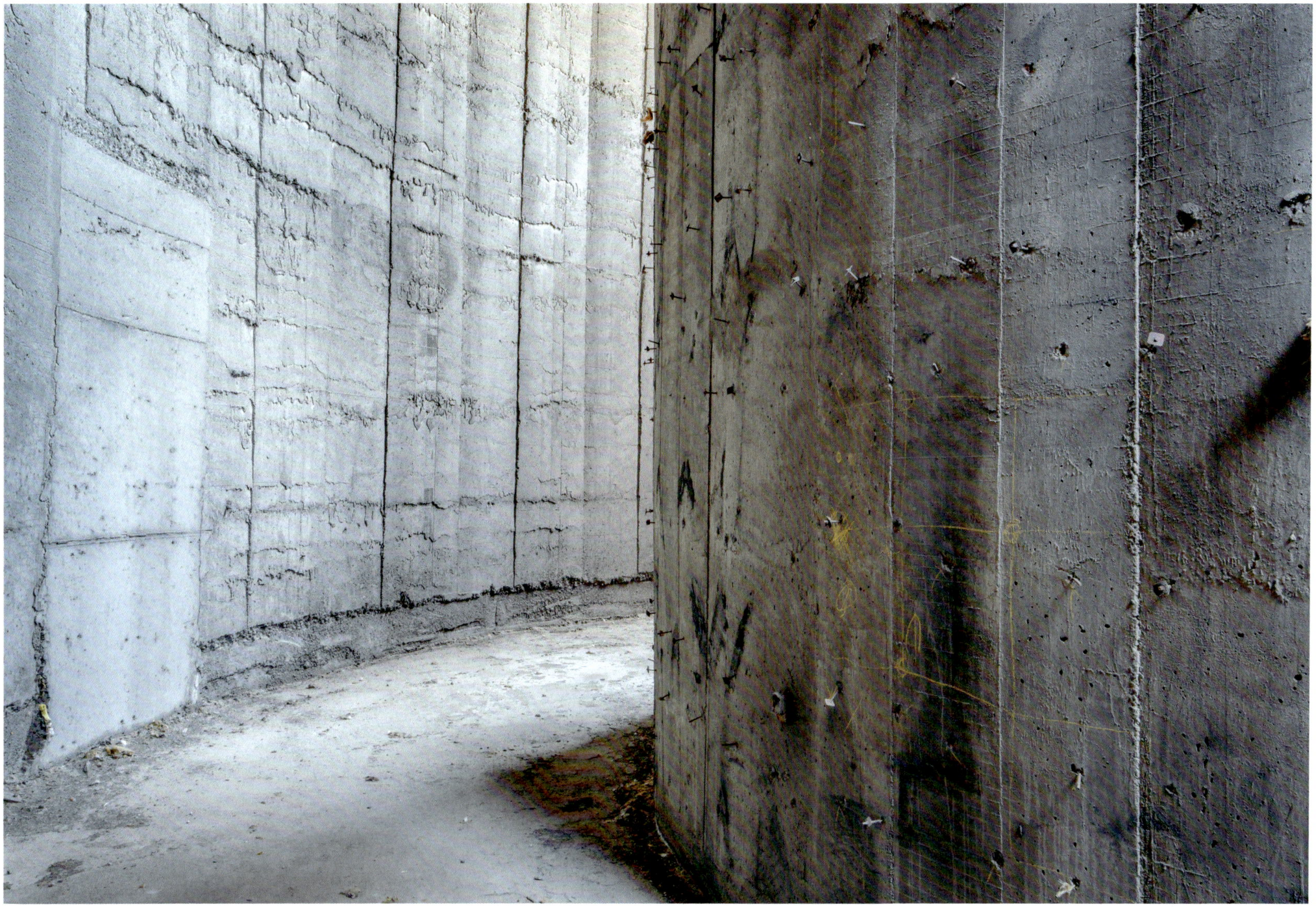

A pre-demolition view of the El Paso ASARCO plant. The image shows the "copper" stack's interior. Of note are these two details: 1) At the far left is a former opening in the concrete outer shell, which was later filled with a concrete pour as indicated by the horizontal plywood form impressions. Access and egress had been essential during construction but were unnecessary once the stack was completed. 2) The chalk drawing on the concrete interior stack at the far right was made during a pre-demolition survey of the structure, to indicate where boreholes for explosives would be drilled to ensure a successful demolition.

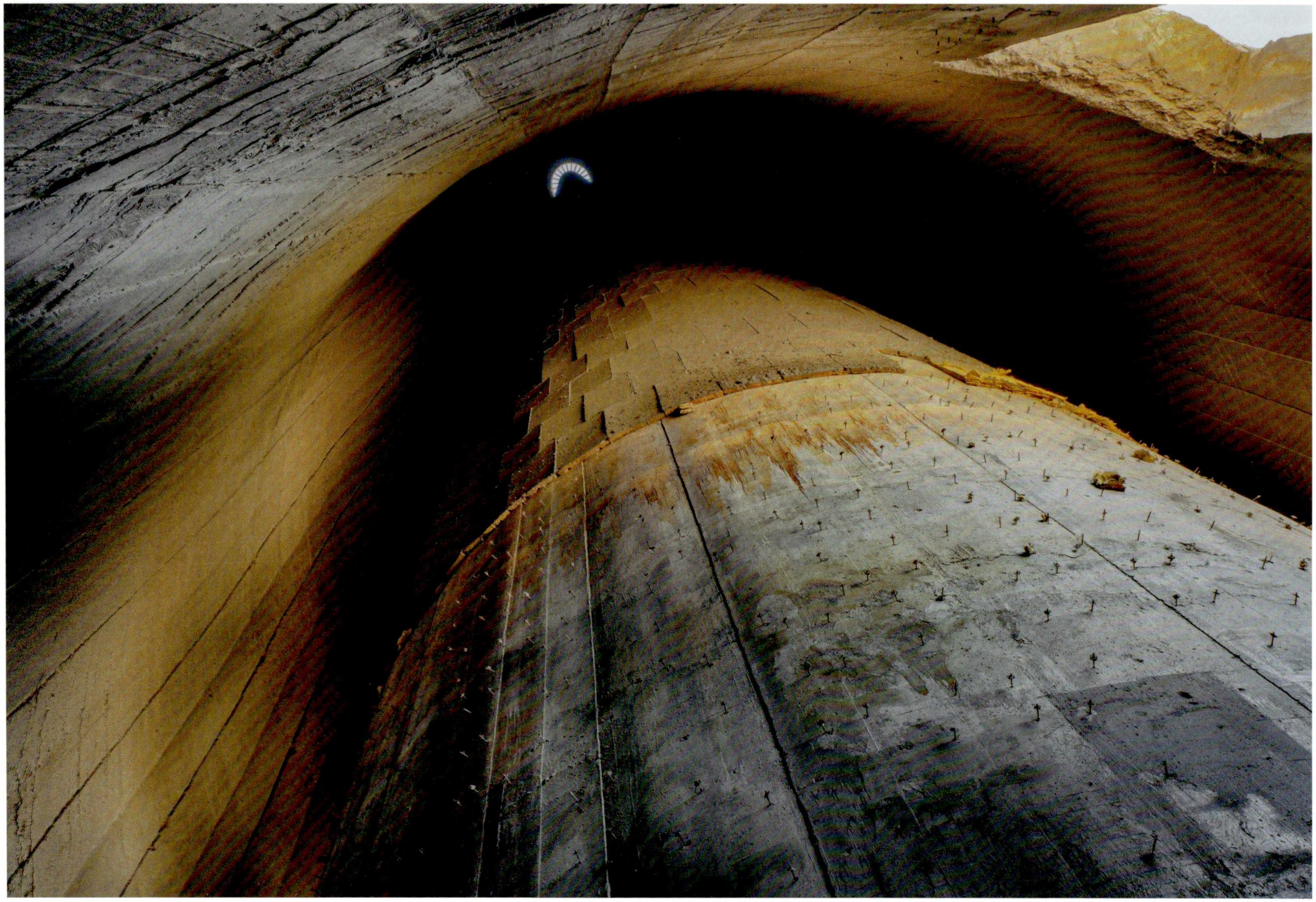

A pre-demolition view of the El Paso ASARCO plant. In this view looking up between the concrete walls of the (once-innovative) double tube stack, daylight pours in through the 12-foot-wide duct opening at the right. The partially intact jacket of fiber insulation remains pinned to the inner concrete wall. The small crescent of daylight in the upper left is 828 feet above the camera.

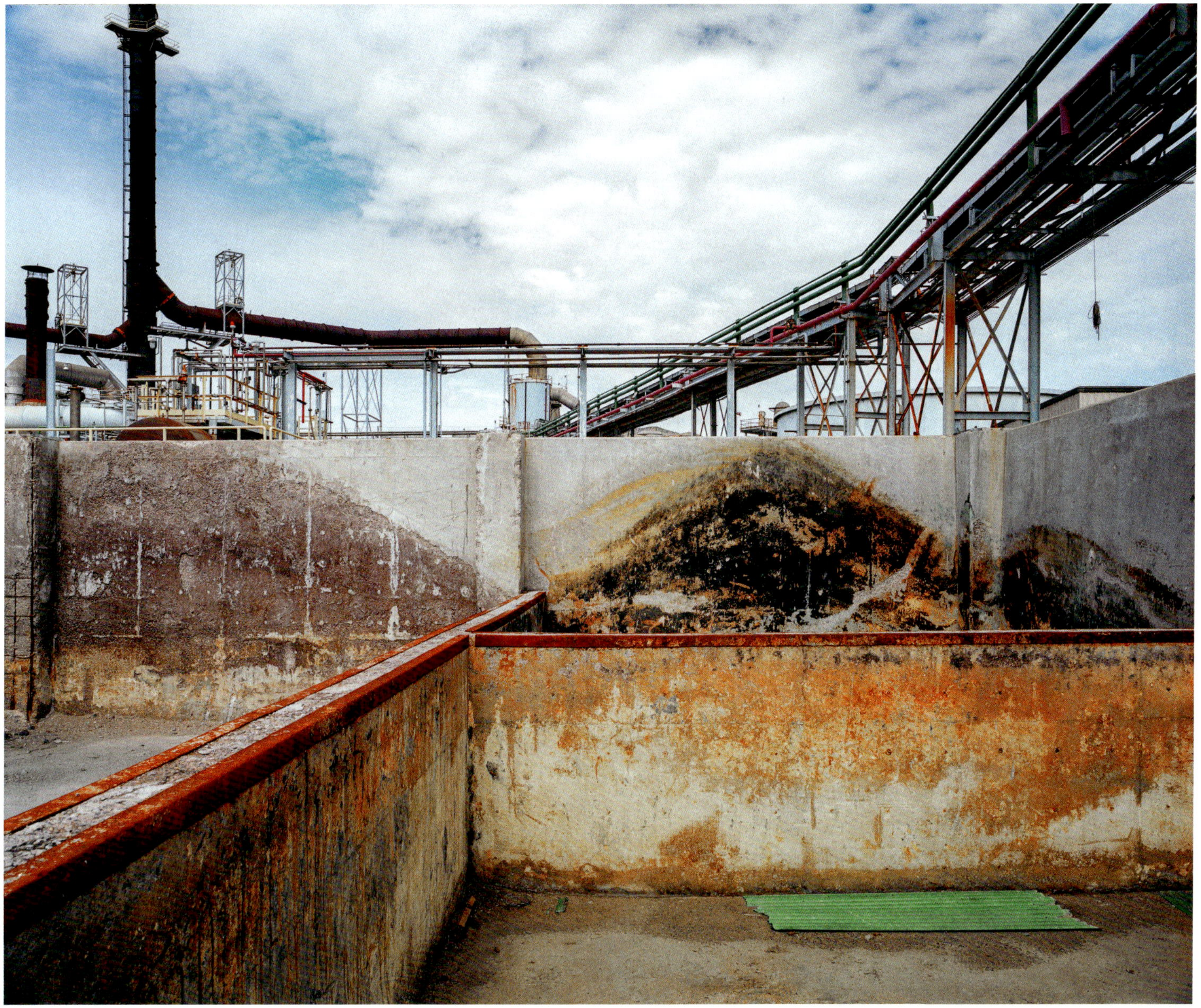

A pre-demolition view of the El Paso ASARCO plant. The image shows concrete bins at a former cadmium plant. This view looks west toward the No. 1 acid plant and the No. 2 acid plant tail gas stack in the upper left.

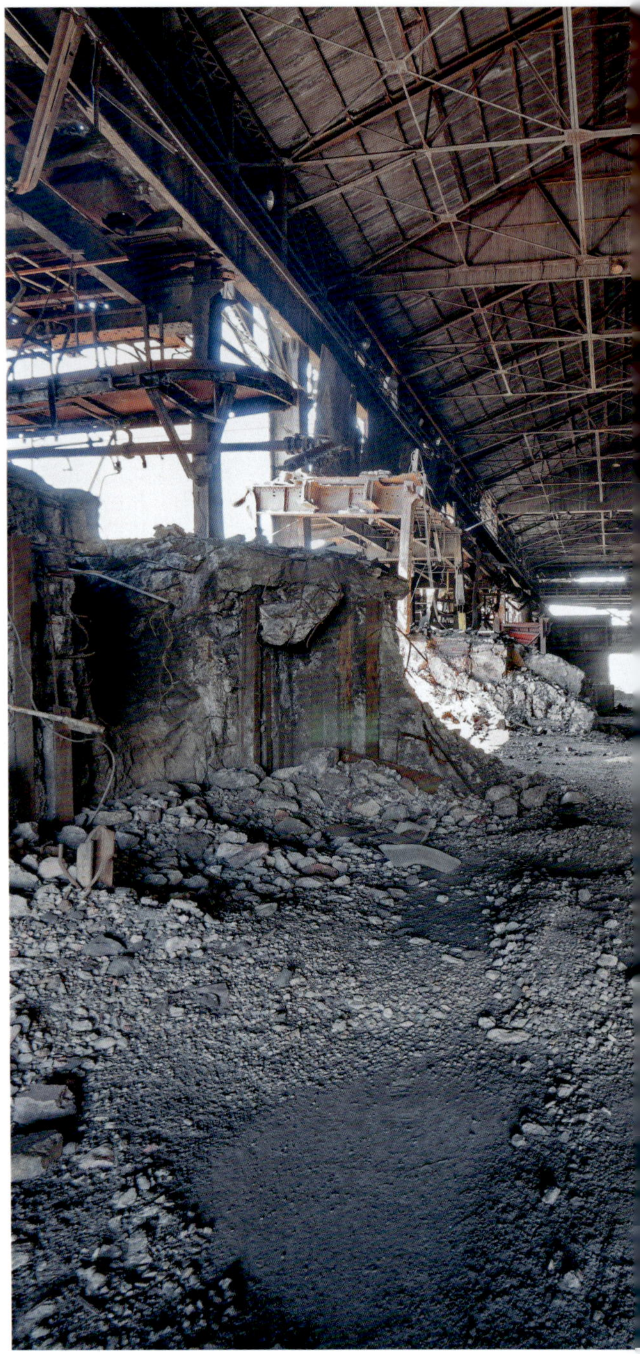

A pre-demolition view of the El Paso ASARCO plant. This view shows the copper converter and ventilation hoods in the main smelter building. Looking down the converter aisle, a major section of the south wall has been demolished. Its removal allowed access for oversized wrecking equipment; the opening offered the added benefit of illuminating a space that had not seen daylight in a century. The photographer stands at the center for scale. At the far right is rotating furnace No. 1, with its massive oxygen supply line penetrating the end wall. Furnaces No. 2 and No. 3 are in the distance on the same axis.

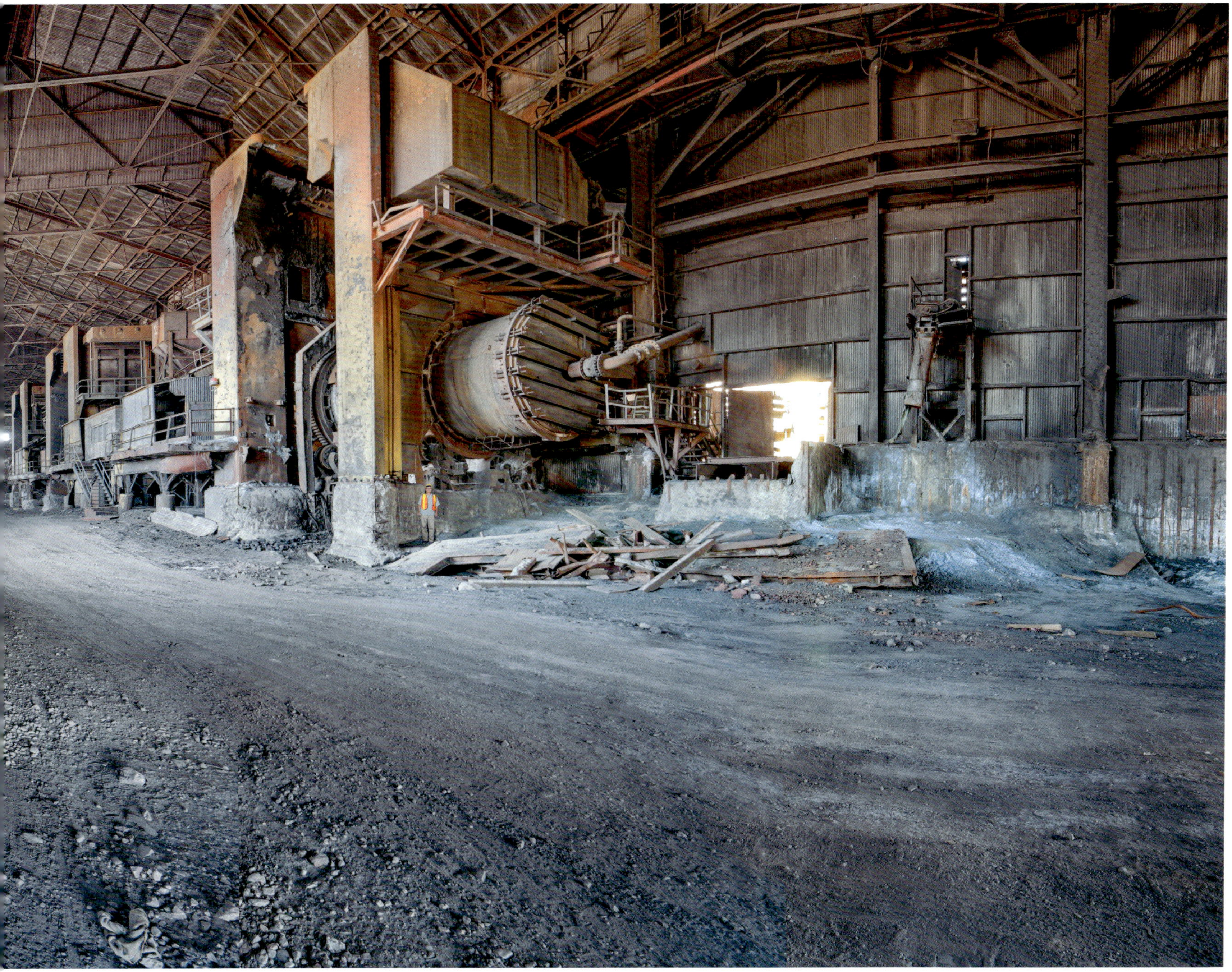

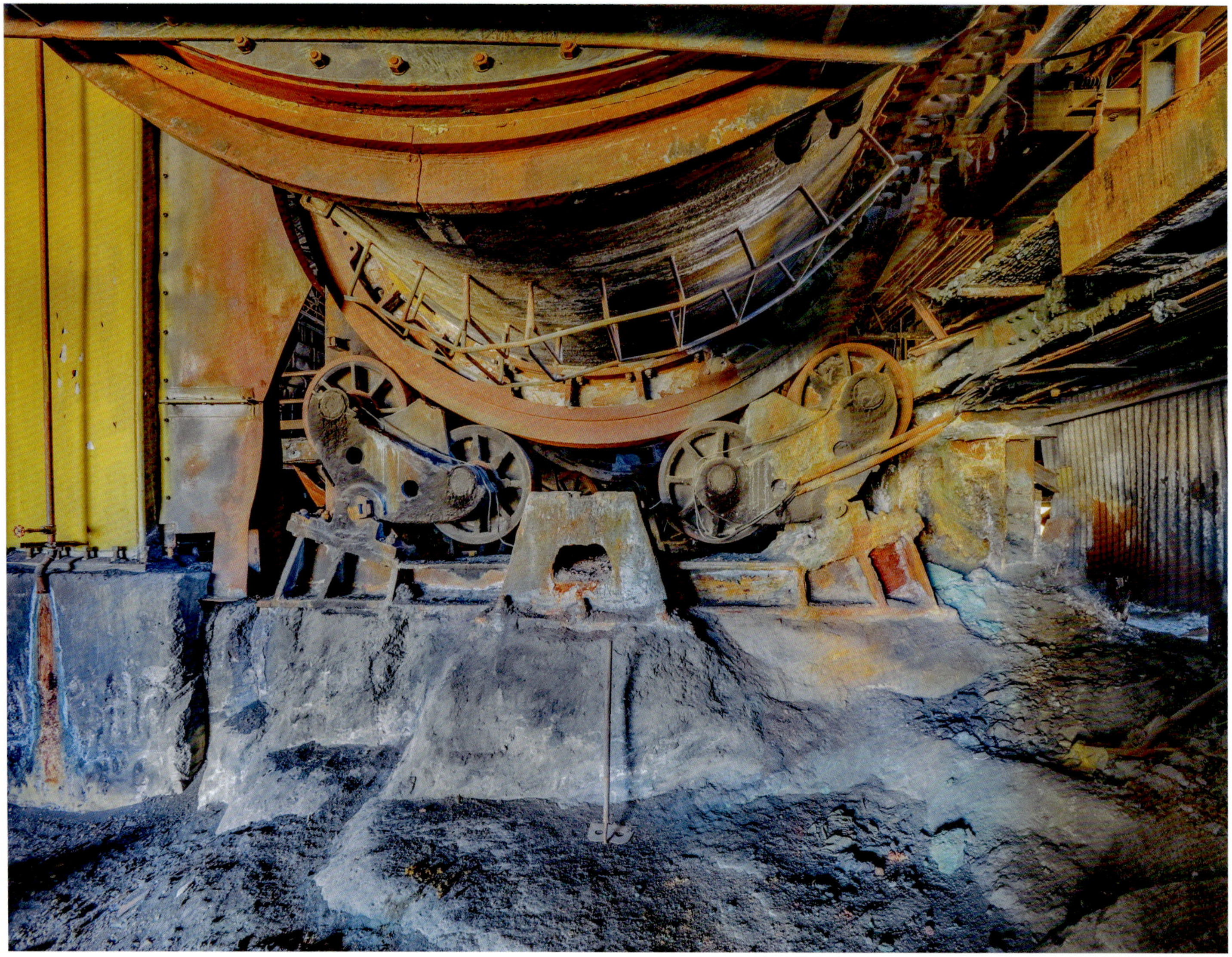

A pre-demolition view of the El Paso ASARCO plant. This copper converter building detail shows the south end of the No. 1 converter furnace. To discharge molten material (copper matte and slag) the cylindrical furnace, girded by these huge steel rings resting on trunnions (the four steel wheels), rotated to allow charging and controlled pour into massive ladles (p. 75) for transfer and further processing or, in the case of slag, disposal to a remote dump site.

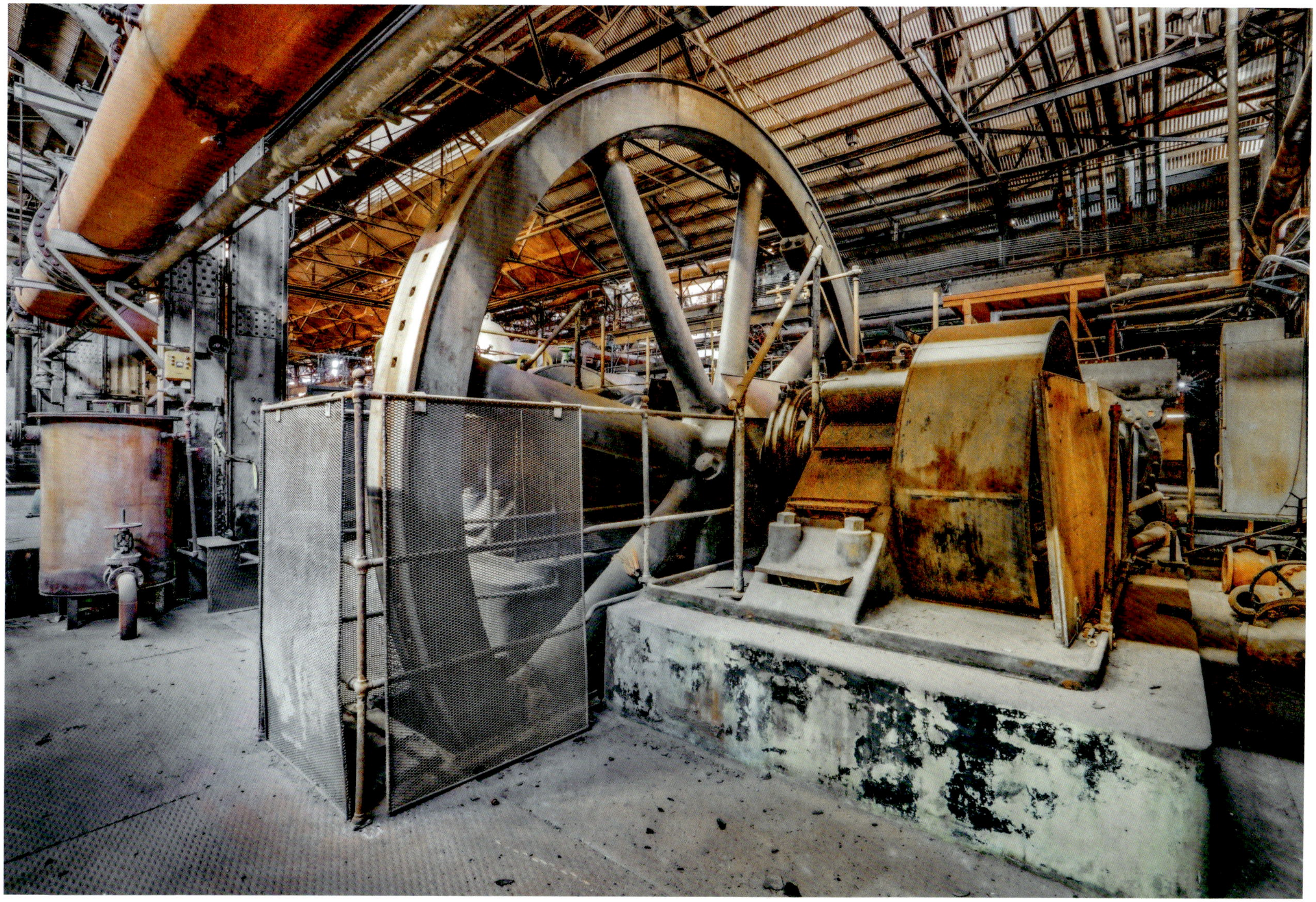

A pre-demolition view of the El Paso ASARCO plant. In the power plant, this twelve-foot diameter flywheel was part of the smelter's steam power-generating system. For decades, electricity for the entire El Paso ASARCO operation was produced solely on-site.

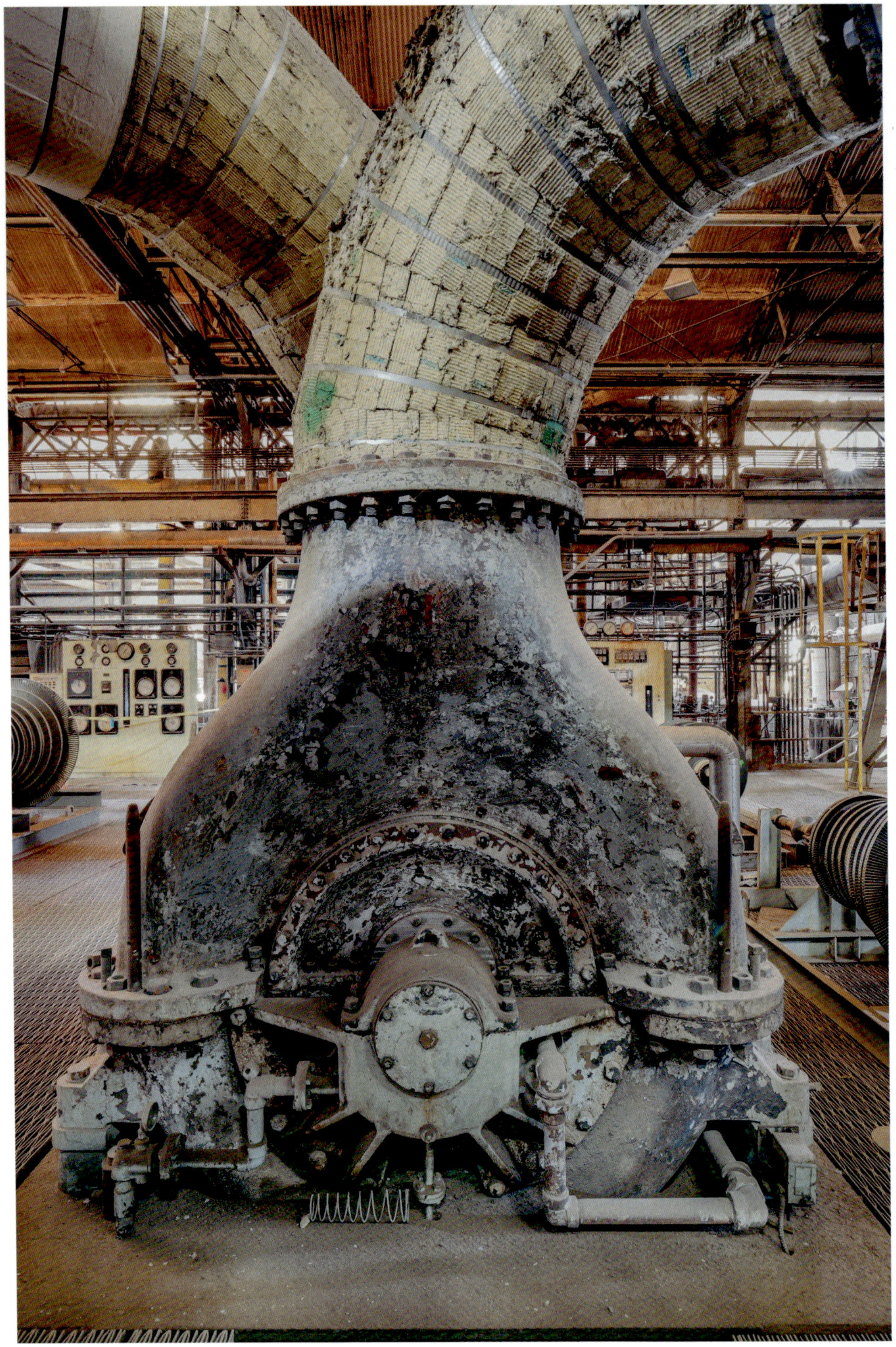

A pre-demolition view of the El Paso ASARCO plant. This image shows an Ingersoll-Rand steam-powered electrical turbine in the on-site power plant. Virtually all electricity used on the ASARCO site was generated here.

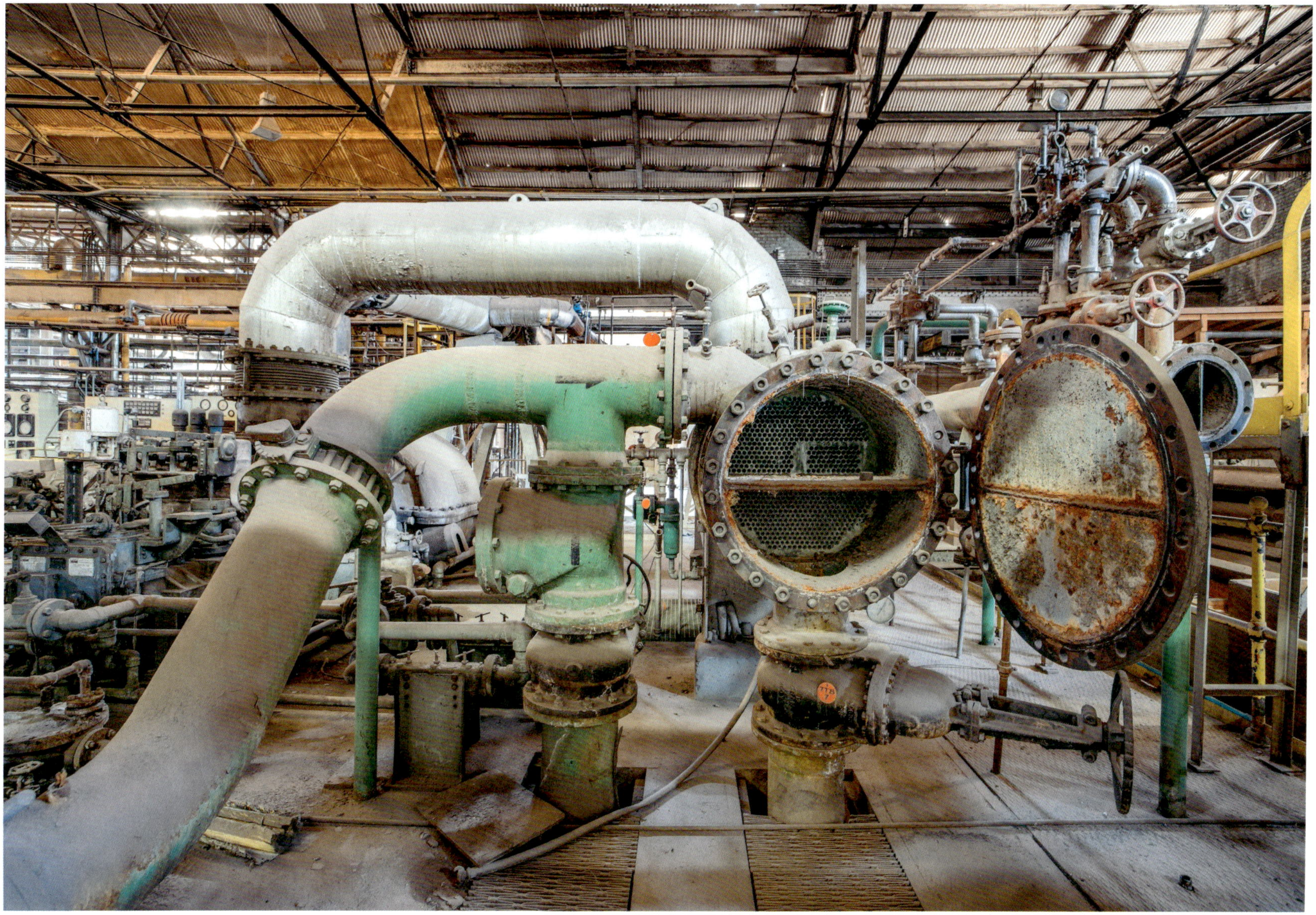

A pre-demolition view of the El Paso ASARCO plant. This image shows the power-plant boiler's interior.

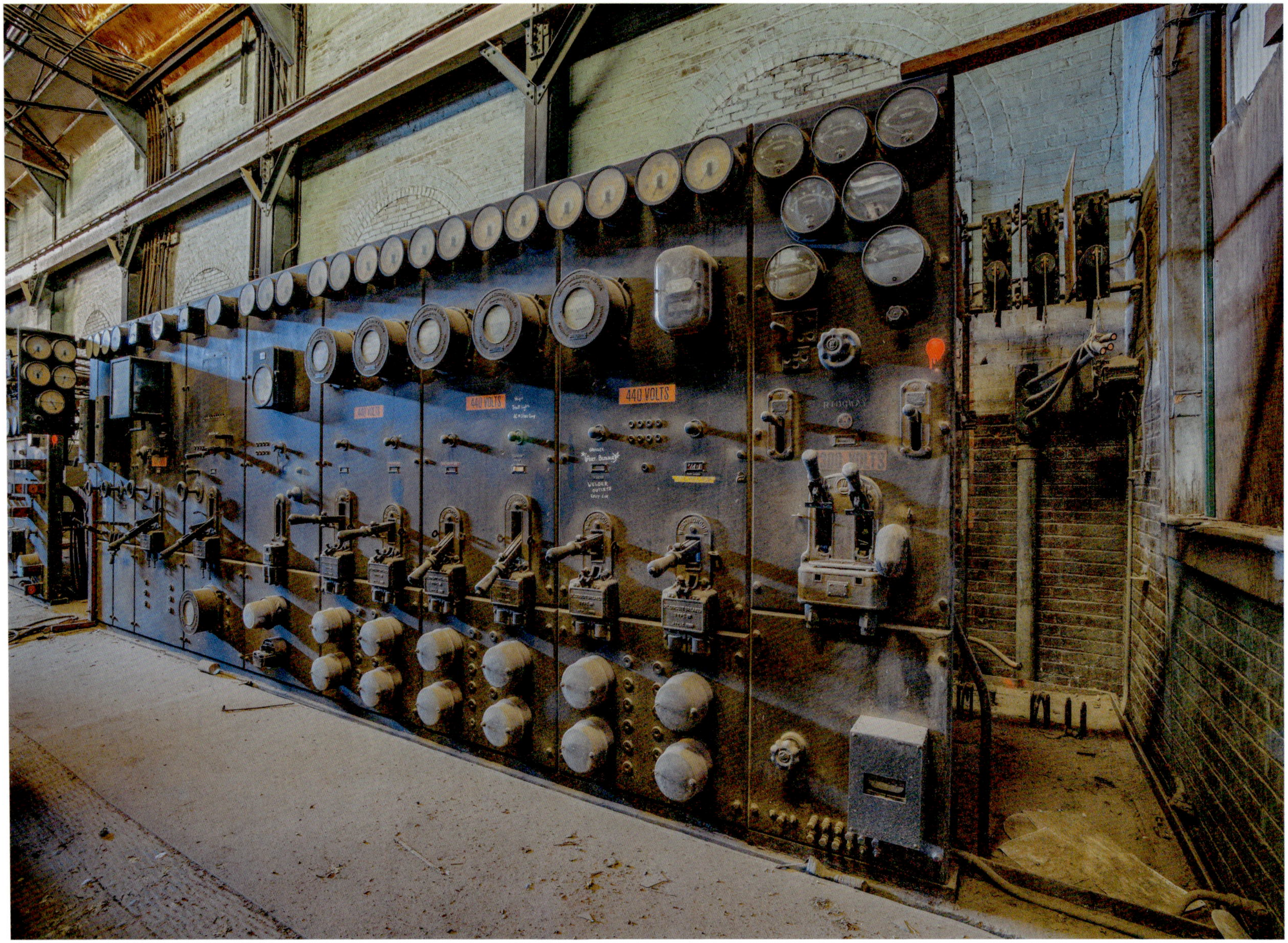

A pre-demolition view of the El Paso ASARCO plant. Distribution, regulation, and monitoring of electrical power throughout the site was controlled in this part of the powerplant. This image shows a panel of Westinghouse breakers and meters dating from the early twentieth century.

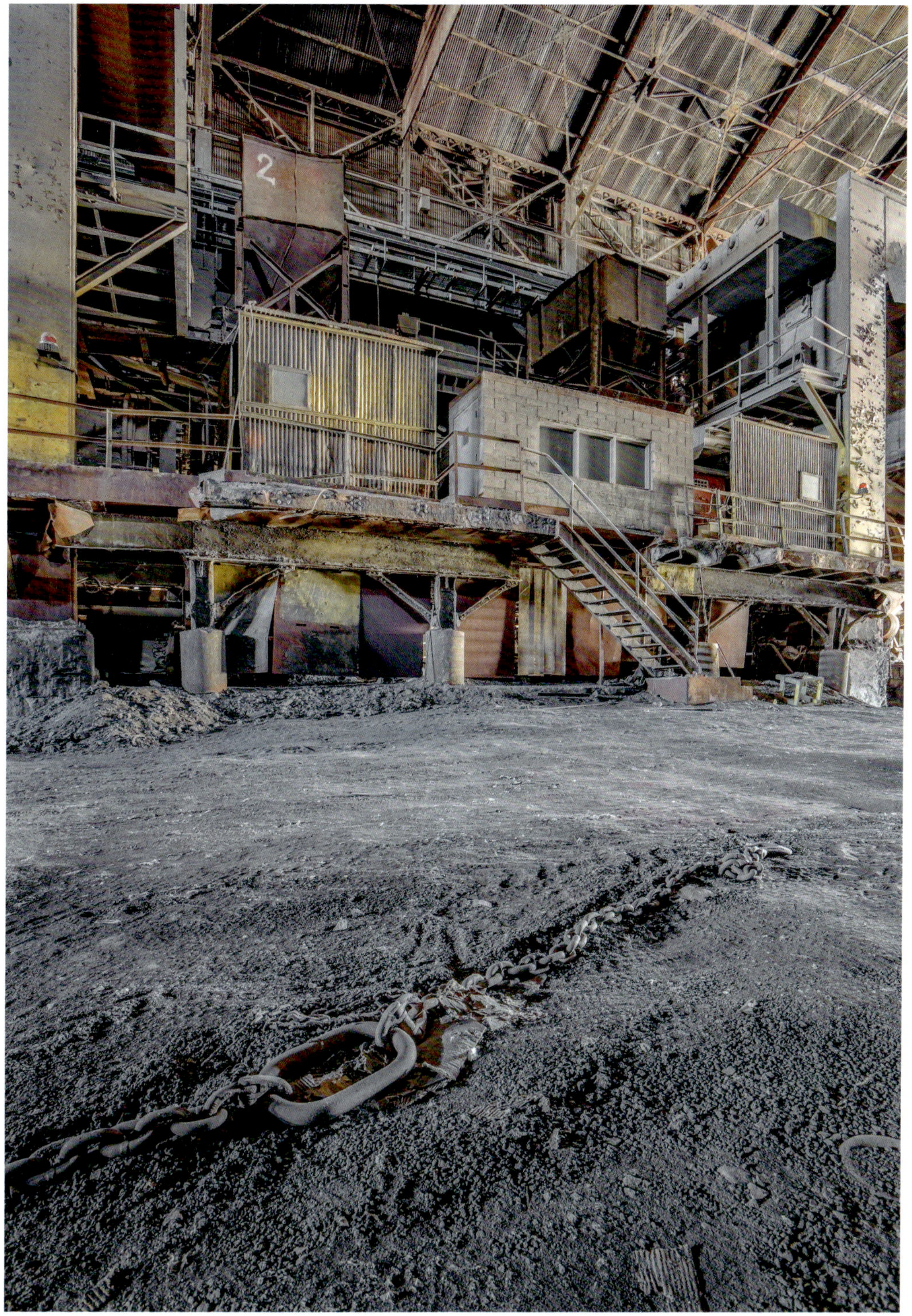

A pre-demolition view of the El Paso ASARCO plant. The image was made in the copper converter building. On the platform at the top of the steel stairs, the masonry cubicle is the copper converter control room.

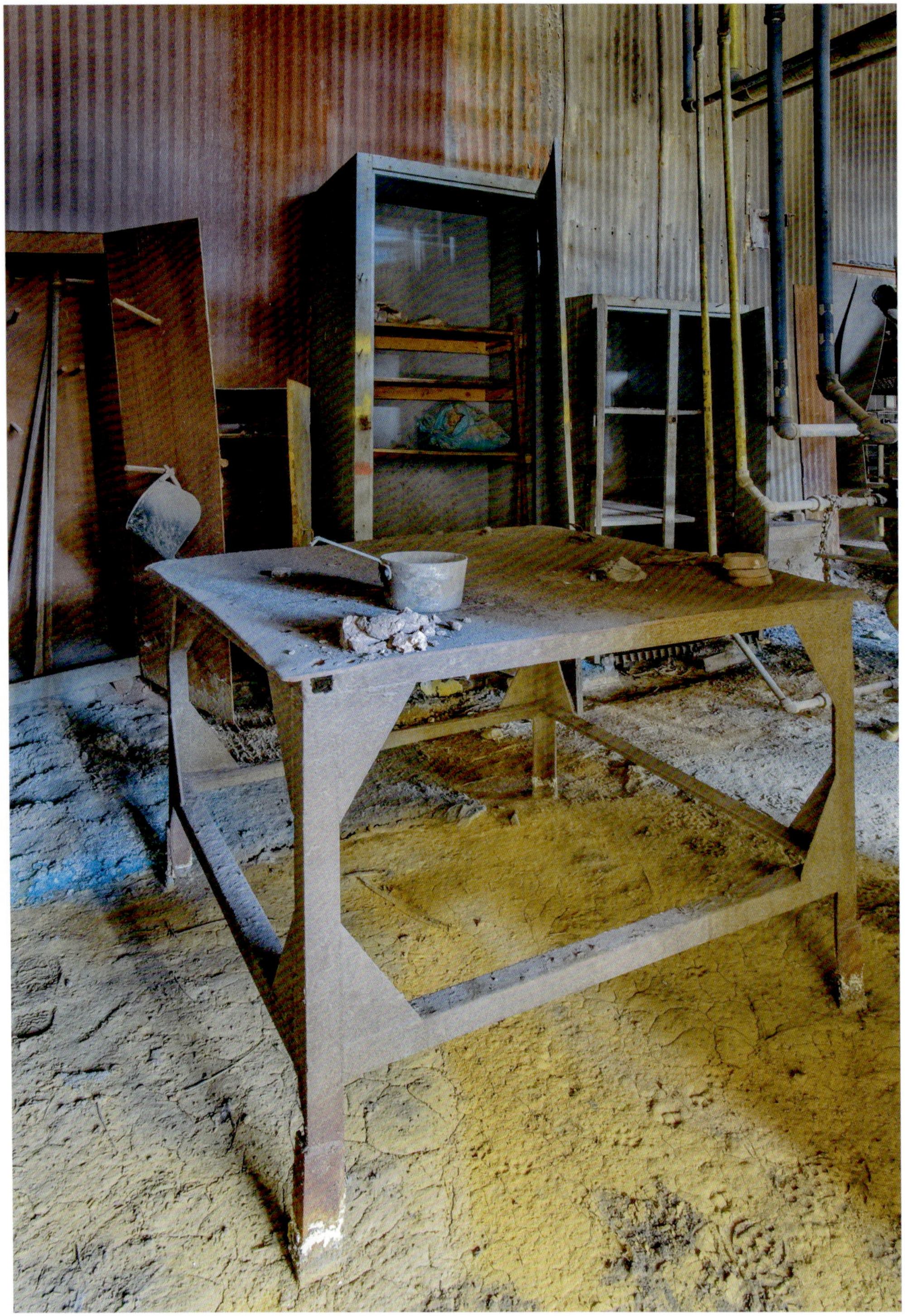

A pre-demolition view of the El Paso ASARCO plant. This image shows the clay-work table as it was left at the end of a shift in 1999, the last time anyone stood here—until this photograph was made eleven years later.

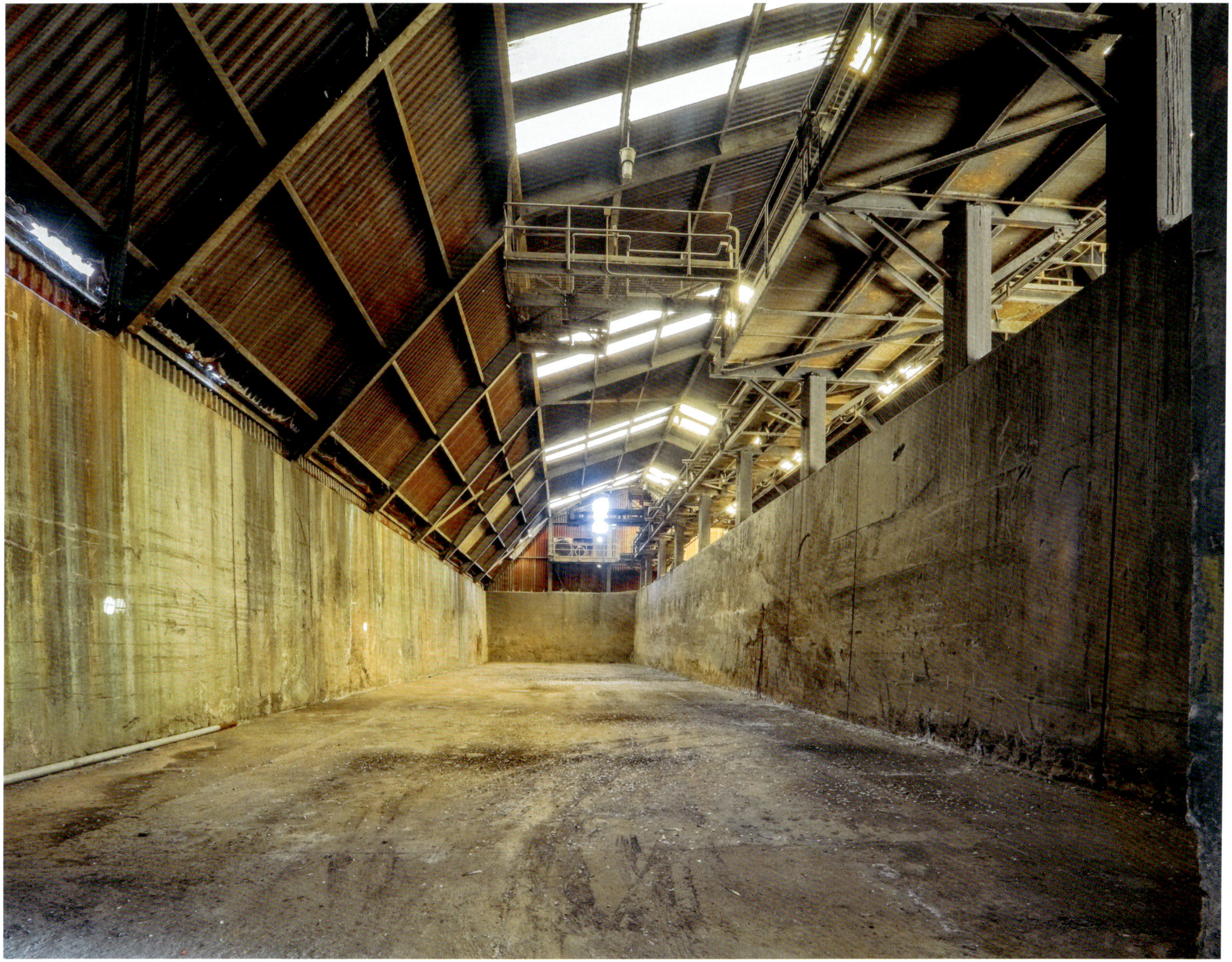

A pre-demolition view of the El Paso ASARCO plant. This image shows one of the seven bays in the ten-thousand-ton ore-storage bedding building. This view is from the west, at the portal through which heavy equipment moved the ore for storage and removal.

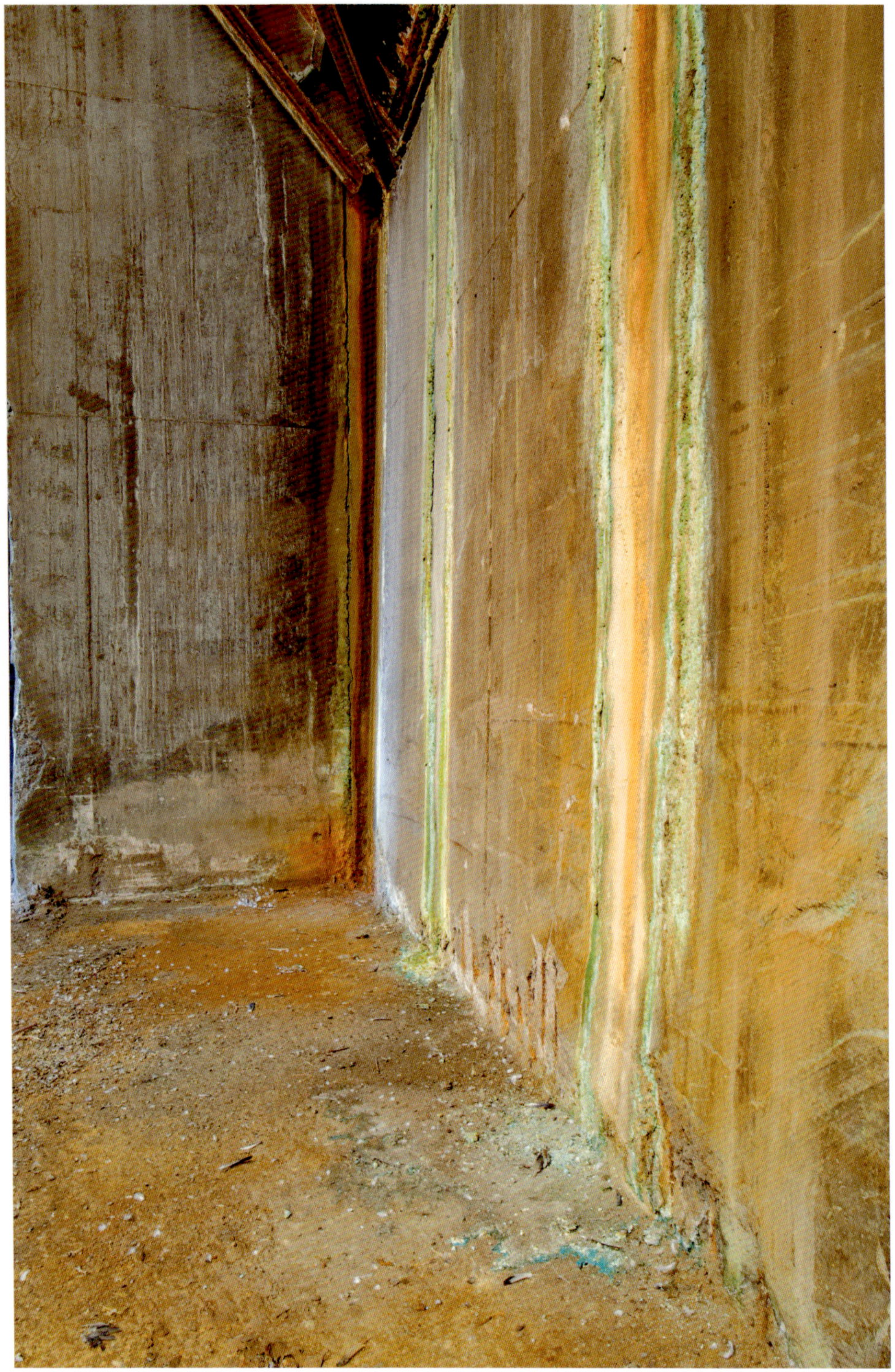

A pre-demolition view of the El Paso ASARCO plant. This view of the same bin shows (though subtly) another element of the structure's functional form: the walls dividing the bins taper as they rise from their thicker bases, accommodating the lateral pressure of hundreds of tons of ore piled against them.

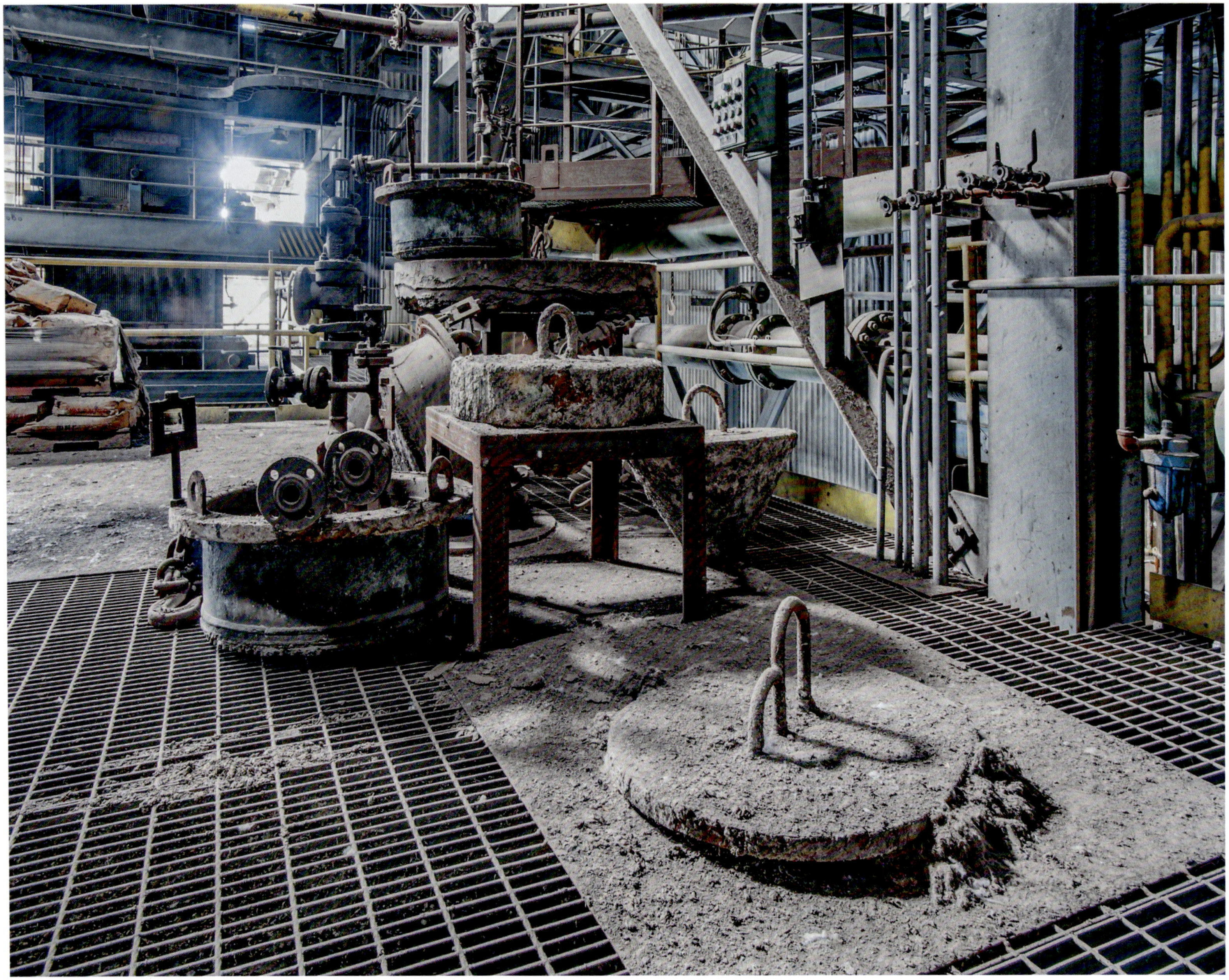

A pre-demolition view of the El Paso ASARCO plant. This image shows the Contop operations deck, looking to the west.

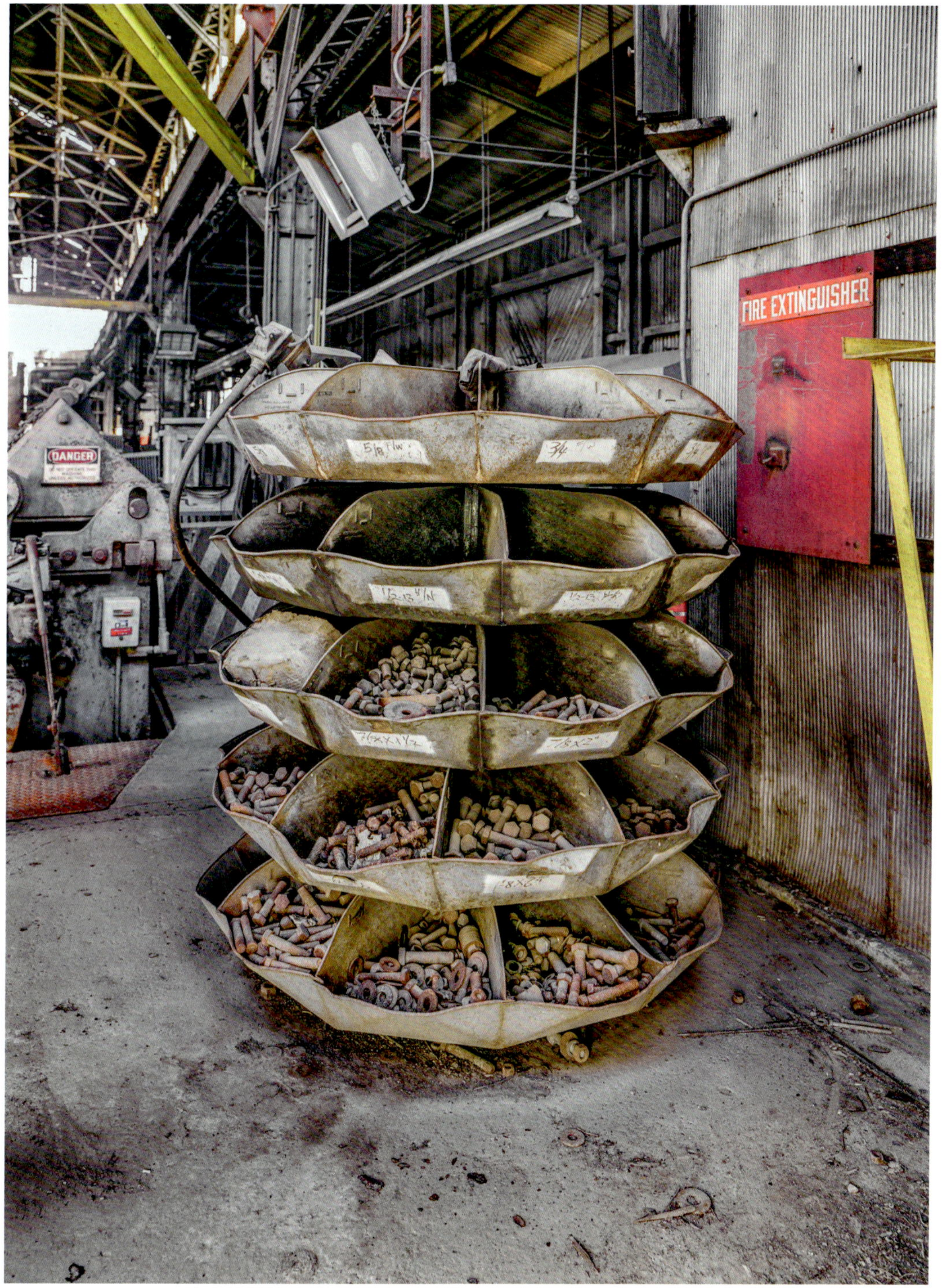

A pre-demolition view of the El Paso ASARCO plant. This image shows a stacked rotating bolt tray in the machine shop.

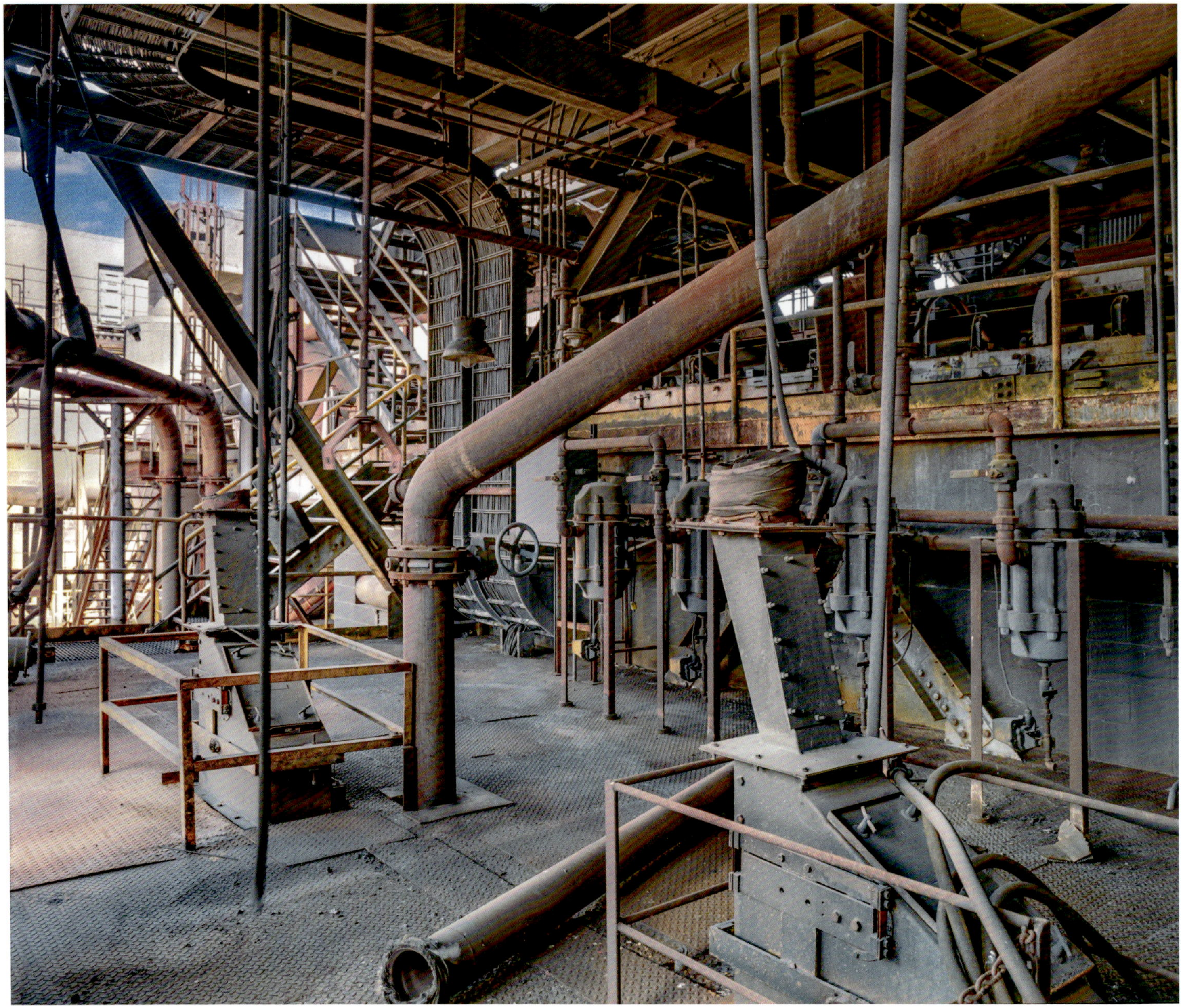

A pre-demolition view of the El Paso ASARCO plant. This image shows an outside work area at the north end of the contop.

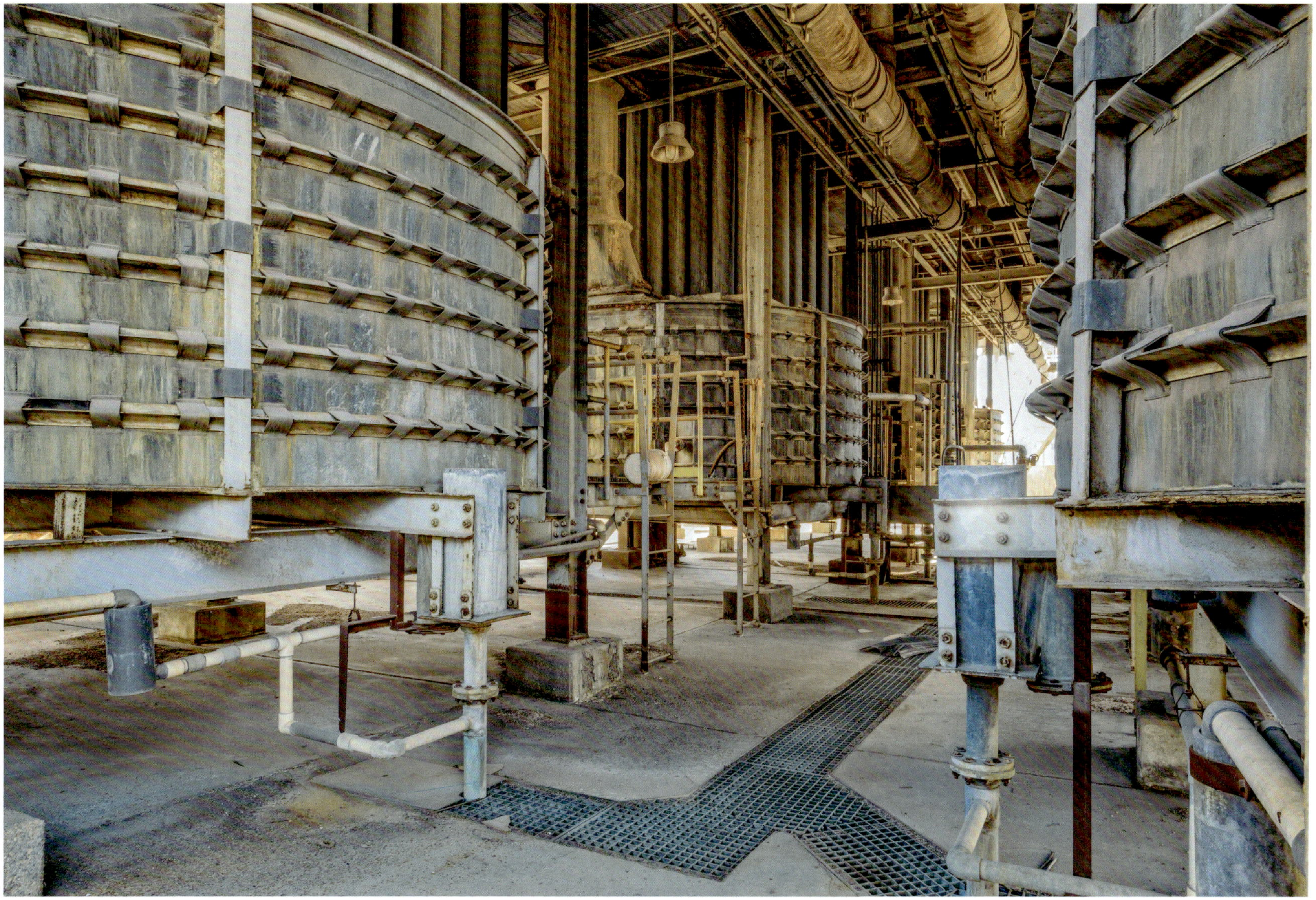

A pre-demolition view of the El Paso ASARCO plant. This image shows the base of the six-cell powerhouse cooling towers.

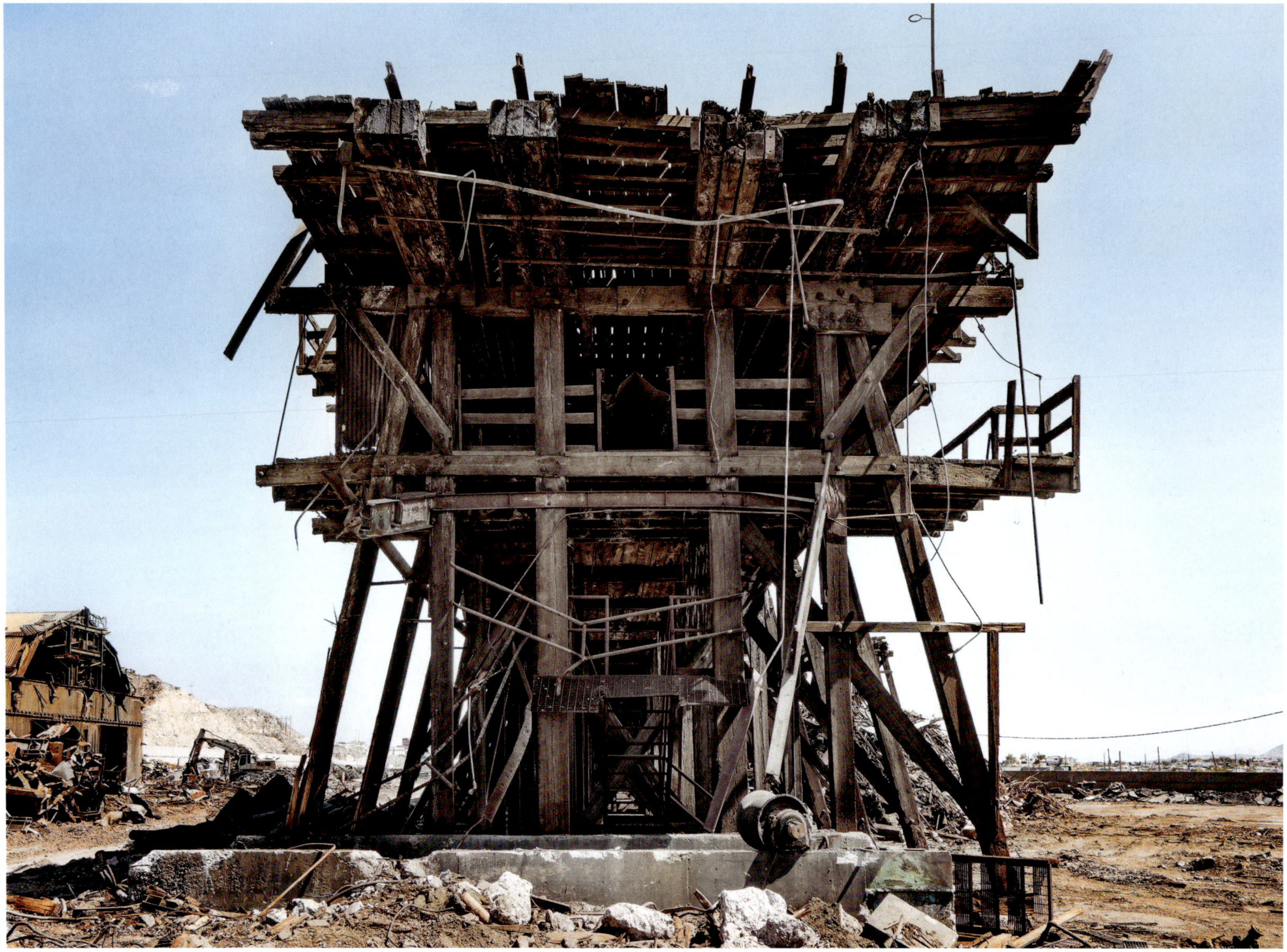

A demolition view of the El Paso ASARCO plant. This image show a rail trestle and ramp during dismantling (see p. 92).

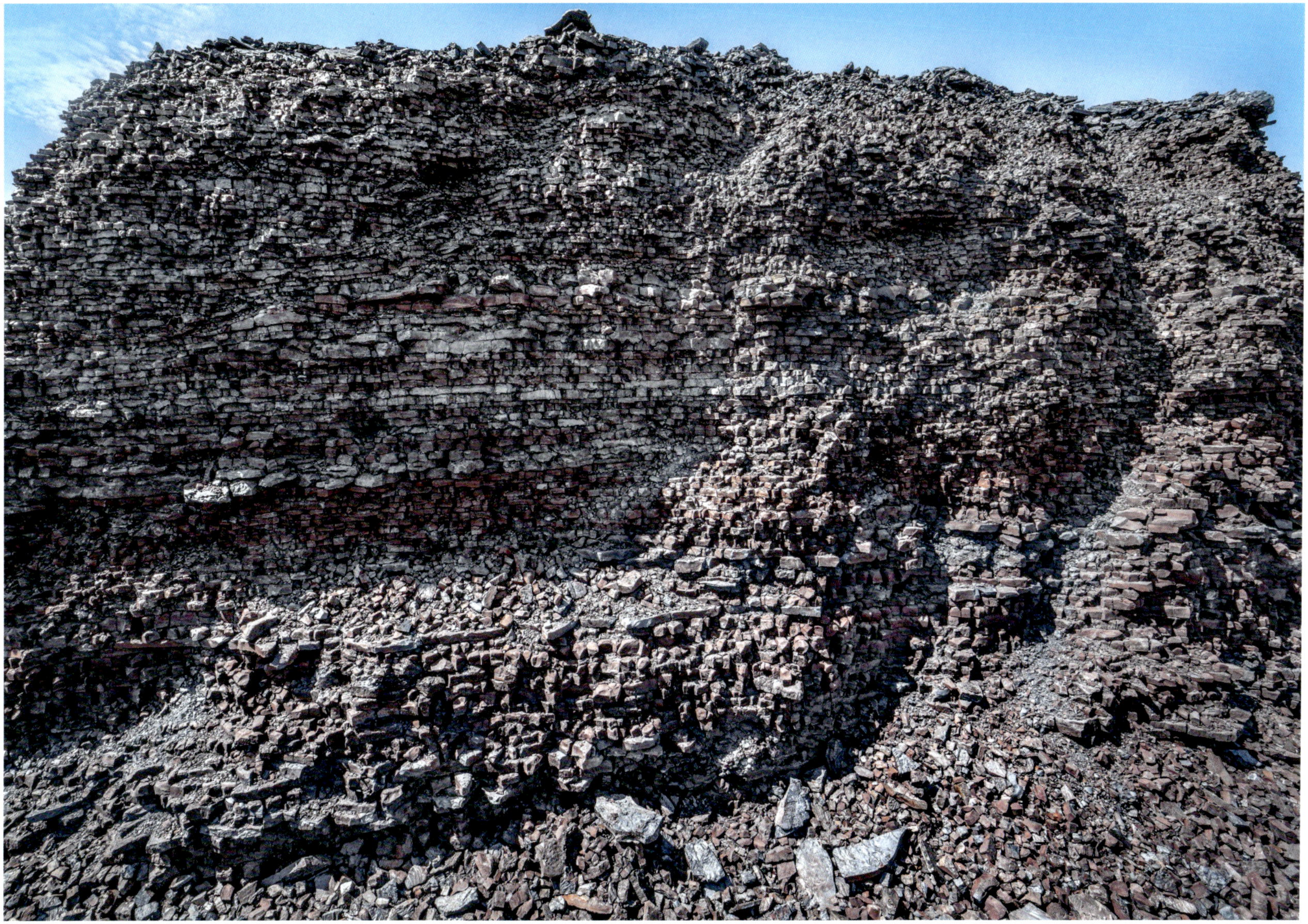

A pre-demolition view of the El Paso ASARCO plant. This mound of slag, typical of many nearby, is on the future site of Cell 4, an encapsulated grave for toxic demolition debris. Each horizontal stratum represents one pour—one ladle of molten waste poured atop previous layers that have cooled and solidified, similar to volcanic basalt cooling after spewing from a fissure or a caldera.

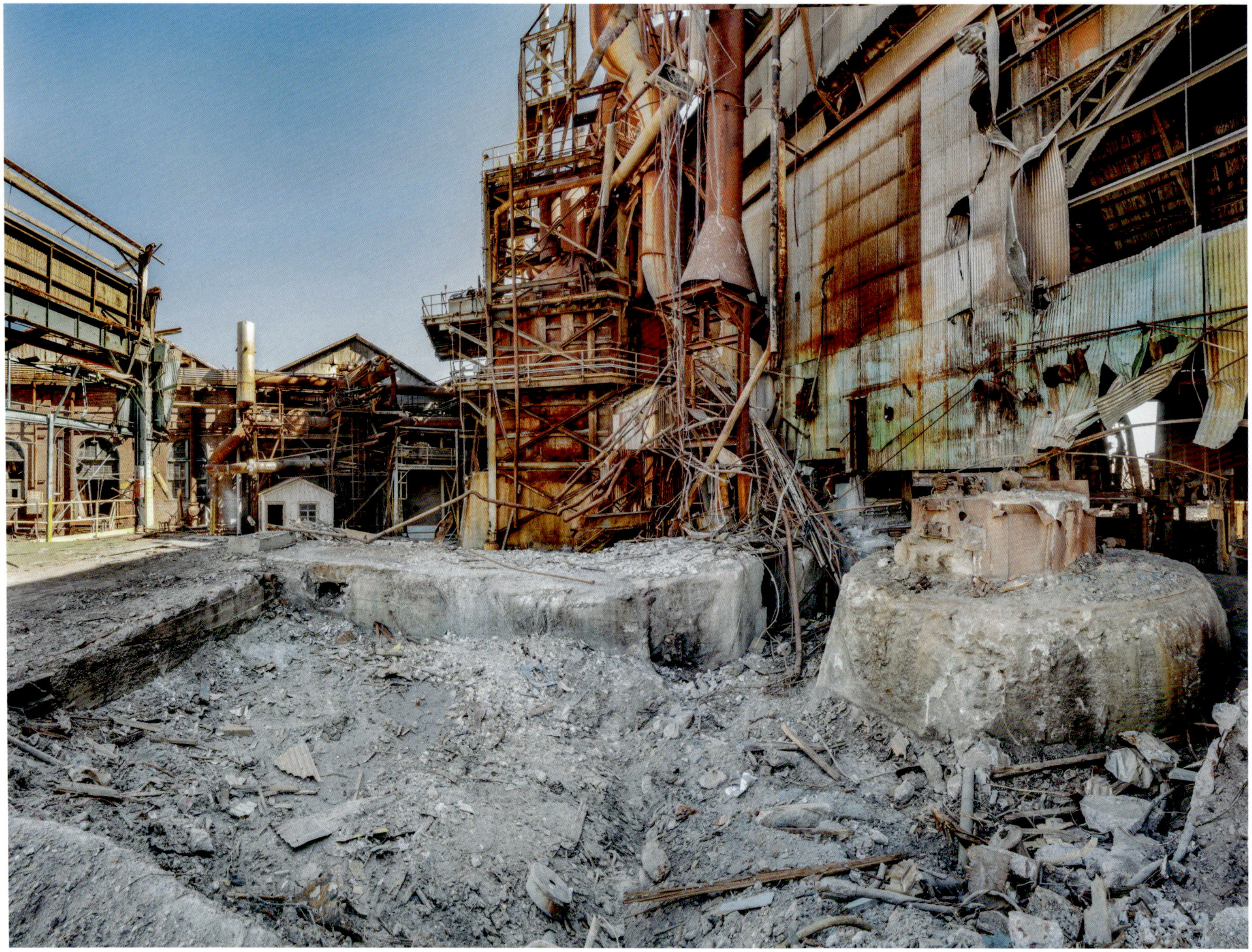

A demolition view of the El Paso ASARCO plant. This view shows the demolished foundations of the copper anode casting area, adjacent to the east side of the converter building's flue-dust chamber. The final step in the smelting process involves making copper anode plates; they are the slabs of nearly pure copper you might see strapped in bundles, chain-winched tight to the bed of a long-haul trailer passing you on the Interstate anywhere in the west from Montana to Mexico.

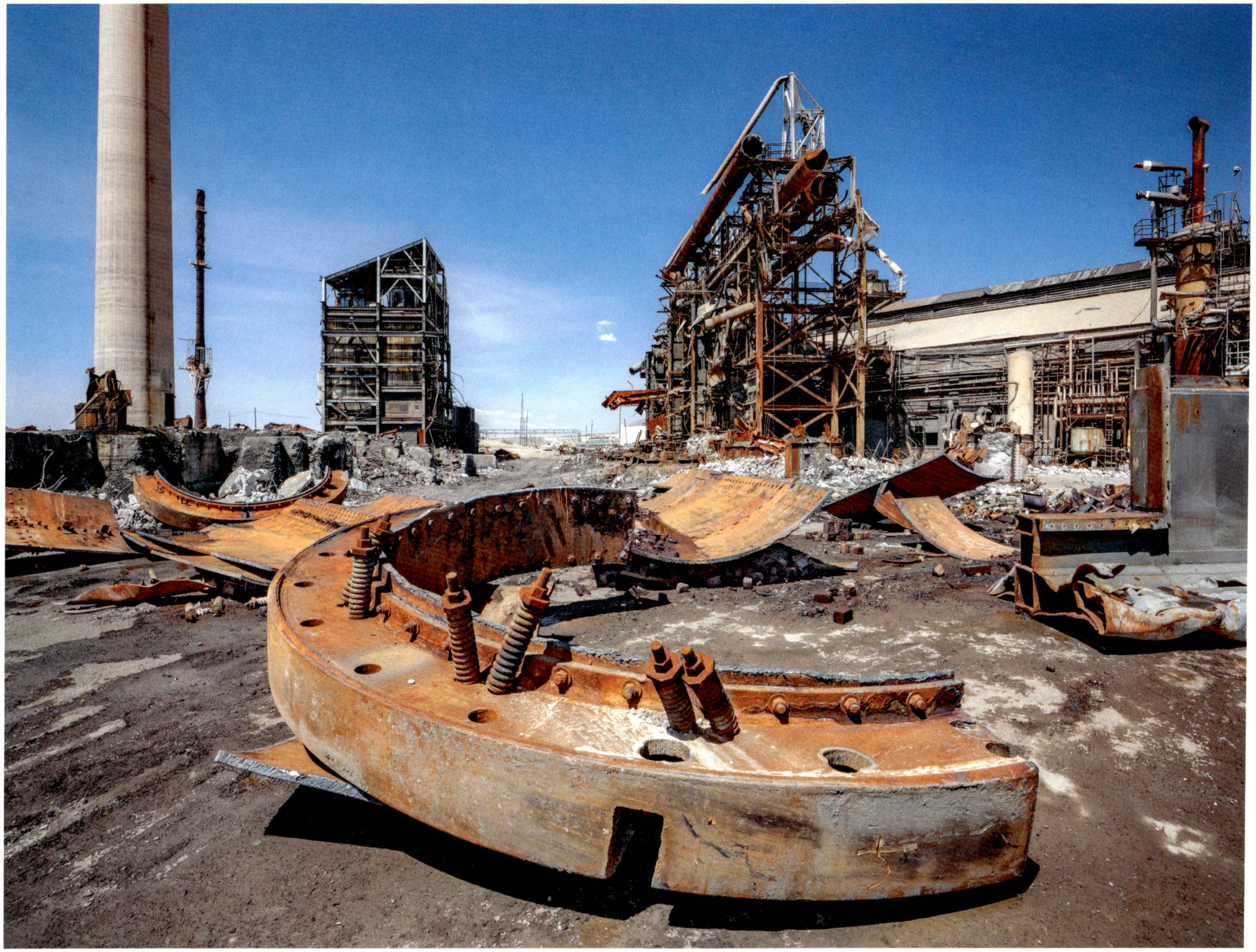

A demolition view of the El Paso ASARCO plant. This image shows a torch-cut section of the converter tires—steel rotary rings from the cylindrical smelting furnace. Fitted with these massive rings, the furnace rolled on steel trunnion bearings, tipping to allow the molten copper to be discharged into ladles for casting into ingots, and for the matte and slag to be poured into ladles for transfer to remote dump sites (see p. 106 for context).

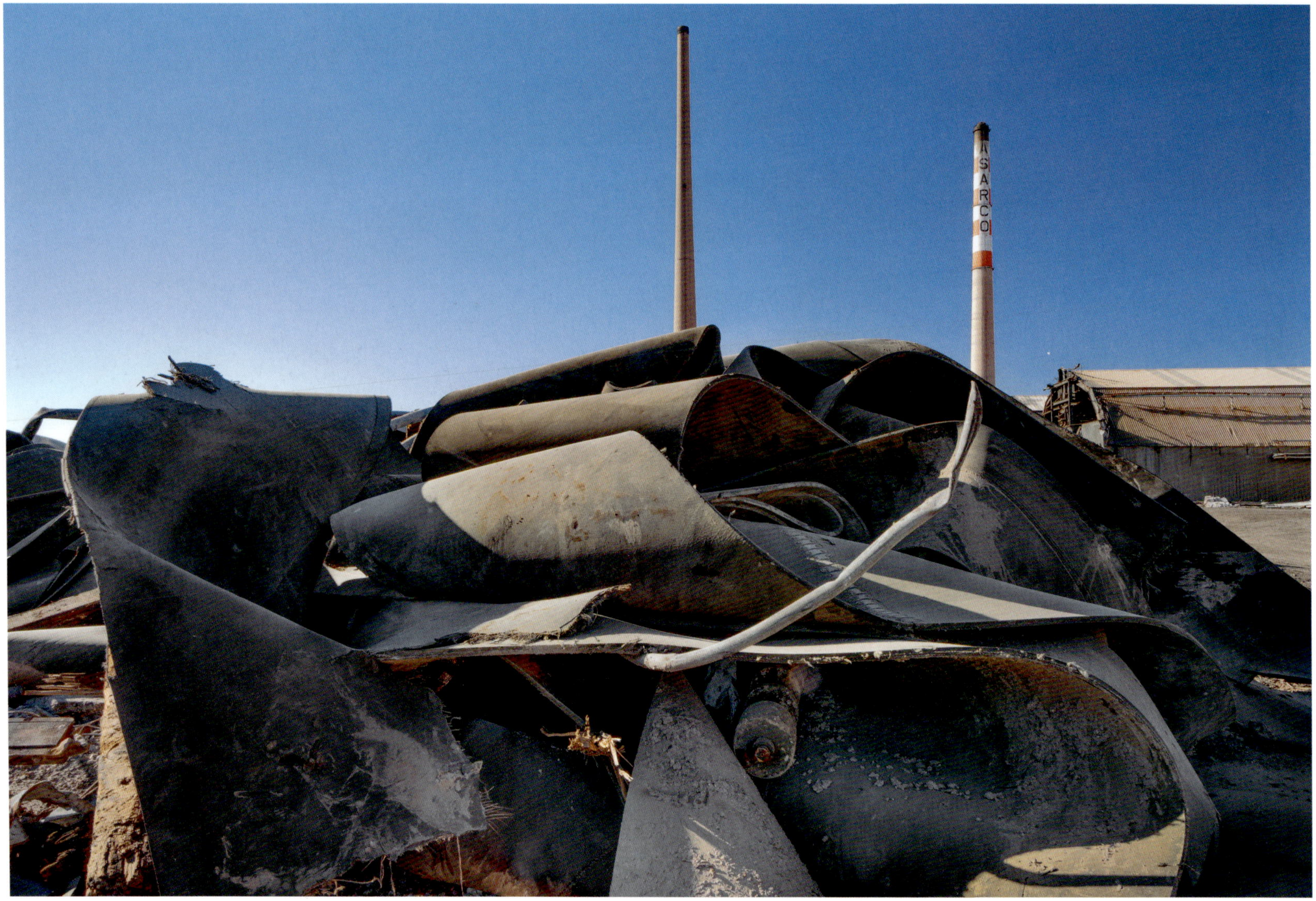

A demolition view of the El Paso ASARCO plant. This image shows long, thick, heavy sections of conveyor belt piled alongside waste timber and scraps of conduit awaiting recycling.

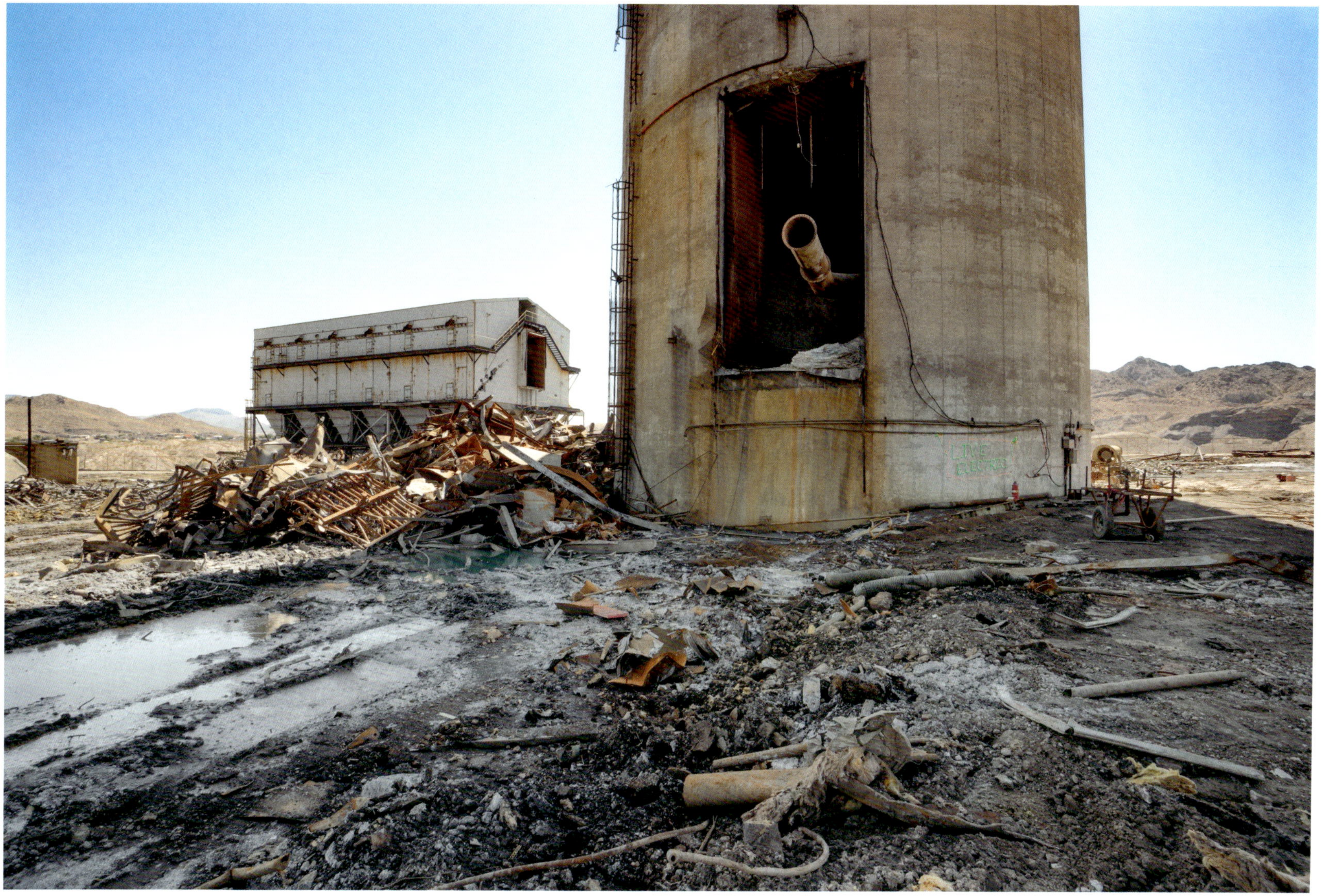

A demolition view of the El Paso ASARCO plant. The last of the major structures remaining include the bag house in the distant left and the main 828-foot-tall copper stack. With the removal of the massive ductwork connecting the stack to the smelter and to the scrubber equipment, we are given a rare view through the outer shell to the base of the inner stack.

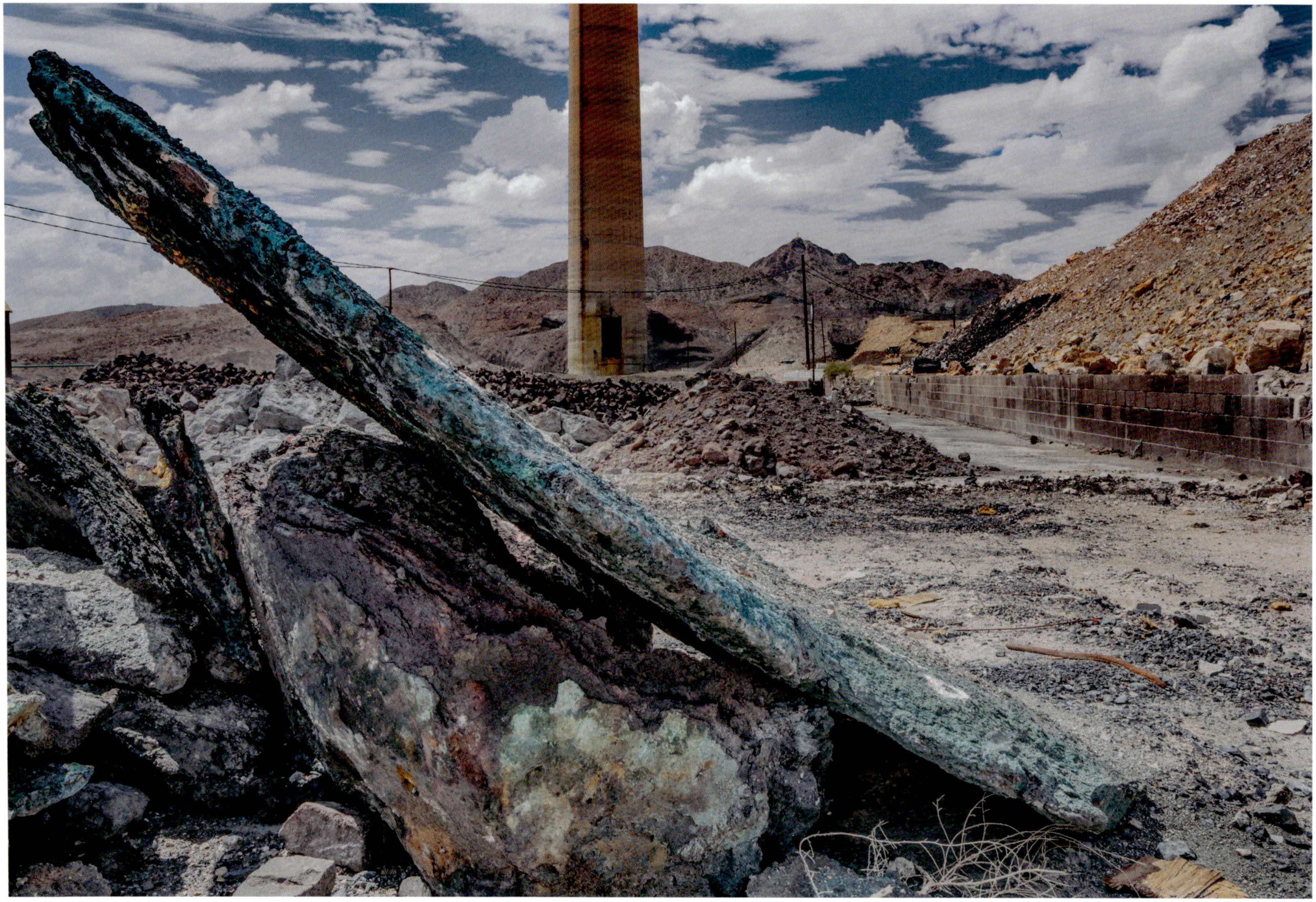

A view during environmental cleanup of the El Paso ASARCO landscape. A normal by-product of any ore-smelting process, slag is loose material ranging from sand-sized grains to massive chunks. At the El Paso ASARCO site, a late phase of building demolition and environmental remediation involved scraping and grading the landscape, sculpting acres of terrain, then shaping mounds of slag and waste rock—some piles as much as thirty feet high. Sometimes, albeit rarely, the process exposed giant slabs and boulders of copper-rich material.

As the site was cleared, stockpiles of surface material were isolated and destined for different uses. Some rock and soils contained economically recoverable amounts of copper and other metals. In this image, the turquoise color indicates exceptionally high concentrations of nearly pure copper, its density far exceeding anything found in the raw ores from which it came. As technologies improved, slags with a pure copper content (matte grade) of less than 2 percent could be re-smelted, rendering a reasonable profit.

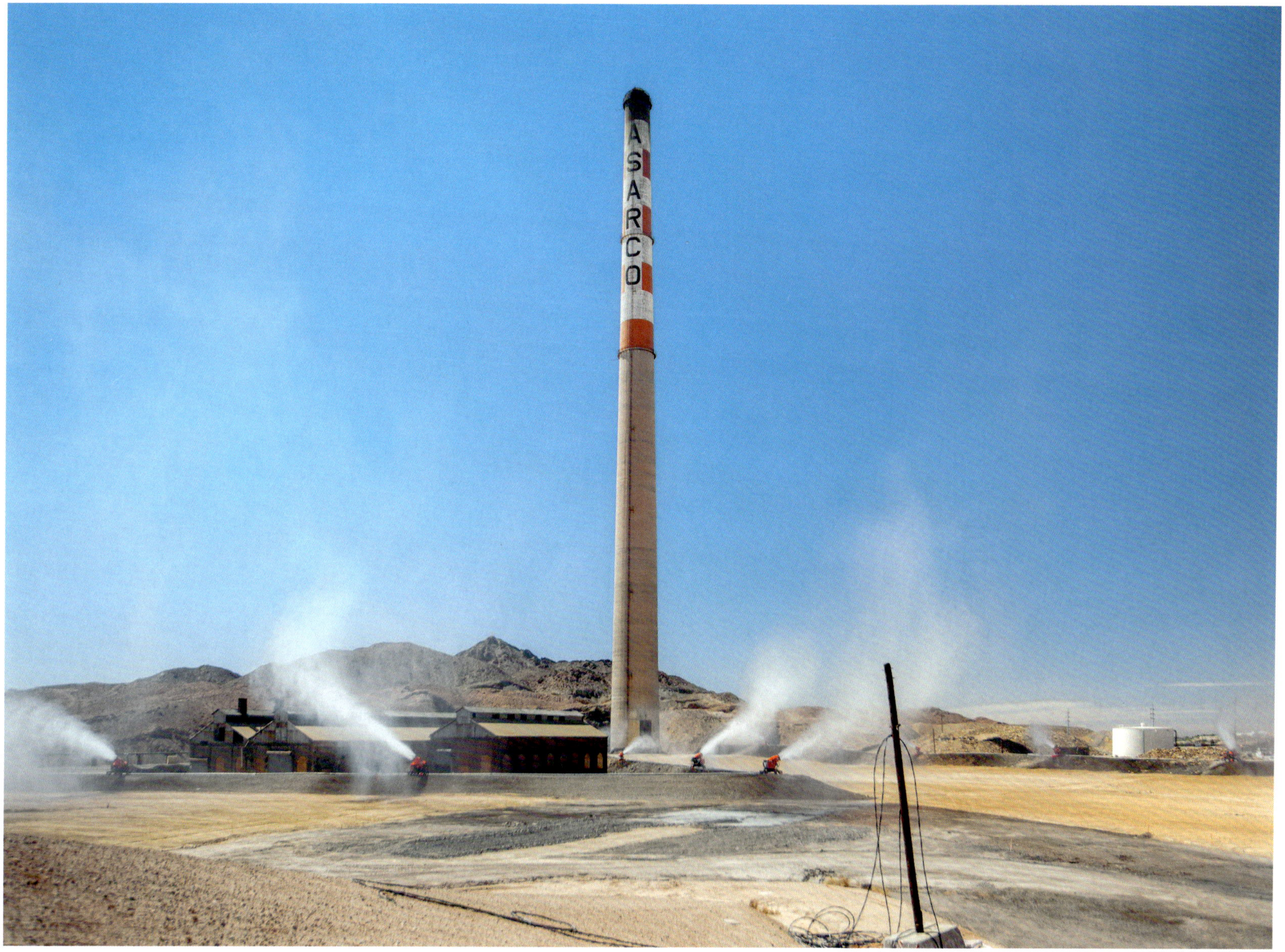

A demolition view of the El Paso ASARCO plant. On the day before their scheduled fall, engineers tested the massive misting fans, intended to dampen and suppress dust roiling from each stack's one-thousand-foot-long drop site in the moments after the two icons toppled and disintegrated.

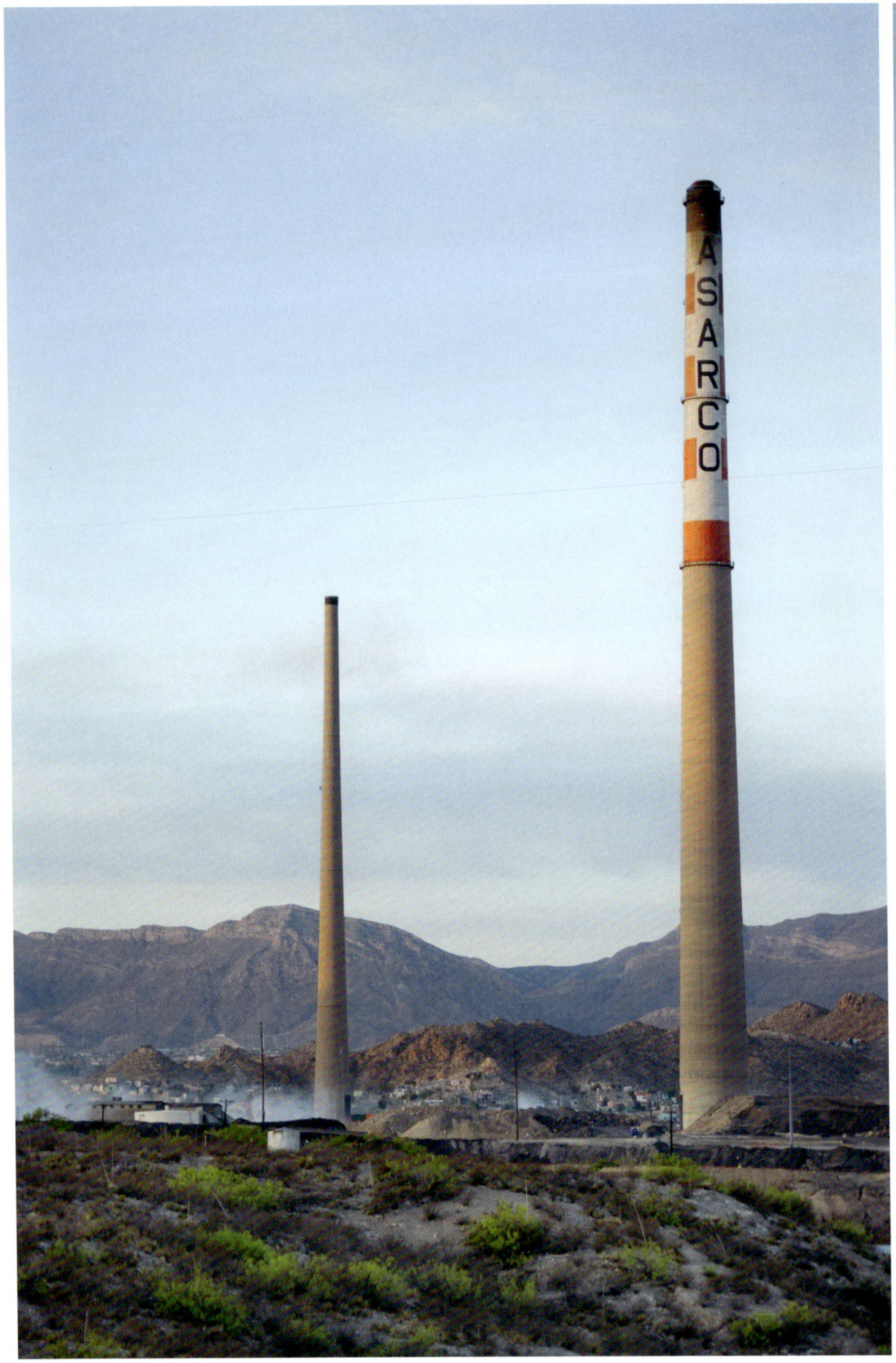
ASARCO

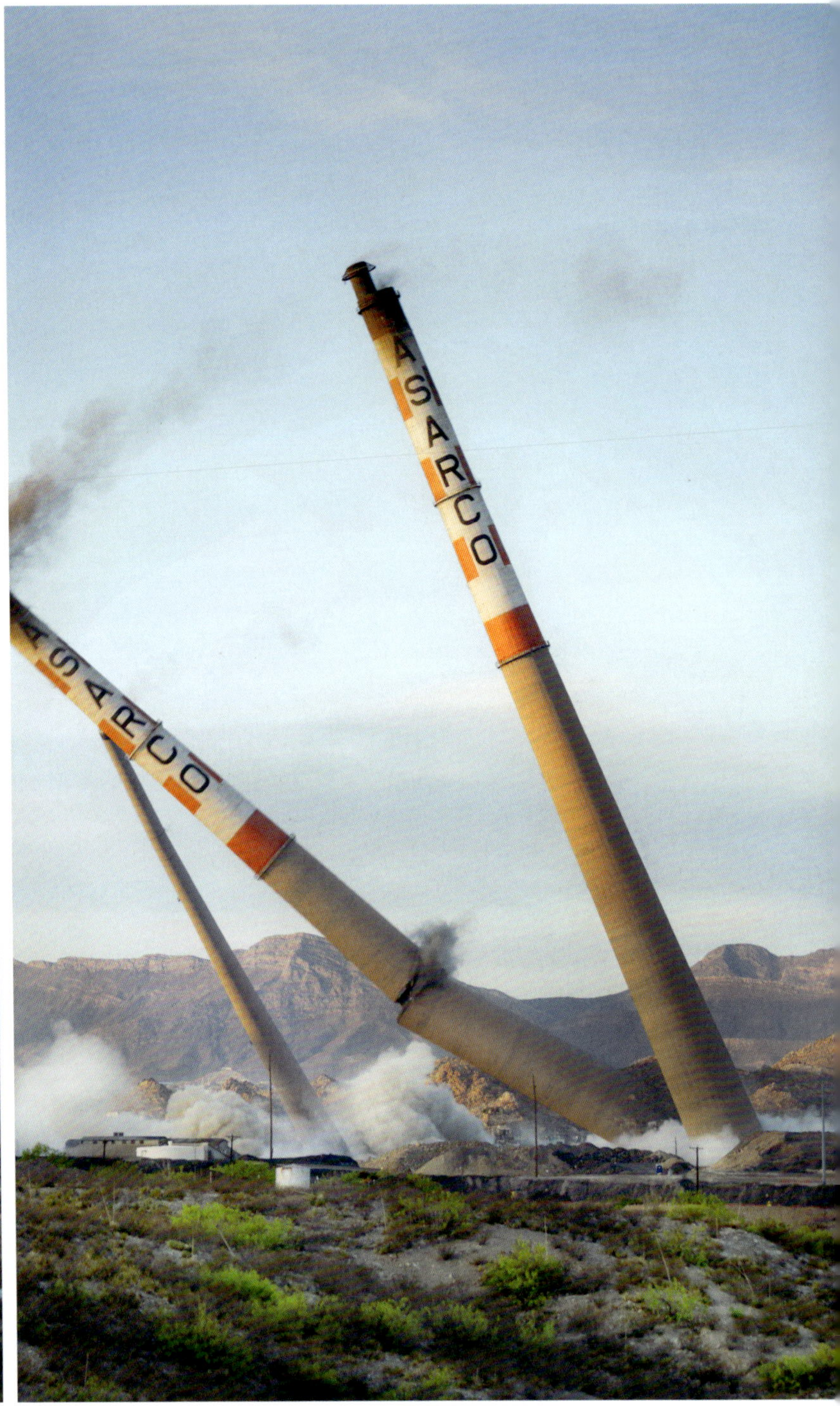
ASARCO

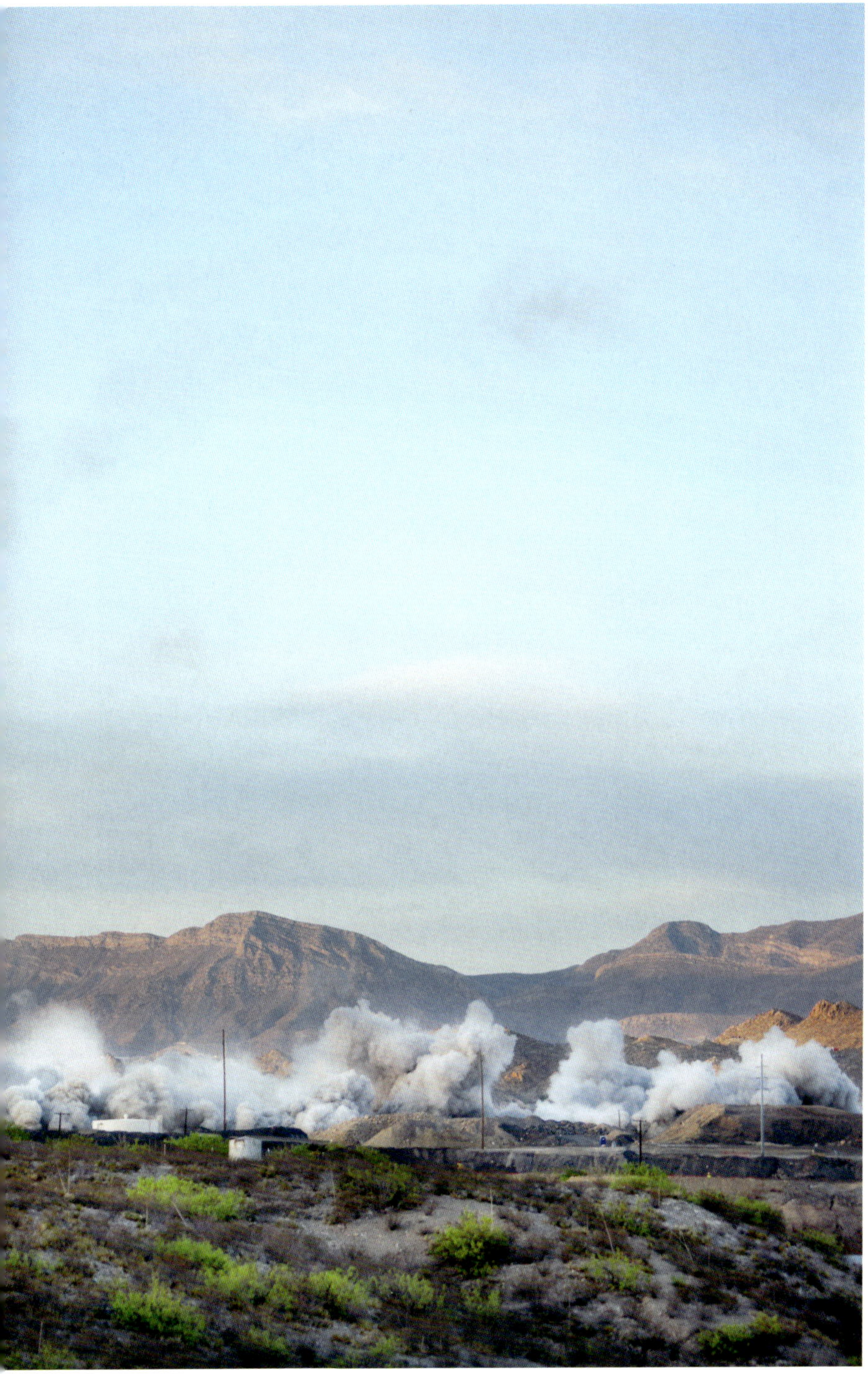

A demolition view of the El Paso ASARCO plant. 06:50, Saturday, April 13, 2013. At dawn, a seventy-second-long series of detonations brought down the "lead" and "copper" stacks.

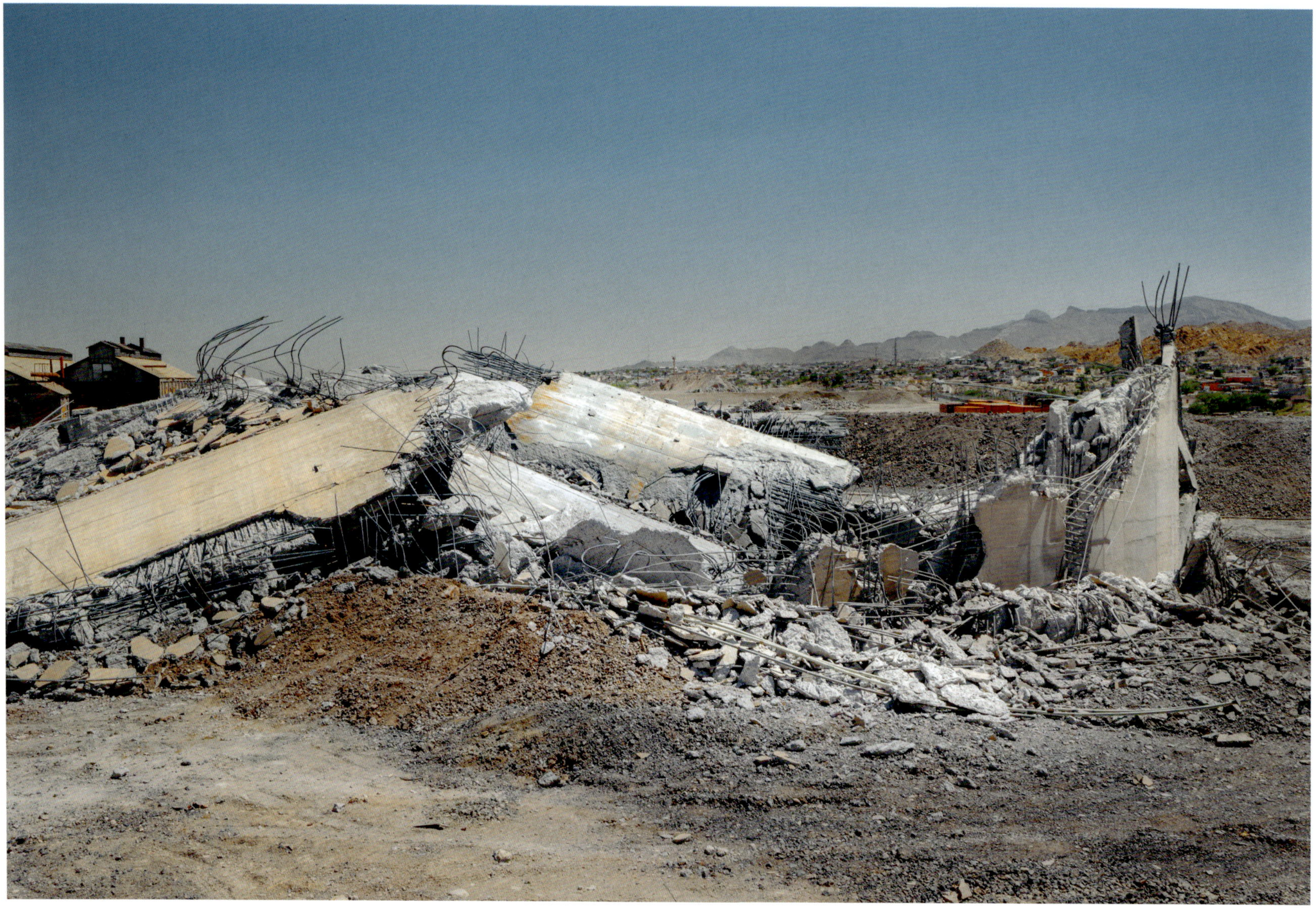

A demolition view of the El Paso ASARCO plant. The detonations that took down the two concrete stacks made them topple, not explode. Toward their bases, thanks to their relatively short trip to the ground, massive fragments remained recognizable as pieces of a cylinder. Giant curved slabs of the stack's concrete shell, some weighing tons, remain knotted together in a tangle of rebar. At the far end of the debris field, the former top of the stack, pulverized by the eight-hundred-foot fall, lay scattered in shards smaller than your fist.

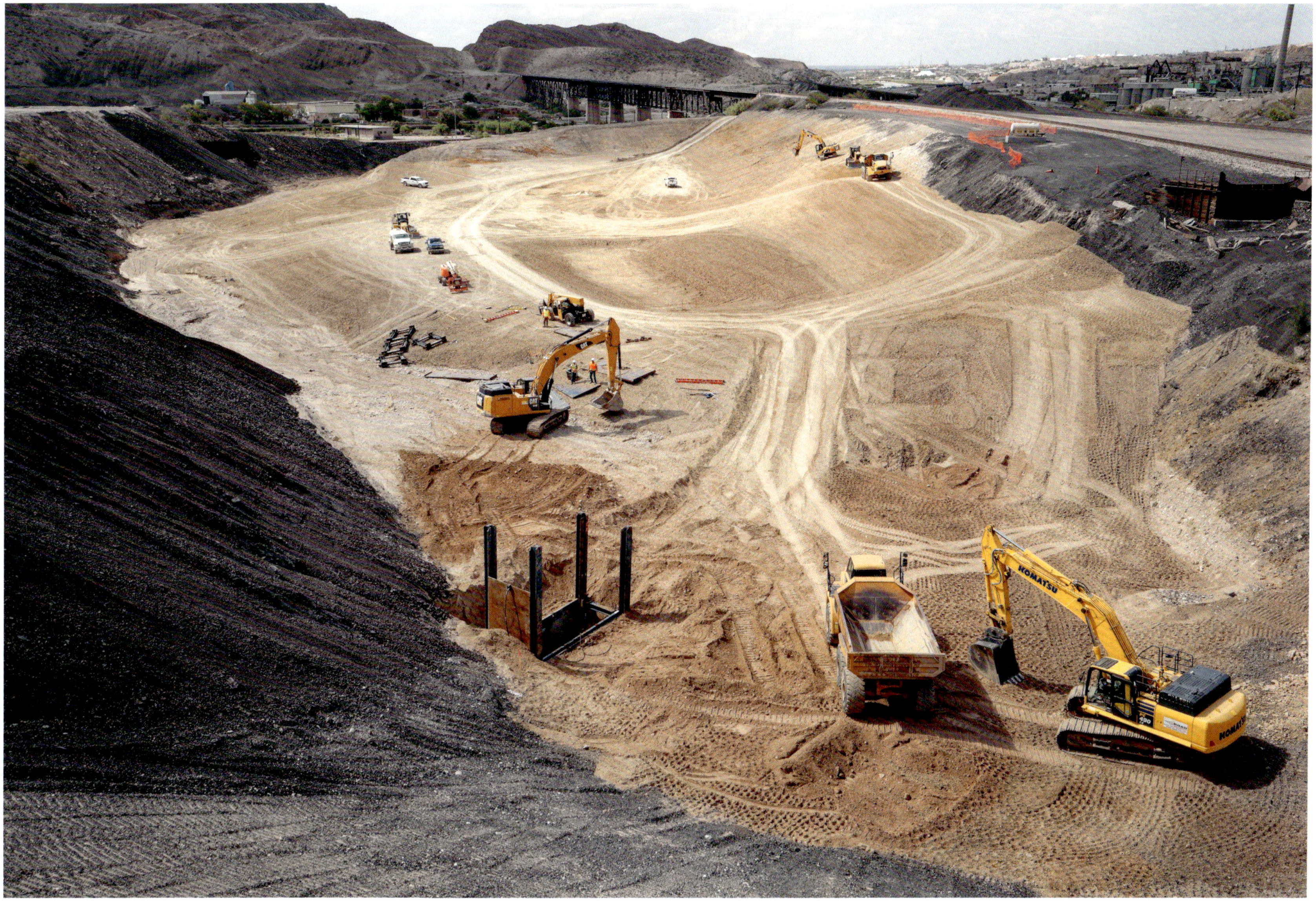

A view of the El Paso ASARCO site remediation. Formerly a slag dump at Lower Parker Brothers' Arroyo, this site is being cleared and re-engineered for the burial of demolition debris before it is capped, ensuring clean flow from the arroyo watershed into the Rio Grande a few hundred yards to the left.

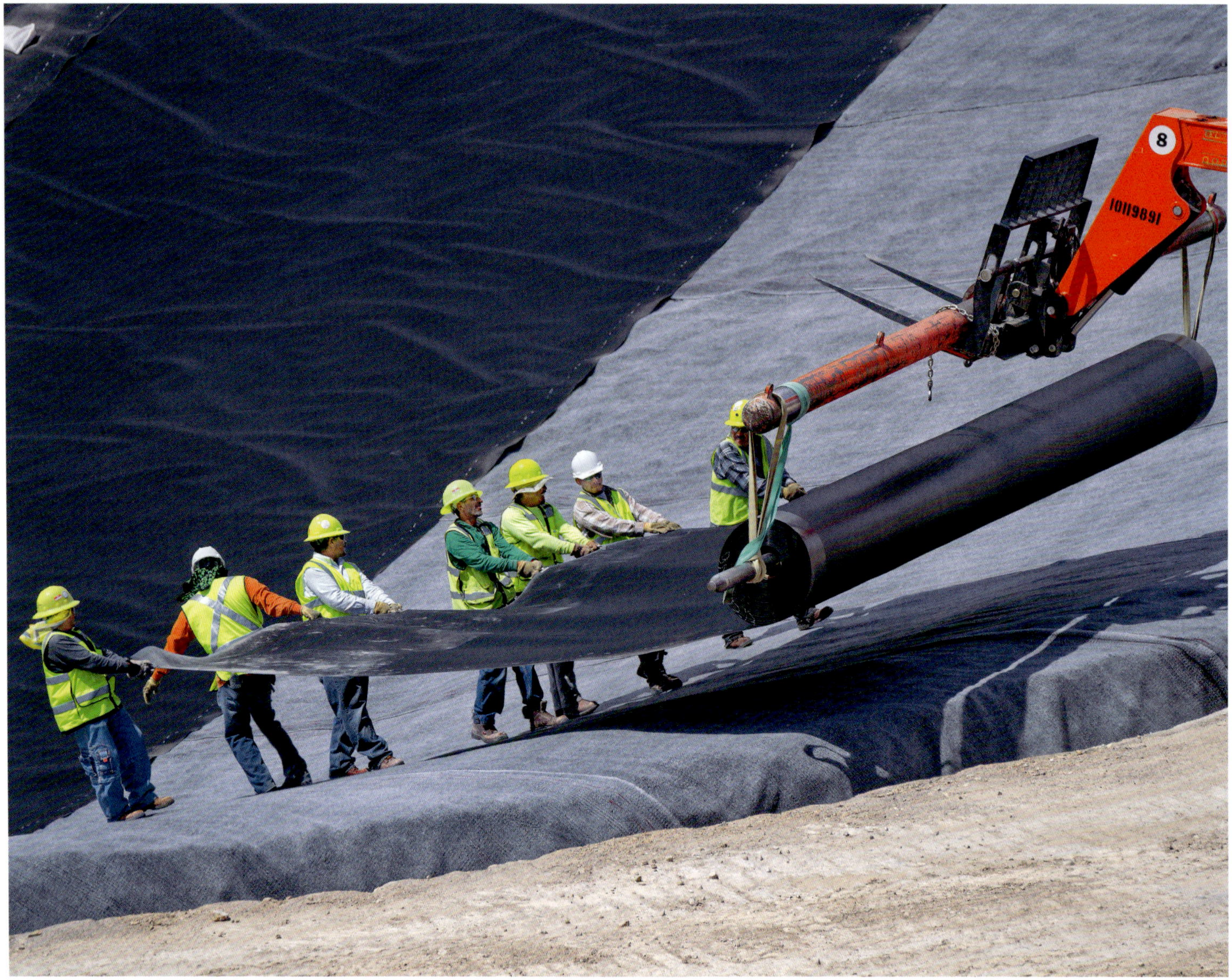

A view of the El Paso ASARCO site remediation. This image shows a crew installing layers of liner at Cell 4—the massive engineered earthen basin at Lower Parker Brothers Arroyo. The cell, a state-of-the-art engineered industrial landfill pit, is lined with thick impervious membrane to ensure that its buried, encapsulated contents pose no threat to the local surface environment, the watershed, and the nearby Rio Grande.

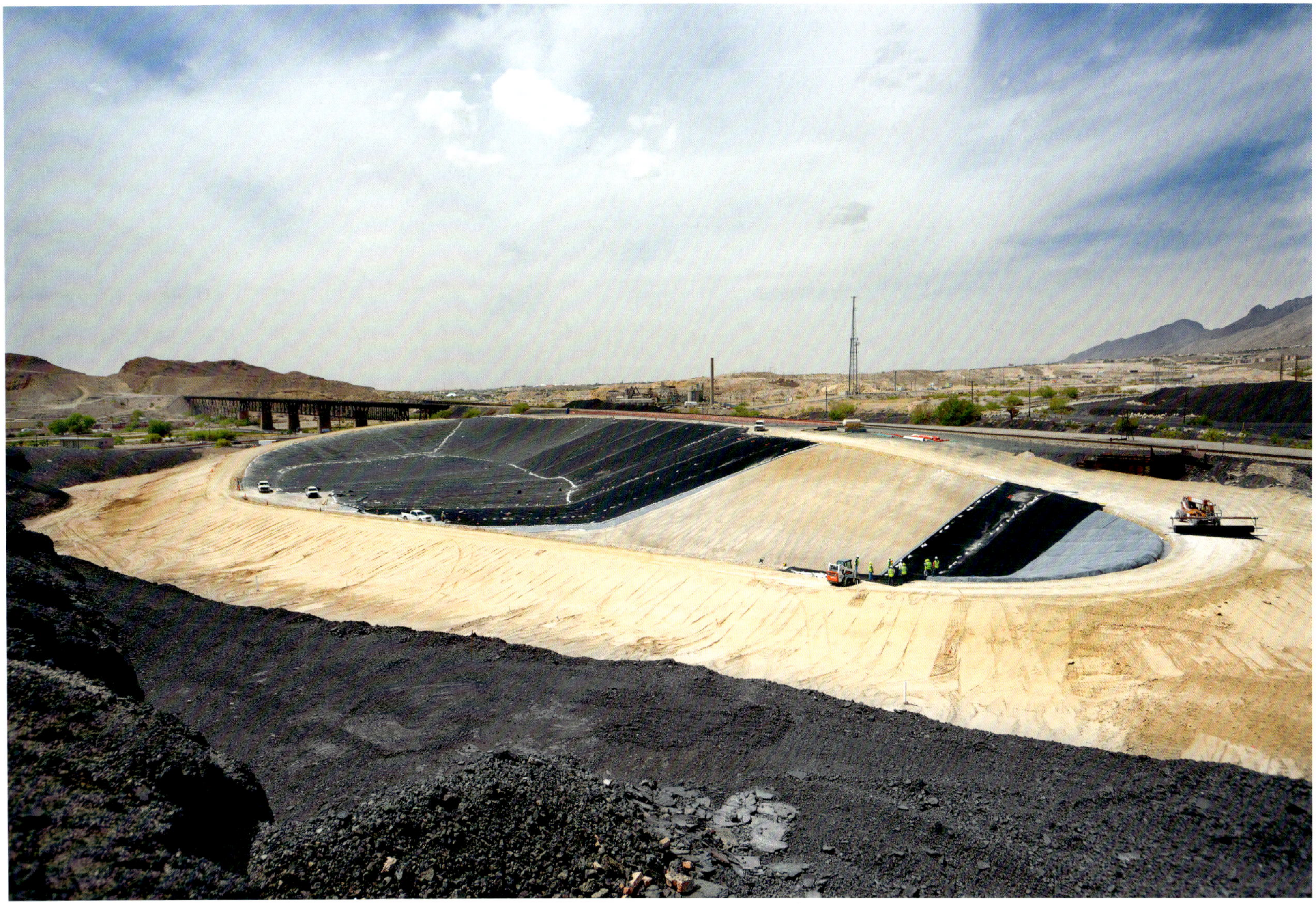

A view of the El Paso ASARCO site remediation. Formerly a slag dump at Lower Parker Brothers' Arroyo, this site is being cleared and re-engineered for the burial of demolition debris before it is capped, ensuring clean flow from the arroyo watershed into the Rio Grande (see p. 132).

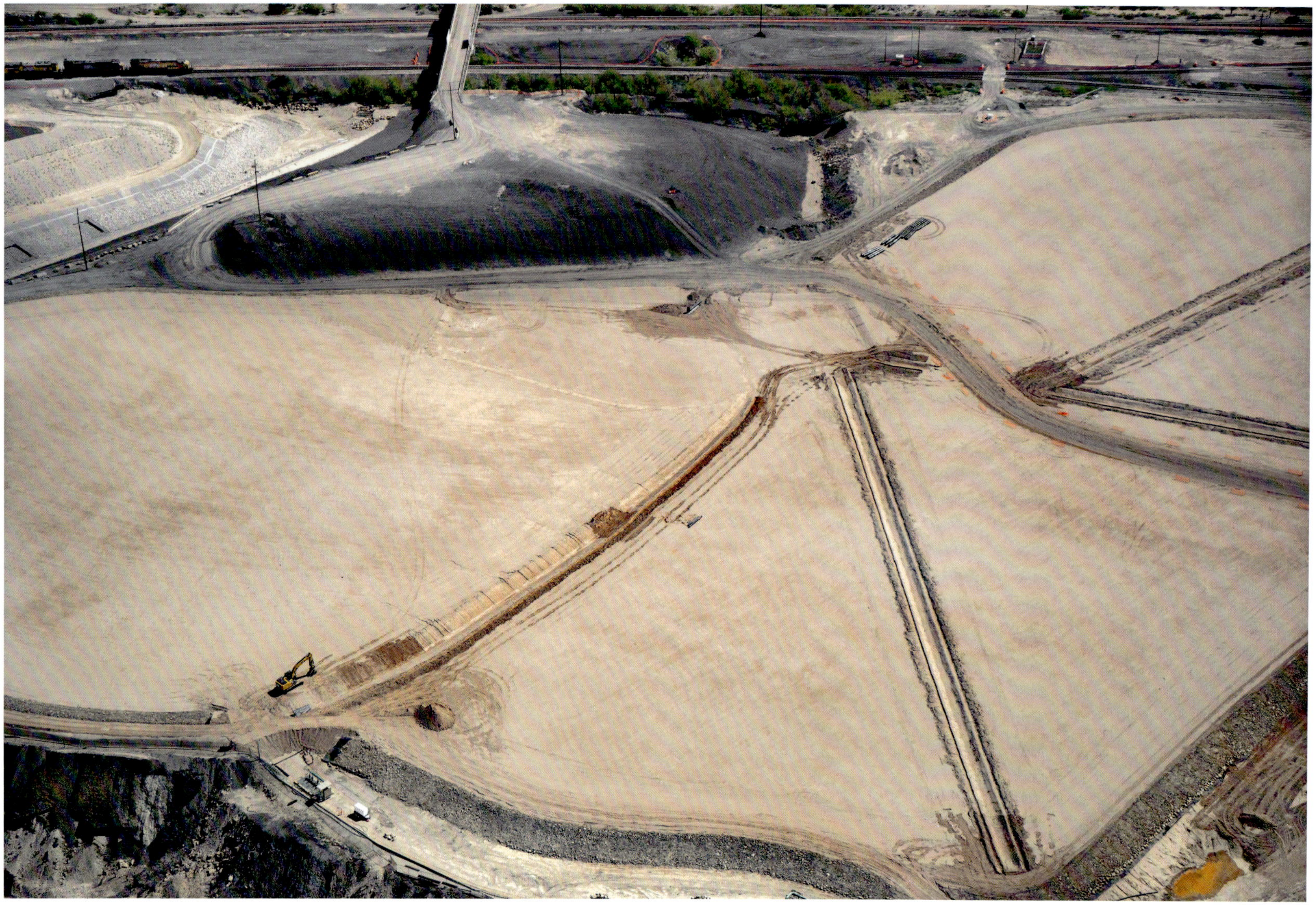

A view of the El Paso ASARCO site remediation. In this 2016 aerial photgraph, re-engineering of the north end of the main smelter property is nearly complete. The former ASARCO landscape awaits its next iteration after its purchase by the University of Texas–El Paso.

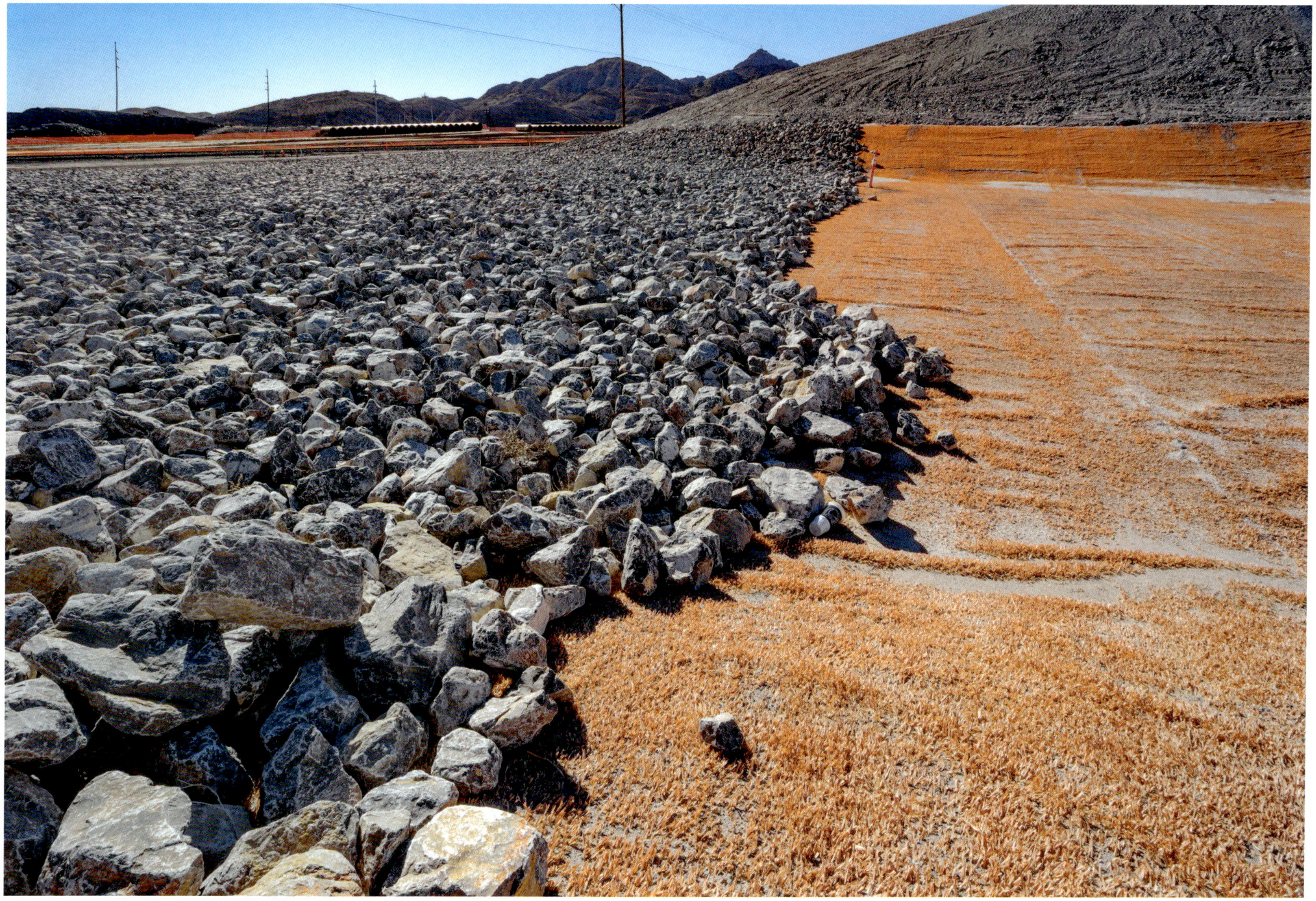

A view of the El Paso ASARCO site remediation. In this photograph rock ballast is laid in the reconfigured Parker Brothers' Arroyo. This lined channel, and the capped slag mound in the upper right, are engineered to passively restore water-table quality to preindustrial levels of purity.

Cokedale, Colorado. Coke ovens (or kilns) are integral to the landscape of nineteenth- and twentieth-century minerals extraction. Cokedale was founded in 1906 as an ASARCO company town. Its ovens relied on local coal mines to feed more than one hundred kilns nearly continuously for a half century. The coke they produced was shipped by rail to fire ASARCO smelters in Pueblo and in El Paso, 450 miles south. The coal came primarily from nearby Colorado mines in Hastings and in Ludlow. Hastings is notorious for an underground explosion in 1917 in which 121 miners died. Ludlow is remembered for its labor strikes and for the 1914 massacre in which the mine owners (headed by John D. Rockefeller Jr.) had slaughtered, by machine gun, twenty-one strikers along with their wives and children.

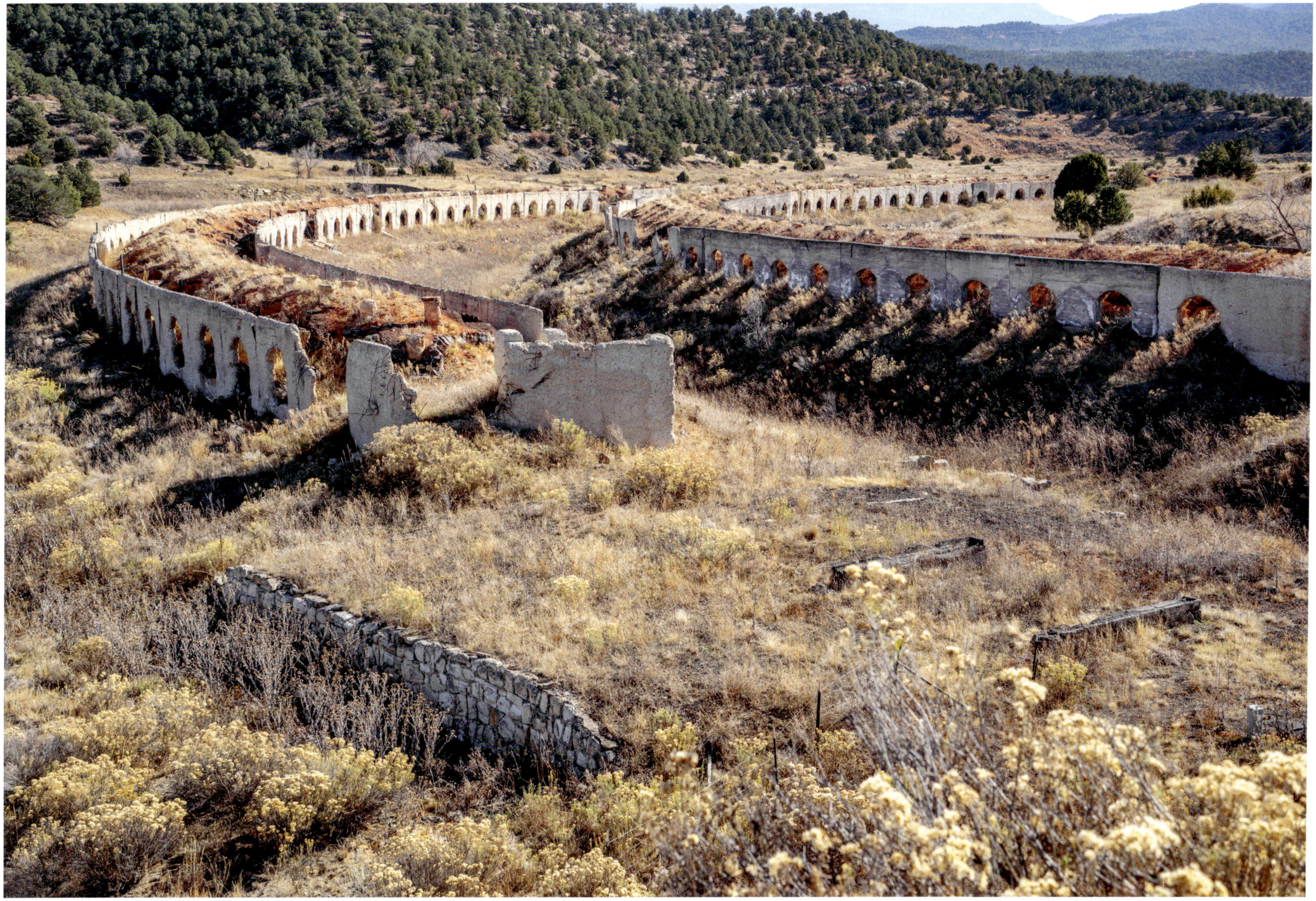

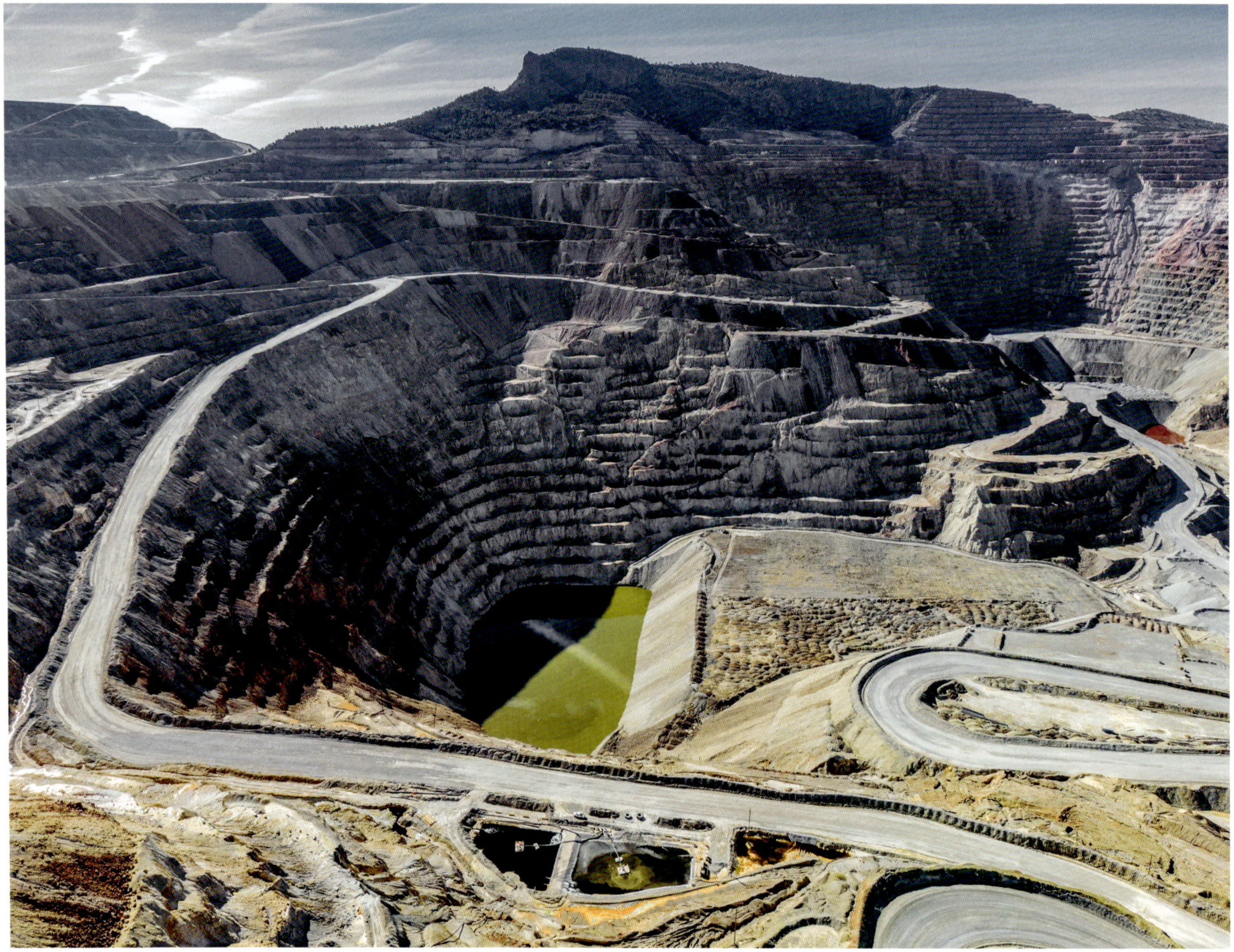

Santa Rita, New Mexico. In 1910, to assure a steady supply of ore for its El Paso smelter during the disruptions of Mexico's Revolution, Guggenheim's ASARCO purchased the Santa Rita mine, near Silvery City, New Mexico, 120 miles northwest of the El Paso smelter. This mine, and the Bingham in Utah, were among the world's first economical open-pit operations—an innovation pioneered by Guggenheim engineers. Those pits remain two of the planet's largest.

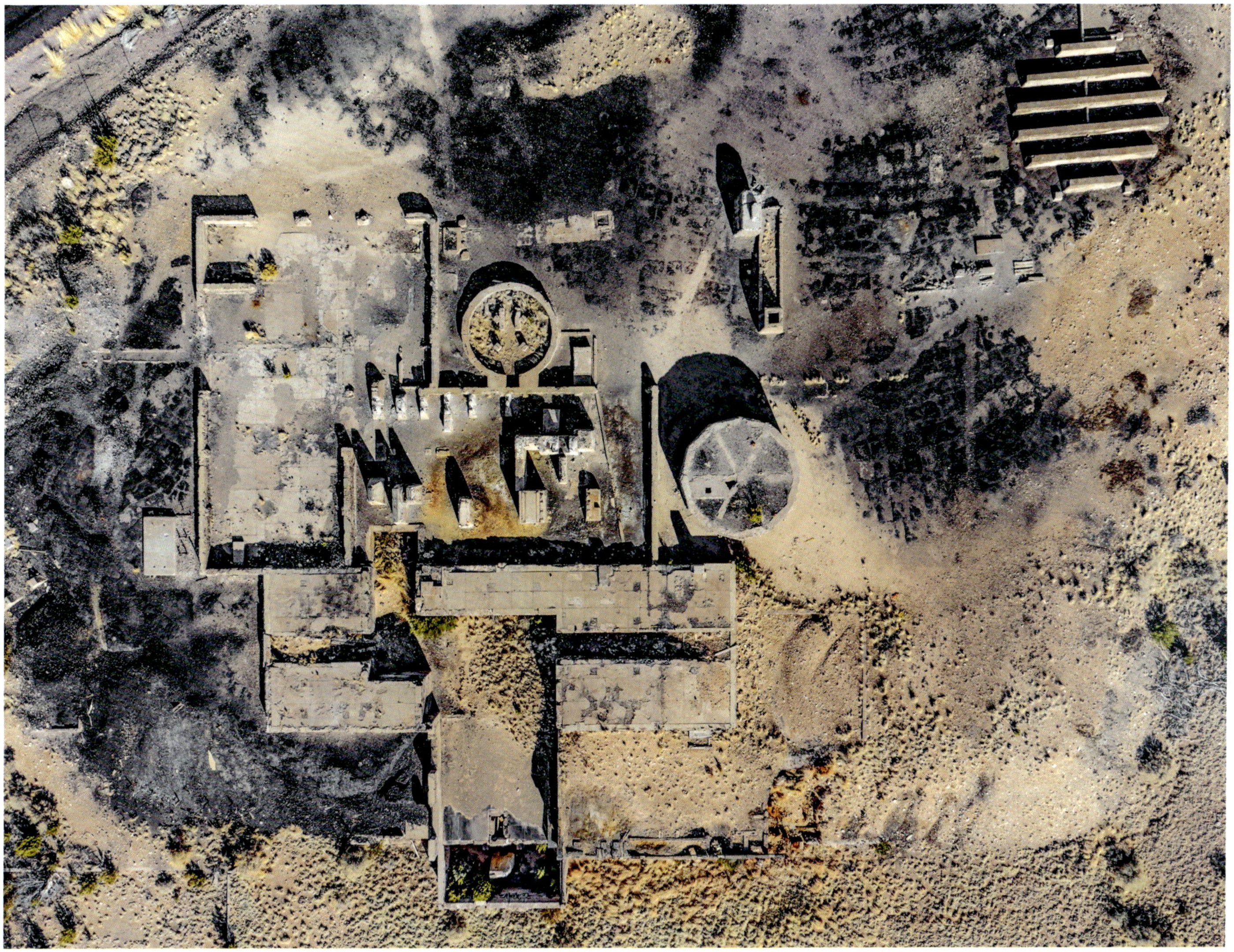

Hop Canyon Mill, New Mexico. In North America, the Guggenheim and ASARCO mining footprint stretched from Alaska and Puget Sound through the Rockies into central Mexico. Here, one mile south of Magdalena, the remains of a 1913 copper and lead refinery gradually melt back into the landscape. These concrete foundation ruins date from the early twentieth century. ASARCO processed ore here until 1947. The property is now part of an EPA Superfund environmental-remediation project.

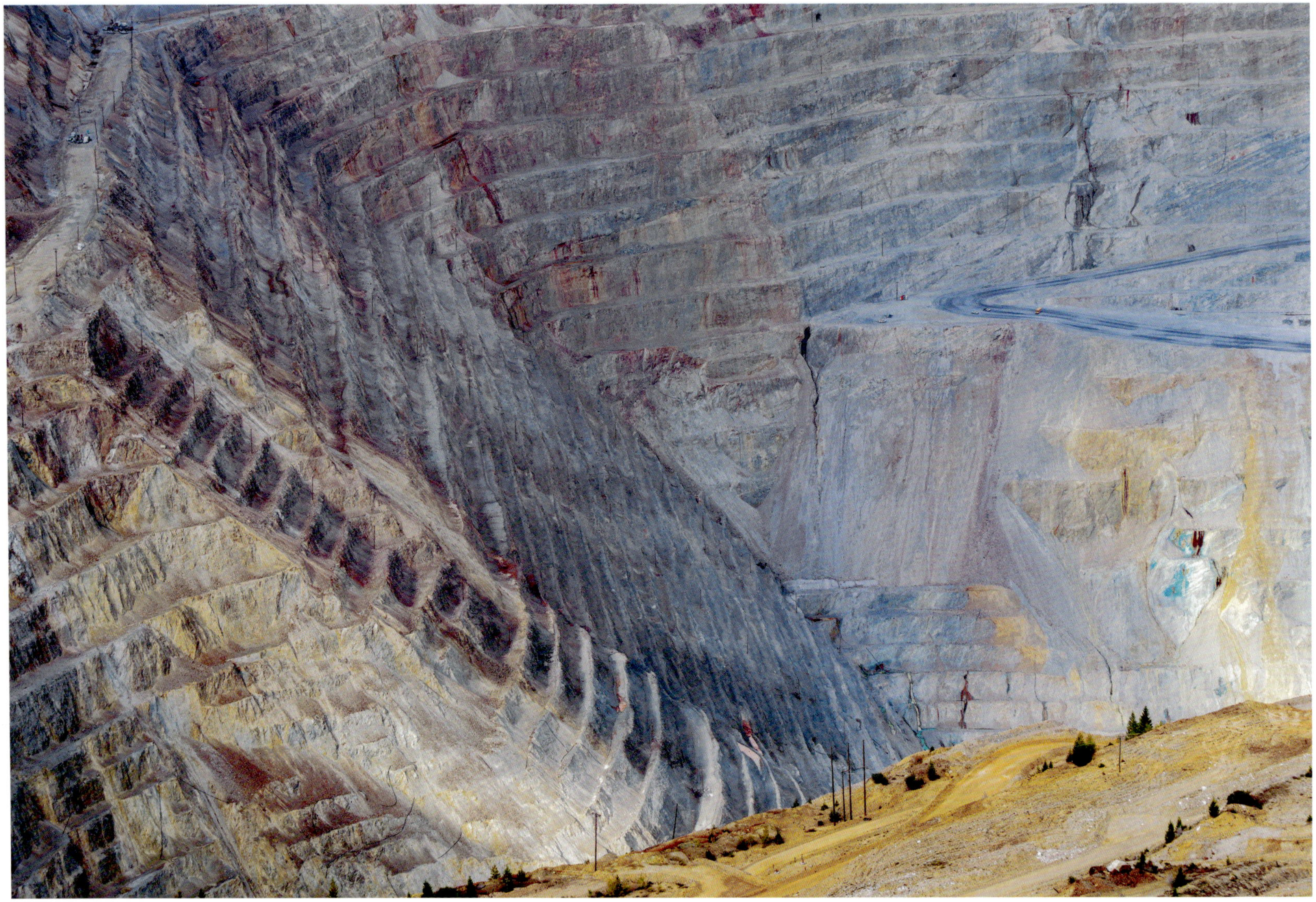

Bingham Canyon, Utah. In 1903 Daniel Guggenheim, representing ASARCO, agreed to invest in an obscure canyon above Salt Lake City, where low-grade copper-bearing ores proved abundant. The Guggenheims' backing, and their faith in the untested method of moving mountains instead of tunneling into them to recover ores, gave the world is first economically viable open-pit copper mine. The Bingham holds the record as the world's deepest excavated pit at 3,970 feet.

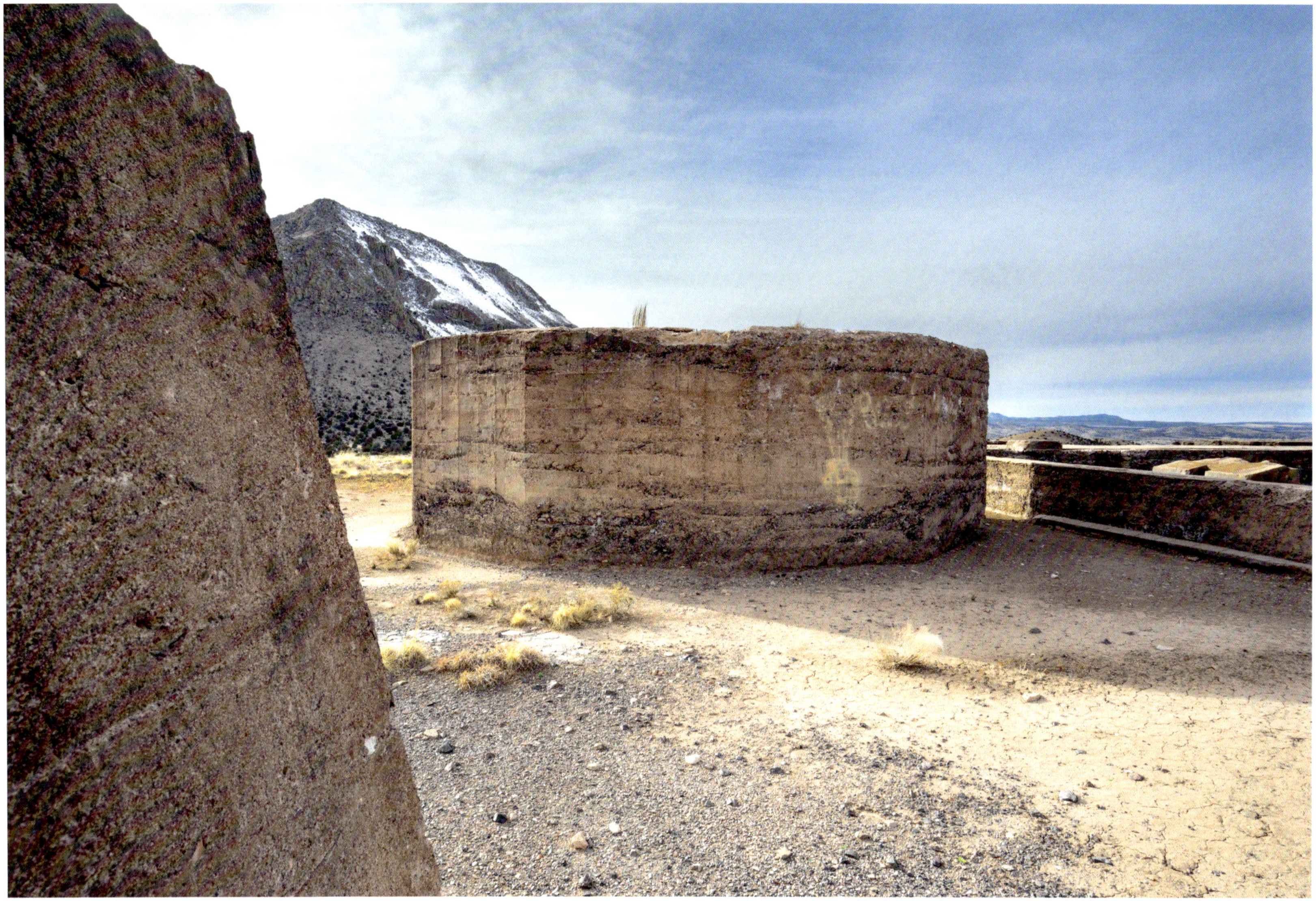

Hop Canyon Mill, New Mexico. These ruins of Hop Canyon Mill, at the base of Magdalena Peak, date from the early twentieth century. ASARCO processed ore here until 1947.

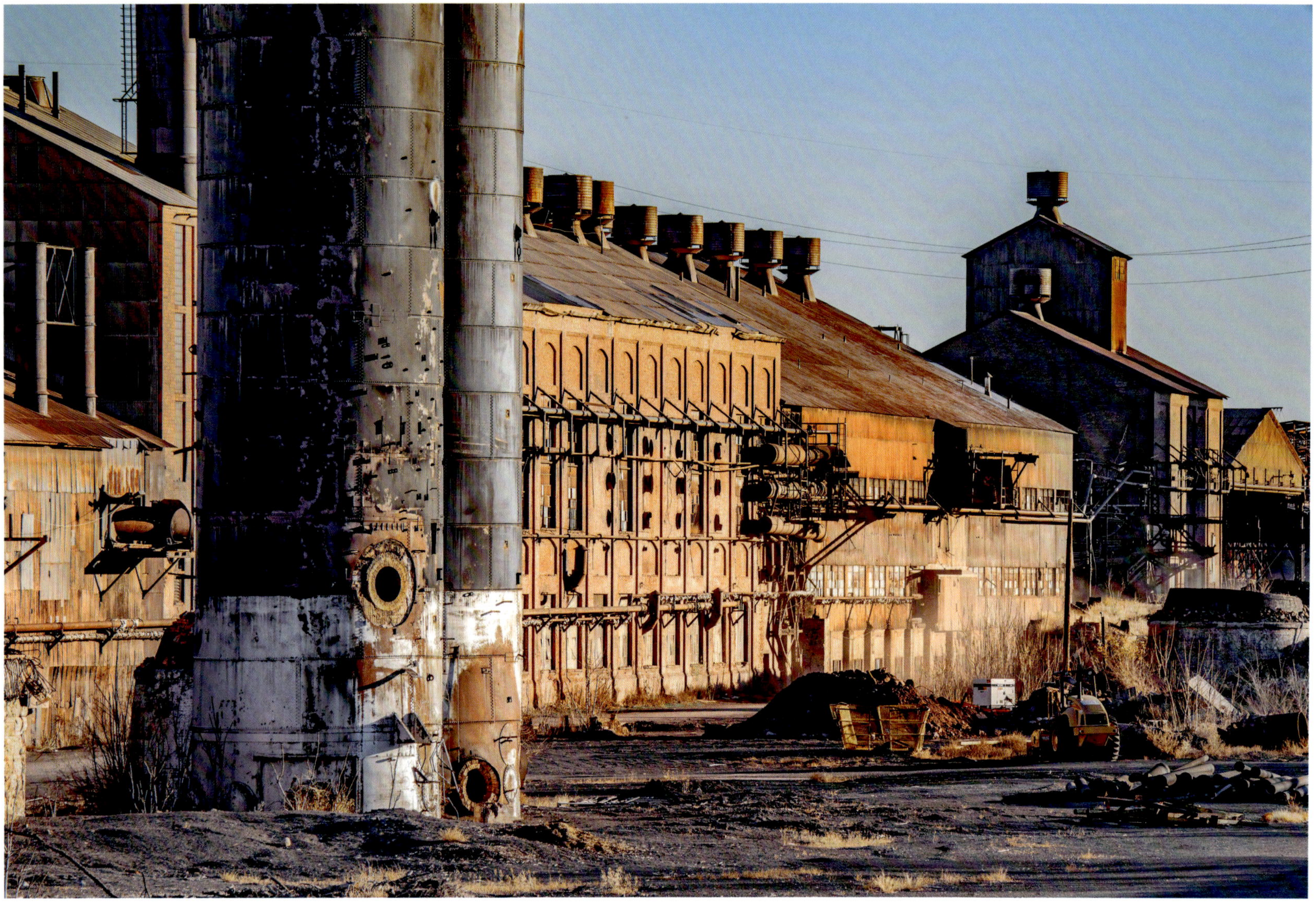

Pueblo, Colorado. In the 1880s the Guggenheim smelter was Pueblo's largest. But it was obsolete by 1909 and was subsequently demolished. A contemporaneous industrial icon, the Colorado Fuel and Iron Company, still stands a century later, hinting at the nature of Pueblo's late nineteenth-century Arkansas Valley smelter landscape.

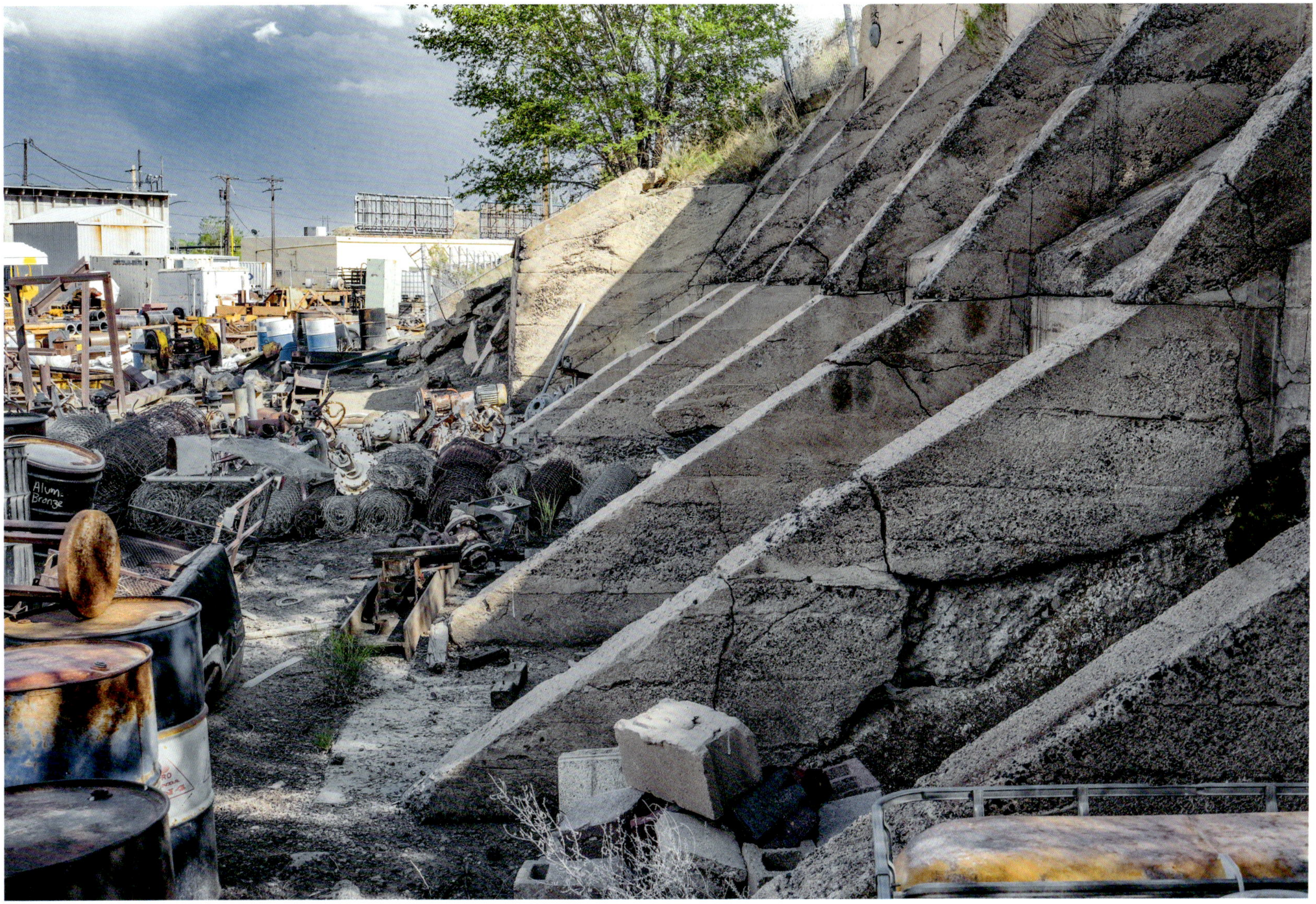

Pueblo, Colorado, smelter site. In 1889 M. Guggenheim Sons purchased an operating smelter in Leadville, but to more efficiently control costs, within months the company built a state-of-the-art smelter in the middle-Arkansas valley—in Pueblo, closer to fuel sources and markets. For two decades it was Pueblo's largest smelter, operating until 1908. This concrete ruin, the remains of a sluice at the north end of the property, is all that stands of M. Guggenheim Sons' Pueblo investment.

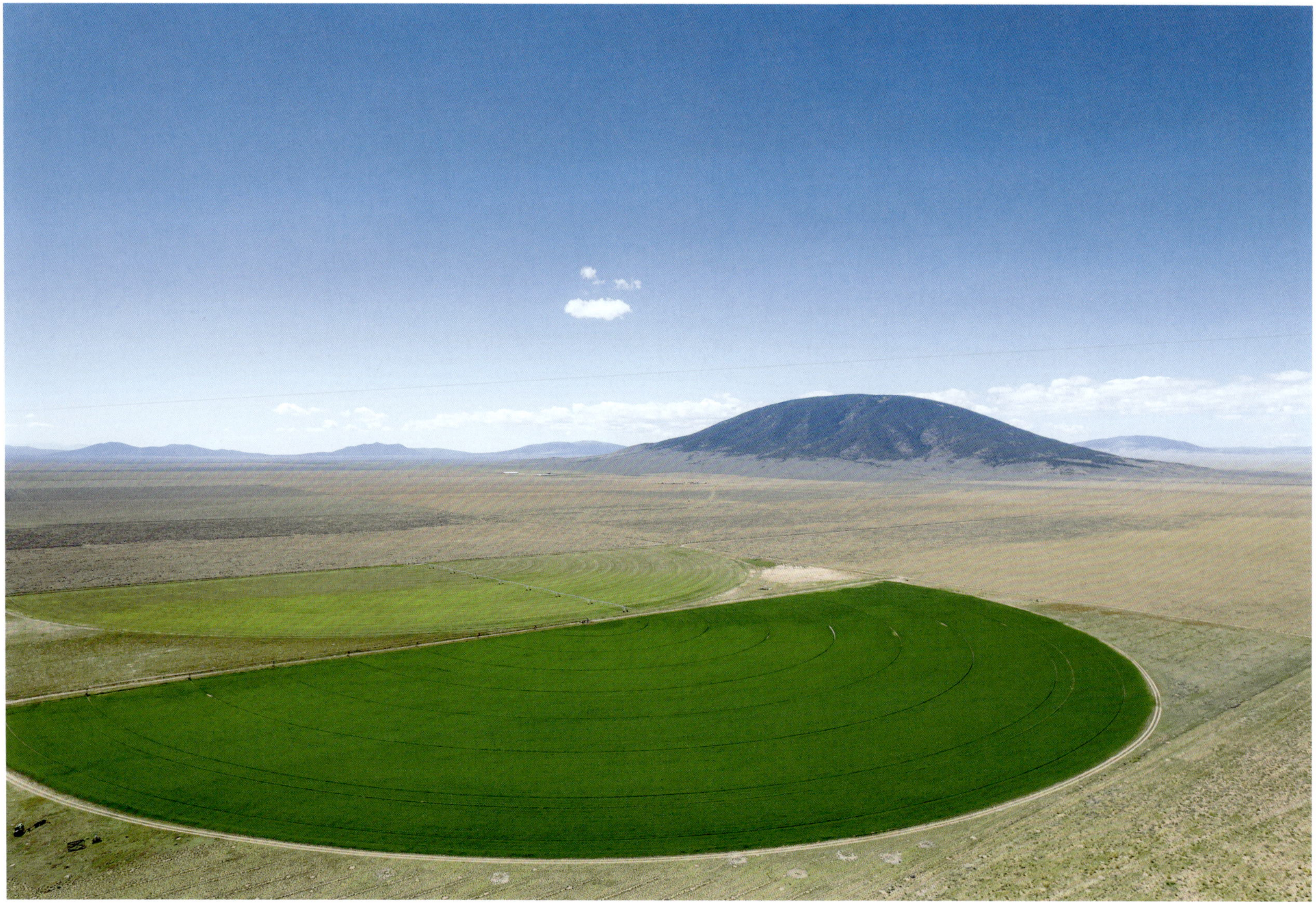

San Luis Valley, New Mexico and Colorado. This landscape, spanning the New Mexico–Colorado line is, according to some, the vestigial northern terminus of El Camino Real de Tierra Adentro. Mid-nineteenth-century farmers and ranchers emigrating from northern Mexico established small communities on the Taos Plateau at Costilla and Jaroso, in the shadow of Cerro del Yuta (Ute Mountain), which rises a half mile above the valley floor.

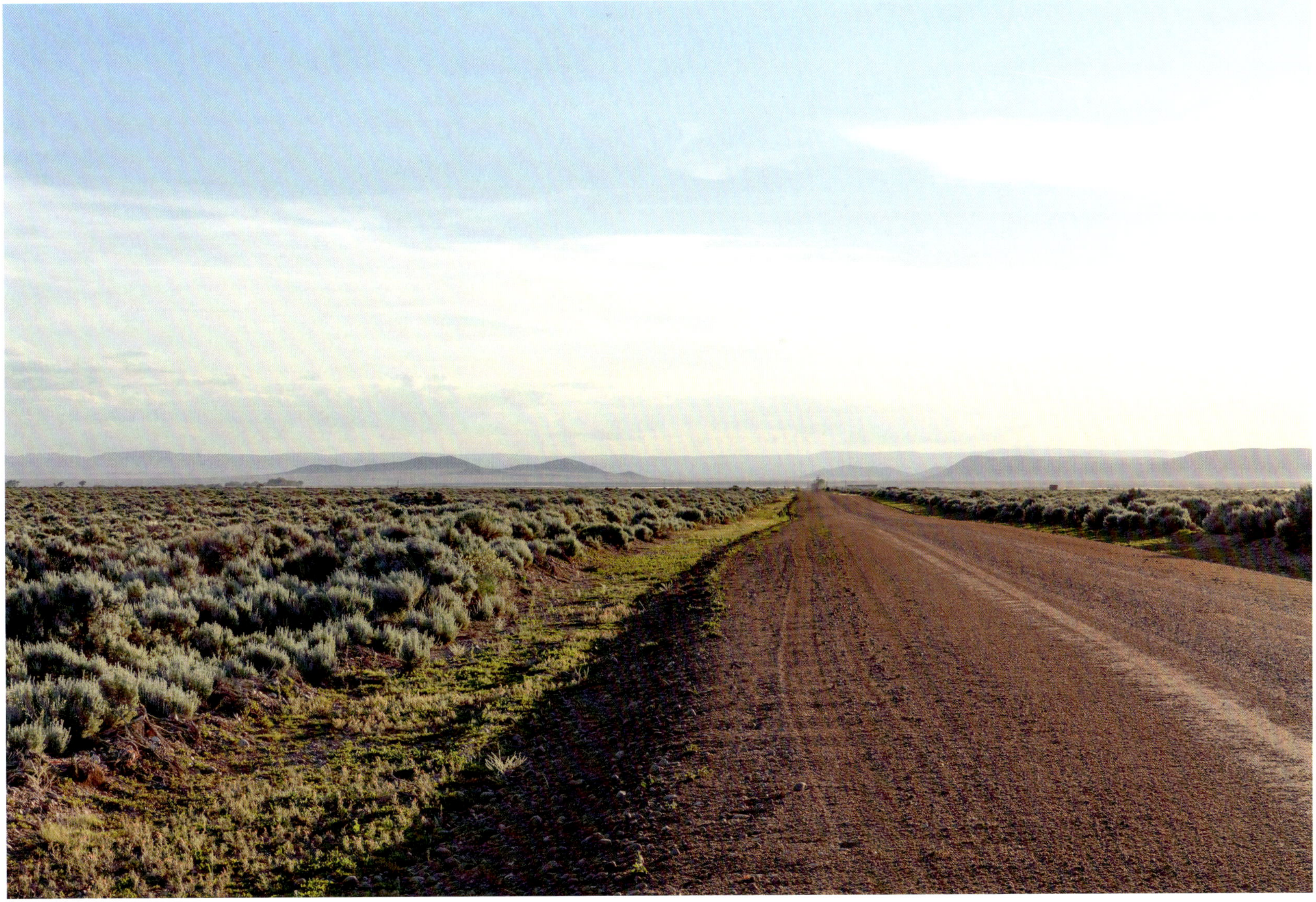

West of Garcia, Colorado, ephemeral Camino landscape. The Royal Road of the Interior begins at Mexico's treasury, a few yards behind the altar of its great cathedral on the Zócalo in the center of Ciudad México. Sixteen hundred miles north, beyond Santa Fe and Taos, the Camino meanders, divides, and thins before it finally vanishes, like an evaporating river delta, into Colorado's vast San Luis Valley.

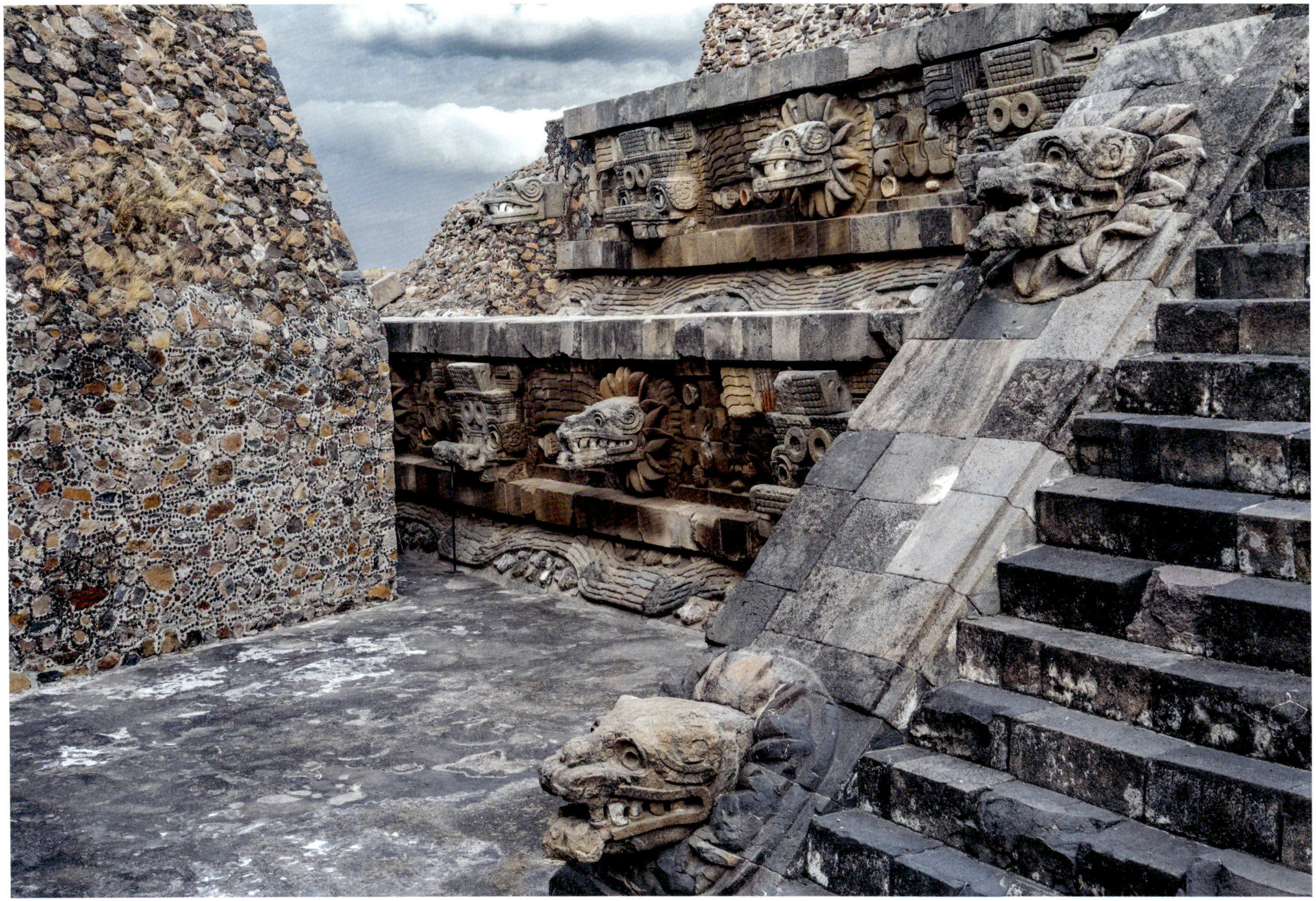

Aztec Temple of Quetzalcoatl (Temple of the Feathered Serpent) near Mexico City, Mexico. Partly intact and partly restored, this temple is one complex of several Teotihuacán pyramids in the Valley of Mexico. Note the wall at the center left where pebbles pressed into the pointing indicate restored versus intact original construction.

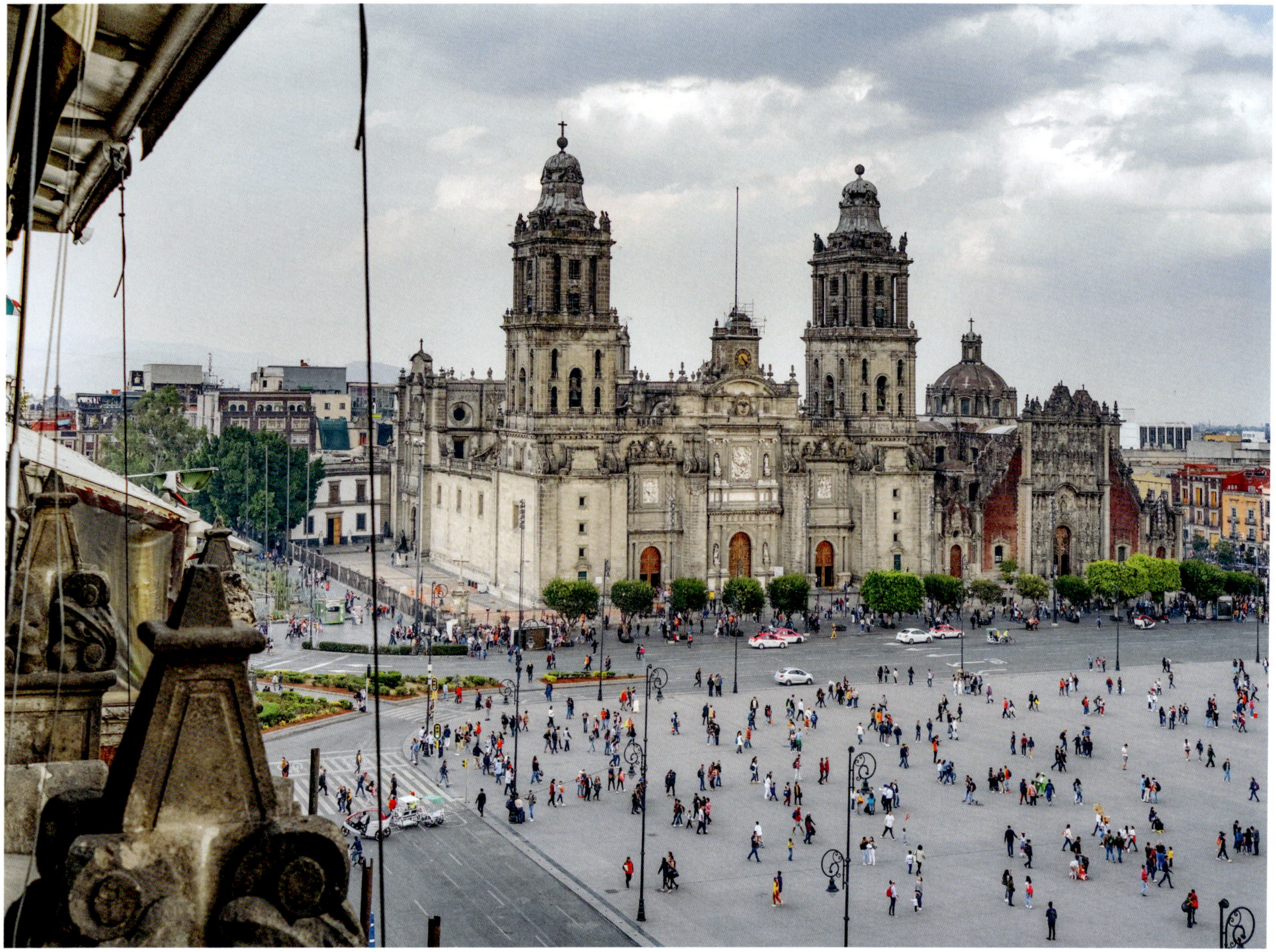

Mexico City, DF, Mexico. The most opulent and the largest Roman Catholic cathedral in the Americas, the Metropolitan Cathedral of the Assumption of the Most Blessed Virgin Mary into Heaven, anchors the south end of the Camino Real de Tierra Adentro, 1,600 miles from its terminus in northern New Mexico. The building's foundations rest upon, and are literally made from, fragments of Aztec pyramids that predated by centuries the Spaniards' arrival.

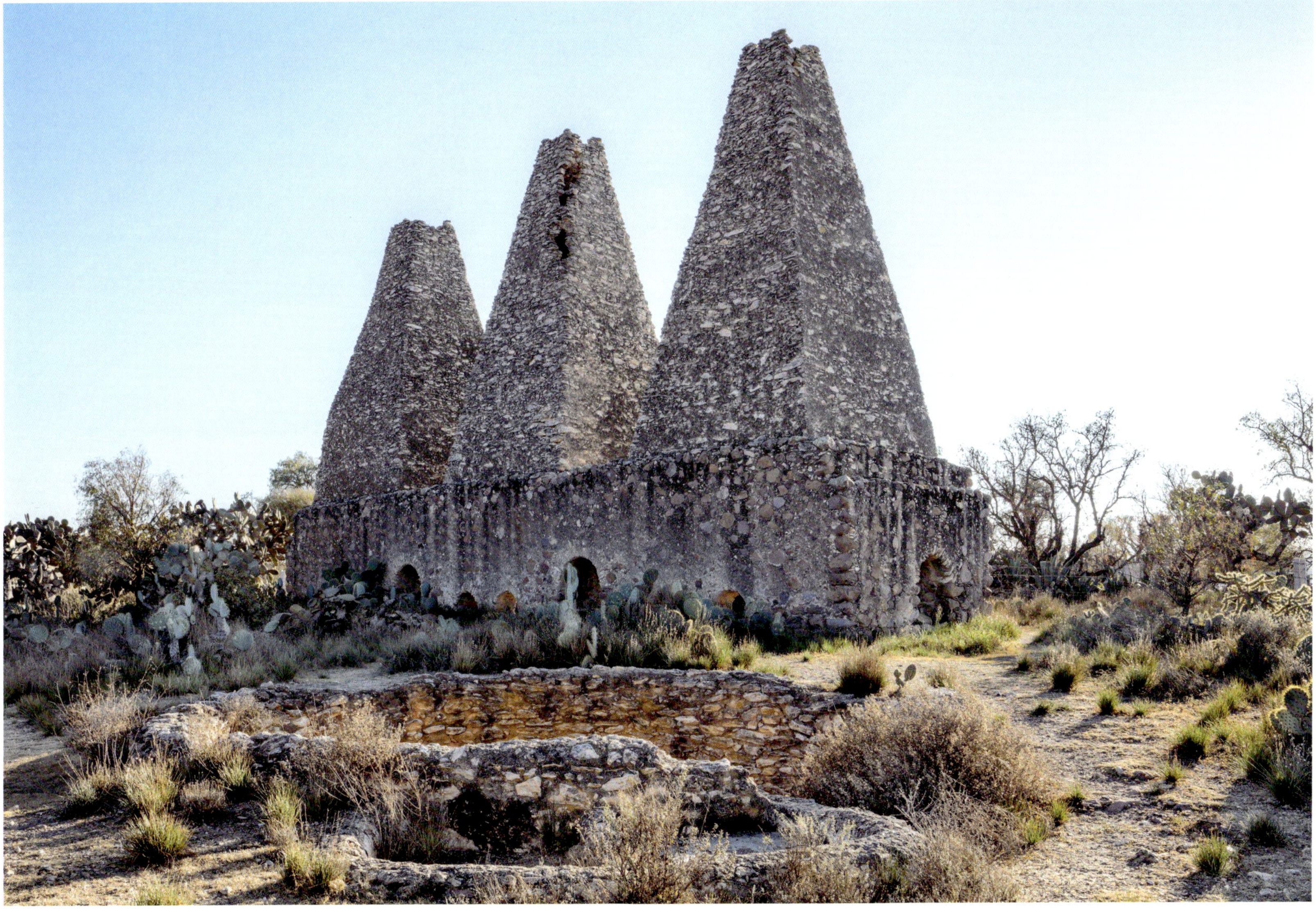

Silver Smelter at Santa Brígida, Guanajuato State, Mexico. In this view, the stone-lined circular pits in the foreground are arrastras, where silver-bearing ore was pulverized. People, presumably not Jesuits, led mules dragging massive stones in endless circles as they stomped over the ore mixed with pure mercury. When the ore was sufficiently crushed, the slurry was transferred to the hornos (the towering stone smelters) for further refining. See the caption on page xiv.

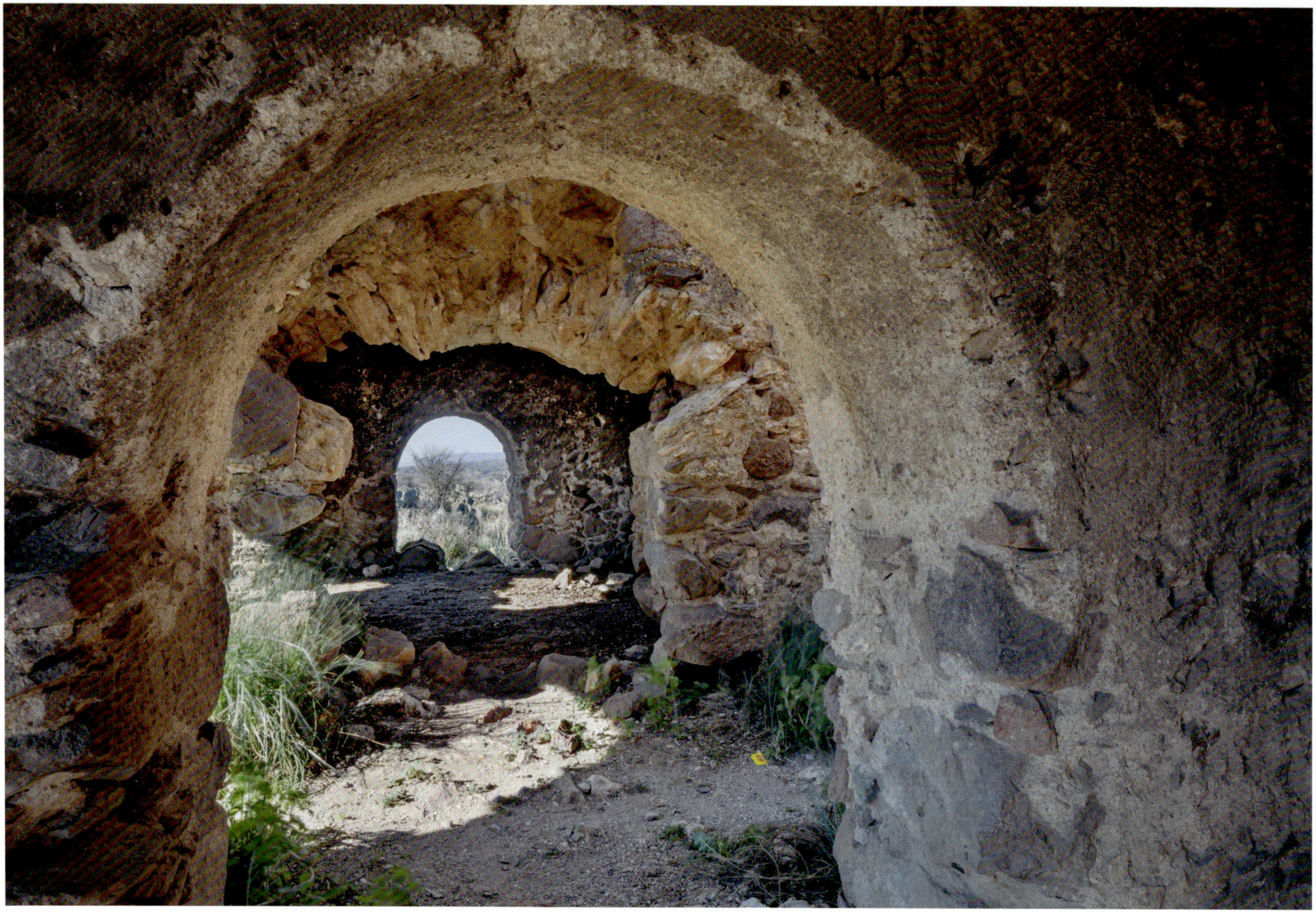

Silver Smelter at Santa Brígida, Mineral de Pozos, Guanajuato State, Mexico. This image shows the smelter oven interiors, or *hornos*, where silver was smelted from ores mined and processed nearby. Built in 1595, the ovens today remain solid, remarkably intact.

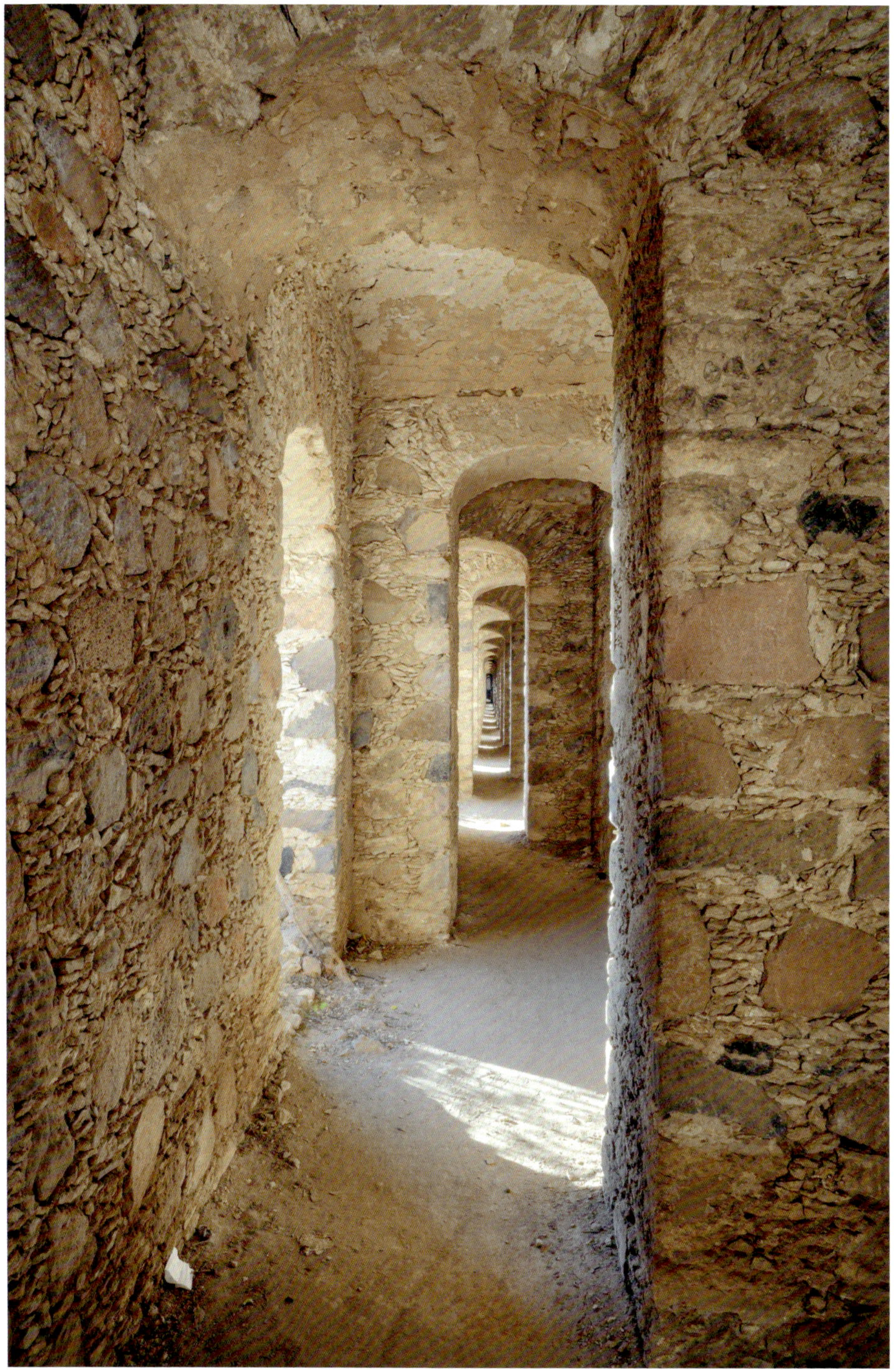

Santa Brígida, Mineral de Pozos, Mexico. Like the twentieth-century Guggenheim operations along the Camino Real de Tierra Adentro in Mexico and the United States, Santa Brígida (also on the Camino) was a major source of local wealth centuries before Europeans commandeered the mines. This seven-hundred-foot-long *respirador* is a seventeenth-century remnant, part of the area's coke production infrastructure and essential to the smelting of silver. This site, in the Mineral de Pozos mining district, was economically viable for four centuries, through the 1920s.

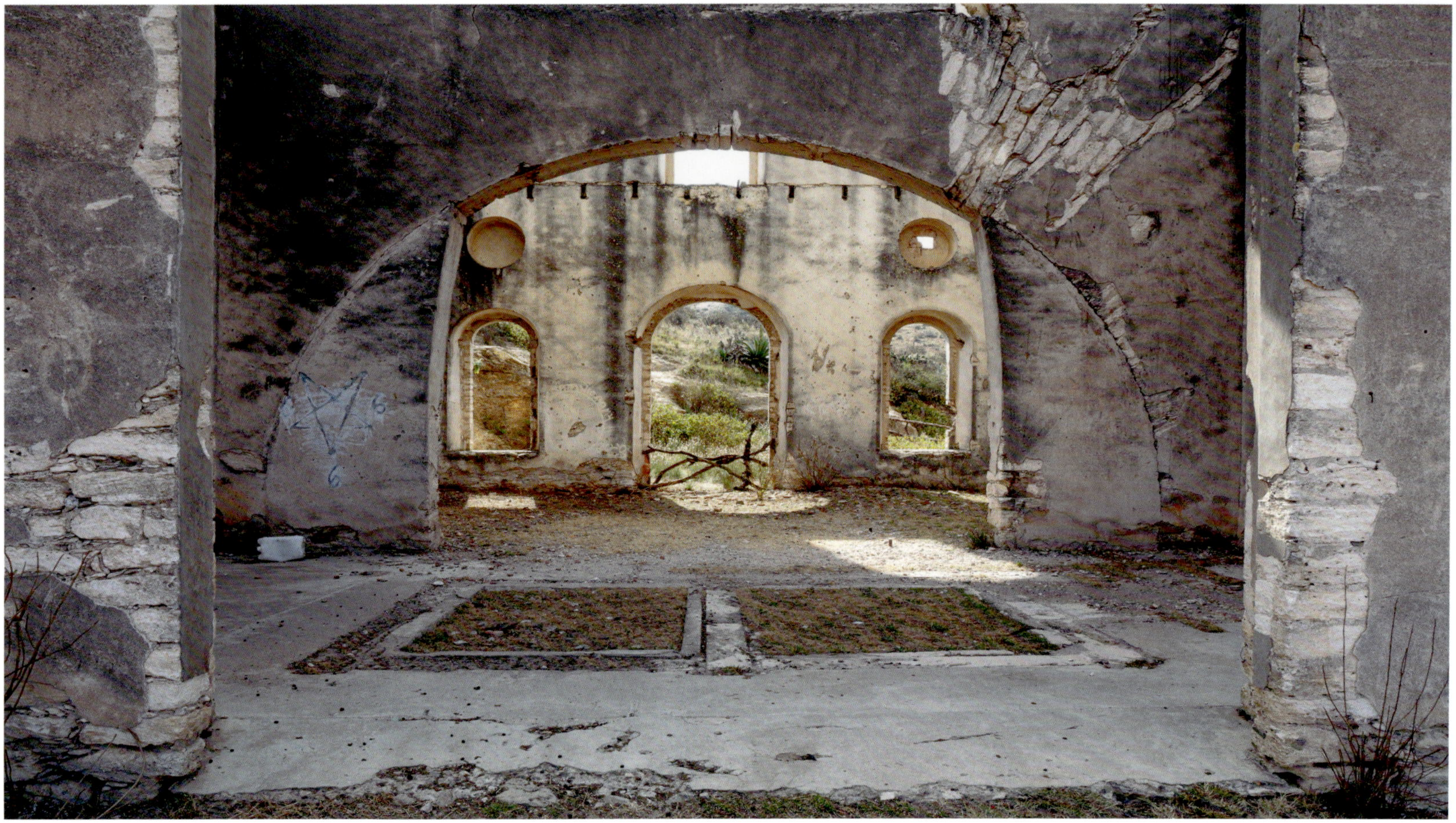

Ex-Hacienda San Baldomero, Mineral de Pozos, Guanajuato State, Mexico. This image shows one of several architectural ruins in this once-thriving nineteenth-century mining district. Founded in the 1880s atop silver lodes that had been productive since before the Spanish conquest, the Hacienda was abandoned in the 1920s.

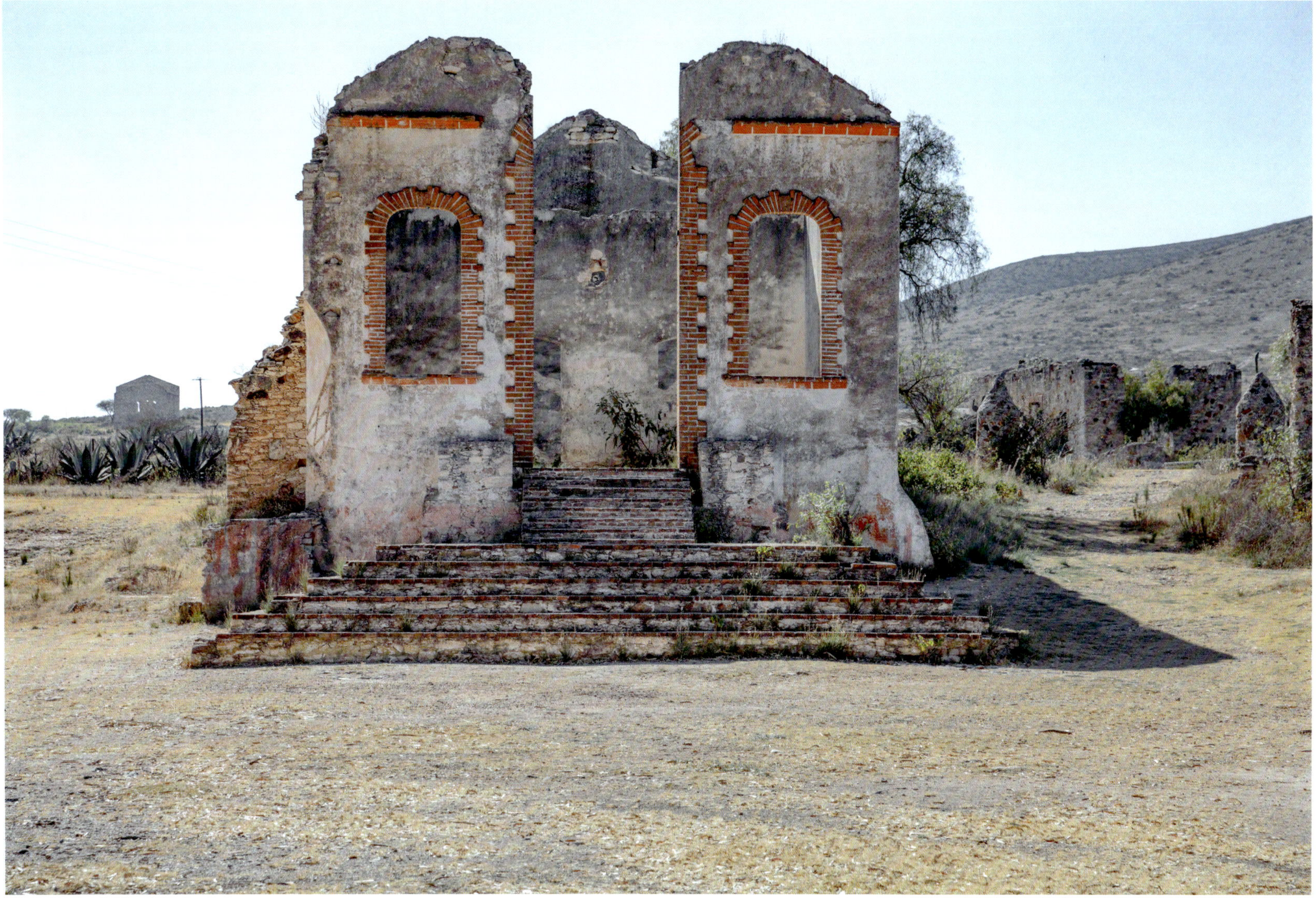

Ex-Hacienda El Triángulo, Mineral de Pozos, Guanajuato, Mexico. This is one of several ruins on the ex-hacienda site. This northeast-facing elevation overlooks the former plaza, a typical feature of these purpose-built "company towns."

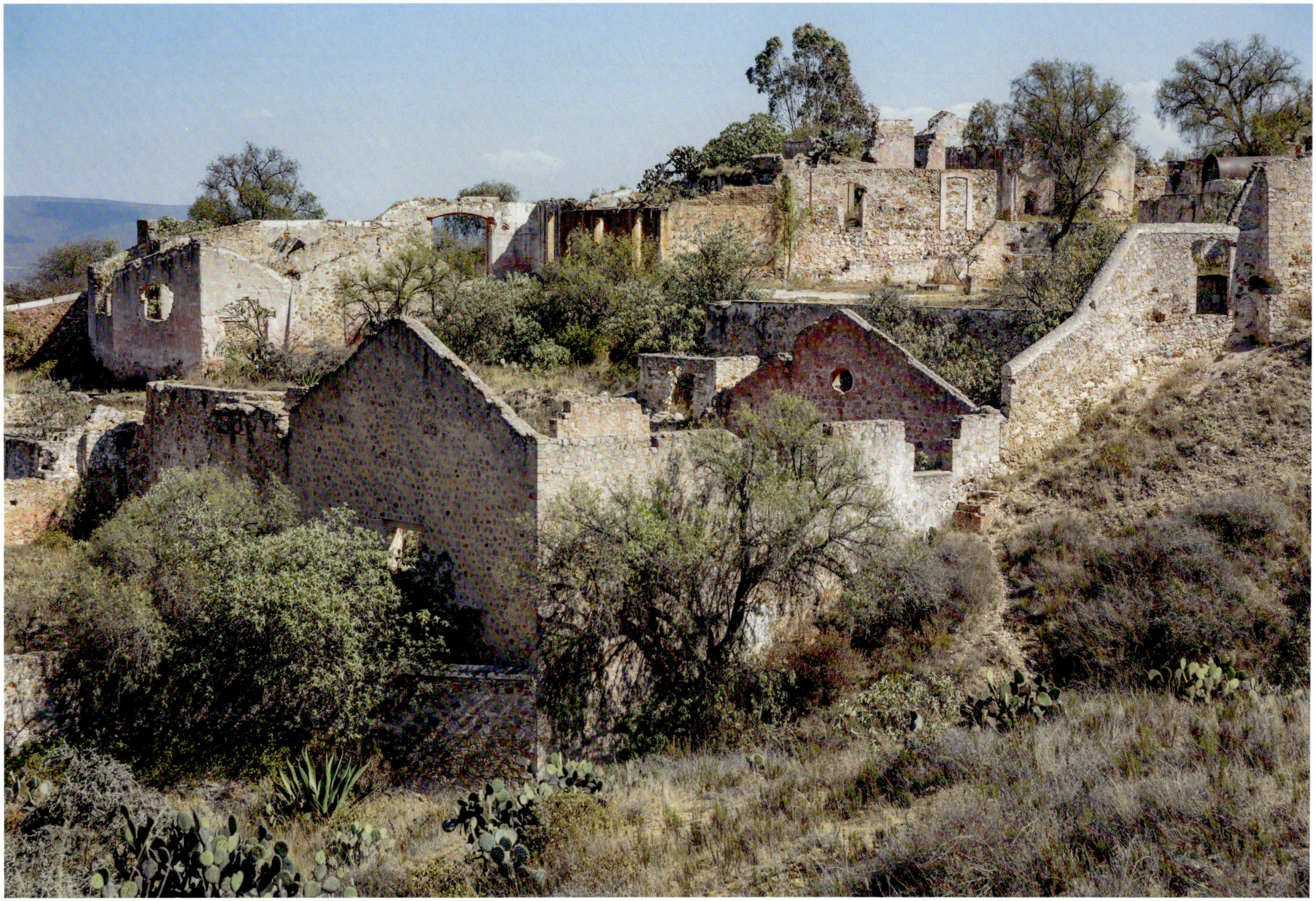

Ex-hacienda El Triángulo, Mineral de Pozos, Mexico. This long view of the hillside site illustrates the reliance of the ore-milling process on local topography. Ore was fed from uphill to the arrastra pits below, on the far left. Established in the late nineteenth century by French business interests, El Triángulo's underground mines operated until 1923, when an active bore accidentally penetrated the shaft wall into the aquifer, immediately and catastrophically flooding miles of tunnels beyond even modern pumps' ability to drain them. The mines closed, and most of the population moved away.

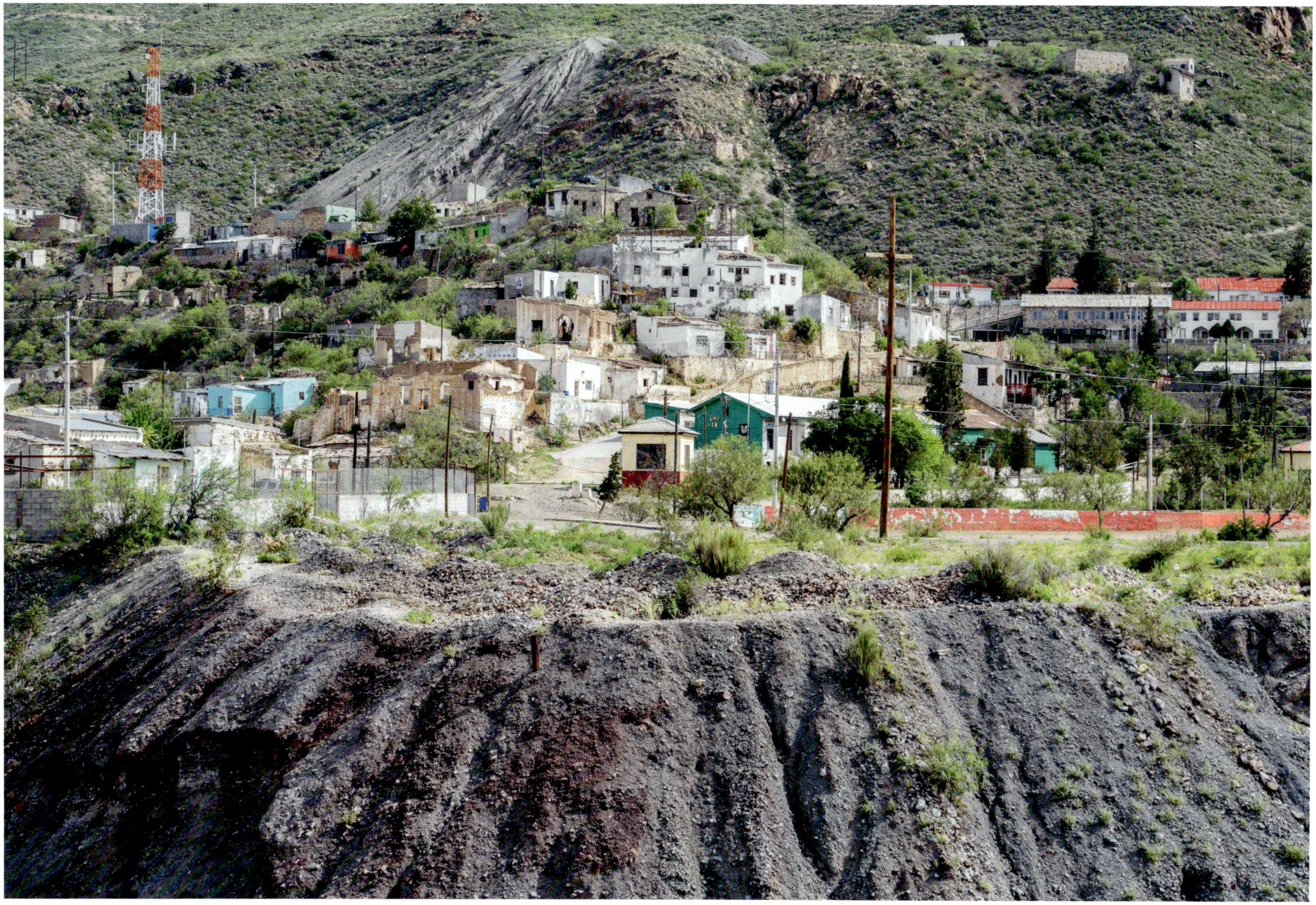

Santa Eulalia Mining District, Chihuahua State, Mexico. Santo Domingo in the Santa Eulalia (Potosí) mining district southeast of Ciudad Chihuahua lies atop silver mining tunnels first worked in preconquest centuries by the region's Indigenous population. The current settlement is built into a hillside, on a tailings dump dating from the nineteenth century. The red wall at the right of center is the north edge of a baseball diamond built in the 1940s for Guggenheims' ASARCO workers.

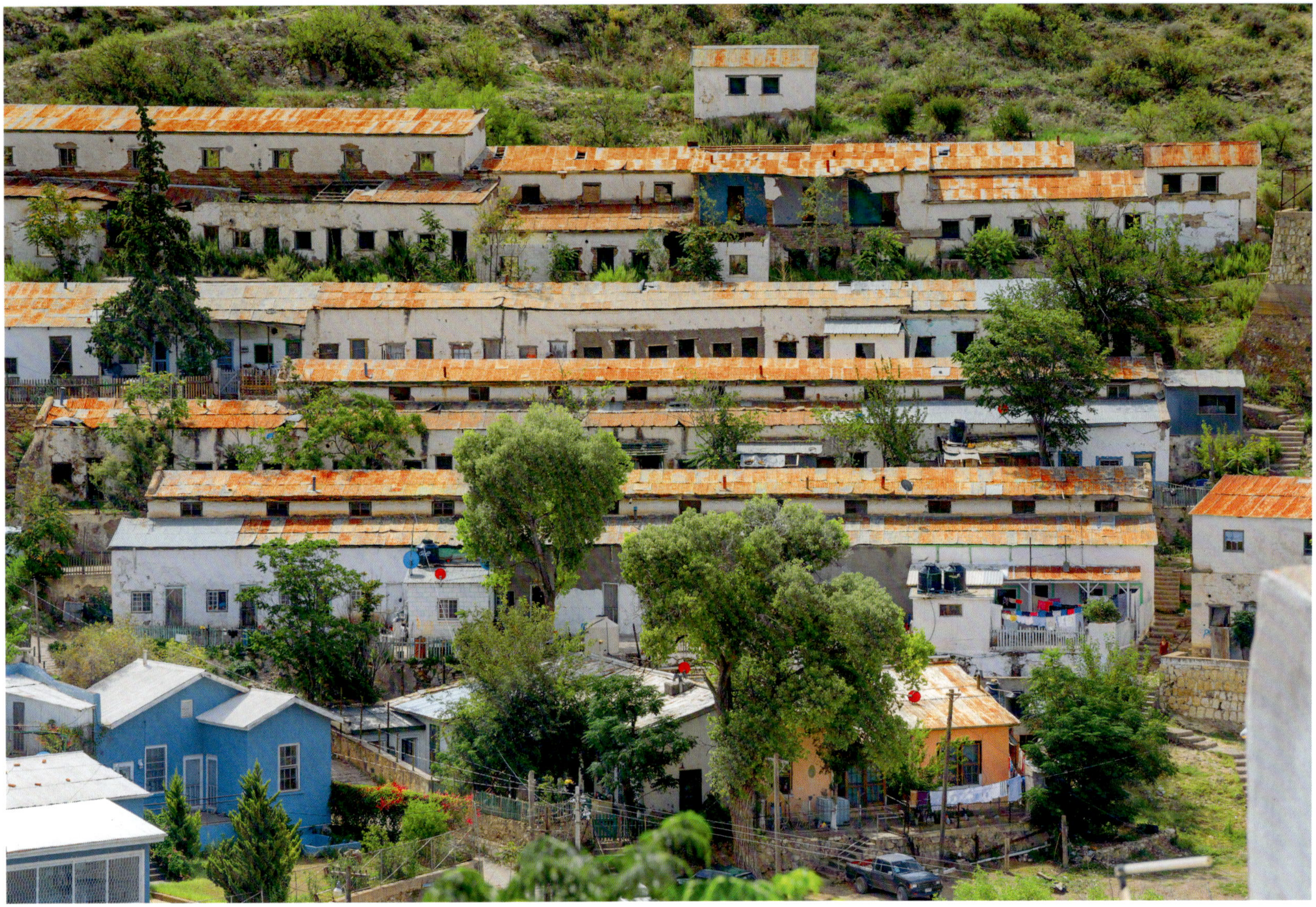

Santo Domingo, Santa Eulalia Mining District, Chihuahua State, Mexico. Worker housing, mostly of adobe, lines the steep hillside overlooking the company town of Santo Domingo. The narrow canyon and its mines are known by many names: Potosí (after the famous historic Bolivian mines), Santa Eulalia, and Santo Domingo. Before Europeans appropriated the mines in the 1500s, local Indians had worked them for centuries. More recently, unable to settle a labor dispute, Guggenheim's ASARCO abandoned its operations here in the 1940s. Some mining, however, continues today.

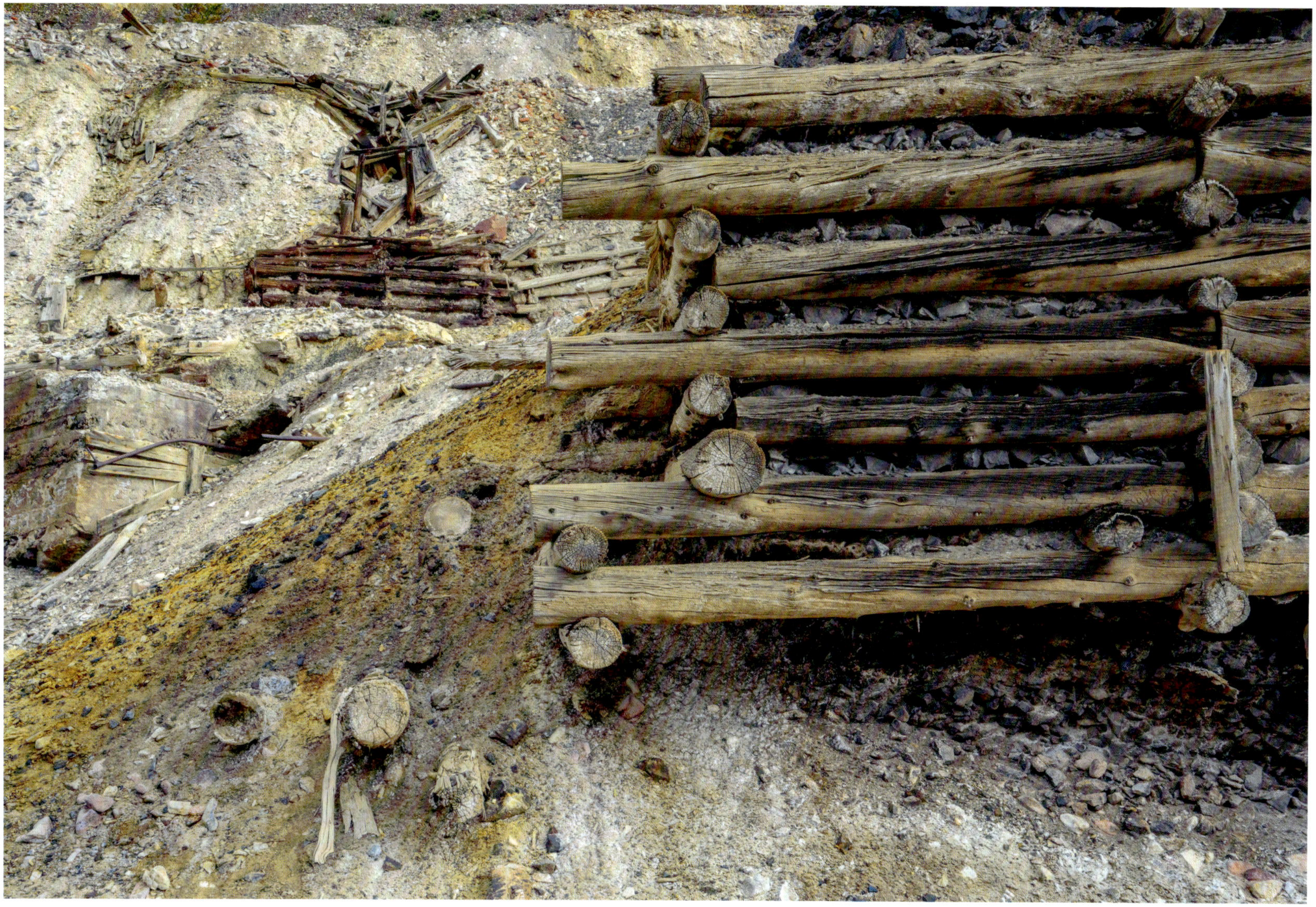

AY and Minnie Mines, Leadville, Colorado. This 140-year-old partly intact timber cribbing at the AY and Minnie Mines is one of only a few remnants of a storied industrial landscape. In the 1880s M. Guggenheim Sons purchased their first modest claims here, high in the Colorado Rockies in the upper California Gulch five miles east of Leadville. The venture prospered, giving the company the confidence, and the cash, to launch an international mining empire, which dominated the industry worldwide for nearly a century.

These 4 × 5 in. photographs, based on Historic American Engineering Record (HAER) protocols, were made during the first two days I had access to the property, in 2010. That was also the last time the OSHA safety officer allowed me to lug the hefty view camera and tripod around his active demolition site. After that I was to use only a smaller tripod and more-nimble digital and film cameras. I made these large-format pictures anticipating a full-scale HAER documentation project. But prohibited from shooting with the large-format camera, and without support from a sponsor or client, reality intervened, leading (surprisingly) to an even more expansive and gratifying project.

The first five photographs are clues to ASARCO's evolution. By 2010 this building's site had been the center of ASARCO's El Paso operations for over a century. In the 1880s a small adobe structure was the first smelter building. Over decades it evolved and expanded, becoming eventually the office space from which ASARCO's demolition was administered.

On the two-hundred-acre smelter tract, architecture ranged in scale from small corrugated toolsheds to the 828-foot tall stack. Even with familiarity and visual clues, it seems implausible that the main stack was half a mile behind and twenty stories taller than its elegant partner (see p. 165).

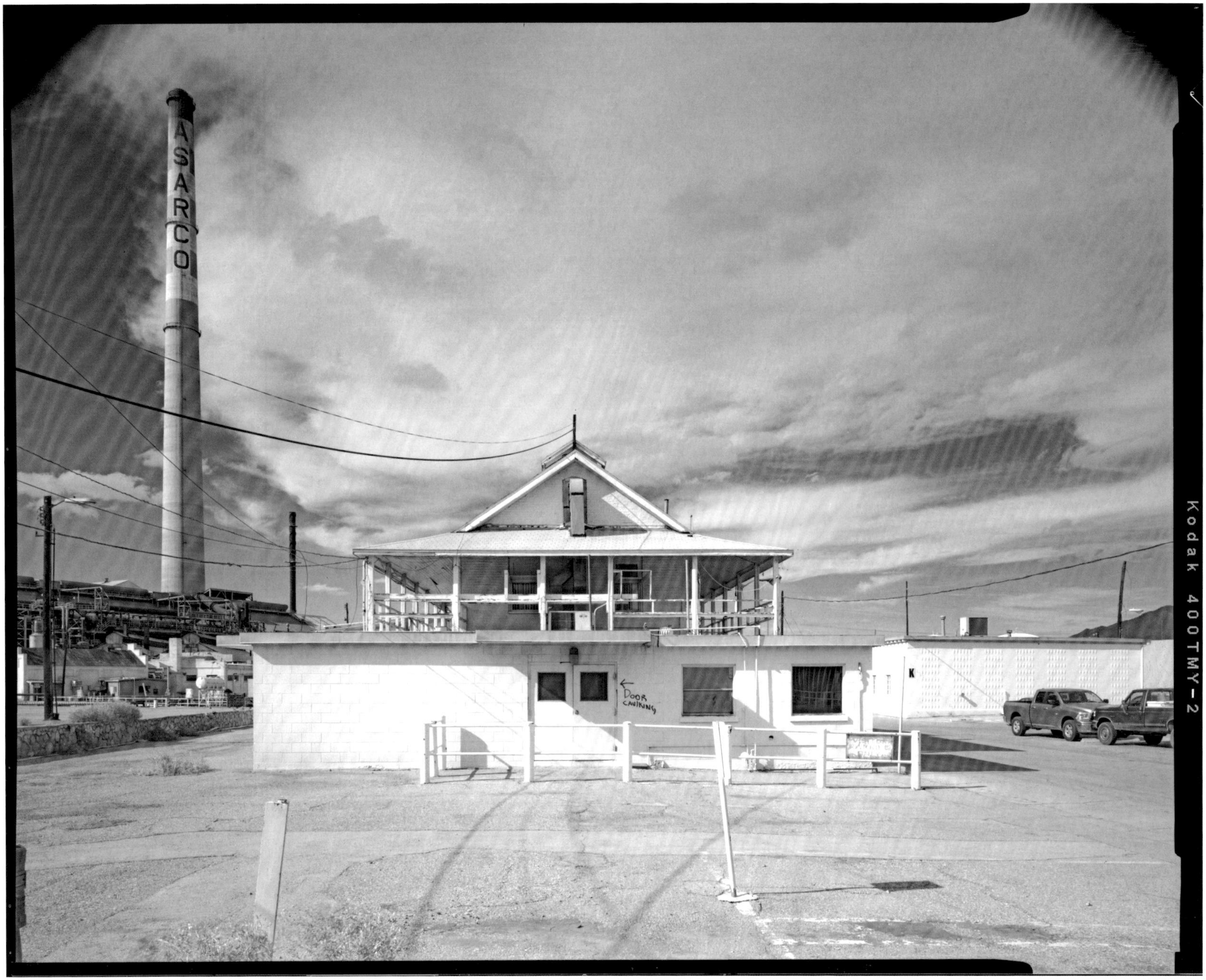
ASARCO
DOOR CAULKING
K
Kodak 400TMY-2

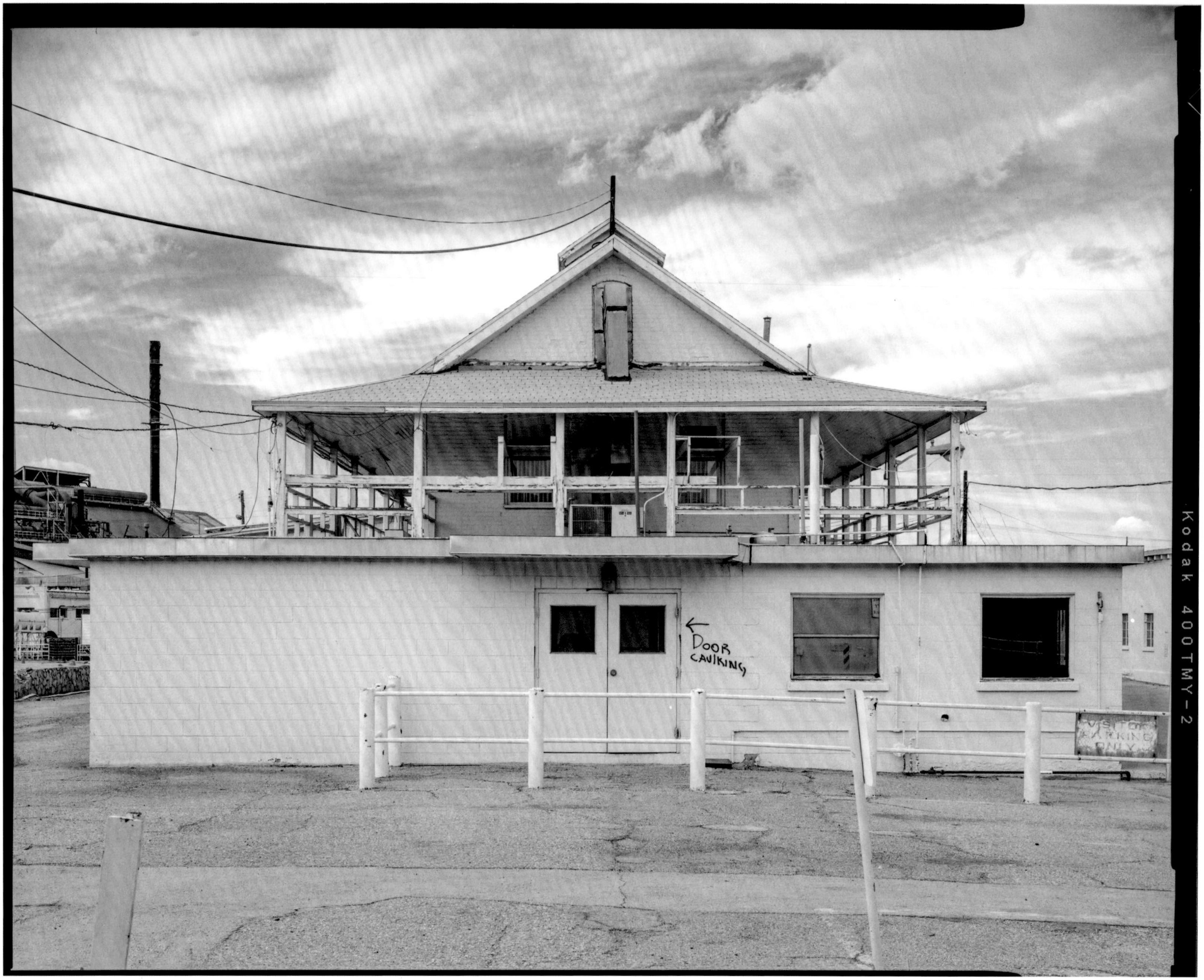
DOOR
CAULKING
Kodak 400TMY-2

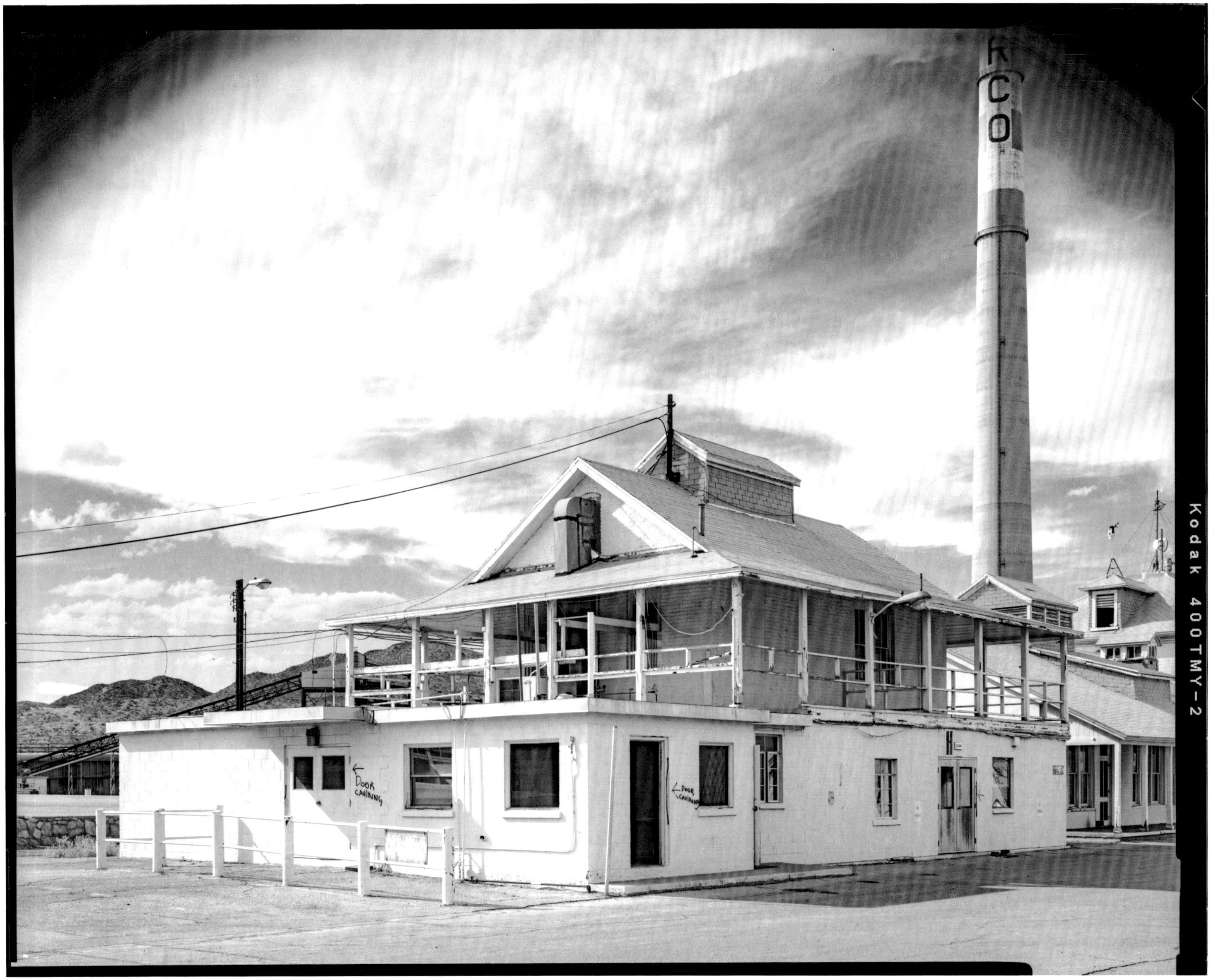
Kodak 400TMY-2

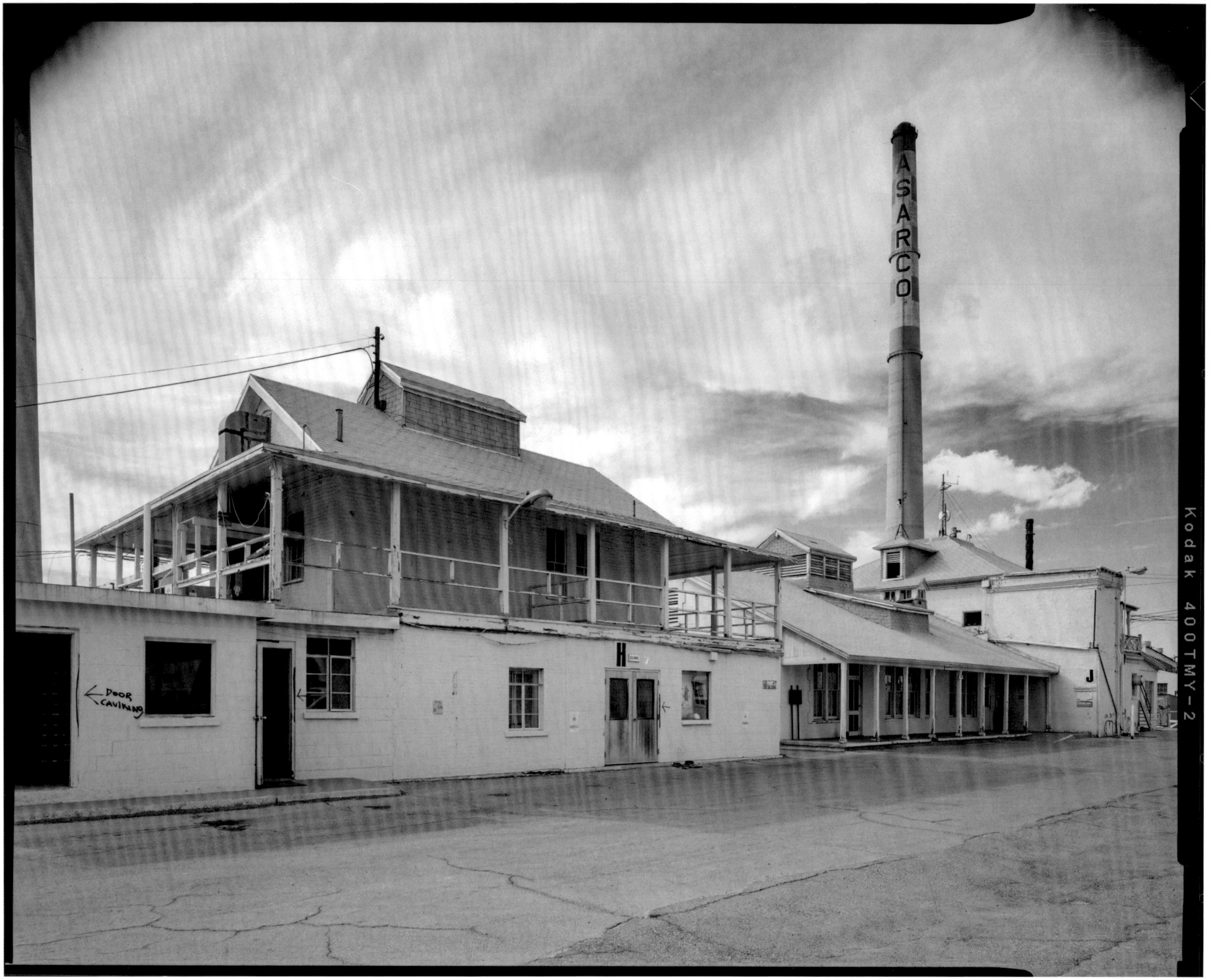
ASARCO
H
J
Kodak 400TMY-2

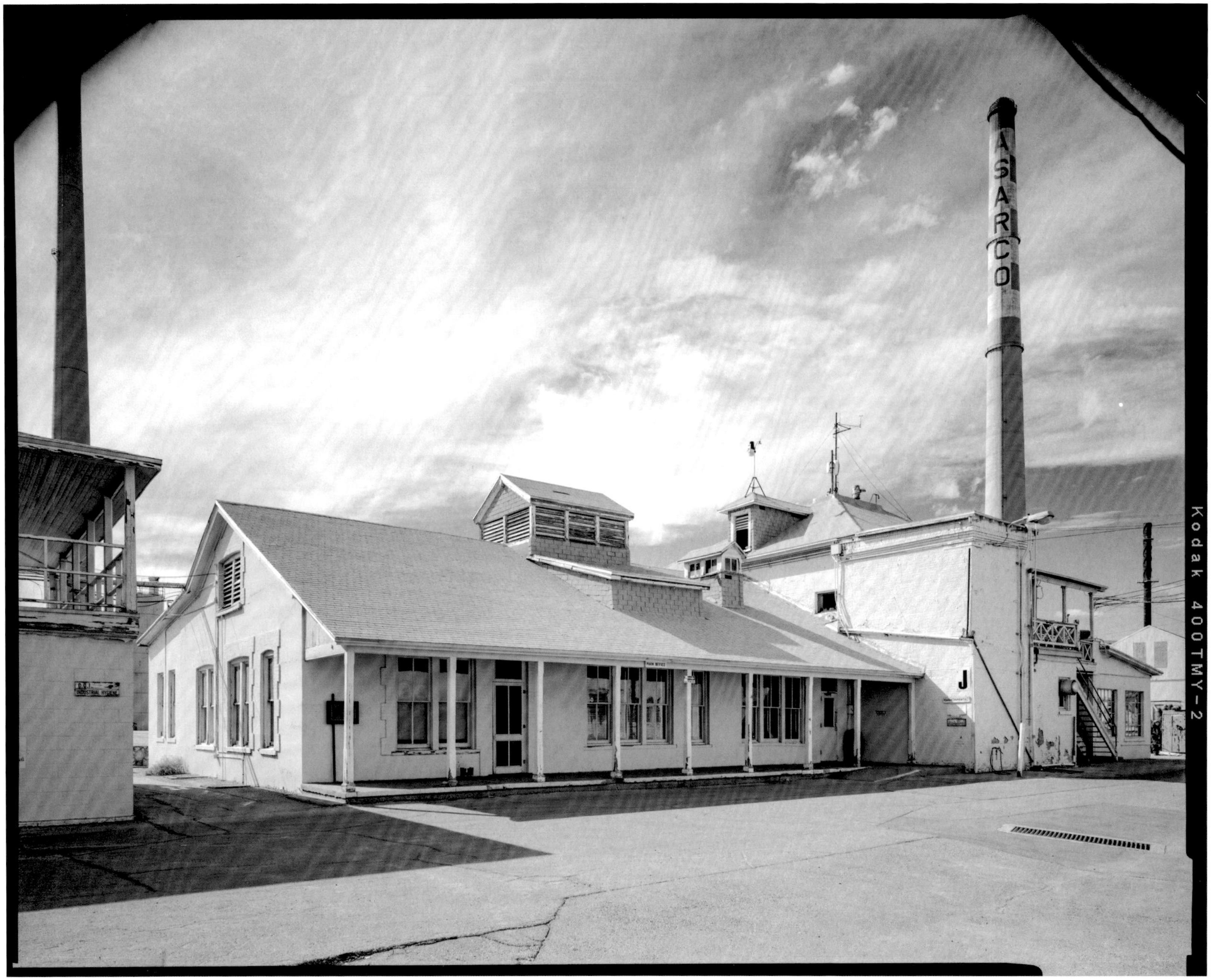
ASARCO
J
Kodak 400TMY-2

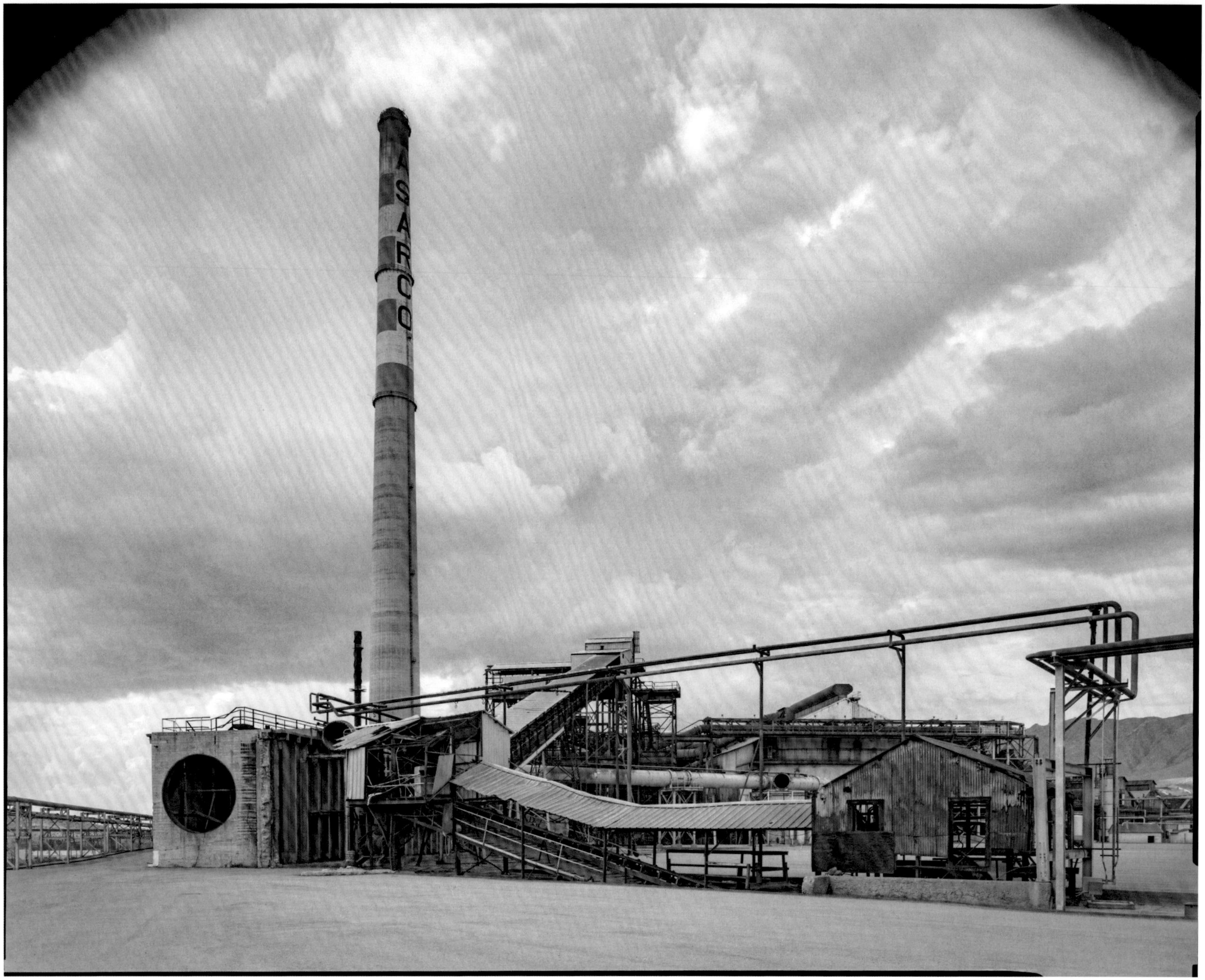
ASARCO

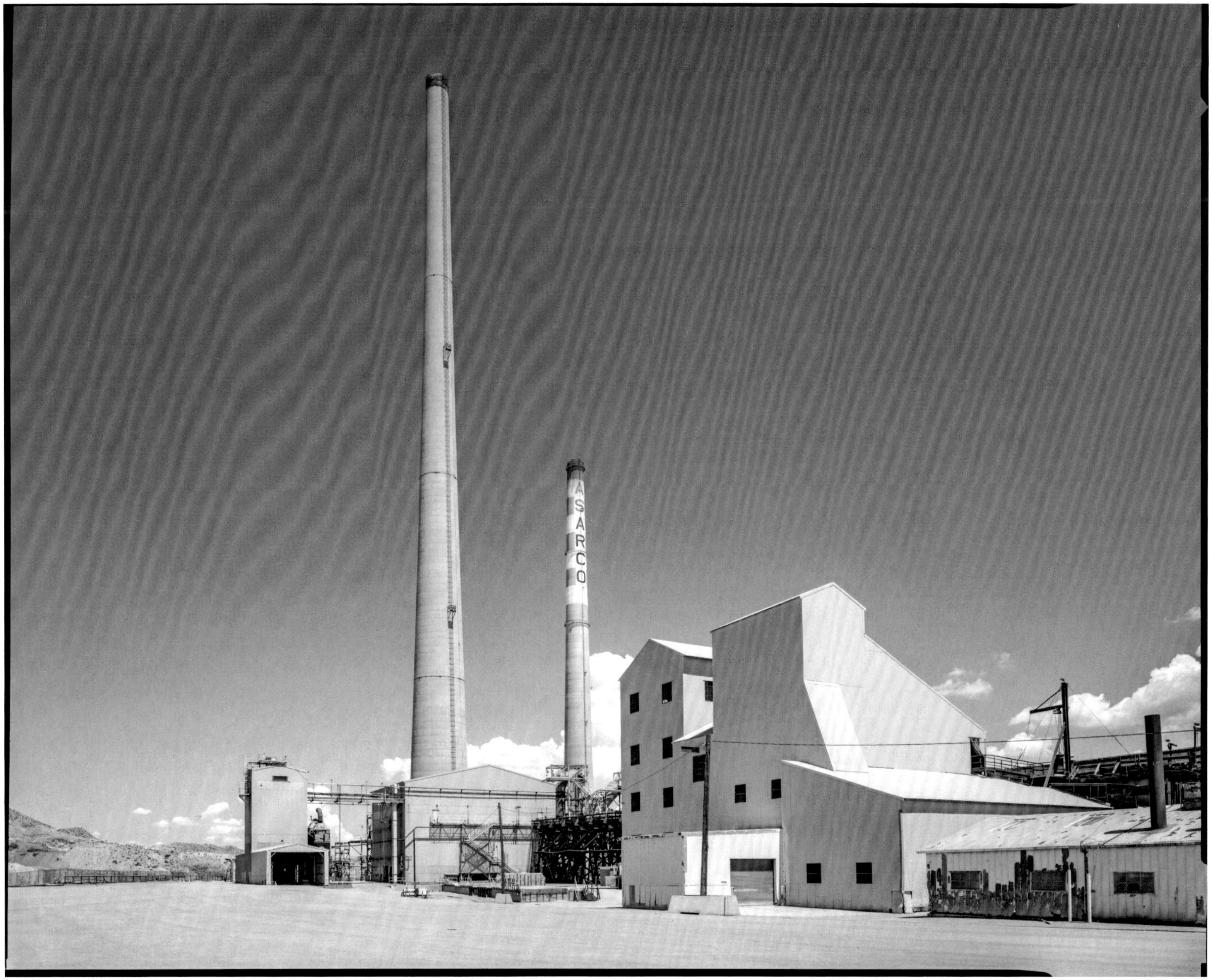
ASARCO

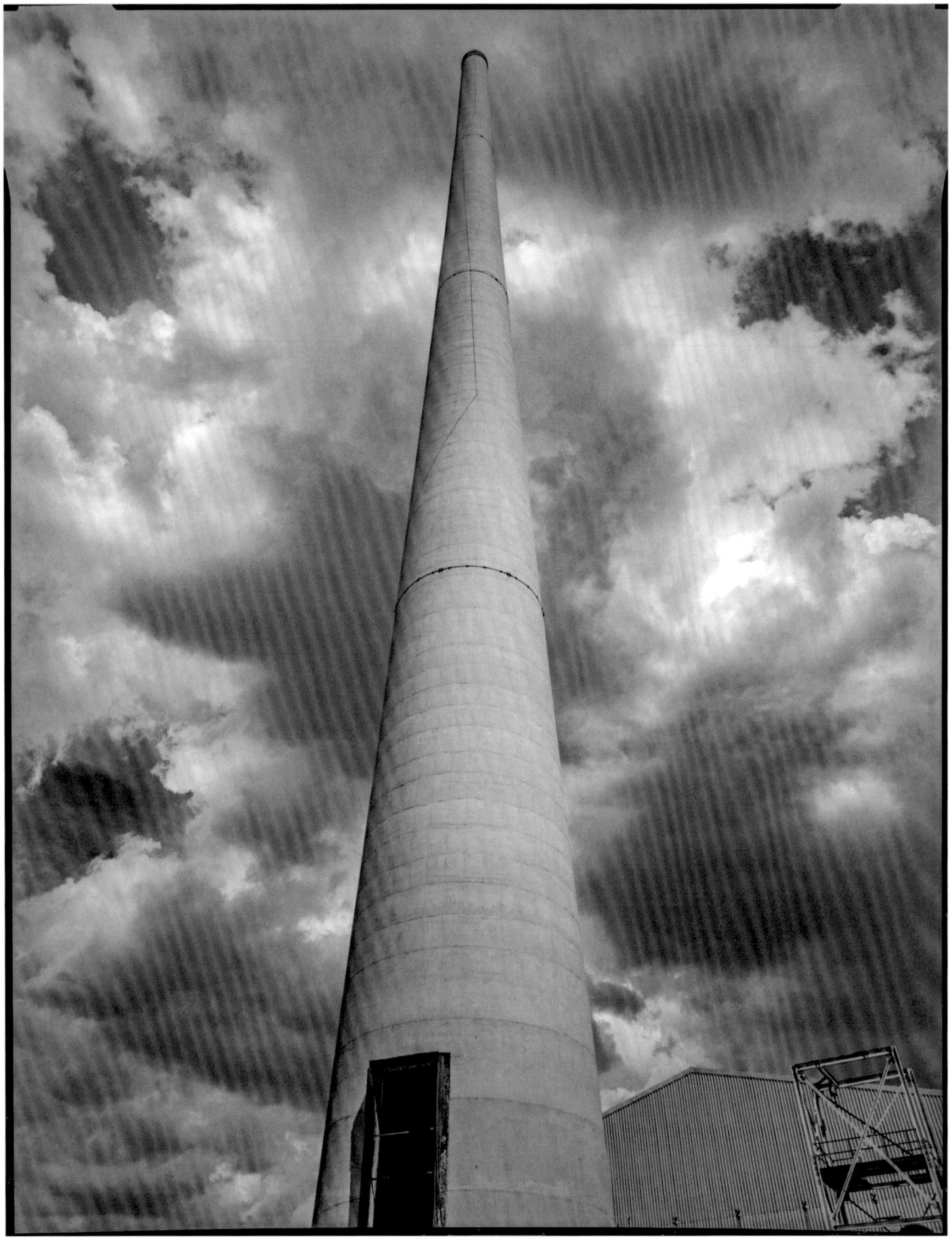

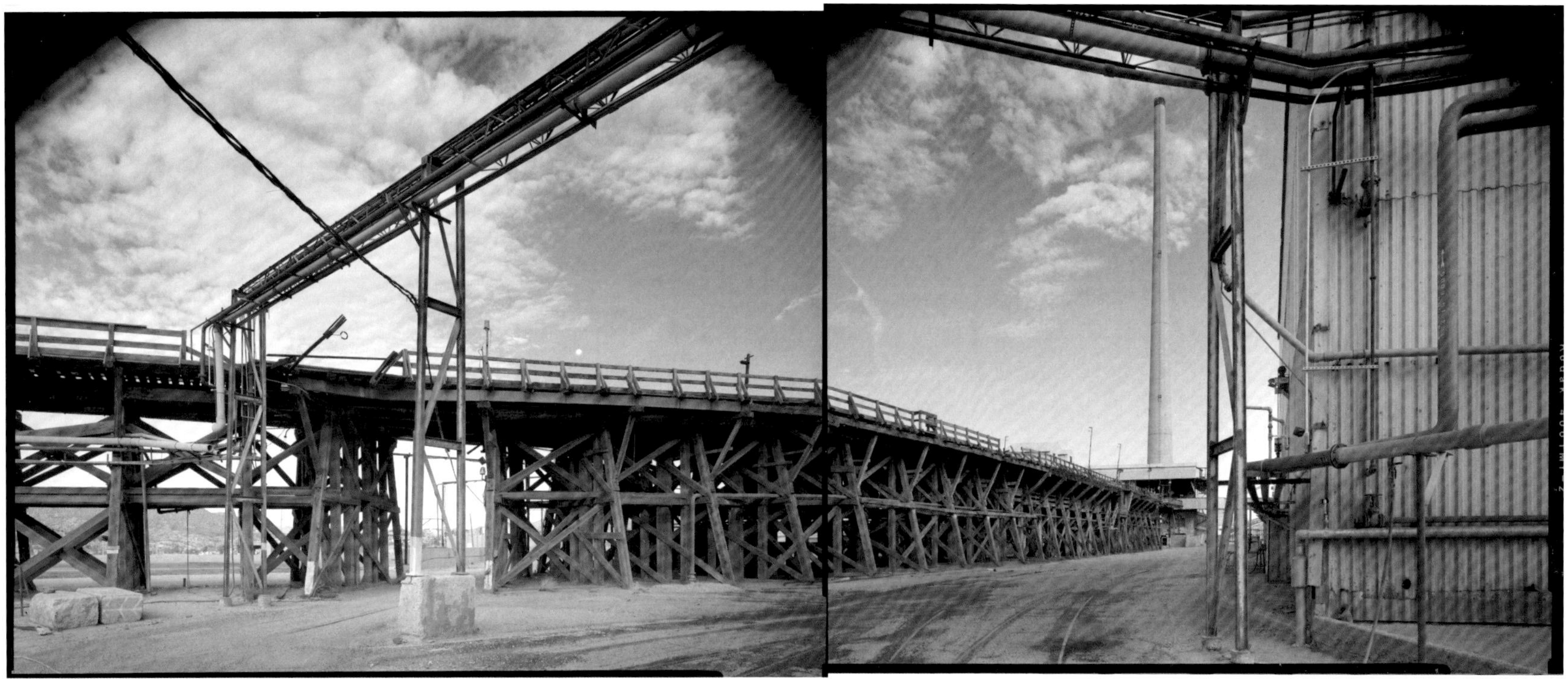

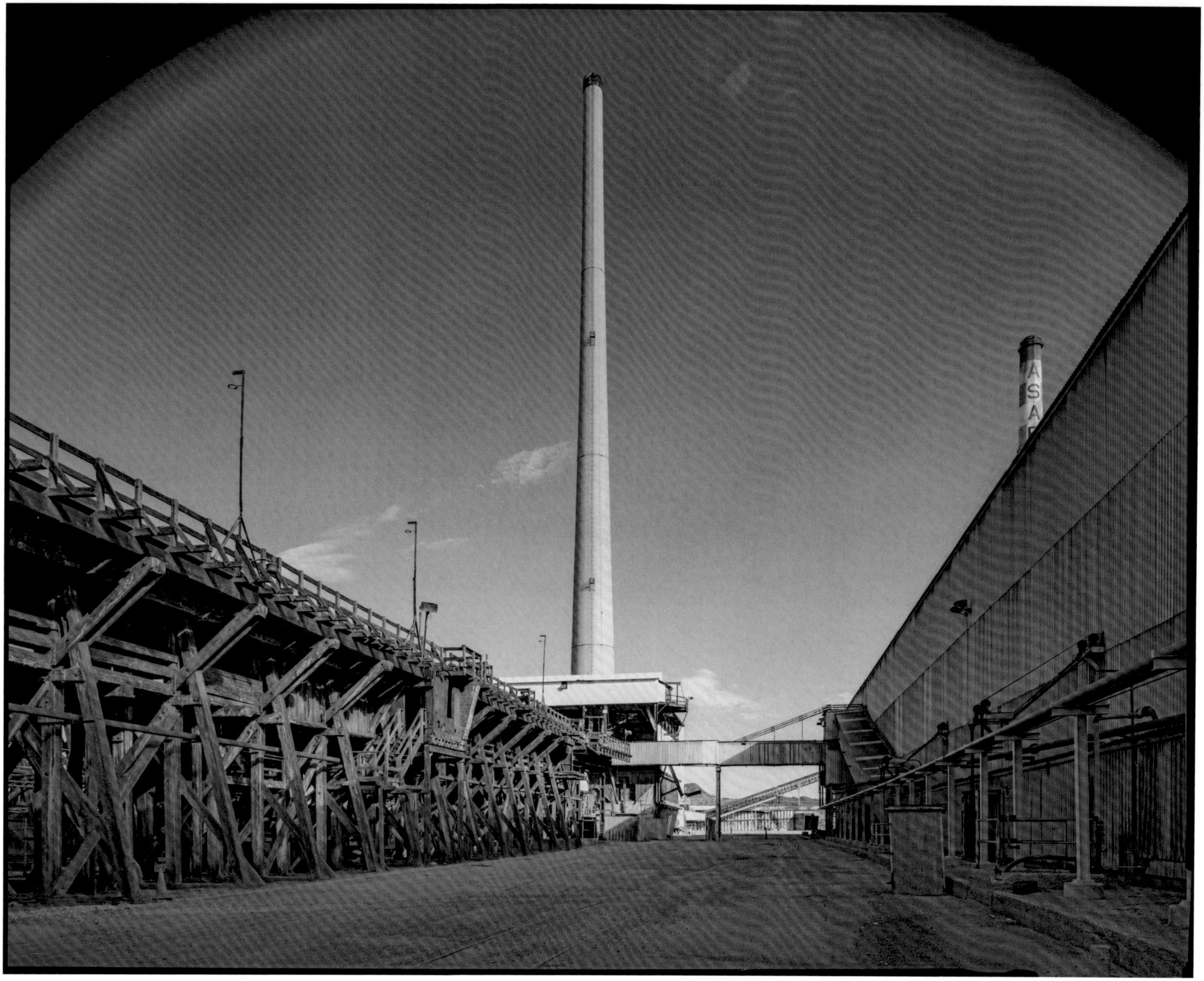
ASA

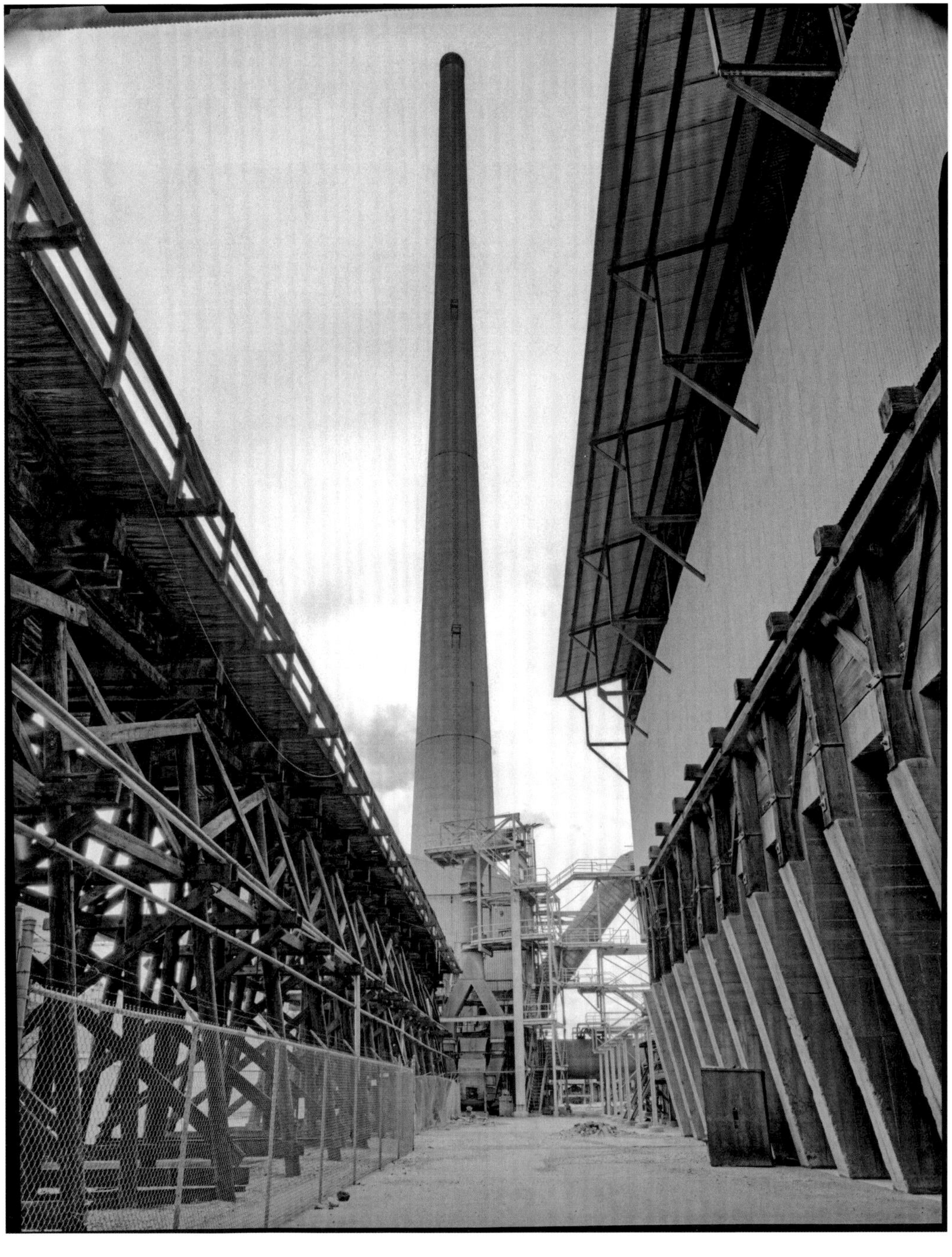

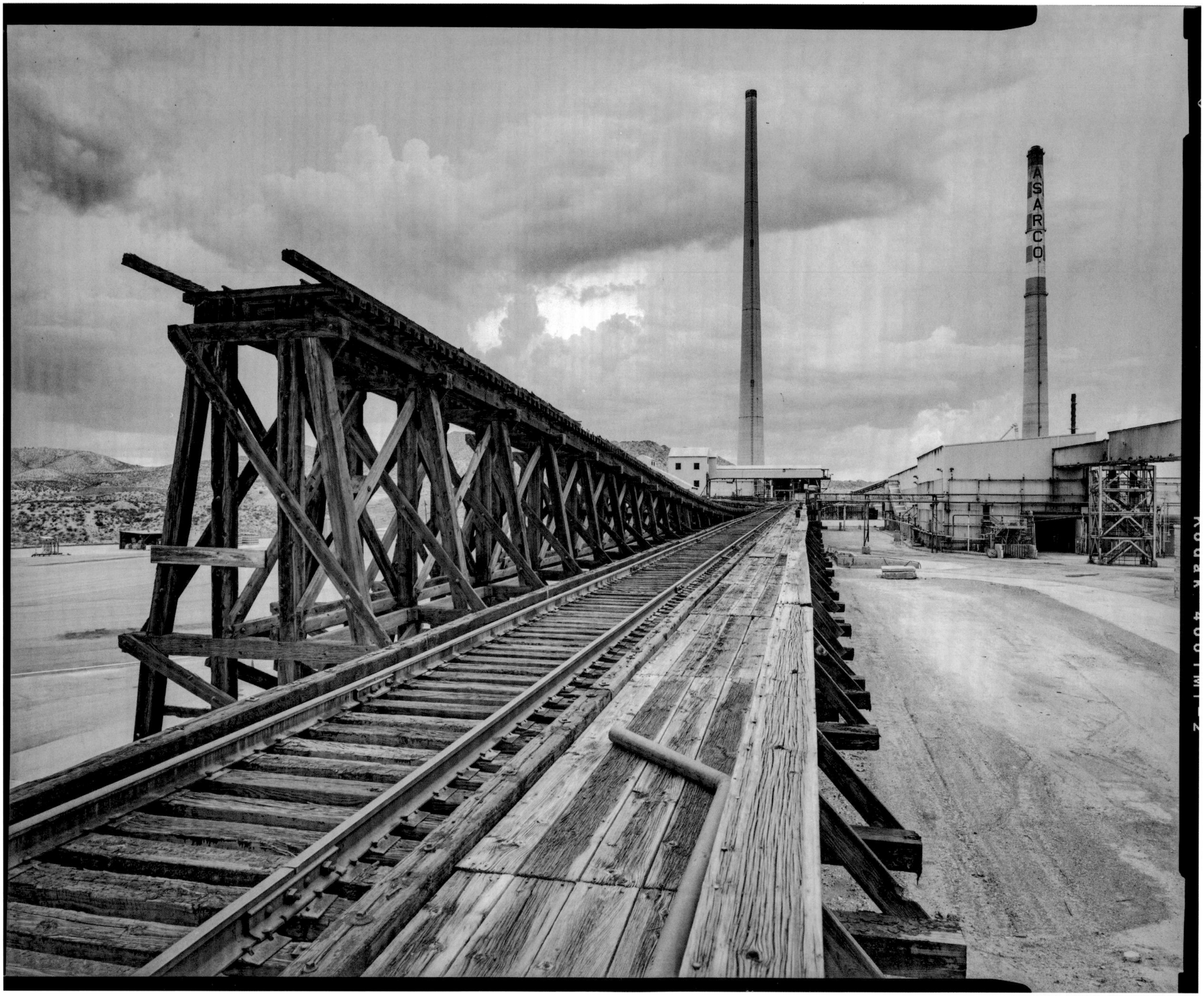
ASARCO
Kodak 400TMY-2

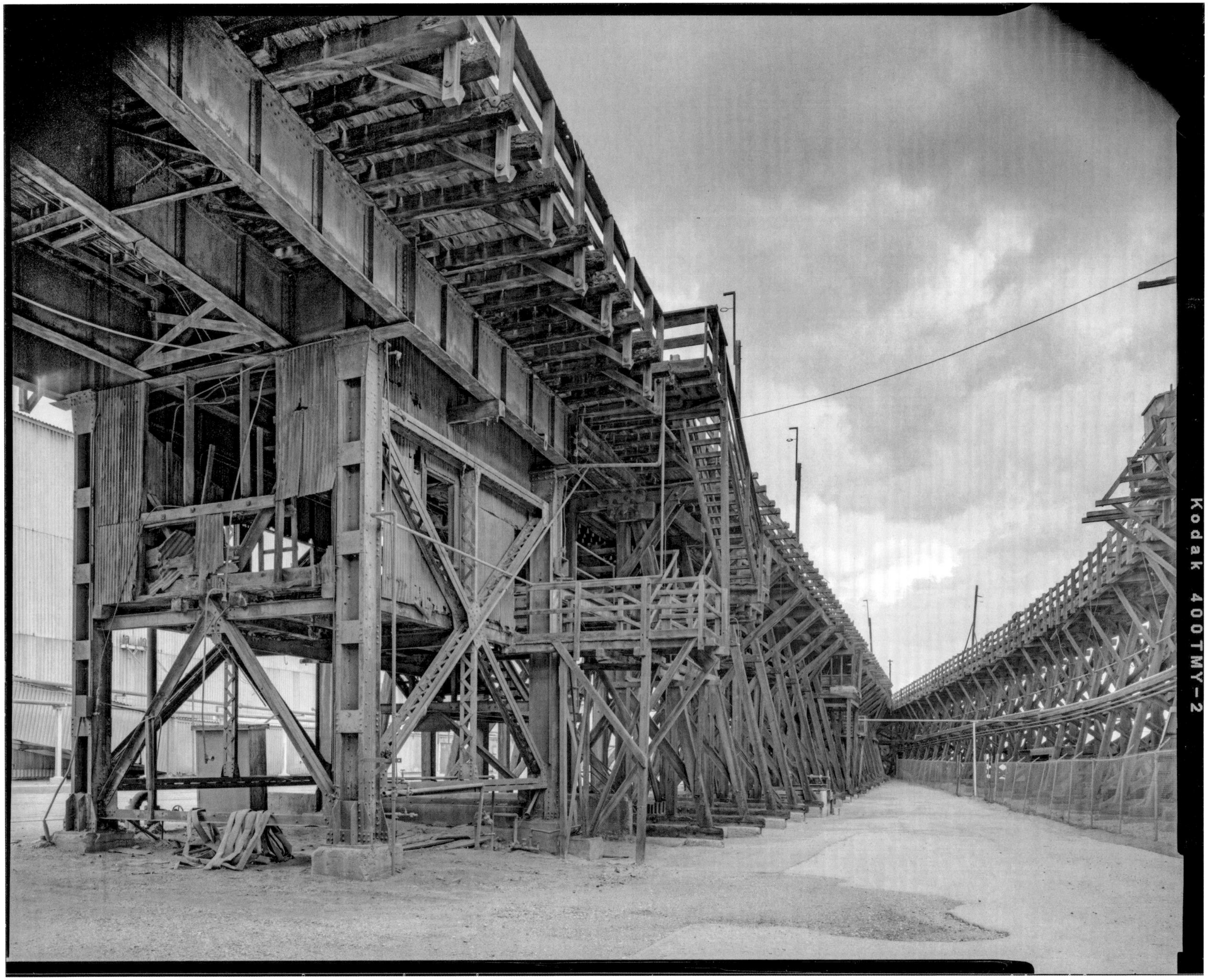
Kodak 400TMY-2

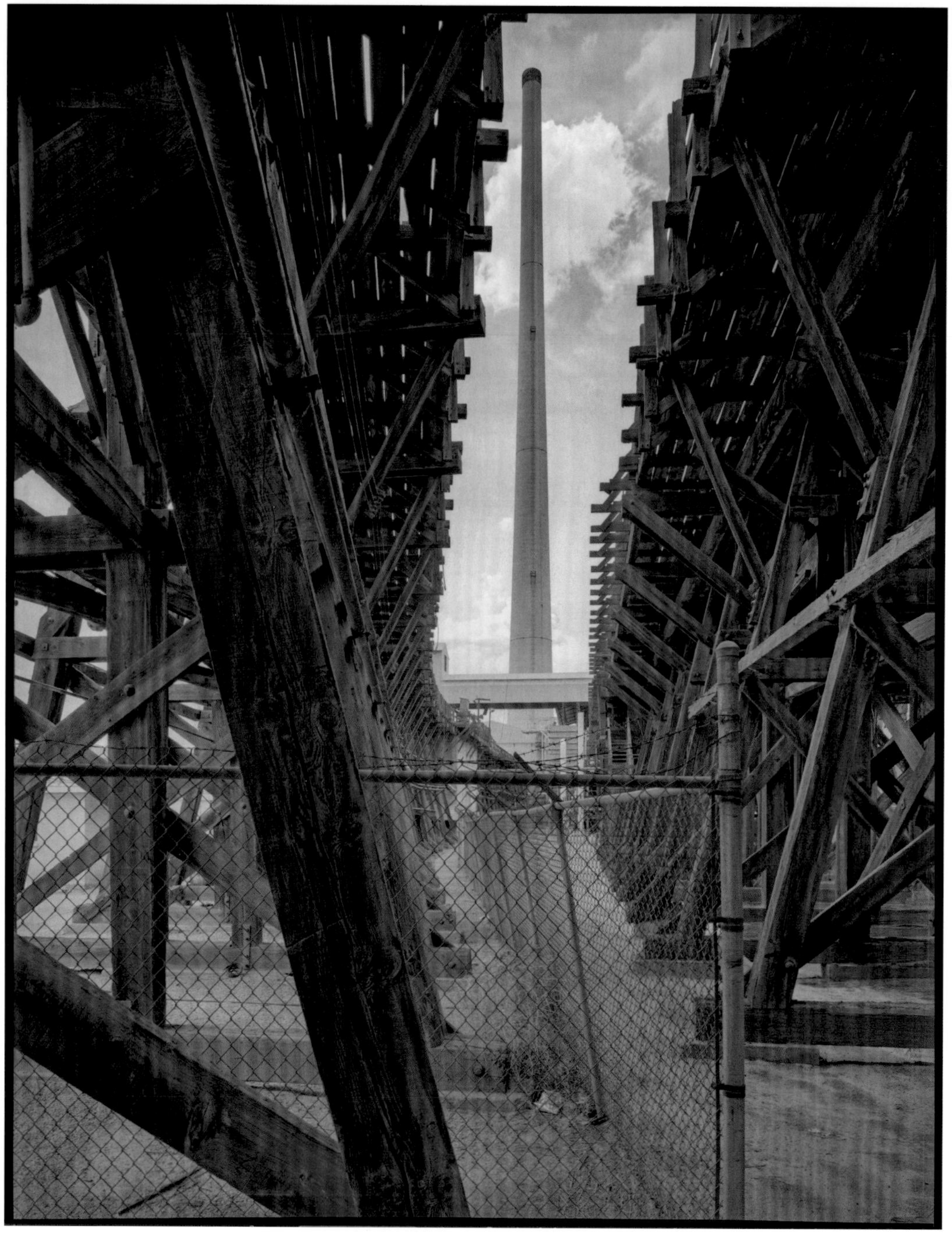

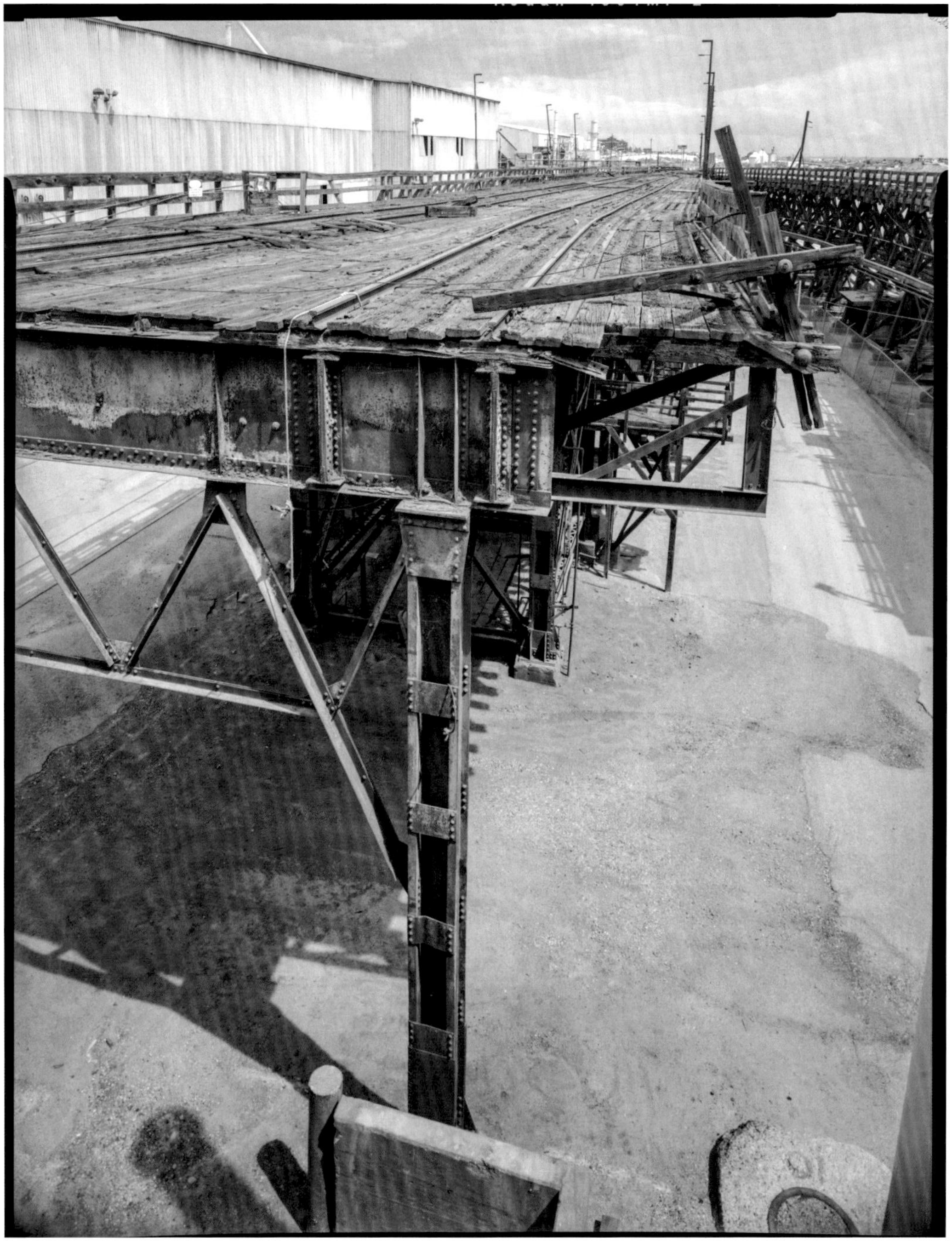

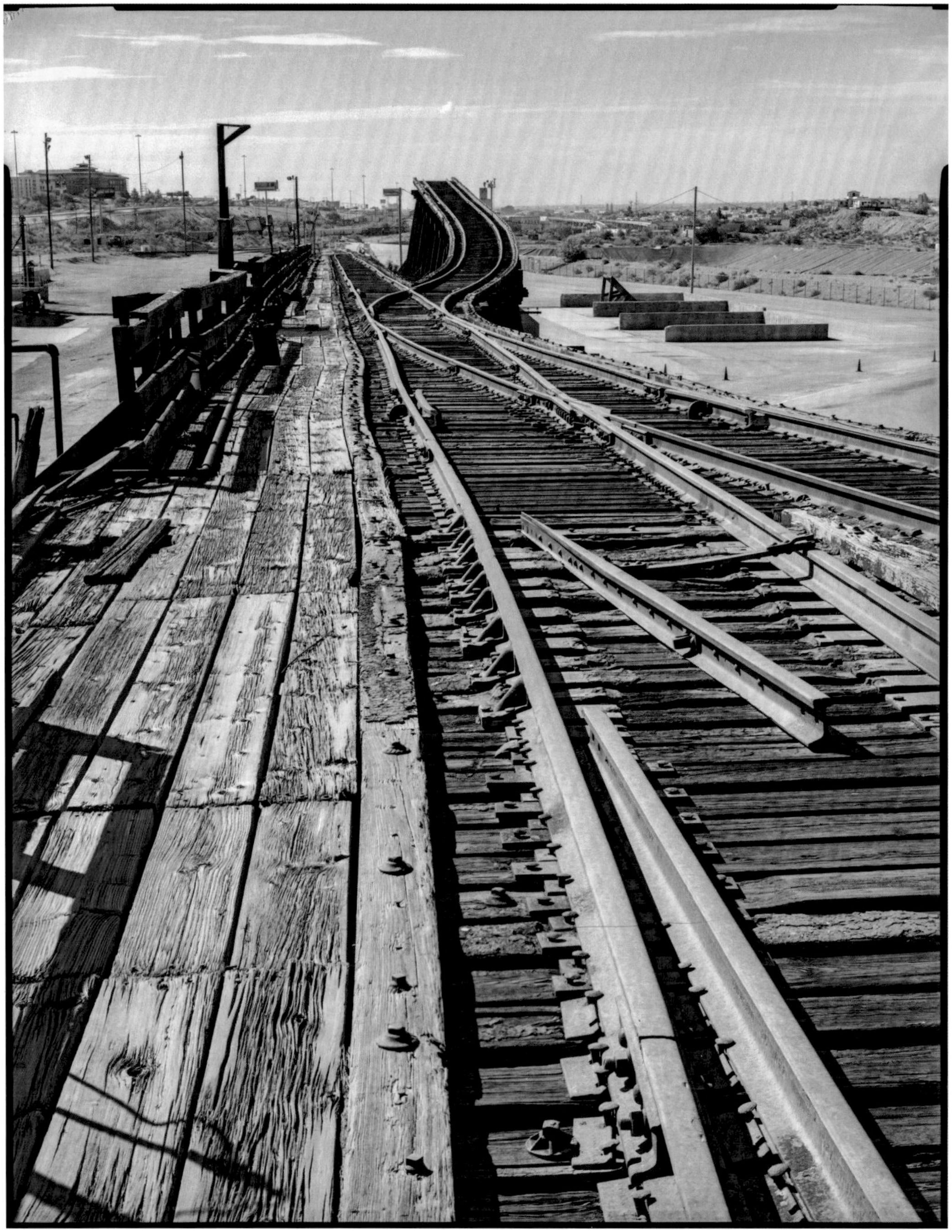

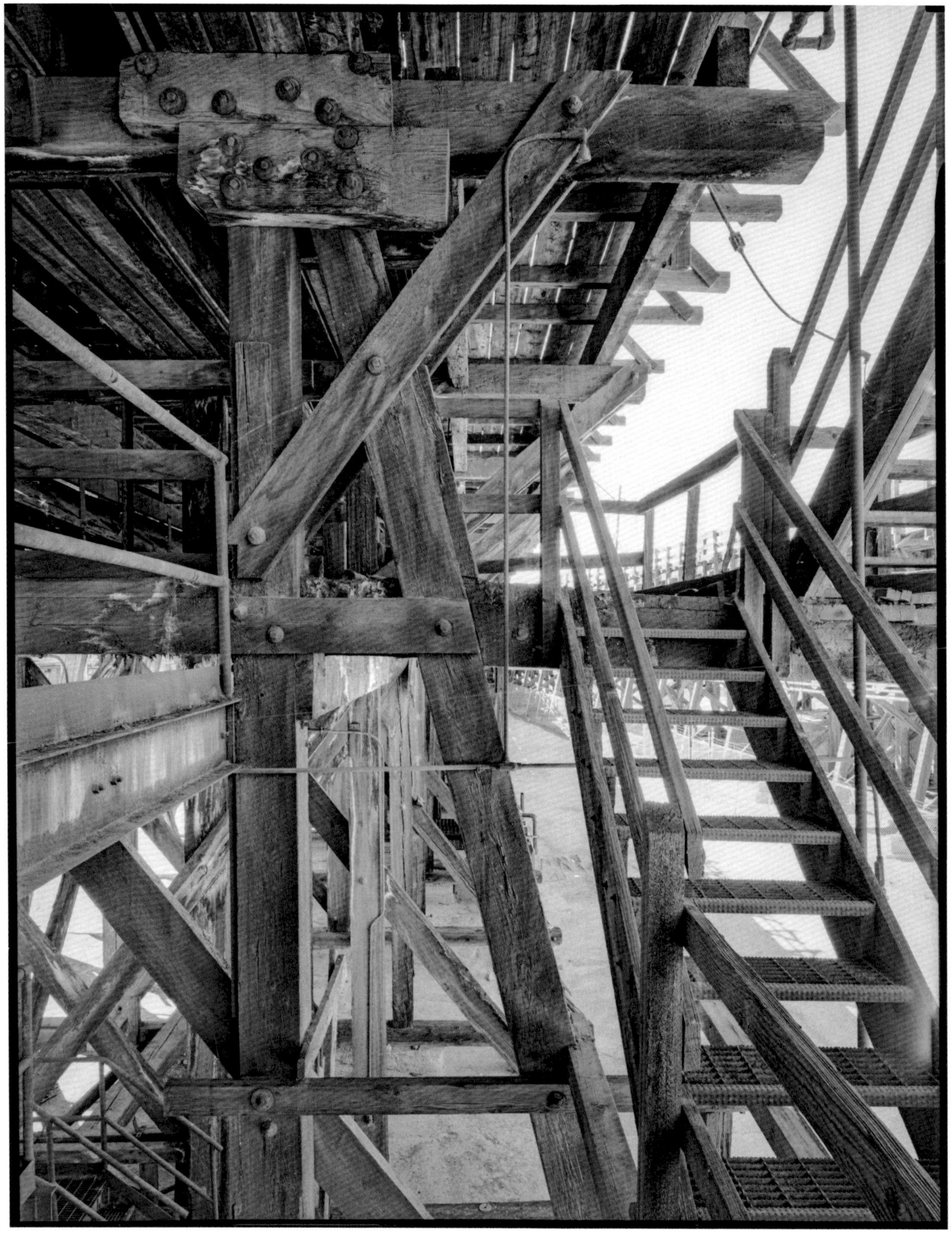

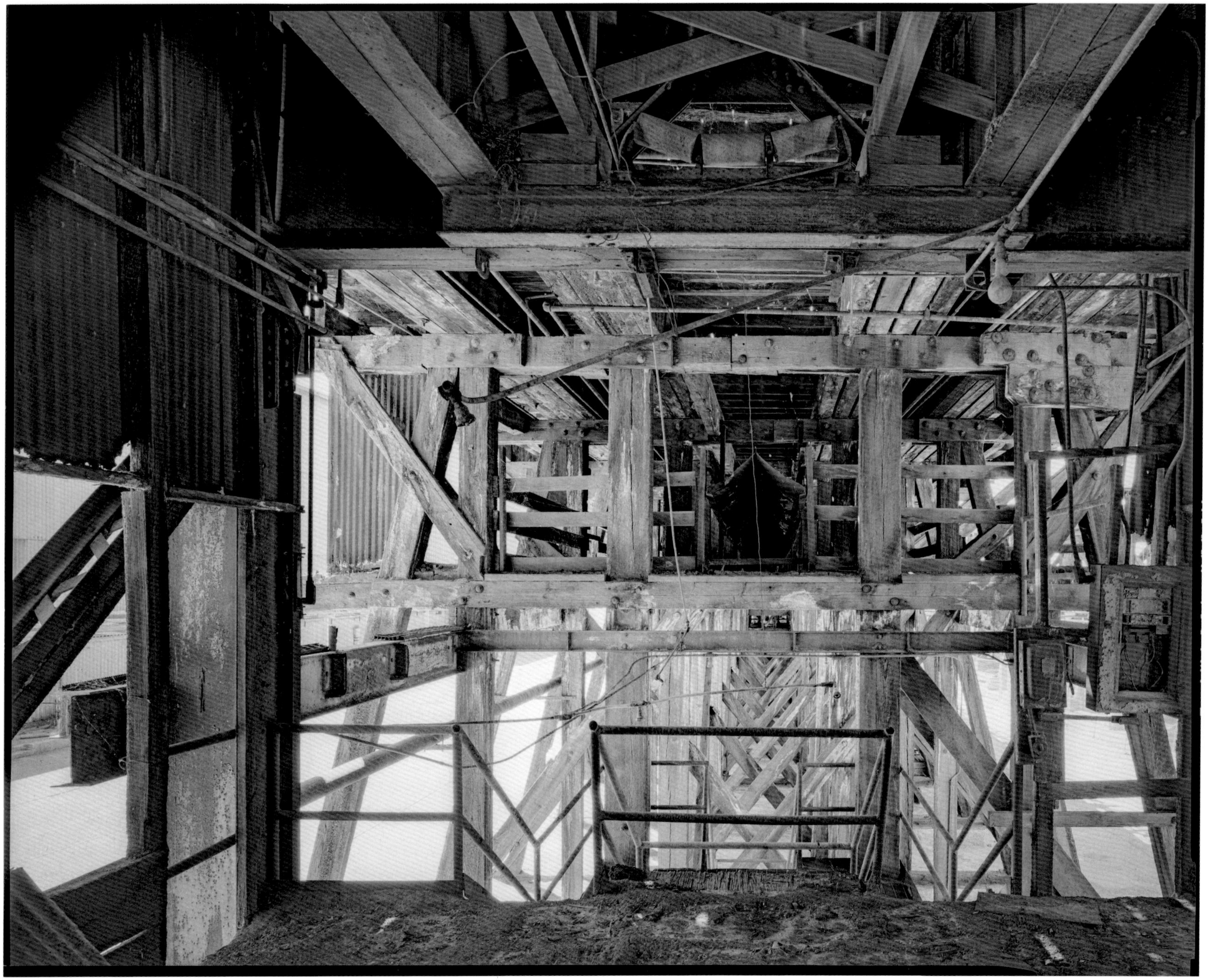

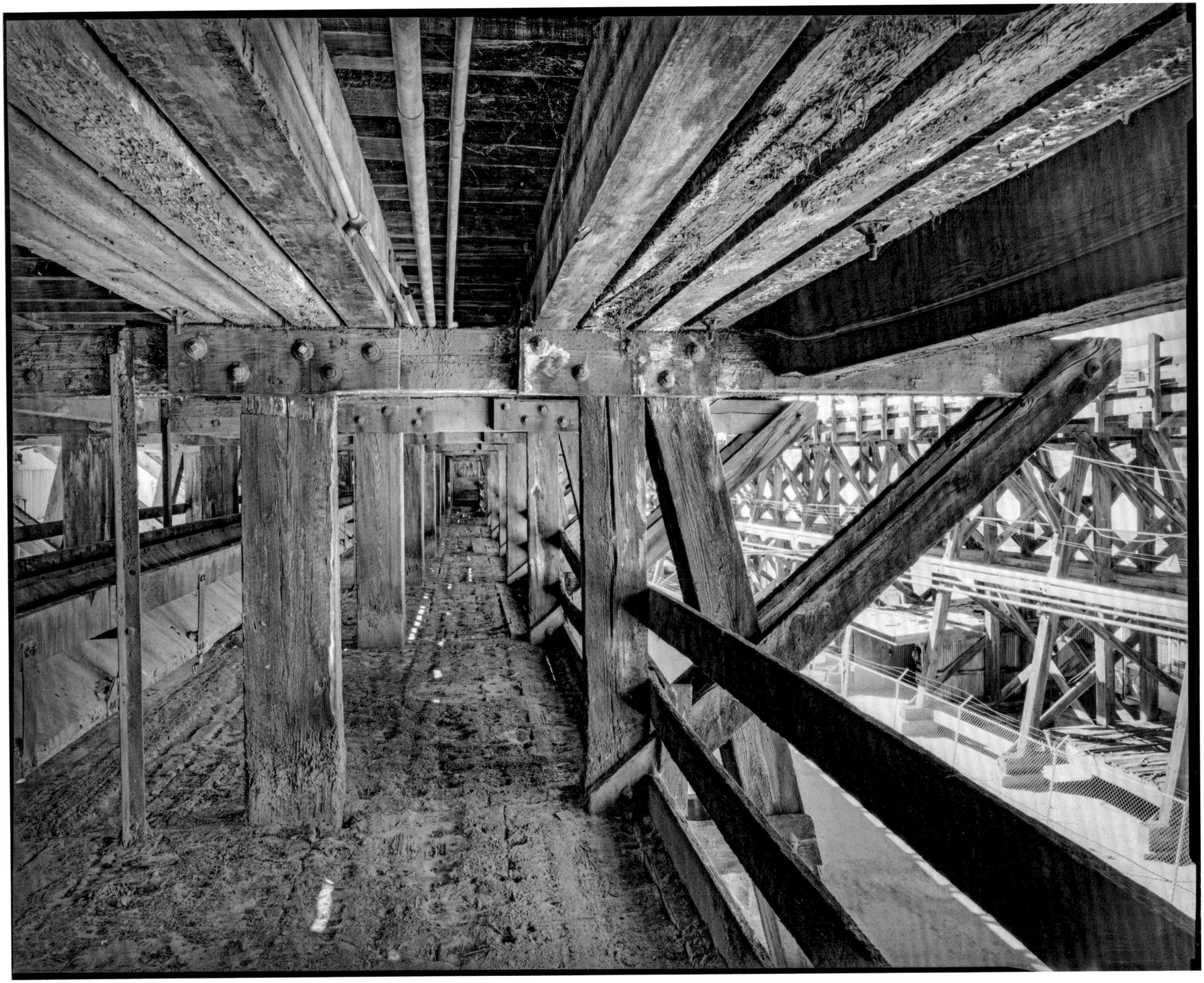

Acknowledgments

The photographs you see here were made between 2009 and 2022. It has been solitary work, but it would have been impossible without the encouragement, advice, and financial support of friends, strangers, and colleagues.

Starting at the beginning, my deepest thanks to David Wright Vaughan, who told me in 2009 of the imminent closure and demolition of the El Paso ASARCO smelter. He went on to be my steadiest and sternest critic in all matters editorial and photographic. Hearty and unending thanks also to Annie Proulx, who, seven years earlier in our collaboration in Wyoming's Red Desert, showed me what real work looks like and taught me that curiosity alone is useless without an appetite for research. She was my guide, plowing head-on into strange territory spurred on by hunches, tattered maps, scraps of historical data, and a trust that where there is a landscape there is a story. Dagoberto Gilb, through Annie's introduction, forced me to look past the landmark ASARCO smokestack and learn the fuller history of El Paso, starting with C. L. Sonnichson and the great University of Texas–El Paso library collections.

Thanks to Sam Sterling for showing me El Paso's H&H Carwash and Coffee Shop (which sustained me on my regular visits) and for his introduction to Martina Lorey, the El Paso–born architect who early on suggested I go to City Hall and seek out Patricia Dalbin—one of the first people to help me understand ASARCO's place in the regional landscape. Ms. Dalbin generously shared her arm-long list of colleagues' names—people who gave me tubes of GIS maps and even more contacts. The ensuing conversations all included "You have to go meet . . ."

I am grateful to Chick Hancock and Lynn Springer, Albuquerque friends who insisted I meet their friend Florence Gillespie, who insisted I contact a cousin who had a friend whose El

Paso helicopter pilot friend knew a guy with a skydiving school and possibly an airplane I could afford to rent. That worked out well, as over the years many pilots flew me in perfect loops over ASARCO and Smeltertown. To all of them, including Bob Kern, Chuy, and Tomas Peralta—my thanks.

In El Paso, one name was on everyone's list of you-have-to-meets: Gary Williams, El Paso Community Foundation Senior Program Officer, whose contagious passion for the deep complexity of El Paso's story makes Oñate's 1598 Rio Grande crossing seem as cogent as a 2025 interview with a migrant family camped in the shadow of the steel border wall. Gary is a gifted storyteller, and his native optimism early on was my north star.

I am forever indebted to Roberto Puga, Texas Custodial Trustee, for granting this stranger years of full access to a hazard-strewn demolition site and for sharing his enthusiasm once the good pictures finally started to happen. Thanks also to his company, Project Navigator, for its generous endowment in 2013, which funded the acquisition of an early portfolio of these pictures for the Special Collections Division of the University of Texas–El Paso Library. That boost made my next years of work easier. At the UTEP Special Collections Library, Department Head Claudia Rivers's immersion in the ASARCO story predates by years my involvement; and her generosity, curiosity, and miraculous ability to recall facts, dates, and names lightened my workload. A bow, too, to the Special Collections Library staff for morsels and giant chunks of help along the way.

On the ASARCO site, I am grateful to Mike Casbon—safety officer and OSHA enforcer during much of the demolition—who knew that my simply owning a hard hat, and confidence, didn't mean I was smart enough to survive there without following the rules (of gravity, for example: "Pieces of the roof may fall on you if the winds gust; so your hardhat *must* remain *on* your head").

My gratitude to Walter Boyle can't be overstated; he was the site liaison for Project Navigator and my guide over years of exploring. Walt comprehends the vast smelter property like an Egyptologist understands a cluster of pyramids. Without his narrating the landscape as we walked it and drove it, I would have grasped almost nothing—of where I was, or of what the sprawling complex had been.

The book's three contributing essayists each gave me more than rich copy.

Collaborating with Betsy Fahlman is like going on a treasure hunt. Her skill as a historian and a sleuth, combined with her genuine delight at poking around the brownfields of El Paso, reminds me that hard scholarship can happen even in the searing daylight of the great wide open and be serious fun. The four days we spent in El Paso burrowing through archives and driving the industrial bottomlands of the Rio Grande between Anapra and East El Paso were invaluable as a vacation wrapped in an adventure.

Michael Romero Taylor knows firsthand the ASARCO neighborhood. His mother and father spent their early years nearby, and Mike spent much of his childhood there. His career for decades as (now emeritus) National Park Service Specialist on Historic Trails, including the Camino Real de Tierra Adentro, makes his narrative as clear and compelling as a conversation with one of Smeltertown's paisanos—like reading history through 3-D glasses.

There are writers' writers and scholars' scholars, and there is an order of photo historian on a plane equal to them but with muddier boots and more miles logged slogging through his subject matter. Toby Jurovics is one of these. He knows intimately the western landscape as well as a century and a half of the region's photography. He insists that good pictures are literate pictures and that craft matters, so his taking my work seriously is a compliment as great as any.

Back on the El Paso smelter site, longtime ASARCO employee Ed Santiesteban spent hours recalling and properly identifying buildings and other features on this landscape. He then wrote their names by hand on panoramic photographs I had given him. His task was to help me label my photos of this place, which was foreign and a mystery to me. Without his help and Walt Boyle's elaboration, writing accurate captions would have been impossible.

I am grateful to Brandenburg Demolition for knocking off precisely at 2:00 p.m. every Friday, which allowed me precious safe late afternoon access to the site during the project's first few years. Later, Arcadis field manager Doug Solon filled in the blanks when I had questions about what (building or trestle or tower) had stood where, and what was soon to disappear—which was very helpful in planning my next shooting sessions.

Among others who contributed inspiration, I am especially grateful to Dr. Estevan Rael-Gálvez, whose passion for history and the importance of storytelling helps me see this project in its full narrative arc, probing the fabric of the lives of unnamed heroic thousands spanning centuries, from pre-conquest Mexico to Colorado's San Luis Valley. Monica Perales, historian and writer, put flesh on the bones of this project by giving us *Smeltertown: Making and Remembering a Southwest Border Community*. The story of her family's home landscape (where they spent their lives working the smelter and raising their families under its infamous toxic plume) helped reshape my project. Because of her book, what I had begun as a photographic document became, finally, an homage.

Far from El Paso, another band of friends and colleagues sustained me, some by simply looking at the pictures as I made them and saying they wanted to see more, to know more about the place and its history. For years these people (some already named here) have encouraged this work by writing letters of support for grants, by purchasing prints, by hosting exhibitions, by acting as guides to unfamiliar places, or by simply offering useful criticism. This all helped nudged this book to life. It adds up to encouragement of the highest order. I thank you, and I apologize to those whose names I might omit here:

Karen Arch and Pablo Miller, Audra Belmore, Ed Boles and Michelle Minnis, Pat and Barbara Carr, Andrew Cecil, Linda Connor, Lisa De Lima and Bobby Alter, Jim Dow, Terry Etherton, Robert Eveleth, Paola Ferarrio, Susan Ferrell and Tony Fines, Miguel Figueroa, Dan Flores, Bill Fox, Aimeé Gonzáles, Peter Goin, Emmet Gowin, Cory Greenfield, Joanna Hurley, Angela Hynes, Kitty Kaupp, Sheryl Kolosinski, Katherine Kurland and John Serkin, Enrique Lamadrid, Rod Lambert, Numair Latif, Lucy Lippard, Jet Lowe, Rob Mangone, Nancy Marshall and John McWilliams, Christopher Marston, Christopher Mead and Michele Penhall, Marcela Medina and Karin De Gier, Steven Moffson, Susan Moldenhaur, Yuriria Morales-Mangone, Jay Murphy, Eric Paddock, Jeff Pappas, Sharon Park, Chris Payne, Jackson Polk, Laura Presley and Center Santa Fe, Walter Rask and Doug Schaffer, Mary Ann Redding, Laurie Rufe, Roger Schluntz, Rebecca Senf, Gary Short, Beth Silbergleit and Dennis Trujillo, Gabe Silva, Bob Spude, Daphne Srinivasan, Mary Statzer, Jim Stone, Sharon Stewart, Wendy Suarez Tena, Mary Virginia Swanson, David Taylor, Selma Thomas and T. Allan Comp, Lisa Tremaine, Elizabeth Turk, Francisco Uviña, Kate Ware, Wendy Watriss and Fred Baldwin, Chris Wilson, and Mary Wyant.

I am especially grateful to my reviewers, whose deep knowledge and historical clarity reined me in by pointing out wrong assumptions and wobbly language. Thank you Samuel Brunk, John Jacob, Enrique Lamadrid, and Robert Morton.

My friends Anne and Bill Frej said late in 2019, "Why not meet next month in Mexico City?" Their easy enthusiasm turned a daunting prospect into an effortless trip a few weeks later. In that extraordinary city I finally saw it, the Catedral Metropolitana, the revered epicenter of Spanish culture in the Americas—the historic beginning of El Camino Real de Tierra Adentro. After our day exploring the city, and a little awestruck, David Vaughan bonked my elbow and pointed up across the Zócalo to a hotel balcony with a view down onto the cathedral plaza and said, "Up there, let's go." We were not dressed for the place, but the Gran Hotel bellman invited us in, led us across the shiny marble ballroom to an elevator, ordered the doors open, and said, "Press three and have a lovely afternoon."

Two minutes later, from the hotel bar's perch, the center of the heart of Mexico lay unfurled at our feet. The map in my head took over; I saw from there the full sweep of my project, the Camino Real from its south end to its far north. There it was, Mexico City's grand baroque church dominating that diorama. And just as clearly, its parenthetical partner, the humble Sagrado Corazón chapel a country away in New Mexico's high desert San Luis Valley. On that spot, my task snapped into focus: instead of connecting scores of wildly disparate historical parts, I needed only to tell this story as one rich loose-knit epic, with a starting place and an end. The work in the middle was still going to be work, but I could now vividly see a procession of conquistadors, indentured and enslaved Indians, soldiers, Guggenheims, miners, and missionaries forging tracks and raising dust clear to the horizon on this suddenly more familiar terrain.

Financial support is the backbone of any long-term project. For this, I am indebted to these partners: The New Mexico Museum of Art, the Phoenix Art Museum, Project Navigator, the University of Texas–El Paso Special Collections Library, the University of Wyoming Art Museum, Jessica R. Aberly, Michael Bade and Rebekah Wolman, Lisa De Lima and Bobby Alter, Jim Frazer, Laurie and Lindsey Gilbert, Chick Hancock and Lynn Springer, Marcela Medina and Karin De Gier, Walter Rask and Douglas Shaffer, and Dr. Robert and Joanne Wood. Thanks also to Bev and Dennis Little, Kitty Kaupp, and Kathryn Story. And at the UNM Foundation, for keeping it all straight, thank you Alaric Bender.

My thanks to these institutions, for permission to reproduce artwork from their collections:

The El Paso Public Library, the El Paso Museum of Art, the Tom Lea Institute, the University of Texas–El Paso Library, the Library of Congress.

At the University of New Mexico Press, Director Stephen P. Hull and Acquiring Editor Michael Millman, with encouragement and focused criticism, guided me through unfamiliar territory. Editor James Ayers lent years of help—massaging an unruly idea into a finished work—and designer Felicia Cedillos assisted in the final stretch.

In 2023 Lisa Tremaine designed the fundraising maquette—the model for what you see here. And even a decade before that, on helping edit my first few dozen pictures from El Paso, she looked up from the pile of prints and calmly announced, "This is a book." Thank you all.

Contributors

Martin Stupich was trained in painting and sculpture in Milwaukee in the 1960s. In the early '70s he studied photography in Ohio with Emmet Gowin and Elaine O'Neil. Then, after two years as a steelworker, he moved to Atlanta to earn a master's degree in photography as a student of John McWilliams. He stepped from graduate school into a career photographing engineered landscape with early grants from the National Endowment for the Arts, held jobs with the Army Corps of Engineers, and worked as a photographer documenting industrial and cultural landscape from Panama to Sitka for the Library of Congress Collections. In 2011 Stupich began a years-long relationship with the Smithsonian Institution, photographing its revered museum buildings, the Washington Monument Grounds, and the National Mall from the air, and on the ground using a traditional large-format view camera. In 2010 he made the first of his *Ore and Empire* photographs at a shuttered copper smelter on the Camino Real in El Paso.

Dagoberto Gilb is the author of three books with the University of New Mexico Press: *The Magic of Blood*, winner of the PEN/Hemingway Award and a finalist for the PEN/Faulkner Award; the anthology *Hecho en Tejas: An Anthology of Texas Mexican Literature*, winner of the PEN/Southwest Book Award; and *A Passing West: Essays from the Borderlands*, winner of the PEN/Diamonstein-Spielvogel Award for the Art of the Essay. His fiction and nonfiction have appeared in both the *New Yorker* and *Harper's*, and his work has been featured in *The Best American Essays* and O. Henry Prize Stories.

Michael Romero Taylor is a native of the Rio Grande borderlands and a retired US National Park Service Cultural Resource Specialist for Historic Trails in the Americas. He served as the New Mexico State Historic Preservation Officer in the early 1990s, and he was the Deputy Director of New Mexico State Monuments from 1995 to 2001. Taylor holds a masters certificate from the Architectural Conservation Course in Rome, Italy; he also was active in the International Council on Monuments and Sites (ICOMOS) for three decades. He frequently lectures on historic preservation, emphasizing traditional earthen (adobe) architecture and historic cultural routes in Latin America, Europe, and Asia.

Betsy Fahlman is a professor of art history at Arizona State University, where she has taught since 1988. She did her undergraduate work at Mount Holyoke College and her graduate work at the University of Delaware, where she earned her master's and doctoral degrees. A specialist in American art, her interests include public art, American modernism, the New Deal, industrial archeology, and the art history of Arizona. Her books include *Kraushaar Galleries: Celebrating 125 Years*, *New Deal Art in Arizona*, *Wonders of Work and Labor: The Steidle Collection of American Industrial Art*, *James Graham & Sons: A Century and a Half in the Art Business*, *Chimneys and Towers: Charles Demuth's Late Paintings of Lancaster*, and *Guy Pène du Bois: Painter of Modern Life*.

Toby Jurovics has been a curator of photography at the Princeton University Art Museum and the Smithsonian American Art Museum as well as Chief Curator and Holland Curator of American Western Art at Joslyn Art Museum. An expert on nineteenth- and twentieth-century photographic surveys of the American West, he has organized over sixty exhibitions by artists including Robert Adams, Lewis Baltz, Barbara Bosworth, and Emmet Gowin, and he has curated numerous thematic exhibitions of both painting and photography. In 2010 he organized a major retrospective on Timothy H. O'Sullivan in conjunction with the Smithsonian American Art Museum and the Library of Congress titled *Framing the West: The Survey Photographs of Timothy H. O'Sullivan*. The exhibition's accompanying catalogue was published by Yale University Press. He has also published essays on Thomas Joshua Cooper, Steve Fitch, John Gossage, William Sutton, and the New Topographics. He is the founding director of the Barry Lopez Foundation for Art and Environment.

Printed in Singapore

ISBN 978-0-8263-6860-7 (cloth)

Library of Congess Control Number: 2025006794

Founded in 1889, the University of New Mexico sits on the traditional homelands of the Pueblo of Sandia. The original peoples of New Mexico—Pueblo, Navajo, and Apache—since time immemorial have deep connections to the land and have made significant contributions to the broader community statewide. We honor the land itself and those who remain stewards of this land throughout the generations and also acknowledge our committed relationship to Indigenous peoples. We gratefully recognize our history.

Cover photograph: *Number 13 Incline Belt Conveyor, 1920s*, by Martin Stupich, 2010.
Designed by Felicia Cedillos
Composed in Garamond Premier Pro